Life Under an Umbrella

The Story of a Bible Translation Support Worker

Shirley Funnell

To my dear friends in the Lord Sam + Lilly

Shirley Funnell
Prov 3:5,6.

Life Under an Umbrella
Copyright © 2016 by Shirley Funnell

Unless otherwise indicated, all Scripture references are from the Holy Bible: New International Version, copyright © 1973p, 1978, 1984 by the International Bible Society. Used by permission of Zondervan Bible Publishers.

ISBN-13: 978-1530761388
ISBN-10: 1530761387

Printed in the United States of America

Edited by Agnes C. Lawless
Cover by Joseph Leman

Dedicated to

Anne West

my coworker and friend of fifty years, whose faithfulness to God and His work in the Philippines has been an inspiration to me.

Contents

Foreword

Have you ever doubted God's faithfulness? If so, you need to read this book.

Read how Shirley Funnell followed God's call and leading a half century ago, and spent most of the years since then serving in the Philippines with the Summer Institute of Linguistics to help bring God's Word to the many dozens of indigenous people groups inhabiting the remotest corners of the country. In the early days she served among an animistic group, former headhunters who still practiced revenge killing, living in a village with very little contact with the outside world. Later she directed the Publications Department, with frequent difficult trips to other remote communities, over almost impassable roads and trails, and sometimes in dangerous typhoon weather.

Many of us, her colleagues in Wycliffe and SIL, have been blessed by her cheerful servant heart. In the Philippines, seeing New Testaments through to publication, and here at the Canada Institute of Linguistics, assisting in the process of recruiting and training a new generation of personnel to work in the Bible translation movement, Shirley has set an example of diligent and faithful service.

There is roughly a chapter for every year of her long career. Be sure to read through to the conclusion, to appreciate how God accomplishes His eternal purposes, far beyond what we can outline in a strategic plan, or even imagine.

Dr. Michael Walrod
Past president, Canada Institute of Linguistics
At Trinity Western University, Langley BC, Canada

Acknowledgements

I have never kept a diary, even though I tried unsuccessfully on several occasions. For this reason, I am grateful to my late mother, Mildred Funnell, who saved all the letters I wrote home from my arrival in the Philippines in 1967 until her death in 1989. I found them all organized by year and numbered as they arrived. Without these letters, I could not have written this book.

I would also like to thank my many Wycliffe and Summer Institute of Linguistics friends who encouraged me to write my life story. Often, after relating some incident that took place during my years in the Philippines or elsewhere, someone would say, "You should write a book."

I am especially grateful to Don Fama, my supervisor at the Canada Institute of Linguistics (CanIL), who allowed me to have one day a week away from my job as his assistant to work on this project.

I want to thank my sisters, Marj and Nell, who helped me remember names and some details of our childhood and who read the manuscript, looking for errors.

And then, I want to thank my dear, longtime friend, Agnes ("Atchie") Lawless Weaver, for her encouragement and for spending many long hours editing this work. She helped to make it readable and a useful piece of history for the work of the Summer Institute of Linguistics in the Philippines.

Agnes's enthusiasm for God's work in the Philippines was one of the major factors that caused me to request that country as my choice of field when I joined Wycliffe Bible Translators.

And most of all I want to thank God for giving me strength and patience to write this book. Without Him I could not have accomplished anything recorded herein. He has been my faithful friend and encourager for my whole life. It is because of Him that many thousands of Filipinos now have His Word in their own language.

Preface

One of my goals in writing this book is to encourage other missionaries who are involved in support roles that may be peripheral to the main objectives of their mission, such as teachers, bookkeepers, secretaries, maintenance people, computer operators, printers, and a great host of other jobs that must be done to keep the work going on the field. I was one of them as I managed the printing that needed to be done and typeset books getting them ready for the printer. Sometimes after spending all day trying to make my department books balance or staring at a computer which didn't want to cooperate, I felt discouraged and very far from the task of giving God's Word to the many cultural communities in the Philippines who were without it. However, at the end of my career as I look back and see what was accomplished, I know that my job was very important since without what I worked at day by day, the long hard work of translating the Bible would not have been available for those who needed it. Every task that God has called us to do is important to Him. Most important is to work with diligence and faithfulness to the best of our ability, realizing that we do everything in His strength.

Now a few words concerning the title of this book. For my whole life I have lived under the umbrella of God's love, care and protection. Through the dark storms He has been there to encourage me and through the sunny times He has been there to keep me from straying from His path.

In a more earthly vein, when I first arrived in the Philippines, I noticed that everybody carried umbrellas. Since it was the dry season, I wondered why. People told me that because the tropical sun is so hot and, unlike us Westerners, nobody wants to get darker, so folks use umbrellas as sunshades.

I thought that was strange and vowed I would wear a hat instead and a raincoat when it was raining. I soon learned that hats are too hot and plastic raincoats, because of the high humidity, make you wetter inside than outside. It wasn't long before I capitulated to the local wisdom of carrying an umbrella and soon, like everybody else, rarely left home without one.

Thus, the title of this book.

Shirley Funnell

Prologue
1967

The darkness pulsed around me like a living, moving thing. Moonlight seeped through the small window over my bed. Rigid with fear, I listened to gongs pounding, voices screeching, pigs squealing, dogs barking outside our house in the little mountain town in the Philippines. *What's going on?*

I shone a flashlight on my watch. Three o'clock, and I hadn't gone to sleep yet.

I crawled from under my warm quilt and peeked out the window over my bed. Breathlessly, I watched men crowding into the space under the neighbor's house where drunken *mumbaki* (witch doctors) were shouting, clashing gongs, and calling on spirits.

Anne, in her bed on the other side of the room, groaned and flung an arm over her ear. I could hear her rapid breathing and knew she was awake too.

My heart beat fast, and my stomach twisted itself into a dozen knots as I watched the activity next door before moving over to Anne's bed.

"How long do you think this will last?" I asked.

"It's hard to say. It started at six o'clock and could go on all night, I suppose."

"I heard them say they were going to make a sacrifice for the sick neighbor boy. I supposed this ritual is to call on the spirits to make him well."

"Yes, that's true, and we need the Lord's protection."

"We sure do!"

Now, as the ritual next door continued, we prayed, "Father, we ask that You put a wall of protection around us to keep us safe. We trust You to do this. In Jesus's mighty name, amen."

As the night wore on, the witch doctors drank more wine, and their chanting and gong playing grew louder and louder.

I could feel the pulsing darkness, not just physically but spiritually. I was discouraged as I thought of the condition of our neighbors.

Dear God, what can You ever do in a place like this?

Shirley at one year

Chapter 1
In the Beginning
1937–1947

Percy Funnell jerked awake early that Saturday morning, March 6, 1937. *This might be the day*, he thought. He snuggled under the warm quilt as long as possible, since the house was freezing cold. He couldn't even see outside because frost coated the window halfway up.

For a week now, bright sun had warmed the days. This made Percy happy, since cold nights and sunny days made the sap in his maple trees flow from roots to branches. This nourished the buds that would pop out in a few weeks.

I should get up, Percy thought, as he tucked the quilt around his shoulders. *I hope Mildred is okay.* As he crept closer to his warm wife, he couldn't help getting excited about his maple syrup business.

Every year Percy tapped one hundred maple trees, collected the sap, and boiled it down to make maple syrup. He transported the sap to the sugar shanty twice a day. Because he'd be busy, he stayed in the woods long hours to keep the fire burning under the evaporator in the shanty. He boiled the sap until it reached 216 degrees F. (102 C.). Then he strained it through heavy felt filters into milk cans before pouring it into bottles and cans for sale.

He jerked his thoughts from his business to his very pregnant wife, still sleeping beside him. Then he turned back the quilt carefully so as to not waken her and stepped onto the braided mat in his long johns and bare feet. He lit the kerosene lamp, pulled on wool socks and bib overalls, and headed to the kitchen. He opened the wood stove door, stirred the warm coals, crumpled up sheets of newspaper, and shoved them in along with cedar kindling. As the fire blazed, he added a few chunks of dry wood and soon heard them crackling.

By this time, Percy heard the eight cows mooing as they waited in the barn to be milked. He pulled on his boots, slipped into his heavy wool jacket, and headed to the barn. He enjoyed milking. The warmth of a cow's belly against his forehead as he squeezed milk into the pail gave him a feeling of contentment.

When the milking was done, Percy skimmed a cup of cream from the top of last night's milking and took it to the house for breakfast. Mildred would mix it with whole milk for use on their oatmeal.

He found his wife in the kitchen, stirring the porridge in the pot. Four-year-old Marjorie was already in her high chair. She waved her spoon at her dad.

He gave his little daughter a quick hug then put an arm around Mildred's shoulders. "How are you this morning?"

"I'm okay, but I think this might be the day. In fact, some labor pains have begun. I think you'd better get the doctor." With effort, she got up and waddled off to bed.

Percy put his jacket back on, cranked his Model T Ford, and headed to the doctor's office. He parked the rattling car but left it running as he hurried up the stairs.

"Hi, Doc! Mildred is ready. She needs you—now!"

He waited until he saw the doctor put on his coat, grab his bag, and head out the door.

Then he climbed back in his shivering "Tin Lizzie" and drove back home along the Lake Road. He didn't hurry, since in those days, fathers were not welcome at the births of their children.

When he arrived, he discovered that he had another daughter. He and Mildred named her Shirley Ann.

I was that baby, and this is my story.

Early Farm Life

When my parents were married in 1929, Grandfather Funnell gave them a down payment on a farm as a wedding present. But the Great Depression (1929–1939) left them unable to make the mortgage payments, and they lost the farm in 1934.

So my father rented another farm. It was located six miles from the village of Port Stanley, Ontario, on the Lake Road that ran along the north shore of Lake Erie.

I loved the farm, especially the barn. This traditional red, hip-roofed building had space for cows, pigs, and horses on the ground floor and a haymow and granary above. A trapdoor from the haymow to the stable below allowed Dad to push hay down to feed the cows and horses.

Dad warned my sister and me to stay away from that trapdoor, and being a timid child, I never went near it. I was also afraid of the hayfork that hung on the inside of the ridgepole. When Dad brought hay in from the field, the horses pulled the wagon up the barn bridge onto the second floor, where a huge, black iron fork ran on a pulley until it was over the wagonload of hay. Then Dad dropped the fork into the hay, and another horse pulled the hay up to the haymow.

A silo sat on the end of the barn for the storage of chopped-up corn, called ensilage, for feeding the animals. We girls liked to climb up the steps inside the silo as we inhaled the sweet smell of fermenting corn.

Everybody had a job to do on the farm. Mine was to feed the chickens and gather eggs every afternoon. This was an easy job, since I just had to take the eggs from the empty nests and put them in a basket. But when a hen was setting, she didn't leave her egg unattended. I got many a sharp peck from an irate mother hen for stealing her eggs. I finally used a stick with which I held the hen's head against the side of the box while I reached underneath to collect her egg. A loud, clucking complaint always followed this.

My favorite time was going to the barn with my dad when he milked the cows. I loved to sit on a milking stool with a cat in my lap and chatter to Dad while he did his job. Sometimes he would squirt milk right into my cat's mouth.

We had three horses that pulled the farm equipment. When we were older, Dad let my sisters and me ride together on the back of Joe, the brown horse. If Dad were using a small plow that only worked one row, he used Joe. A dappled team, Min and Jerry, pulled the big equipment.

Behind the house was an orchard with different kinds of apple trees—Sweet Apples, Northern Spies, Transparents, Snow Apples, Russets, McIntosh, and in the corner a "grape tree." A grape vine had grown up an old pear tree and produced luscious bunches of Concord grapes. I loved to climb that tree and pick the ripe grapes, sucking the juice and spitting out the tough skins and seeds.

I learned a lot about farming from living on a farm. When I was in high school, I felt sorry for city kids who didn't know anything about farm life.

In the winter of 1938, my mother said, "It's time for me to go home to visit my family. I haven't seen my mother for nine years."

Dad couldn't leave the farm because he had to feed the cattle, horses, pigs, and chickens, milk cows, and gather and sell eggs. So in the spring when I was a year old, Mom packed up, took Marjorie and me, and caught the Canadian Pacific Railroad train to Saskatchewan. We arrived in Gull Lake three days later and stayed for six weeks. This was still during the massive drought that ravaged the western prairies in the 1930s, giving them the name the "Dirty Thirties." It was also during the Great Depression, and nobody had any money.

I don't remember much of my younger years. I was a sickly baby and took a tonic until I was six years old. One of our neighbors told my mother that she would never raise me. The only drawback from my poor beginning was that I never grew beyond five feet tall.

One day after I had turned four, Mom sent me to school with Marjorie. Dad came to pick me up after lunch. When we got home, I found a new baby sister in the bassinette in my parents' bedroom. She was very tiny and cried a lot. Her name was Nellie Marie.

Making Maple Syrup

My only other preschool memory was when my grandma and uncle came to visit from Saskatchewan. I was about five, and it was maple syrup-making time. When the sap was running well, the trees produced many gallons of sap every day. To collect it, my dad poured the buckets into a round galvanized vat on a stone boat (a platform with runners), and the team, Min and Jerry, pulled it through the woods.

Because the stone boat was rectangular and the sap holder was round, a five-year-old could stand in a space at the corners. One day when my uncle was driving the horses and I was standing on that little corner, the horses pulled the stone boat over a fallen tree branch. Unfortunately, the sap holder was nearly full, and the jarring set off a big wave in the sap. It washed over the back and poured over my head. Being March, the liquid was icy cold. My dad rushed me to the house to get me out of my wet clothes before I caught pneumonia.

Early School Days

Boxall School was a one-room country school where all the children in the community attended grades one to eight for several generations. Since kindergarten was not offered there, everyone began in grade one. My birthday was in March, but the teacher allowed me to begin school in September when I was five-and-a-half instead of waiting until the next year. I always liked stories and would bring my mother books to read to me from the time I was very little. When Marj went to school and learned to read, she read to me, but she soon decided I should learn to read for myself. By the time I went to school at age five, I was already able to read all of the grade-one books.

Miss Elizabeth McLennan, a spritely Scottish lady, had been the teacher at Boxall School for many years. She loved her students, and we all loved her. Since most of what was taught in grade one was reading, and I already new how, she put me into grade two immediately. Unfortunately, this put me two years ahead of everybody else my age. Since I was smaller than average and quite shy, I didn't fit in very well socially.

We lived a mile-and-a-half from the one-room school and always walked both ways on a gravel road. In the winter when it was cold and snowy, Mom bundled us up in snow boots, ski pants, woolen coats, mittens, knit caps, and scarves and sent us off to tramp through the snow. Sometimes the snow reached halfway to our knees.

Our school had a furnace in the basement that sent hot air through a three-foot-square register in the floor at the back of the classroom. Every morning wet mittens, scarves, and hats covered it. We hoped they would get dry by lunchtime so we could put them on and go out to play again.

Dad was not a believer, but you wouldn't know it from how he lived. He didn't smoke or drink, he was honest, and he cared about people. In his youth, he attended the United Church where he didn't hear the gospel. Eventually, he listened to Christian radio programs. Through Dr. M. R. DeHaan and the Radio Bible Class, Dad found the Lord as his Savior. He was eager to learn more and studied a number of the Radio Bible Class courses.

When I was eight in 1945, my brother, Arthur John, was born, completing our family. Mom didn't like nicknames, so she never allowed us to call him Art. He became Art after he left home to go to school, Marjorie eventually became Marj, and Nellie became Nell.

During most of my years living on the Lake Road, the world was at war. Since Dad was a farmer, he didn't have to join the armed forces. A number of my schoolmates' older siblings joined the army or the air force, and some went overseas.

Since we were able to grow almost everything we needed to eat, we didn't suffer from rationing like people who lived in the city. We bought only gasoline for the car and sugar.

Victory in Europe Day

When Victory in Europe (VE) Day came on May 8, 1945, my folks heard on the radio that the war in Europe was over. They also heard about a ticker-tape parade and other celebrations to commemorate the end of the war, so they decided we should all go to town to join in the fun. They stopped by the school to pick us up and sent Nell in to get us. She ran in the door and stood at the back of the classroom. At the top of her voice, she yelled, "The war's over! It's time to go to town." So off we went.

Harvest Time

We lived in a fairly close-knit community, especially during harvest time. Every year a group of men banded together and moved from farm to farm to thresh the grain. When the men came to our farm, they hauled a threshing machine near our barn. Dad had already cut, bound into sheaves, and stacked his wheat crop in the fields. He and the other men loaded it on wagons so horses could pull the wagons to the threshing machine. There the wheat was separated from the chaff and straw. The wheat went into the granary, and the straw was blown into a stack to be used for bedding for the cows.

Mom cooked for the ten or twelve men who came to work, and we girls helped. We set up galvanized washtubs in the yard with soap and towels so the men could wash before coming in to eat. Since Mom always cooked lots of food, we had plenty of leftovers for us to have special dinners. All during harvest, we only saw Dad at breakfast and night time, since he helped the other men get grain into their barns.

Our best friends among the neighbors were Jim and Tilly Fulkerson, who lived about a half a mile away. We often visited them and their four children—Erwin, Burt, Mason, and June. They were all grown by this time, since June, the youngest, was twenty-one when I was born. They all lived at home, except Erwin, so I got to know them well. I especially liked June. She was kind to us girls and played an important role in my life many years later.

Another special time was butchering day. Every year Dad butchered a cow and a pig or two, not usually at the same time. For a cow, Dad cut the carcass into roasts to be placed in the freezer locker in town, since we had no electricity. He brought all the extra chunks of meat to the kitchen where Mom, Marj, and I cut them into small pieces, packed them in jars, and canned them. Sometimes we had one hundred quarts of canned beef for the coming year. The beef made wonderful sandwiches, and heated with onions and gravy, it was one of my favorite meals.

When we butchered a pig, we made ham, bacon, and sausage. We had an extra, unheated bedroom upstairs that we used for storage, and Dad hung the hams there to cure.

I loved summers with long days to play outside. I preferred playing with the cats to playing with dolls. When I was about six, I received a baby doll for Christmas. Instead of playing with it, I put her to sleep in the bassinette in the guest room upstairs. About once a month, I changed her clothes on a Sunday afternoon, since she had two sets. Then I put her back to sleep for another month. I have that doll to this day, and she is in such good condition that she is now worth thirty times her original cost.

Since I liked to read, I spent long hours lying on a blanket in the shade of a tree with a book. Our front yard had six tall pine trees and a white picket fence along the road. I was never very brave, but one time I did walk the picket fence without falling off.

When I was ready for grade six, Miss McLennan left Boxall to teach in another school. I couldn't believe it. How could I go to school without my beloved teacher? In September the new teacher came, a young woman not many years out of normal school. Her teaching methods were very different, and I didn't like her at all. But I was shy and usually well behaved, so I managed to get along with her.

A New House and Dad's New Job

Then late that same year, Mr. Locke, who owned our farm, informed Dad and Mom that he wanted to sell it. His price was nine thousand dollars, and we didn't have that much money. So we had to move.

After Dad searched for another farm to rent without finding one, his brother Les persuaded him to give up farming and get a job at the Roads Department of Elgin County where he worked. Dad found a place to rent that had a barn and an acre for a garden, a big yard, and a medium-sized house. On March 20, 1947, we moved to the fifth concession of Yarmouth Township.

Lake Road house

Boxall School 1946
Shirley third in first row, Marj last in first row

Chapter 2
School Days
1948–1957

"Let's go!" called Mom. "I'll walk to school with you this first day."

Mom, Nell, and I set off to Coles School, just a half mile down the road from our new house, which we usually called "RR5," our rural mail-route address. Coles School was a one-room school like Boxall but not as nice. It had a big yard though, with a ball diamond and lots of room to play.

When we walked into the school the first time, I couldn't believe my eyes. My beloved Miss McLennan sat at the teacher's desk! She hugged me, and we both cried. I was so happy to have her as my teacher again.

Life at RR5

Life at RR5 was different from our farm on the Lake Road. For one thing, Dad wasn't there during weekdays, since he drove a road grader, keeping the gravel roads in good driving condition.

We had brought a dozen chickens, three cats, and one cow that had a calf soon after our move. Since Mom was handy with tools, she made part of the barn into a chicken house.

We had a big yard at both the front and back of our house. Mom planted two maple trees and a number of flowers in the front yard, and Dad planted an acre of garden vegetables in the backyard. Nell and I helped him by dropping in seeds and covering the rows with hoes.

When I used a hoe, I found that I was left-handed for doing a swinging motion. Although I write with my right hand, I do things like hoeing, sweeping, batting a ball, or playing golf left-handed. I also can write backwards with my left hand. I thought this was a skill everybody had, until I later found out that it's an unusual ability.

Through his work, Dad met people who invited us to attend the Hiawatha Street Baptist Church in St. Thomas. In 1949 Dad and Marjorie were both baptized and, along with Mom, became members of that church.

Visiting Grandma

In the winter of 1948, my mother said, "It's time for us to go to Saskatchewan again to visit my family. It's ten years since we were there last."

This time Mom took four children on the train, since my brother Art was born in 1945. On July 4, Dad took us to London, Ontario, where we caught the Canadian Pacific Railroad (CPR) train for Toronto. We changed trains there and rode through the forests of northern Ontario and the prairies of Manitoba and Saskatchewan. We didn't have berths but slept in our seats. Since we didn't eat in the dining car, we carried a big box of food. Mom had packed sandwiches, apples, and hardboiled eggs. We got off the train to buy milk when we pulled into a station for a brief stop. The hilly landscape of northern Ontario was beautiful, but the ups and downs and the rocking of the train upset my stomach. For most of the trip, I suffered from motion sickness.

We arrived in Gull Lake, Saskatchewan, at midnight after two nights and two days on the train. Uncle Earl, Mom's youngest brother, met us at the station. He drove his truck as close as he could, carried our heavy bags, and piled as many of us as possible in the cab and the rest in the back. And away we went to Grandma's house. When we drove into her driveway, we made lots of noise getting out of the truck and carrying our bags up on her porch. But that didn't bother her a bit. This amazing lady threw her covers off, got up out of bed, and shoved more wood in the stove to heat up a chicken dinner for us. Since the table was all set, we pulled up chairs and enjoyed a real meal in the middle of the night.

The house was always full of people, coming and going. Grandma often had ten or twelve for a meal at her long table. Mom not only helped with the meals and housework, but she joined us in visiting neighbors and family, picking Saskatoon berries, and riding in Uncle Earl's truck to shop or to see a movie.

One day Mom was picking green peas in the garden, when she looked up with surprise to see Dad walking in her direction. "Percy! What are you doing here?"

He gave her a big hug. "I missed you so much! I had a two-week vacation from work so rode the bus here."

We enjoyed having Dad with us on the farm until August 15, when we all rode home on the train.

Beginning High School

The spring after I turned twelve, I finished grade eight and was ready to begin high school in the fall. Fortunately, the school bus came down the Fifth Concession, so I could ride the bus to the St. Thomas Collegiate Institute (STCI).

As a child, I'd always been shy and afraid to do things on my own. The thought of riding the school bus and going to a big school with hundreds of students was more than I could handle.

So every morning for the first week, I could hardly eat my oatmeal then lost it before getting on the bus. Eventually, I made friends and managed to cope.

Dedication to God

The pastor of our church, Roy Campbell, was an evangelist. We used the hymnbook produced by Ira Sankey, evangelist D. L. Moody's song leader, and I learned many of the old hymns, which are still precious to me.

Two years later we got a new pastor, Rev. Balfour Pittaway. During the summer, our church constructed a new building. On December 2, 1951, Dedication Sunday, the pastor held a baptismal service, and I was baptized.

Although I didn't know when I was saved, it didn't matter. I knew that Jesus was my Savior and that He died for me and took away my sins.

Youth for Christ was at its peak in the early 1950s, and most of our youth group attended faithfully. When I was sixteen, a dynamic speaker urged us to turn our lives over to God for His leading.

As the speaker prayed, I was so moved that I prayed silently, *Dear God, I promise that I will do anything You want me to do and go anyplace You ask me to go. I just have one request—that You will not let me become involved with any man that is not Your will for me.*

I never forgot that promise.

Teacher's Training

High school in Ontario went to grade 13 in those days. After five years, graduation loomed, and I needed to decide what to do next. Some of my friends planned to attend London Teachers' College. Since my folks didn't have enough money to send me to the university and the teachers' college was free, I applied there. At the graduation ceremony, I was presented with a bursary for $250 to help pay my expenses. That amount would be worth $2,500 now.

Teachers' college was a one-year course, consisting mostly of methods, not content. In the fall I joined the choir for a Christmas concert. The first number we worked on was Handel's, "And the Glory of the Lord," from *The Messiah*. That was my first experience singing Handel, and I soon grew to love his music, even though it was difficult. I was chosen to join a small group that sang carols at the concert. We wore capes and bonnets to look like nineteenth-century carolers.

Elementary Teaching

In the spring of 1955, school-board members from various districts in Ontario came to the London Teachers' College to interview new graduates for their schools. The Grantham Township school board in St. Catharines hired me to teach grade three.

I was only eighteen, and teaching was the hardest thing I had ever done. Our school had two grade-three classes, mine and the other one taught by an experienced teacher. The children were divided according to their abilities, and I ended up with twenty-five poorer students.

My teaching job became more and more difficult as the months went by. In the fall of 1956, I was again given a class of difficult students.

Because they didn't teach typing at my high school, I had never learned to type. I decided this might be a good time to learn, so I enrolled in a night-school course in beginning typing, using Royal manual typewriters with blank keys. After I had become somewhat proficient, I purchased a Smith Corona manual portable typewriter that I used for many years.

During the year, I became less and less enamored with teaching. I began to feel that God was leading me to go to Bible college. Our church in St. Thomas had contact with the London Bible Institute and Theological Seminary (LBI and TS) in London, Ontario. Students came to speak on occasion. Since the school was less than thirty miles from home, that was the logical place for me to apply.

When I wrote for application papers, I found that I needed to have a physical. Part of that was a routine tuberculosis test. I went to a local clinic where they did a miniature x-ray and was shocked to receive a report that indicated I had TB. I had to go to the sanitarium to have a sputum test and a larger x-ray. When the final tests came back, however, I was clear. The report said I had scarring on my left lung from an unknown cause, possibly pneumonia.

In the late spring of 1957, I received my acceptance to attend LBI. I enrolled in the bachelor of religious education program and looked forward to going back to school.

I left Maplewood School, feeling as if I never wanted to teach again as long as I lived.

Chapter 3
London Bible Institute
1957–1961

After spending two of the worst years of my life teaching in St. Catharine's, I now was entering three of my best years. I loved sharing a room with three other girls.

At that time, London Bible Institute was a small school with about 125 students. We got to know everybody and enjoyed great times of fun as well as studying the Word of God.

As I look back, I realize that one of the most important things I learned was to establish a habit of a daily quiet time with God. I hadn't learned this at home because my mother believed that we shouldn't talk about two items—sex and religion. So the only time we prayed together was saying grace at the table. But now my teachers told us that the main way to grow spiritually was to read God's Word and pray each day, preferably the first thing in the morning. I'm eternally grateful that this habit became an important part of my life.

The professor of music, William Carey, directed a fine choir, which I joined my first semester. We worked hard, learning and memorizing our repertory of Christian music in preparation for a weeklong tour in the spring. Choir practice was one of my favorite times.

While tuition and room and board were low at LBI, I had almost no money saved, since my teaching salary had been just enough to live on. My parents were not able to help me, so I needed to work.

LBI classes were all held in the mornings to allow students to work in the afternoons. My first job was cashiering in a grocery store, but bagging heavy items hurt my back. My next job was in a ladies' wear shop, but because the store was not doing well, I was let go. The last job I had that year was working as a family housekeeper.

Two weeks before school started in the fall, I arrived at LBI to look for another job. I was able to move into my new dorm room, which I was to share with classmate Marg Kenney. Marg had worked on the housekeeping staff at LBI during our first year and planned to continue.

The first day I was there, I met Miss Edna Lockhart, the women's dorm mother, in the hall.

"What are you doing here so early?" she asked.

"I've come to look for a job. I didn't have a good one all last year, and I hope to find something that will last through the school year."

"Would you like to work in Marg's place on housekeeping for a week? She just wrote to say she will be arriving late, and I need to get the dorm rooms ready for the students."

My heart sank. "I need to be out looking for a regular job," I said, "but if you really need me, I guess I could work for a week or so."

The next day, I grabbed a mop and pail and began scrubbing dorm room floors. At 10:00 a.m., the staff gathered in the dining room for a coffee break. Doug German, the business manager, made an announcement: "If anyone hears of a student who is looking for a job, we will have one in the office when school starts. Have her contact me."

Is it possible that I could get that job? I wondered. Immediately after break, I went to Doug's office and enquired about the job.

"Do you have any office experience?" he asked.

"I know how to type, but that's all."

"That's probably enough. The main job will be as a receptionist, answering the phone, and taking care of people who come to the window. You might have to do some bookkeeping, but it will be basic, and you can learn it as you go."

Doug told me the working hours and the amount I would earn. He said I could have the job if I wanted it.

I wanted it!

Looking back, I realize that this incident changed my life and helped me to look for God's leading instead of following my own way. My natural inclination was to reject Miss Lockhart's request and look for a job on my own. But I felt God telling me to fulfill that request. Had I not, I would not have heard about the opportunity in the school office. That job led me to discover that office work was really where God wanted me and where I was to spend the remainder of my life.

The days and months flew by quickly, and soon my second year at LBI was finished. I enjoyed my job in the office immensely, learning not only how to run the PBX switchboard but also the mimeograph, the scanner, and the big adding machine. I typed receipts, posted accounts payable invoices, answered students' questions, and did any number of other small jobs. I also disagreed with my mother's opinion of office work. It wasn't just for dumb kids but could be a necessary and fulfilling occupation.

With morning classes, four hours of work in the afternoons, and homework in the evening, I didn't have much time for anything else.

Since I didn't have any other plans for the summer between my second and third years at school, I was hired to work full-time at my job in the business office.

During my third year at LBI, I faced my first real experience with death. Dr. Percy Harris served as the much-loved president of LBI as well as professor of Bible and Christian education. Polio was still fairly prevalent, and in November of 1959, Dr. Harris was hospitalized with bulbar polio, the worst kind. He was placed in an iron lung, and the student body and staff prayed earnestly for his recovery. It was not to be. After three weeks, the Lord took him home at the age of thirty-seven. The whole school mourned, along with his wife, Kay, and children, Paul and Elizabeth. At times I would look down the hall expecting to see Dr. Harris coming in the front door. I seemed unable to accept that he was gone forever.

During Dr. Harris's illness and death, I really learned to pray. As he lay in the hospital, we students formed a prayer chain and prayed for him around the clock. Getting up at four o'clock in the morning to spend a half hour in prayer was not something that I would have chosen to do, but God met with me there. Although He didn't choose to answer our prayers as we hoped, afterwards I felt God's presence and comfort as we mourned for our beloved president.

In my third year, I took a course in Christian writing with Ann Winslow. As a course project, we wrote and produced a monthly newspaper for the school, a task I spent many long hours at and which I thoroughly enjoyed.

As graduation neared, I wondered what I would do next. My degree was in Christian education, but I had no desire to work in that field. I had enrolled in that course because I wanted the Bible study classes and a degree, and the straight Bible program provided only a certificate. So when I had an offer from LBI to continue at my present job full time for the next year, I accepted it happily.

Graduation was a time of excitement and great celebration. We were honored at a banquet for which I had saved enough money to buy a stunning new white-and-pink silk dress. For the first time in my three years there, I had a date for that banquet, although I found out later that two other girls had already turned down the young man I went with.

At the graduation ceremony, I received my degree, the first one in my extended family who had ever done so. I also received the Jean C. Scott Memorial Scholarship for the highest grades in an English course.

Teaching Again

One day, the dean of faculty, Frank Koksma, called me to his office. "We're looking for someone to teach a remedial English course in the fall," he said. "We want to bring incoming students, who didn't score well on their English exams, up to college level. Since you did very well in English and have had some teaching experience, we would like to offer you the job. It's just one course and is only for one semester. Are you interested?"

Little did he know that my teaching experience had made me say that I would never teach again. I wanted to shout no, but for some reason I couldn't. I told him I would think and pray about it. I talked to Ann Winslow, who had become my mentor in all things English. She promised to help me with the course. She had taught it before and had lots of class notes and student exercises that I could use.

After praying about this opportunity, I felt the Lord saying that if I were ever going to get over this fear of teaching, I would have to do it again. Here was an opportunity to heal a wound that could become a hindrance in the future. Perhaps teaching adults rather than children would be better. So I agreed to teach remedial English in the fall semester along with my work in the business office.

True to her word, Ann was a great help. I not only managed to get through that semester, but all of my students passed the course. I did lose my fear of teaching, but I didn't gain a love for it. I realized that I much preferred office work and that I did not have the gift of teaching.

A Door Opens

In October I received an application form from my mother for a contest she thought I should enter. CHLO, the radio station in St. Thomas, was sponsoring a Christmas short-story writing contest. The winner would receive one hundred dollars, and the station would produce the story and air it on Christmas Day. I tossed the application on a pile of unanswered letters and didn't think much about it. I had no time with my office work and teaching to think of such a thing.

Two weeks later, classes were cancelled for the fall spiritual emphasis conference, giving me some time off from teaching. To please my mother, I wrote a short story for the contest and sent it off. I was shocked when at the end of November the radio station sent me a one-hundred-dollar check, saying I had won first prize, and my story would be read on the radio on Christmas Day. Later, it was published in *Trails,* the Pioneer Girls magazine.

This got me thinking. Did God want me to be involved in a literature ministry in the future? I knew I didn't want to spend the rest of my life working in the LBI office, much as I enjoyed it.

In the spring of 1961, Harold Street of the Evangelical Literature Overseas spoke in chapel. His message challenged me, and I talked with him afterwards. After listening to me, he said, "If you are interested in literature production, you need further education in journalism. I'm on my way to Syracuse, New York, to visit an old friend, Dr. Frank Laubach. He is head of the Laubach Literacy Fund, which teaches people to read around the world. His son, Bob, teaches a course in literacy journalism at Syracuse University. If you like, I will talk to them about you and see if they can help you."

Within two weeks, I received a letter from Bob Laubach, telling me that the Laubach Literacy Fund was setting up an assistantship for a foreign student wishing to earn a master's degree in journalism from Syracuse University. Since I'm a Canadian, I qualified for that assistantship. First, I would need to get accepted into the master's program at the Syracuse University School of Journalism. Then I would be considered for the assistantship.

How could I be accepted to attend a big American university? I had only a bachelor of religious education degree from a small Canadian Bible institute. However, a few years before, LBI had received membership into the Accrediting Association of Bible Colleges. Partly because of this, when I applied to Syracuse, I was accepted. I immediately sent in my application for the assistantship and was awarded the first Laubach Foreign Student assistantship. This paid all of my tuition and gave me two thousand dollars a year to live on. In return I was required to work twenty hours a week at the Laubach office as assistant editor of their weekly literacy newspaper, *News for You.*

How is this going to affect my future? I wondered.

LBI choir

LBI school building

Chapter 4
Syracuse University
1961–1963

In the summer of 1961, Mom, Dad, and I drove to Massachusetts to visit Mom's brother and his wife, Uncle Wilfred and Aunt Arlene. Since the route took us past Syracuse, New York, I arranged to meet Bob Laubach. He graciously invited us to visit him at his home on a tree-lined street close to the university campus. It was a hot summer day, so we appreciated the tall glasses of iced tea that Fran, Bob's wife, served us on the front porch. Since they welcomed us as though we were longtime friends, I could see that the nervousness I had felt about studying in the States was unfounded.

One of my first tasks in Syracuse was to find a good church to attend. Someone suggested I try South Presbyterian, since I could walk to it in nice weather. There I found a vibrant, evangelical church with a strong ministry to college students. They also had a choir, which I soon joined. Every Sunday night, the college crowd met at someone's house for food, fellowship, and study. The pastor, the Rev. Don Wallace, was an excellent preacher, and I soon felt at home there.

Graduate school was not easy. Most of the students studied seven days a week. But I decided that God's plan for us to have a day of rest wasn't cancelled because of too much work, so I never studied on Sunday. In spite of this, I always completed my assignments on time. The programs at church and the friends I made there helped to keep me sane during those days of school and work.

Since journalism was a new field for me, I had to take prerequisite courses to enter the graduate program. One was photography, which I found both challenging and enjoyable.

My favorite course in all my journalism studies was graphic arts. While I am not artistic, I am quite mechanical, and this course covered the intricacies of printing and designing print. I learned how to set type by hand and how to operate a clapper printer, a linotype machine, and an offset printer. This was in the days before computers were in general use, since most computers filled up a whole room.

Literacy Journalism

My major was literacy journalism taught by Professor Bob Laubach. We learned to write materials for adult new literates, using a limited vocabulary and simple sentence structures. Our goal was to make our writing suitable for a sixth-grade level audience. We were assigned articles on many topics from current events, geography, science, politics, and any other topic that might interest adults who were just learning to read. These articles were printed in a weekly newspaper entitled *News for You,* published by the Laubach Literacy Fund. The fund used this small paper in their extensive literacy programs, especially throughout the southern states. The circulation eventually grew to many thousands of copies.

As a graduate assistant with the Laubach Literacy Fund, I worked twenty hours a week as assistant editor of *News for You.*

Caroline Blakely, the editor, had received her master's degree a couple of years before. She was wonderful to work with, and we became fast friends. She was a hardworking single mother of five children who loved her job and her family. I learned much from my work on *News for You,* and my experience in writing for new literates has had a permanent effect on my writing skills.

Dr. Frank Laubach, Bob's father and the founder of the Laubach Literacy Fund, was still living then. He had been a missionary in the Philippines for many years where he formulated the Each One Teach One method of teaching people to read. He became known as "Mr. Literacy" through his work not only in the Philippines but around the world. Bob followed in his steps and became head of the Laubach Literacy Fund after his father's death.

Most students who had undergraduate degrees in journalism could complete a master's degree in one year, but since I took several prerequisite courses and worked on *News for You*, my course load was limited to nine semester hours. It took me two years to complete my degree.

After the spring semester in 1962, I returned to Ontario and found a summer job at the headquarters of the Fellowship of Evangelical Baptist Churches of Canada in Toronto. I worked on their magazine, *The Fellowship Baptist,* and assisted the director in a number of secretarial projects.

When I returned to Syracuse in the fall of 1962, I moved into a new apartment with two women I had met the year before. One of them was a Mennonite. Since no Mennonite church could be found in the area, a group of Mennonite students met on Sunday mornings in our apartment for worship and Bible study. Some of them were in the religious journalism track, so I had classes with them. I enjoyed them and attended some of their functions.

During my second year at Syracuse, I continued working on *News for You* at the Laubach office. One of my classmates in Bob's "Writing for New Literates" course was a missionary, Agnes Lawless. She too was working on a master's degree and attended the Christian Journalism Club, where we became lifelong friends.

One day when she saw me typesetting, she said, "We could sure use you in the Philippines!" She told me about the work of Wycliffe Bible Translators and the need for someone to typeset literacy primers, Gospel portions, New Testaments, and Bibles. I tucked away this information for a future date.

One course required for graduation at Syracuse was research methods taught by Dr. George Bird. This course had a strong reputation for being the proverbial straw that broke the camel's back for journalism students. It consisted of library research in which we learned how to access all the resources of information in the library, since this was before the days of the Internet. The bulk of the course was a ten-page research paper to be written every week of the semester.

To complete work on our master's degrees, we wrote comprehensive examinations the end of March. They were divided in two sections, three hours for the general journalism section in the morning and three hours for the literacy journalism section in the afternoon. Because I had so little extra time to study, I knew I wasn't ready when the day came. But I was determined to finish that spring, so I had registered to write the exams.

We took our typewriters and dictionaries to the exam room and typed as fast as we could for each section. Our magazine-article writing professor had said, "Absolutely no spelling errors are allowed. Some people are poor spellers, but that's no excuse. If you don't know how to spell a word, look it up in the dictionary."

Two weeks later when the results came out, I found that my premonitions had been correct. I passed the literacy journalism section with no problems but just missed passing the general section by a few points. That meant I would have to take it again. I was upset but not surprised. I made arrangements to return to Syracuse in August to retake the exam, which I passed fine the second time.

Graduation was scheduled for late May, a beautiful time in central New York. My parents came to see me graduate, although it was an impersonal ceremony. Because the entire university had 2,500 graduates, the only ones who had their hoods installed and shook the chancellor's hand were the PhD candidates. The rest of us sat in chairs in the front section of the stadium, stood, and turned the tassels on our caps when the time came. Our degrees arrived in the mail three months later.

Dear God, now what do You want me to do?

Bob Laubach, Caroline Blakely, and Shirley in 1987

Chapter 5
Back to London
1963–1964

I loaded my parents' car with my personal belongings and left Syracuse after two years of hard work. Although I was sorry to leave many good friends behind, I was happy to be through with the studies. I would especially miss Bob and Fran Laubach, Caroline Blakely, and my friends at South Church. As I look back, their friendship helped me as a struggling foreign student to survive through two years of hard work and a bit of culture shock at the beginning.

I had been seeking the Lord's wisdom for several months to know what to do next. Bob Laubach suggested that I work with them overseas in their literacy projects, but I didn't have peace about that. I believed that teaching people to read was important, but I felt that the number-one priority of the organization I was to work with should be spreading the gospel of Christ.

I wrote to the London College of Bible and Missions, the new name for London Bible Institute where I had worked before, to see if they might have a job I could do. I received an answer, saying that they wanted someone to work in the alumni office, edit the alumni news magazine, and advise the yearbook staff, as well as teach the Christian journalism course. After praying about this, I agreed to return to LCBM in September of 1963.

Work in the Alumni Office

I enjoyed my work in the LCBM alumni office. I could put to use many things I'd learned in my graphics arts class at Syracuse by designing a new alumni news magazine. I wrote articles and worked with the printer to get it into production. I loved going across town to the print shop and watching the big presses spit out literature. I got printer's ink in my veins there, which has lasted for the rest of my life. One day I said to the print shop manager, "Murray, do you ever have women apprentices in your print shop?" He looked at me with amazement and said, "No, I can't imagine any woman would want this job." How wrong he was!

I also appreciated working with the yearbook staff. The staff all worked hard, and we put out two excellent yearbooks during my two years as advisor.

I taught the Christian journalism course the first year I was at LCBM, but I didn't enjoy even teaching a course where the material was familiar and the students were motivated. I came to the conclusion that teaching was not a gift I had been endowed with, and I shouldn't keep trying to do it.

A Near Fatal Accident

In November 1964, the LCBM alumni chapter in Kitchener requested a speaker from the alumni office for their regular fall meeting. Elmer Cassidy, field representative for the London area, Helen Hofstetter, secretary to the dean, and I were selected to attend this meeting. Elmer would be the speaker, and Helen and I would interact with the alumni.

It was early evening as we turned off one highway onto another highway approaching the city. This was a four-lane highway but without a median. A car heading south stopped in the inside lane, waiting for us to pass so it could cross into a gas station.

Just then another car driving very fast smashed into the back of it and forced it into the path of our car. We collided at the left front of our car, flipping the other car around in a circle. Our car had a bench seat in the front. I was in the middle where I had no seat belt. My left arm was thrown against the steering wheel, and my face hit the windshield, which shattered and left a large hole. I have no recollection of hitting the windshield. The first I can remember was sitting with my head against the dashboard and realizing that blood was dripping on my new winter coat.

Helen sat in her seat, stunned.

I pushed her a bit. "Get out, Helen."

She hesitated. "I can't open the door."

I undid her seat belt and reached to open the door, but it was jammed.

Elmer wasn't able to open his door either, but he climbed over the seat and got out the backdoor.

Soon someone forced our door open, helped us out, and laid us on the side of the road. A woman from a car behind us pressed tea towels on my forehead. "Don't worry," she said. "It's just a nosebleed."

A nosebleed? I thought. *Since when does a nosebleed run in your eyes?*

Before long an ambulance and the police arrived. The woman in the middle car that had hit us had back injuries, and the ambulance took her to the hospital.

Helen had a small cut on her chin where she had hit the dashboard. Policemen helped both Helen and me into the backseat of the police car.

The officer placed the drunk driver, who had caused the accident, in the front seat of the police car. He had a dislocated thumb. Elmer wasn't injured at all.

The police took Helen and me to the hospital emergency room, where she had six stitches placed in her chin. I was injured the most and was taken care of last. I had a gash across my right forehead and another through my left eyebrow. In all I had thirty-six stitches and was admitted to the hospital overnight.

The young doctor had just graduated from medical school the year before. Since he was very careful, he did a marvelous job of sewing me back together.

The next morning when I opened one eye that wasn't under a huge pressure bandage, I couldn't see anything clearly. *Has my eye been damaged?* I wondered. Later, I learned that swelling had caused my blurred vision. When the swelling went down, my eyesight was good again.

As I lay in that hospital bed, I prayed silently, *Thank You, God, for saving my life. I could easily have been killed. Were You trying to get my attention? Do You have something else You want me to do for You?* One word immediately came to mind: *Missions.* I suddenly realized that since I had gotten entrenched in my job at LCBM, I had set aside my interest in missions.

Later in the morning, Carol Wilson, one of our alumni, took me home for a day and drove me back to London. The doctor had removed the bandage, since he wanted my wounds to be left open to encourage healing. I was a sight! In a week my doctor in London removed the stitches, and I looked a bit better but not much. I wanted to go back to work to meet some deadlines. I felt fine, so I went. Lillian Scobie, one of my fellow staff members, refused to look at me for several weeks. Eventually, the healing was complete, but the long scar across my forehead had puckered and drawn in, leaving a small river of scar tissue across my face.

The insurance company was slow in processing my claim. They required me to go to Detroit, Michigan, for an evaluation for possible plastic surgery to remove my scar. Fortunately, I didn't need it. It was well into the next year before the claim was settled.

Missionary Call

Part of my job in the alumni office was to answer letters we had received from alumni. Many were missionaries serving around the world. As I read their letters, God impressed on me that instead of sitting in a comfortable job and writing letters to these missionaries, I should be out there joining them.

During the years I had spent at LBI and LCBM, I had heard many missionaries who had come to speak to our students in chapel meetings and missionary conferences. As I thought about the missions I was familiar with, one stood out in my memory—Wycliffe Bible Translators. I had been impressed with the stories I had heard about the changes in people's lives when they received the Scriptures in their own languages. I had also been impressed with the literature they left behind.

The time had come for me to find the organization God wanted me to become a part of. I planned to write to a number of missions to see where I would fit best, and perhaps God would show me the one He wanted me to join. Wycliffe was on the top of my list, so I sent a letter to their office in California, asking for information about their work.

By return mail, I had a packet of information in my mailbox. With it was a preliminary questionnaire, a form that would give them basic information about me, including my education and interests. I filled that out and sent it back. For some reason, I didn't feel led to write to any other mission.

Before long I received a letter from Wycliffe, saying that the information on my preliminary questionnaire qualified me to apply for membership with Wycliffe. If I were interested in becoming part of the Bible translation ministry, I would need to attend the Summer Institute of Linguistics in Norman, Oklahoma, during the summer for training in linguistics and Bible translation. They recommended I begin the membership process immediately, since the board met at the end of August. The process needed to be completed before summer school began because of the heavy workload at SIL.

I felt confused and unsure. I didn't even know what linguistics was, and I was afraid it might be something I didn't like or couldn't do. So I wrote back and said that I would plan to attend the summer course at Norman, Oklahoma, but I would wait before beginning my application to see if this was really something I wanted to do.

The next week I attended the annual missionary conference at my church. I don't remember who the speaker was or what he spoke about. All I remember was hearing God inwardly saying, *Why aren't you willing to trust Me? You don't want to begin the application to Wycliffe until you see whether this is something you want to do. But this is what I want you to do. It is important that you obey Me.*

The next week I sent a letter to Wycliffe, saying that God had changed my mind, and I requested application papers.

All that spring I filled out those papers, contacted references, and wrote my doctrinal statement. The latter turned out to be sixteen pages long, declaring what I believed about many different aspects of theology. A big job! Finally, I finished filling out the papers and sent them to the headquarters of Wycliffe Bible Translators in Glendale, California. Wycliffe didn't have an office in Canada that accepted new members yet.

All the time this was going on, I was asking God to supply the funds for me to go to SIL. At that time, LCBM was having financial difficulties. We had all-night prayer meetings, asking God to provide the needed funds for operating the school and meeting the payroll. My salary was very minimal, only enough to live on and nothing left to save. I knew that God would have to do a miracle to provide my travel funds, tuition, and room and board for the summer. He did! By the time I was ready to leave for Oklahoma, all the needed funds had come in.

One humorous incident regarding God's supply still makes me laugh. Our staff and faculty were aware that I needed funding. One day I received an anonymous gift in my mailbox, so I wrote a thank you note to the donor and gave it to our business manager, Doug German, thinking he could pass it on.

The next day our history professor, Horace Braden, stopped me in the hall. "I got your thank you note. You weren't supposed to know where that gift came from."

"I didn't until now," I replied.

I have never forgotten the chagrined look on his face. He hadn't noticed that my response was a "to whom it may concern" type of note.

Chapter 6
Heading toward Work with Wycliffe
1965–1966

I got permission from LCBM to take a summer break away from my job to attend SIL. They promised to save it for me in the fall. When school was over, I spent time with my parents and then began my trip to Norman, Oklahoma.

Oklahoma in the summer is hot! It was my first experience with really hot weather, and I found it hard to take. We lived in dorms that had been wartime barracks without air-conditioning. Pat, my roommate, had brought a ten-inch electric fan, but that was the only cooling we had other than the dining hall, which was air-conditioned. One day the temperature got to 106 degrees F. (41 C.), but most days it was in the nineties.

To keep our expenses down, everyone had to work an hour a day at various jobs. When we arrived, we filled out forms stating the kind of work we would like to do or were trained to do. I said I would like to do secretarial work or work in the library. I was assigned to a typing job. After one day, I received a notice in my mailbox, saying my job had been changed to cleaning refrigerators. *Cleaning refrigerators? Why the change?* I wondered.

The kitchen had a number of large stainless-steel refrigerators that needed to be washed down every day. Jello was a popular meal item, and the cooks must have had shaky hands because almost every day they had spilled jello on the refrigerator shelves. By the time I arrived after supper each night, the jello was well dried on and took a lot of scrubbing to remove. I also had to wipe the outside of the doors with lemon oil to remove the finger marks that had accumulated through the day.

On Saturdays I had to clean the big walk-in refrigerator. I enjoyed that job, since it let me get cooled off once a week. One Saturday when the heat was at its worst, I walked across the campus wearing a long-sleeved sweatshirt to keep warm while I did my job. I met a number of students on the way who stared at me with open mouths. They must have wondered why anybody would wear a sweatshirt when the temperature was over one hundred degrees.

I often wondered why my job was switched from one I was experienced in to the mundane job of cleaning refrigerators. Although I have no proof of this, I suspected it was because I was a candidate, and staff members were watching me to see how I would handle such a situation. Just in case that was so, I decided to use my cleaning time to do a little singing practice. I sang my way through that job all summer. Later, one of the team who interviewed candidates said to me, "I've never seen anybody do that job so joyfully before."

Linguistics was difficult. It took me a while to discover that some terms were the same as those used in English grammar, but the meanings were different. In spite of the fact that I worked long hours to complete assignments and get papers written, I did enjoy my summer. I attended numerous extracurricular activities and made good friends among the students and staff, most of whom were translators in Mexico who came to Norman every summer to teach.

Every day a volleyball game seemed to be compulsory. I loathed volleyball. I was never good at it when we played in high school. I always seemed to come away with a red hand and arm from serving and was never good at getting the ball over the net. One day it occurred to me that nowhere had I read in the candidate literature that you had to be a volleyball player to join Wycliffe. So at that point, I stopped playing and haven't played a game since.

In our language-learning course, we had two weeks at the end of the summer when we worked with speakers from Oklahoma native languages. We were to elicit information from them and learn the basics of their language without using English.

A Providential Meeting

I had only two days of working with a language helper when I came down with the mumps. As a child, I had almost every childhood disease there is, but I didn't have mumps. Only one other case was on campus, and I didn't have any contact with her, so I don't know where I picked it up. I was very sick in bed for over a week with swelling on both sides of my face. Looking in the mirror, I thought I knew what I'd look like if I gained fifty pounds. The doctor gave me Demerol to ease the pain, but it made me so light-headed I could hardly walk. I had to be in bed most of the time.

Since I wasn't allowed to go to the dining hall, one of the students on the nursing staff brought me my meals. Anne West was a graduate nurse who was also a candidate for Wycliffe, and we got to know each other while I ate. Later, I realized that this was part of God's plan.

One day when I was in bed, a board member informed me that Wycliffe had accepted me as a member. That was a joyful day.

As soon as I was well again, I went back to classes in time to write final exams. Also, a staff member talked to me about my next steps. Although I had passed all of my courses, I didn't have a mad passion for linguistics like some students had. I discovered that the mission had a long list of other things that could be done besides linguistic analysis and translation. Perhaps I would be better suited for one of those jobs. When I suggested this, the staff member said that since I had done well and already had a master's degree in another field, I should take another year of SIL. But first, I had to go to Wycliffe's jungle camp in southern Mexico on the border of Guatemala.

Even the thought of that was scary.

Anne West

Chapter 7
Excitement in Jungle Camp
1966

After the summer course in Norman, Oklahoma, was finished, my roommate and I loaded up my car and headed back to southern Ontario for the fall. Pat returned to her last year of classes at LCBM, and I returned to my job in the alumni office.

This time I knew it would be for just one more semester. I also began raising support, now that Wycliffe had accepted me as a member.

Raising Support and Prayer Partners

Almost immediately, Faith Baptist Church in St. Thomas, where I grew up, and Wortley Baptist in London, where I was now a member, took on a good part of my support. Other individuals also came on board when they heard I was support-raising.

In October I received a phone call from Rev. Don Wallace at South Presbyterian Church in Syracuse, asking me how much support I still needed. I told him. He said that his missions committee was meeting, and they would get back to me if they decided to take on some of my support. About an hour later, he called again and said they would cover all the rest that I needed. Faith Baptist in St. Thomas is still supporting me more than fifty years later.

Beside my work at LCBM, I got ready to go to jungle camp in Mexico in February. I received a long list of specific items that I needed to buy—a duffle bag, sleeping bag, air mattress, pistol belt, ammunition box, plastic ground sheets, water purification tablets, a canteen cup, mosquito net, insect repellent, cotton skirts and tops, and hiking shoes. It sounded as if I were joining the army, since I found many of these things at the army surplus store. I was preparing for living outside in the jungle for three months, a training that would prepare me for primitive living wherever I ended up. All of my equipment had to fit inside one duffle bag, since that was all we were allowed to take with us. I learned how to pack efficiently as I struggled to get everything I would need for three months into one bag.

My trip to Mexico gave me another new experience. I had never flown before nor had I needed a passport or visa. My visa for Mexico was delayed until the very last minute. The day before I was to leave, I finally received a call from the travel agent in London, saying I could pick it up.

Travel to Jungle Camp

I had moved out of my apartment and was home at RR5 by then, so Mom and I went to London to collect my passport and visa. We had a great deal of snow, and overnight a new dump had made the highway very slippery. Halfway there, I hit a slick spot and skidded until I faced the direction I had come from. Fortunately, no cars were in sight, so I turned around and continued on my way. The next day, my parents drove me to Toronto to catch my flight to Mexico City. I was nervous to fly since this was my first time in an airplane but also excited. The flight was smooth except for a short way over the Gulf of Mexico. We had just finished dinner, and my seatmate, suffering from airsickness, deposited her dinner in the bag provided for such things.

I arrived in Mexico City in the late evening. Fortunately, someone from the SIL center met me and took me to the Mexico branch headquarters. There I stayed with Canadian Helen Ashdown, who worked in the office. I not only met my fellow campers, but I sat through several orientation sessions and a three-day translation seminar. We new recruits also saw the sights of downtown Mexico City, visited the pyramids, and prepared to travel seven hundred miles south to the state of Chiapas, the site of jungle camp.

We traveled to Tuxtla, the capitol of Chiapas, a nineteen-hour trip by bus through the mountains. The bus was hot, so we were happy for a stop about two a.m. for a drink from fresh coconuts. Vendors punched holes in the eyes at the tops of the coconuts and inserted straws, another new experience. The juice was slightly fizzy and refreshing. For breakfast, we stopped at a roadside restaurant, where we ate fried eggs and tortillas.

Main Base

From Tuxtla we flew with a Missionary Aviation Fellowship (MAF) pilot in a single-engine plane to the main base of jungle camp on the Jatate River. Main base was a rustic camp with one main building used for a dining hall, kitchen, and classrooms surrounded by a number of thatched-roof mud cabins. The cabins had wooden shelves for beds where we spread our air mattresses and sleeping bags. My cabin mate was Ginny Larson from Minnesota, who was assigned to work in the Philippines. Our group consisted of forty-five campers plus their children, one of the largest sessions since jungle camp began.

The first day was steer butchering day. In the afternoon, everyone gathered in the corral armed with sharp knives, and we helped skin the animal after it was killed. The next morning we cut it up and canned seventy-five quarts of beef, ready for eating during the next six weeks.

Since campers did all the cooking and maintenance, the leaders divided us into crews of six each for planning and cooking meals. Each crew had a chief who organized it and made sure the meals were cooked and served.

Ray Posey was the head chef in charge of the kitchen. He had worked in Mexico for a number of years and was an excellent cook. He taught us how to bake bread in the big black wood-fired cook stove, how to cook beans, and how to make plain food palatable. A small paper-covered cookbook contained the recipes that were used and distributed to each person. Later, that book was enlarged and published in a 475-page hard-covered edition that sits on my bookshelf. I still use it for favorite recipes that can't be found anyplace else.

The indigenous people who lived in the area were Tzeltal Indians. Since they were accustomed to dozens of Gringos living in their neighborhood, they came by often to sell eggs, bananas and other fruits, tortillas, and vegetables. They lived in villages and practiced slash-and-burn farming, cutting down the jungle and burning the wood to make clearings for their corn crops.

Days were packed full, from lights on at 5:00 a.m. to lights out at 9:00 p.m. Our everyday classes taught us how to live without electricity or running water, how to operate and repair our equipment, and how to keep healthy. We used oranges to practice giving shots. We also had classes in the Tzeltal language and were expected to use it with the local people when we had contact with them. We had swimming classes in the Jatate River, which was icy cold, since it was early March. The weather was about like early summer in Ontario.

I had never learned to swim well, even though I had taken swimming lessons during high school. I could float on my back and sidestroke for a short distance, but I had never learned to breathe properly so ran out of breath and stamina quickly. I was classed as a beginner, but in spite of regular lessons, I didn't progress very much.

We had several conditioning hikes to get into good shape for the one big hike of the session, a two-day, thirty-mile trip to visit the Lacandon Indians. The translators for this group were Phil and Mary Baer, so our leaders called this the "Baer Trip." At the end of the first day's hiking, we camped overnight in the jungle, sleeping in hammocks tied between trees. These hammocks had roofs and netting sides, so when we were zipped inside, mosquitoes and other jungle creatures were excluded. It was tricky to sleep in these hammocks, because it was easy to flip right over if we weren't careful.

We traveled with several mules and one horse, which we took turns riding. Some of the trail was in deep jungle and very muddy after the winter rains. Sometimes the mules would get so mired up to their knees that they needed help to get going again. Some trees had spikes on their trunks, and on occasion the mules would pick their way through the mud and rub riders against those trees if they didn't watch carefully. Most of the time I preferred to walk.

A translation project was in progress among those people, but the Lacandons had not responded to the gospel. The Baers had learned their language but found it difficult to obtain a translation helper to work with them. Later, when Phil and Mary had translated the New Testament, a small church was in existence. The Baers worked for fifty years with the Lacandons.

Advanced Base

After returning from this trip, we prepared to move from main base to advanced base. One of our last activities before leaving was an overnight canoe trip up the river. We paddled upstream to a pre-designated location in several large dugout canoes. Each canoe carried about six people, including one who stood at the back to steer. One canoe held the box containing our food for the trip. Unfortunately, the food canoe hit a rock and overturned, throwing all the passengers into the river. The screams from the onlookers were not "Save the people" but "Save the food!" After camping for the night, we returned to main base to get ready to hike to advanced base.

We packed everything in our duffle bags and set off to walk twenty miles in one day to the advanced base on the Santa Cruz River, which was much larger than the Jatate. This time we had the children along. Many of them were too small to walk far, so whoever was currently riding a mule or the horse held a child.

Since we were the third session of jungle camp that year, we were using the same location as the previous two sessions, so a clearing in the jungle for the central area was already there. Here we had classes and met for group meetings, including Sunday services. From this clearing, trails led in three directions where the leaders told us to build our *champas,* shelters we would construct from whatever jungle materials we could find. My *champa* partner for the six weeks was Julie Van Dyken.

In previous years, campers had to cut cane and forage for leaves to thatch their *champa* roofs. However, the administration decided that since it was not likely that we would need to do this in field situations, we should learn how to supervise someone else who spoke a language we didn't understand.

We were assigned Tzeltal men to be our construction engineers. We had to design our own *champas,* using guidelines we were given. Two single women were not allowed to place their house posts more than six feet by six feet apart.

However, Julie and I got extra space on both sides by extending the roof to the ground to make an A-line construction. We put the platforms for our beds in that space, which gave us a full six feet in the center of the building. We made the end walls and framework of the roof of cane that grew profusely in the area, and the thatch was leaves from the cane that we tied onto the framework. We made shelves at the back for our clothing and left the front open. We built a table with a bench on the left side and a mud stove on the right side. Over the table and stove, we hung a big sheet of plastic to protect us from the rain.

We built the mud stove on a cane platform with a firebox in the center and an iron plate on top for cooking. An opening at the back allowed the smoke to rise through a stack of tin cans with the ends removed. These mud stoves worked very well if we followed the instructions carefully. Julie and I didn't make our firebox deep enough, so I spent a great deal of time fanning the fire to give it enough draft to keep burning.

While we were building our *champa*, we slept in jungle hammocks slung between trees at our campsite. We were happy when the work was done, and we could sleep on a flat bed again. We blew up our air mattresses, spread out our sleeping bags, hung our mosquito nets, unpacked our clothing from our duffle bags, including the minimal number of dishes and cooking pots we were allotted, and settled in to living for the next five weeks in our *champa*. We dubbed ours, "The Bird Cage," because Julie and I both liked to sing.

Since we were the third session who had camped in this location, our predecessors had gathered and burnt the handy firewood, and we had to go farther afield to find wood for cooking. In Mexico a certain tree burns fairly well when it's green. Someone had cut one down not far down the trail, so we chopped it up and brought armloads to our *champa*. What we didn't know was that the wood was extremely hard. We had an axe, but I didn't have the strength to make much of a dent in that hard wood. Julie was bigger and stronger, so I made a deal with her. Since she didn't enjoy cooking, I agreed to cook all of the breakfasts if she would cut the wood. That worked fine.

Later, a group of us rowed across the river to a *milpa*, a field that had been burned ready for planting. We found lots of wood from trees that had only partially burned. From then on, we had plenty of firewood.

When the bell rang, indicating food was available for distribution, we hurried to the center. The leaders gave us canned food and other dried staples, but we had to buy fresh food when it was available. Tzeltal women brought eggs, cooking bananas, greens, tortillas, and vegetables from time to time. We learned to cook bananas with onions for a vegetable, but we longed for good eating bananas, the kind we had at home that were sweet and didn't need to be cooked.

One day some Indian women delivered several big hands of eating bananas to the center. The bananas were still green, but we looked forward to enjoying them. We took our share to our hut and hung them on the end of a roof slat to ripen. We waited and waited, but they took a long time to turn yellow. Then one day I pinched one and discovered that it was very soft. That was when we learned that green bananas were delicious if we didn't let them get rotten first. Our disappointment was great when we discovered that our bananas were well beyond the eating stage and were only good for making banana bread. That variety never does get yellow.

We had pressure cookers to boil our water and cook fresh meat. One day a male camper brought us a turtle he had found at the river. I knew that turtle was good for eating but had never cooked one before. Using a machete, I opened the shell with great difficulty. I discovered that nothing but the turtle's inner parts were inside the shell. Only the legs, neck, and tail were edible. We cooked him up and had turtle stew on rice for supper, quite passable.

Six single men were in our session, which was more than usual. Jim Musgrove lived at the other end of the campgrounds, so we usually only saw him at class. One day he said that he had bought a live turkey from a Tzeltal woman, and he was going to cook it Texas style in a pit in the ground. He invited us to attend his turkey party.

Julie and I looked forward to a good meal of roast turkey, until we heard that Jim had failed to tie it up tight enough, and the turkey had fled.

One of our activities was to spend an extended time with a Tzeltal family. Some campers moved from place to place, staying with several families. Since Julie is a nurse, the leaders assigned us to stay with one family where the wife had recently lost a baby. They lived in a village less than an hour's hike from jungle camp, so we hiked there in the morning. When the baby had been born, it had come transverse with one arm out first. Nobody could help turn the baby, so it died. Later, the husband took his wife several hours away to a hospital where the baby was removed. The mother needed strong antibiotics for some time to take care of infection, but the family couldn't afford for her to stay in the hospital, so she came home. Julie's job was to teach the father how to give her injections in a sterile way. It took several tries, but eventually he caught on. It wasn't easy, since our knowledge of Tzeltal was very limited, and he didn't speak any English. We don't know what happened after we left, but hopefully the mother survived.

The family was very hospitable and gave us a room to sleep in. The room was bare of furniture, but they had spread leaves on the floor and gave us blankets. The floor wasn't smooth, so we had a bumpy bed but managed to sleep well even so. One morning we woke up to a commotion outside our door. The older sons of the family were shooting rats that had gone up a tree. I have never seen such big rats, the size of small dogs.

These men were excellent shots. One day the sons went hunting with their father and shot a *tigre* (ocelot). The skin was valuable if it was in good condition. This one was beautiful with no bullet holes. The shot had gone in through one eye and out the throat, so when it was skinned, the center cut went through the throat bullet hole. The men worked all morning, removing the pelt and getting it ready for market. They gave the carcass to the mother to prepare for supper. It was delicious!

Survival Hike

Another noteworthy activity of jungle camp was the survival hike. The date for this hike was kept secret from us campers. Men and women went on separate hikes. Our leaders told us that it would be within the next week, and we had to be prepared to go at a moment's notice. We packed food items that we were allowed to have and left them in our *champas* to be delivered to us later. On the day it was our turn to go, we were sitting in class at the center. Suddenly, our instructor said, "This is it! The women are going on a survival hike now. Divide into two groups. Assemble on the trail, and one group will follow me. The other will follow my 'brother.' We are 'Indians' and don't speak your language. We will guide you to the places you are going to sleep tonight."

Off we went with only our canteens full of water that we had been carrying to class all week in case we were called to go. We hiked down trails we hadn't been on before, following our "Indian." All day we had nothing to eat except whatever we could find in the jungle. For me, that was nothing. Late in the afternoon, we came to the riverbank and spotted an island in the middle of the river. We had to wade through the river, which was only half-way to our knees, and locate spots on the island to build shelters and spend the night. We had to be out of sight of anybody else.

I found a spot, and taking my machete, I began cutting branches and cane that I found in the area to make a bed with a roof over it in case it rained. I had a length of nylon cord on my web belt that I wove back and forth through the cane poles to keep them together for the bed. I found four forked sticks for the legs of the bed to keep it off the ground. I tied leaves on the frame over the bed to make a roof. Then I built a small fire and settled down to wait for morning.

That was probably the longest night of my life. Soon it began to rain, and I found that my bed wasn't waterproof. I had a plastic poncho on my web belt, which I put on, but it didn't keep me very dry either. I spent most of the night fanning my fire to keep it from going out. I didn't know what kind of creatures might be living on that island, and I didn't want to have an encounter with one in the dark. At one point, I saw big eyes staring at me from the opposite side of the fire. I prayed a lot that night and later found out that the eyes were from a large land toad that had been attracted to the fire.

Finally, morning came. Although we weren't supposed to get together, everybody was so miserable from the rain that we all decided we'd had enough. By calling out, we managed to find one person who still had a good fire burning. We all gathered there to comfort each other and try to get warm and dry.

Later in the morning, we saw a canoe coming down the river. It pulled up where we were and dispensed one of our staff members and our food bags that we had left in our *champas*. But before he gave us those, he gave each of us a chocolate bar. That was the best chocolate bar I have ever eaten.

Now came the next part of our exercise. We were divided into two groups and given the following scenario: We were supposedly a group of botanists in a balloon who were following a group of butterflies as they migrated south. The balloon had crashed on the island, and we were lost. One of our number was injured. Someone had to stay on the island with the injured person, and the rest had to wade to the shore of the river and start looking for help. In order not to get lost, they were to cut notches in the trees as they went, which could be used by searchers who might be looking for us. I was chosen to stay behind on the island.

We discovered later that the other half of the women were given the same scenario, except they were the searchers who were looking for a group of botanists who had crashed their balloon in the jungle. They were excellent searchers, since before the afternoon was over, they had found the notches on the trees and were able to follow them back to our island and rescue us.

Usually, people on survival hike stayed out at least two nights, but since we solved our problem early, we were taken back to camp in the late afternoon. As we rowed to a nearby bend in the river, we saw that the camp was just around the bend. We had walked all day only to end up almost within shouting distance of the base.

As time went by, we became more confident that we could live and survive in difficult situations. We made good friendships, some that have lasted our lifetimes, and we all looked forward to when we would put some of this learning into real-life practice.

The last task we had to perform was to build several balsa wood rafts on which we would float downriver to the MAF airstrip where we would be flown out to Tuxtla and back to Mexico City and home. While balsa is light and floats well, the logs needed to be quite large to hold us all with our baggage. We were glad for the men in our midst who could do the heavy lifting.

Eventually, the rafts were completed, and the day came to say good-bye to advanced base and head downstream. It was a beautiful day with the sun on the jungle trees and the water rippling under us as we poled our way toward our destination. I felt a bit sad to be leaving all this beauty but glad it was over and the next step was not far ahead.

We spent a day in Tuxtla in a hotel and then went on to Mexico City. Again I stayed with Helen Ashdown for a couple of days until I flew back to Toronto and home.

I had spent my twenty-ninth birthday at jungle camp. It was time to go forward to the task to which God was calling me.

Chapter 8
Linguistic Studies in North Dakota
1966

Two weeks later, I packed up my little brown Volkswagen and headed to Grand Forks, North Dakota, for my second summer of linguistic studies at SIL. I stopped just south of the Straits of Mackinac in Michigan and picked up Jackie Bernhardt, who had been at Norman the summer before and who was also taking her second year at North Dakota. We drove across the Upper Peninsula of Michigan, the corner of Wisconsin, and all of Minnesota to reach the University of North Dakota (UND) at Grand Forks.

Halfway across the north of Lake Michigan in bush country where we hadn't seen a building for miles, we had a flat tire. I had a spare, but for some reason I didn't have a tire wrench. Right across the road was a gas station. *God is taking care of us*, I thought, but when we checked, they didn't have a tire wrench that would fit my Volkswagen wheel nuts. But God did take care of us. Soon a car came along, and the driver had a wrench that fit. He changed our tire, and since the old tire was destroyed, he insisted on giving us money to buy a new tire when we got to the next town. Was he an angel or just a kind man who wanted to assist two damsels in distress? I don't know, but God used him to take care of us, whichever he was.

After the heat and primitive conditions at Norman the summer before and three months of living in the jungles of Mexico, the campus at UND was pure luxury. We stayed in a fairly new air-conditioned dormitory. The classrooms, dining hall, library, and all the grounds looked beautiful.

North Dakota is in the middle of the prairie, so trips out of town took me back to the times I had crossed these prairies with my parents on the way to visit my grandmother. Part of the summer was hot, but most of the time the temperature was reasonable. I enjoyed my second year of SIL much more than my first. My work job was setting tables in the dining room and occasionally assisting the cook, which I enjoyed doing.

I also liked my courses. We studied transformational grammar that was more like geometry, which I could do, while tagmemics that we studied at Norman was more like algebra, which I wasn't good at. One of our teachers, Austin Hale, was enthusiastic about the subject and made the course interesting, almost fun. Transformational grammar uses tree diagrams. When Austin had to leave before the summer was finished, the students had a farewell party for him. We made a twenty-foot-long poster wishing him goodbye and designing our message into a tree diagram.

45

Toward the end of the summer, we celebrated a wedding. Two of our students from Toronto were engaged and planning to get married later in the fall. They were from Germany originally and were very poor. When it was nearly time to travel home, they didn't have enough money to pay for two motel rooms. They decided they would quietly get married in Grand Forks so they could have just one room.

One of Uwe Gufstassen's friends got wind of this, and we all helped them have a proper wedding. The wife of one of the students was a good seamstress, so she made Elke's wedding dress. We asked the pastor at the East Grand Forks Baptist Church to conduct the wedding in his church. We arranged the school dining room like a reception with a head table and flowers.

On the wedding day, the whole student body flocked to the church to see Uwe and Elke Guffstasson get married, and we celebrated at a lovely reception in the dining room. This didn't cost them a cent. We sent them off home to Toronto with our blessings, knowing they were part of the large Wycliffe family who would spend their lives serving God in Bible translation.

Assigned to the Philippines

During the summer, members from a number of countries gave presentations. One was the Philippines. Because of my connection at Syracuse University with the Laubachs and their beginnings in the Philippines and also because of my friendship with Agnes ("Atchie") Lawless who worked there, I had become interested in working there too.

The North Dakota SIL group had an agreement with the Philippines branch. Members who wanted to work there were requested to take at least one summer at North Dakota SIL, working on a Philippine language. The Philippines branch was greatly in need of translators, so when I expressed an interest in going there, I was assigned with no difficulty.

But what would my next step entail? I wondered.

Chapter 9
On My Way
1966

I didn't know what life would be like or what I would need on the other side of the world. At Grand Forks that summer, I had talked with Marilou Weaver who, with her husband, Dan, had spent five years with SIL in the Philippines. Marilou gave me a great piece of advice, one I've never forgotten. When I asked her what kinds of things I should take, she said, "Take whatever you need to make you happy. Some people need certain types of things; others can live with very little. Decide what kind of person you are, and take what you think you can't get along without."

Getting Ready

I didn't know where I would be living but expected it to be in a village in the rural Philippines. So I stored my good china and silverware at home and bought Melmac dishes, stainless steel cutlery, and pots and pans. I bought a cot-sized foam mattress, basic tools, sheets, towels, tablecloths, kitchen utensils, baking pans, and much more.

Our leaders had told us to pack in forty-five gallon steel drums with locking rings, since our shipments would go by freighter. Dad got three steel lard drums free at the bakery. When well washed, they served me fine. They didn't have the proper rings that would take padlocks though, so Dad drilled holes through the tops and out the sides of the drums, through which padlock hasps would fit around the rings with screws to tighten them. Another set of holes and padlocks on the other side of each drum secured them safely.

Packing these drums was a big job. The mattress just fit when rolled, leaving space to tuck in other things that needed padding. Eventually, I packed everything in, attached the shipping labels, and sent the drums to Home of Peace in Oakland, California. The drums would go on a freighter with members Joe and Marilyn Waddington as part of their shipment to the Philippines. They planned to sail in January.

When not shopping and packing barrels, I spoke at meetings around southwestern Ontario, about the work of Wycliffe, what I was planning to do, and about my experiences in jungle camp. I also waited for my Philippine visa to come from Vancouver. It was delayed because of a mail strike, so by the time it arrived, I had to advance my departure date to December 4.

Then the Philippine director sent me a letter, telling me I shouldn't plan to come until December 20. The branch was having their biennial conference at Nasuli, the southern center on the island of Mindanao. Nobody would be in Manila to meet me or to give me directions. Since that was so close to Christmas, I decided to spend Christmas at home. I looked forward to this last celebration with my family.

An Important Visit in Hawaii

While working at LCBM, I had become good friends with librarian Betty Roberts. Her brother was studying at the University of Hawaii in Honolulu. She suggested that since my flight had a stop in Honolulu, I should spend a few days there. She would ask Tom to show me around. I made contact with him, and he agreed. I also asked him to make reservations for me at the local YWCA.

When I arrived in Honolulu, Tom was at the airport to meet me with a friend. He had mentioned that I was coming to a classmate of his, Dick Elkins, who was also working on his PhD at the university. Dick and his wife Betty were translators with SIL in the Philippines. When he heard where I was going, he and Betty decided that I should stay with them instead of the YWCA. So Dick had come to take me home.

I loved my stay with the Elkins and my time touring around Honolulu. We went swimming on Waikiki, visited tourist shops, and drove all around the island of Oahu, stopping to see the sights. It was the first time I had seen pineapples growing.

I was scheduled to fly to Manila late on New Year's Eve. We spent the evening at Tom's apartment high up on a mountainside where we had a wonderful view of the fireworks that lit up the sky. My flight left at midnight, with a two-hour stop in Guam, and arrived in Manila at 7:00 a.m. on January 2. Because we had flown across the international dateline, I completely missed New Year's Day in 1967.

That was to be a momentous year in my life, in spite of its not having a beginning.

Chapter 10
Arrival in the Philippines
1967

When I stepped off the plane in Manila, I felt as if I had stepped into a sauna. Although it was January, the coolest month of the year, the high humidity and the temperature in the eighties F. (26 C.) felt very hot to me after coming from Canada's winter.

I soon had to learn a whole new system of measurements, since the Philippines was on the metric system. Canada didn't adopt that system until the mid-1970s. The average temperature in Manila in January was 30 C. (86 F.). The humidity was the big problem. In January it ran an average of 68 percent, and that felt damp to me.

Waiting at the airport to welcome me were Ed Ruch, the administrative officer for SIL in Manila, Joanne (Jo) Shetler, Donna Hettick, and Carolyn Kent, translators who worked in the northern part of the Philippines. Donna and Carolyn worked with the Northern Kankanay people and Jo with the Balangaos. They were all in Manila for a break from their language work.

On our way to the SIL guesthouse in San Juan, a suburb of Manila, Jo announced, "We're planning to stop at the Cherry Supermarket to buy a few things." I didn't know what to expect but thought the store might be something like Safeway. Instead, it was quite small, more like a Mom and Pop store at home.

We soon arrived at the SIL guesthouse in San Juan, a large nineteenth-century Spanish house set on a hill. We drove up a steep drive and unloaded my bags. A young Filipino man picked them up and disappeared inside with them.

The guesthouse was a two-story building with a wide center stairway. Downstairs were three bedrooms, an office, and the men's bathroom. Upstairs were four more bedrooms, two on each side, a *sala*, (living room), dining room, large kitchen, and the women's bathroom. Jackie Ruch, Ed's wife, as the guesthouse manager, warmly welcomed me to Manila.

One of the bedrooms on the second floor was designated as the "girls' dorm." This had three bunk beds, each with its own white mosquito net. We had used khaki-colored mosquito nets at jungle camp, and I had loathed them because they gave me claustrophobia. At the end of advanced base, I had burned mine with great glee. But these were sheer white.

Jo informed me that Willis and Ginny Kramer had invited us for dinner at their home. Willis was the radio technician and operator. At 5:00 p.m. Jo,

Donna, Carolyn, and I climbed aboard Willis's vehicle and drove the few blocks to their home.

Ginny served us a delicious meal of ham with raisin sauce and scalloped potatoes, but that is all I can remember of that evening, since I experienced my first jet lag. I went to sleep once at the dinner table and fought to stay awake the rest of the time. Willis finally took pity on me and drove us back to the guesthouse. Since then, I have experienced many more bouts of jet lag, something that I have never gotten over. In fact, the older I get, the worse it becomes. Travelling halfway around the world upsets my sleep patterns for about a week every time I take a trip.

ఴఴ

The next morning I sat up on the top bunk bed and peered through the mosquito net. Jo, Donna, and Carolyn were dressed and ready for breakfast. I threw back the netting and climbed down the ladder to the floor.

A Visit with Jo Shetler

As I dressed, Jo asked me, "How would you like to go home with me in a couple of days? I understand that Anne West, Marge Draper, and Ginny Larson won't be here for three weeks, and you need to wait for them before going to Nasuli for orientation. I'm starting back to Balangao day after tomorrow, and I'd love to have you go with me if you would like to. That way you could see my place and meet my Balangao friends."

"Could I? That would be great!" I hadn't imagined that I would get to visit a language project so soon after arrival.

"I'll send a radio message to the director at Nasuli to check it out, and we should know by this afternoon. I imagine he will say 'Go ahead!'"

Jo walked to the radio shack and gave a message to Willis to send by single sideband radio to the director at Nasuli, requesting permission for me to join her for three weeks. Late in the afternoon, we received his okay.

Before leaving Manila, I needed to get paper work done at immigration that would make my stay legal. Ed Ruch took me downtown to take care of that. Since this process took us nearly all day, I was grateful that I didn't have to do it by myself.

The next day I went with Jo to the grocery store to buy food and film. Jo's village had no such store. Everything had to be flown in.

At 5:30 a.m. on January 5, 1967, Jo and I caught a bus to travel 155 miles and six hours north to Baguio, the Philippine summer capital situated at

5,000 feet in the mountains. The temperature was in the eighties in Manila and very humid, but Baguio was pleasantly cool. After arriving, we took our baggage to the airport and then returned to the farmers' market to buy fresh fruit and vegetables to take to Natunin.

Soon after lunch, the SIL plane arrived to fly us to Bagabag, our northern center. It was a four-passenger single-engine Helio Courier, especially designed for short takeoffs and landings (STOL). These planes are ideal for the kind of flying needed to navigate mountain airstrips where only short flat spots can be found.

We arrived at Bagabag after about twenty minutes of flying over rugged mountain peaks. The center was about 1.8 miles from the town of Bagabag, which was situated in a valley surrounded by mountains. The center housed the SIL translators who were working with language groups in northern Luzon, the big island at the north of the Philippines. Numerous support services were there, including the hangar for the airplanes, a storage area called a *bodega*, a maintenance department, and a small library.

Jo had a beautiful two-bedroom house, which had been built for her and her partner, Anne Fetzer, when they had arrived five years before. Unfortunately for Jo, after two years, Anne returned to the States and married longtime friend Tommy Hopkins. Since then, Jo had been working alone.

After two days at Bagabag, we flew to Natunin, high in the mountains of Mountain Province. The airstrip was very short and seemed to go uphill as we landed. From the airstrip, we hiked for twenty-five minutes to the village over trails that ran along the tops of rice-terrace walls, some as much as eight feet high.

Balangao is like the Banaue rice terraces of northern Luzon. These terraces were built by hand more than two thousand years ago and are considered one of the eight wonders of the world. They have provided fields for planting mountain rice to feed their people. The views as we walked were breathtaking, since we were about halfway up the mountain, and we could see for miles across the valleys.

Jo's house in Natunin was small—two rooms and a bath, consisting of a water-seal toilet and a tin washtub hanging on the wall. When Jo and Anne arrived in Natunin, their house owner's uncle, Canao, lived close by. Balangaos are family oriented and thought it wasn't safe for foreigners to be living alone. They needed protection, so he said he would be their father ("Ama").

Ama's niece, Tekla, became like a sister to Jo. She had a three-year-old girl, Ana, when I arrived there. The first night, Tekla invited us to eat with her family. Being in the tropics, the sun goes down almost the same time all year, so when we arrived at Tekla's house around 6:00 p.m., it was nearly dark.

The house was built on posts, five or six feet off the ground, and had only one room. We climbed a ladder to get up to the living quarters and sat on the floor not far from a fireplace. A large kettle steamed over a fire of small sticks. In a short time, the rice was cooked, and Tekla served us bowls of soup with pieces of meat floating in it. She dished rice into a big bowl in the middle of the circle of diners, and we ate it with our hands. The meat was good, as was the rice, and I was hungry so enjoyed it very much.

I asked Jo later what kind of meat we had, and she said it was pork entrails. So much for my first meal in Natunin!

The weather was rainy much of the time I was there, with temperatures in the fifties F. (10 C.). In preparing to go to the Philippines, I had never heard it could be cold there so had brought only a light summer sweater. Jo loaned me a warmer one that helped a bit, but with no heat in the house, I was cold all the time, except in bed at night and when hiking on the terraces.

Most of the older men wore g-strings and perhaps tee shirts on top. The women wore skirts and cotton blouses, if they were not nursing babies. Otherwise, they wore nothing on top. I asked Jo how they could stand the cold, and she said, "Oh, they are 'face all over.'" It took me awhile to understand what she meant, and then I realized that my face doesn't feel cold until it gets well below freezing. But I certainly wasn't "face all over" as these people were.

One morning we woke up to the sad news that a fire in the night at the school compound burned all four of the teachers' houses to the ground. We walked the ten minutes to the school and heard that the fire had started in one of the houses. But because they were built of split bamboo, the fire spread quickly to the other houses too. No one was injured, but the teachers lost everything they owned.

People in the village fed them, and several days later, the SIL plane came from Bagabag with clothing to help out. The village men later rebuilt the houses.

My time with Jo and her people soon came to an end. It was a wonderful experience that I'll never forget.

Chapter 11
Life as a New Recruit
1967

My three weeks in Natunin with Jo Shetler went by quickly, and soon I was on the SIL plane to Bagabag. Jackie Ruch had been there and was returning to Manila by bus with her two children. I went along with them, so I didn't have to travel alone. Since the bus was crowded and the young children had no seats, we had to hold them on our laps. They were hot and tired, so we had an uncomfortable trip.

We arrived the day before Anne West, Marge Draper, and Ginny Larson sailed into Manila Bay. Stu Hussey, a translator who worked on the island of Palawan, met their ship. On the way from the docks, Stu stopped at the Magnolia ice cream parlor to introduce them to Manila's famous ice cream. "It was delicious," said Marge. "I had a mango parfait. M-m-m-m!"

Jean Haggar, who worked in the SIL office in the Department of Education building downtown, took us new members on a memorable sightseeing trip. A hydrofoil transported us at rapid speed across Manila Bay to the island of Corregidor. This had been the headquarters of General Douglas MacArthur during World War II. A tour bus then drove us around the island, stopping at landmarks that told what transpired there during the war.

One of the most amazing sites to me was the Mile Long Barracks, which housed servicemen who were stationed on Corregidor. We also saw the huge guns and the Malinta Tunnel, which housed a 1,000-bed hospital and the headquarters of General MacArthur.

A Trip to Headquarters

We were now ready to travel to the large southern island of Mindanao, where the headquarters of SIL Philippines was located. At the center called Nasuli, we would see the director and find out where we would be working.

"Everybody goes to Nasuli on the Night Mercury flight," Jean told us. We discovered that the "Night Mercury" was a Philippine Airlines (PAL) flight from Manila to Cagayan de Oro, a city on the north coast of Mindanao. Nasuli was located in the province of Bukidnon, south of the capital, Malaybalay, some 71 miles (115 kilometers) from Cagayan de Oro.

Ed Ruch bought our tickets and told us that we would have an all-night trip. The plane left Manila at 1:30 a.m. and flew to Cebu City on the island of Cebu, about halfway to Mindanao. There we changed planes and sat for two hours in the airport waiting for another flight. Then we flew to Cagayan de Oro. It was now morning, and the sun was up.

We had a five-hour wait in Cagayan de Oro for a flight to Malaybalay. We took a taxi into town and found the recommended hotel where we got breakfast and waited for our flight. Soon we all needed to use the bathroom. When we asked for it, we were shown the shower. We tried *toilet* and got to the right place but later found that the correct term was *comfort room*. My English language file now had one more entry to join the terms for this facility. In Canada it's *washroom*, and in the US it's *restroom*.

Breakfast consisted of fresh papaya, fresh pineapple, fresh bread rolls, and coffee. What could have been better? I soon learned that Del Monte had a huge pineapple plantation just south of Cagayan de Oro over which we flew every time we went to Nasuli. Papayas grow everywhere—on plantations, in backyards, even on street corners.

By now we were very tired, having been up all night. Eventually, the five-hour wait came to an end, and we took a taxi back to the airport to find that our plane for Malaybalay was a DC3. When we boarded the plane, the aisle went uphill to our seats. We flew very low over the mountain ridge just south of Cagayan and over the Del Monte plantation. We could almost count the pineapple plants! It took about thirty minutes to fly to Malaybalay, where we landed on a grassy strip that headed straight for a mountain. Fortunately, our pilot brought our plane down before we got that far.

Our Time at Nasuli

Nasuli staff members, John and Karen Beitzel, were waiting at the small Malaybalay airport for us. We caught a jeepney and bumped our way to Nasuli, about 10 miles (16 kilometers) down a dirt road. A pig was tied on the outside of the jeepney. It let us know of its presence all the way, since it was hanging upside down and must have been uncomfortable.

We soon arrived at beautiful Nasuli with its green lawns, fruit trees, and flowering bushes.

We learned that we were to stay with Mary Granaas. Mary had only recently arrived herself. She was a woman in her sixties from Burbank, California, who had come to manage the Manila guesthouse. She had been at Nasuli for the conference and for some orientation herself. A wonderful hostess, she loved to entertain.

Our days were filled with getting to know our way around the center. We learned to take a siesta after lunch and then go for a refreshing swim in the large natural pool fed by artesian springs—one of the delightful features of Nasuli.

We also met the support workers who lived there. A number of translators who had houses on the center were in from their language allocations for a time of rest, for shopping, or to take care of business. We new members decided on partnerships and the language groups we would be working with.

I was very interested in the publications department, where the Scripture and literacy materials were printed for each language group where work was in progress. When we were given work to do, I was disappointed when Marge Draper was assigned to work there. I was asked to type up anthropology notes for the director, Les Troyer, who, with his wife, Maddy, had been translators for the Ga'dang people of northern Luzon.

Mary was a wonderful hostess. One night she invited all the other single women for a tasty Chinese dinner. I still use her recipe for sweet-and-sour pork.

Assignment to the Amganad Ifugao People

The house we stayed in had only three bedrooms, so we were assigned two to a room. My roommate was Anne West. Since we were good friends already, we decided after much prayer and discussion that we would like to become partners. Then we had to decide with which language group we would work.

The directors presented us with some choices. One was the Ivatan people with whom Morrie and Shirley Cottle had been working. They wanted someone to go to the Batanes to work on the home island. Since one of their children had a serious illness, they needed to stay at Nasuli.

Another was the Amganad Ifugao people who live in the mountains of northern Luzon among the famous rice terraces near the town of Banaue. Since my degree was in literacy journalism and I was interested in helping in the branch literacy program, the director suggested that we might consider working with the Ifugao people. This would place me nearer our northern center, Bagabag, where workshops were often held. So Anne and I chose Amganad Ifugao, and Marge and Ginny chose the Ivatan people.

Two weeks after our arrival at Nasuli, Anne and I flew to Manila to prepare for our trip north. We spent a few days there buying staples that we would need for our new life in the mountains. Then we caught a bus to Baguio where we stayed overnight at the Shanghai Hotel, an inexpensive but clean establishment that seemed to be the favorite of SIL people. The next day we met the Missionary Aviation Fellowship (MAF) pilot who was stationed in Baguio, and he flew us to the SIL center at Bagabag. We had requested our barrels to be shipped there, but it took several days after our arrival for them to come. A few days of sorting and repacking kept us busy until Dick Hohulin arrived to take us to Amganad.

What would we find there? I wondered.

Chapter 12
Off to the Mountains
1967

When the Hohulins finally arrived, Dick arranged for a jeepney driver to transport us, our boxes, and our bags to Bokoh, a small village south of Banaue. We loaded up early in the morning on March 4, 1967, two days before my thirtieth birthday, and headed north.

The narrow, unpaved road wound through two lowland towns before climbing into the mountains. In places, the road was too narrow to pass another vehicle. Fortunately, we encountered almost no traffic. The farther we went, the steeper the road became as it switched back and forth.

Soon we saw the amazing and beautiful rice terraces climbing the mountainsides. Since it was early March and in between rice-growing seasons, most of the fields were filled with water and brilliant green patches of tiny rice plants.

After we had travelled about three hours, Dick stopped the jeepney at a small cluster of houses on both sides of the road. "This is it," he said.

First Impressions of Amganad Country

As I looked around, I felt as if I had literally come to the end of the earth! The houses were made of wood planks, some with thatched roofs and some with corrugated galvanized iron (GI) roofs. Some were positioned on four tree trunks about five feet off the ground, and others were built right on the ground. Those on posts, we learned, were native houses called *bale*.

As we climbed out of the jeepney, a smiling white face topped by a motorcycle helmet greeted us. Janet Davis was a missionary with the Far Eastern Gospel Crusade, which had been working in this area for a number of years. Janet was from London, Ontario, where I had attended Bible college. Her younger sister, Elaine, was a fellow student of mine, and her two older sisters were also alumni of LBI. It was wonderful to see someone from home, even if I didn't know her yet.

Dick had sent Janet a radio message, saying we were coming and would be looking for a place to live. She had checked the area to see what was available and had several choices for us to see. We unloaded our baggage and left it in a store nearby, where the storekeeper assured us it would be safe. After a trip to Banaue to have lunch with two missionary nurses, we returned to Bokoh.

Janet parked her motorbike, and we walked down a trail that descended into Amganad. We learned that this was a *baranggay*, like a township, made up of many *situs* or villages scattered among the rice terraces. The trail, which was fairly wide, wound around the side of the mountain. Where it bent sharply to the right, a smaller trail dropped down a steep hill. This trail took us to the Amganad school and the village of Huyuk.

Hiking that trail was no easy feat but was easier than it was to become. Recently, Otley Beyer, an American anthropologist, had died. He had lived and studied in the area for many years and had an Ifugao wife. As was the custom, his body was carried down the trail to Huyuk where it was set up under a house for a wake that lasted many days. In order to make it easier to transport the body, men had cut uneven steps in the trail.

It was dry season, and we were able to take advantage of the steps. We had been given walking sticks at Bokoh, which kept us from falling. Later in June when the rains began, the steps washed out from the tramping of many feet and rivers of water.

The first house Janet had found was in the main plaza of Huyuk. It was a two-storied house made of galvanized iron siding and roofing. It had one room downstairs and one room upstairs with a porch along the front. The house was built on five-gallon kerosene cans filled with cement as house posts. Its dimensions were about ten feet by twenty feet, which seemed enough.

We hiked along the banks of the rice terraces to several other villages but didn't find any other house we liked as well as the one in Huyuk so decided to rent it. The landlord, Ambugawon, lived in a *bale* in the village. We knew we would need to do some renovations to make the house livable, so he agreed that the rent, equivalent to fifteen dollars a month, could go toward the house repairs until it was used up.

The Far Eastern Gospel Crusade (now Send International) operated a hospital and clinic in Banaue farther up the road. They had a nice guesthouse on the hospital grounds where we stayed until we could get our possessions carried down the hill.

Janet was a great help to us during those early days as we assessed what needed to be done to the house. She helped us find carpenters to do the work, carriers for our baggage, and a house helper named Elaina. Our landlord had a seventeen-year-old daughter named Hilda. She and one other woman were probably the only Christians in Huyuk when we arrived. She became like our little sister and helped us too, since she lived in the village.

Huyuk had no streets, just a trail that ran down the four levels of the village, which was built on dried-out rice terraces. Our house was on the third level from the top, right next to the trail.

Hilda had gone to school and was presently enrolled in Ifugao Academy in Kiangan. She had learned to speak quite good English so was able to help us in the early days when we struggled to understand the language.

House Repairs

Soon the work began on our house. Gumidlu, a carpenter and a wood carver, agreed to make the needed repairs. Along with his helper, Ongallan, he soon was busy sawing and nailing the materials we had shipped to do the job.

Since the whole house was made of galvanized iron, we could hardly talk to each other when it rained. A lining of plywood helped to cut down the noise. We also had a partition made upstairs, so we could have a bedroom and a study. We had two glass windows installed on the lower floor, since the window openings were covered with hinged doors that made the house dark in the daytime if closed. If not, we got wet when it rained. Upstairs the windows were glass.

We also needed furniture, which we gradually collected, either from people at Bagabag, who had some to spare, or through the handiwork of the carpenters. They made desks, beds, and cupboards. When the work began on the walls, I was surprised to hear a rhythmic noise one day coming from Ongallan's hammer. He had music in his soul and used his hammer as a musical instrument to play tunes as he worked.

At first, bathroom facilities were a problem for us. Ifugaos usually bathe in the open near a stream or a waterfall. Since we wanted more privacy, we asked the men to build a two-room addition on one end of the house. One side would be a bathroom and the other a storeroom.

With the help of our friends at Bagabag, we bought a five-gallon tank with ten-inch legs on the bottom. A showerhead with a tap was welded near the bottom on one side. We set it on a head-high shelf at one end of the bathroom and ran a hose from one of the four fifty-gallon drums that were at the back of the house to catch rainwater. Under the small tank, we placed a one-burner kerosene stove. By running the burner under the tank for an hour or so, we could get a hot shower.

Unfortunately, since it was a closed system, when the hot water ran out through the showerhead, cold water came in from the outside tanks and soon cooled the inside water. Fortunately, I liked a very hot shower, and

Anne preferred hers a bit cooler, so I showered first, and we were both happy.

We also had a water-seal toilet installed in the bathroom and a septic tank behind the house. When we first arrived, some men built an outhouse for our use. This was fine except they refused to place it in the village, so we had to walk across our level of town, climb a fence, walk a short way down a trail, climb another fence, and go down a hillside to get to it. Needless to say, night trips were out, so we had a *gezunder* ("goes under") the bed in our bedroom, a return to childhood, at least for me.

Language Learning

Life soon settled down to a daily routine. Our number-one goal was to learn to speak Ifugao in preparation for translating the Bible. We spent large parts of each day visiting, writing down what we heard, and working with Oscar, a young Ifugao man we hired to help us analyze the language. Oscar spoke some English, so we were able to communicate with him fairly well.

Sometimes we ran into surprising meanings to the words we had heard and written down. One day I gave Oscar a list of words, and when I came to the last one, he said, "That one is English." The word I had written down was *palawel,* which wasn't in my English vocabulary.

After thinking about what I had learned about Ifugao, I realized he was right. Ifugao has no *f* and no consonant clusters. In borrowed words, *f* becomes *p* and a vowel is placed between consonants in a cluster. Ifugao also has no *r*. In borrowed words, *r* becomes *l*. So using these rules, my *palawel* became "flower."

Language learning was difficult for me. As a child I had been very shy, not wanting to talk with people I didn't know. As I matured, I overcame most of that shyness, or I thought I had. But when in a situation outside of my experience, my shyness returned, and I didn't want to visit with people.

When we walked to villages to find people to talk to, I forced myself to go, knowing that was the only way to learn the language. But I usually sat on a little block of wood and said very little. Anne, on the other hand, talked freely and soon was far ahead of me in her ability to speak and understand. I was better than Anne at cooking, baking, and fixing things, but that wasn't what we were there for.

I soon became discouraged. I know now I was also suffering from culture shock, which can be debilitating. But eventually, I realized that God has made us all different. Even though I wasn't as good as Anne at the language,

I could do what needed to be done around the house and learned to accept myself for what I was.

My inability to learn another language worried me during all my years in the Philippines. Later, when I worked in Manila, I could use English, as it's the trade language. I tried to learn Tagalog, the language spoken there, but I found that working full-time and taking language courses at night were too much for me.

I never did learn to speak Tagalog. Much to my embarrassment when Filipinos would ask me, "How long have you been in the Philippines?" and I told them, "twenty years" or "thirty years," they would almost always ask, "Oh, you speak our dialect?" My response was *Konti lang*!" (Just a little.)

Work at the Clinic

One day during our first few months in Amganad, Dr. McCurry, the American doctor, asked us if we could work in the clinic for a week or so. Nurses Mary and Marilyn, as well as he and his family, needed to go to Manila for the Far Eastern Gospel Crusade (FEGC) conference. Drs. Eleazar and Elma Sarmiento, the Filipino doctors on staff, would be staying, but they needed a nurse to help with the walk-in clinic and in-patient care.

Anne is a nurse and we were ready to have a break from language learning and our spartan lifestyle and enjoy Western-style living for a bit. We moved into Mary and Marilyn's apartment while they were away. Anne worked in the clinic and hospital, and I took care of the library and drove patients home when they needed transportation. I cooked our meals, took care of the house, and helped people who came to the clinic for other than medical needs.

One night we got a call from Dr. Eli, saying that a woman had come in with a severe bolo slash to her wrist. I went with Anne to the operating room where the doctor would sew up the wound.

First, he cleaned out the chopped-up grass that had been packed into the wound to stop the bleeding. This plant seemed to have anti-bleeding properties and may have saved the woman's life. When Dr. Eli finished cleaning the wound, he discovered that the tendon had been cut and gone up inside her arm. After putting in a local anesthetic, he searched for the upper end of the tendon.

This took a long time, and soon I could see that the patient was in pain. I'm not usually too squeamish when it comes to blood, but realizing that she was hurting affected me. Soon I felt faint, moved away, and put my head down quickly.

Dr. Eli looked at me. "Are you okay?"

"I think so. I just felt faint for a minute."

"Come back here. I have a job for you." He told me to get a cloth, wet it, and hold it to the patient's head. As long as I had something to do, I had no problem with fainting.

Before long, the doctor sewed up the wound and sent the woman home.

Language Help

Several months after Anne and I moved to Amganad, SIL translators Len and Doreen Newell returned from a year of furlough in Canada. While there Doreen had been diagnosed with chronic leukemia. The Newells worked in Batad, a beautiful valley on the east side of Banaue, over a 1,200-foot mountain. They had been translating for the Batad Ifugao for ten years. They arrived with a new Jeep Cherokee so they could drive to Manila when Doreen needed to see her doctor.

They built a garage for the jeep at the bottom of the trail to Batad. From there they had a two-hour hike over the mountain to their home on the other side, overlooking the Batad Valley. This valley sat in a huge bowl of rice terraces with a small village at the bottom. A spectacular waterfall spilled into the far side of the valley.

In past years, three single women, Shirley Abbott, Trudy Pauwels, and Margaret Cunningham, had worked in Amganad on our dialect, and we had the helpful grammar papers they had produced. But we still had a long way to go to complete the needed linguistic analysis.

Although the Batad dialect of Ifugao was different from ours, it had many similarities. Len was a seasoned linguist and translator, so when he offered to help us and invited us to visit them, we accepted gladly.

We set off for Batad on a Sunday. We walked to Banaue early in the morning and took Oscar with us, since we wanted him to help us with the language and to carry our suitcases over the mountain. Mary and Marilyn invited us to have lunch with them after attending the Banaue Evangelical Church. When we sat down to our meal, we were delighted to see roast beef, mashed potatoes, green beans, and strawberries. We usually ate a lot of rice and sometimes longed for a good Western meal.

Oscar, however, was not delighted. He observed that the menu contained no rice. In the opinion of Ifugaos and most rural Filipinos, if you haven't eaten rice, you haven't eaten at all. He wondered how he could carry our suitcases up the steep trail and over the mountain without his daily dose of strength. He expressed his concern when we set out in Mary and Marilyn's van for the trail to Batad.

"Don't worry," I said. "You had a nutritious meal of meat and vegetables, so you won't be hungry."

He looked at me with a worried look. We reached the trail and began the hour's climb. At the top, we stopped to rest and have a drink.

Oscar was quiet then said, "You know, you were right. I'm not tired."

We spent several days with the Newells, where Len not only gave us linguistic help, but we helped Doreen put together several copies of a literacy book she had prepared. We sewed the spines with needles and string so the pages would stay together.

Soon it was time for us to tackle the mountain again and return to our own village.

Patty, the Cat

Since our neighbors were rice farmers, each year after harvest, they stored the seed for next year's crop on shelves over their fireplaces. These storage places for grain attracted rats, and everybody in town wanted cats, including us. When we were back at Bagabag for a time, translators Tom and Janet Headland gave us a cat, and we took her home. She was a pretty calico named Patty, who had just one flaw; she had only one eye. We soon discovered that Patty was a good ratter. From then on, we never saw rats or mice in our house except those she brought in herself.

One time Len and Doreen came to visit us. Being good hostesses, we gave them our beds upstairs, and we slept in sleeping bags on the kitchen floor. Since Patty liked to come in and out of the house at will, I had cut a hole in the floor and made a ladder so she could get in and out when the door was shut.

In the middle of the night, Patty brought in a rat. The trouble was, it was alive, and she let it go so she could play with it. The rat ran for its life over our sleeping bags with Patty behind. I was soon up and helped with the chase. I grabbed a long wooden spoon off the wall and rounded the rat into a corner. But the spoon was too big to touch the rat as it crouched against the wall. When Patty caught Mr. Rat, I picked them both up and threw them out the door. My sympathy went to Len and Doreen trying to sleep upstairs with all that noise below.

Patty was not only a good ratter, but she was also good at having kittens. I had never had a close relationship with a pregnant cat before. Our cats on the farm always had their kittens in secret corners of the haymow, and we didn't see them until they were several weeks old. When Patty was nearing her time to deliver, I put an old towel in a cardboard box and placed it at the top of the stairs in our study. I thought she would make it a good bed for her babies. Of course, she wouldn't have a thing to do with it.

One night after supper, we were washing the dishes when Patty bounded down the stairs and rubbed on my legs. Then she ran to the stairs and started up. About three steps up, she stopped, looked at me, and meowed. When I ignored her, she came back and went through the whole routine again. This time I got the impression she wanted me to go upstairs with her. I left the dishes and climbed the stairs behind her. She went right into the box I had prepared and began to push. I realized she was about to deliver her kittens, and she did get the message that the box was for such a purpose.

Even though I had grown up on a farm with lots of cats and kittens, I had never seen them born. So I sat beside the box to watch the procedure. Shortly, the first kitten came out. Patty chewed off the cord, licked the kitten, and waited for the next one. It was taking a long time, so I got up to finish washing the dishes. When I started down the stairs, Patty got out of her box and followed me, all the while meowing loudly. I felt that she was saying, "Don't leave me now. I need you." So I sat with her until she delivered three healthy kittens.

Patty proceeded to have a batch of kittens twice a year. When our neighbors heard we had kittens to give away, they got on a list to receive them from the next batch. We were happy to give them, except we felt sorry for the cats. When they were fully grown, people tied them inside their houses to keep the rats away. Sometimes they even clipped their ears so the cats wouldn't go outside in the wind.

Life in the mountains was interesting, to say the least.

Chapter 13
Omens, Rice, and Storms
1967

The Ifugao people have strong beliefs in omens. Many things in nature—from a red bird singing, to a green snake crawling across one's path—mean bad luck ahead and require that the person turn around and go home. Sometimes friends or family members would be carrying a sick person to the medical clinic when they would see a bad omen and return home. Occasionally, people died needlessly because of their beliefs in omens.

Death Customs

Death rituals were hard for Anne and me to adjust to. Not long after we moved into our house, Kinadduy, an elderly man who lived one terrace below us, died. We learned that when a person died, family members nailed a piece of bamboo across the house posts. Then they placed the body in a sitting position on the bamboo and tied it to the bottom of the house to keep it upright. Fortunately, Kinadduy's family made a coffin, so they placed his body under the house, the coffin slightly raised so the fluids could drain out as the body decayed. The more affluent the family was, the longer the body stayed unburied.

When a person died, all the family and friends within walking distance came to mourn. The immediate family had to feed everyone. When they had no more money for pigs or rice, they took the body to a cave or an open tomb, if one was available. A raised tomb made of cement sat on one side of our village plaza and was presently unoccupied, so family members would place Kinadduy's body there with wood over the opening to keep animals out.

Another part of the death ritual was family picture-taking time. Almost every house had a photo of a body with family members around it. Someone in the family hung the photo by the door so visitors could see it.

Since we had cameras, someone asked us to take a picture of Kinadduy and his family four days after he died. First, they removed his body from the coffin, washed it, and sat it up for the picture before returning it to the coffin.

On the fifth day, they removed the lid from the coffin. Since the body had not been embalmed, the stench was unbearable in the tropical heat. We closed our windows, burned incense, and held perfumed handkerchiefs to our noses as we sat down to coffee break that day.

After eight days, the family removed Kinadduy's body from the coffin and placed it in the cement tomb near our house. They left it there for about a year until the flesh had decayed.

Then they cleaned the bones, wrapped them in a new piece of Ifugao weaving, and stored them on a shelf under the eaves of his house. The bones were then ready to be retrieved for a sacrifice when a member of his family got sick and the witch doctor *(mumbaki)* said it was his spirit that caused the illness.

Growing Rice

Ifugao people leave the production of rice to the women. Each year after the harvest, they store bundles of rice in their houses over their fireplaces to be used for seed the next year. In January women place these stalks of dried rice in fields full of water to sprout new seedlings. By March the seedlings have grown to about ten inches in height. The women pull them up and transplant them in rows in the owners' fields. The water is usually less than knee deep, but the bottoms of the rice paddies consist of soft, sticky mud.

As newcomers, Anne and I watched the transplanting and wanted to try it out, so a neighbor let us work with her. It didn't seem too hard a job, since we simply pushed seedlings into the mud. But we found it was backbreaking work after a few hours as we bent over in water almost to our knees.

At one point, a woman from another village walked along the path on the terrace wall. When she got to us, she stopped and watched us for a bit and then laughed. "Look at that! Americanos planting rice!" she said. "Doesn't anybody know that Americanos don't know how to plant rice?"

We felt a bit insulted but continued on with our jobs. We thought we did quite well, but later in the season when the rice had grown tall, our neighbors said they could tell which rows we planted, since they weren't quite straight. After that, we decided to stick to language work.

By July the rice was ready for harvest. On the first day, everyone worked in the fields of the richest person in the community. In Amganad that was Anna who had seven fields. Our neighbor, Catalina, came by at 8:00 a.m. to take us to watch. About eighty women started at the far side of a big field and worked toward the village. They cut the rice just below the first leaves with special crescent-shaped or short straight knives. The women held the rice until they cut several stalks. Then they pulled the leaves off, tied the stalks in bundles with strips of bamboo, and placed them on the terrace walls. The men and boys secured the bundles on the ends of long poles and carried them over their shoulders back to the village where they put them in an open area between the houses. By noon when the whole area was filled with hundreds of bundles, they left them to dry in the sun for three days.

While the women worked, they sang the "Hudhud," an epic poem that can go on for days. Only the old women sang the hundreds of verses. Everyone joined in on the chorus, which they sang after each verse.

Except for the few men and boys who carried the rice back to the village, the men stayed at home and looked after the children. They also performed a *baki* to persuade the rice god, Bulul, to bless the rice harvest. They drank great quantities of rice wine until they were quite drunk.

During the *baki*, one man brought the Bulul statue out of the granary. They killed a pig, cut it up, and placed pieces around the statue. Then they poured blood in a half-coconut shell with cooked rice, and the oldest *mumbaki* ate the mixture. The men inserted pieces of pork on sticks, set them afire, and took them quickly to the *mumbaki,* who clasped the burning meat in his hands before eating it. Other men cut up the part of the pig for the crowd and cooked it in a big pan over the fire where one person had been cooking rice all morning.

When the women arrived from the fields, they each carried several bundles of rice on their heads, which looked like frilly hats with rice heads dangling over their eyes. The men gave the women pork and rice to eat.

After this first day of harvest, the women worked in their own fields. Since July was the rainy season, and rains usually began around 3:00 p.m., the people collected all the rice bundles and carried them inside. After the rice was dry, they stored it in a granary, usually an old house that was not being lived in or a smaller one especially built for grain storage. Anne and I tried harvesting but found it much harder to do than planting.

When the bundled rice is needed for food, the women have more work to do before they can cook it. They take the bundles from the granary, strip the kernels from the stalks, and sometimes tie the stalks in bunches to be used as whisks or small brooms. They place the rice kernels in large wooden mortars and pound them with long wooden pestles to remove the husks. Then they pour the kernels into flat baskets and winnow them to let the husks fly away, leaving the kernels ready for cooking.

Ifugao rice has a delicious nutty flavor and a beautiful aroma that can be enjoyed all over the village when it is cooking.

Rainstorms and Typhoons

When Anne and I first arrived in Ifugao, it was still the dry season. We were able to hike to the various villages over the rice terrace trails and up the steep mountainsides.

In late June, the summer rains began. Usually, the sun shone brightly in the morning, but by early afternoon, large clouds gathered over the mountains. Soon the rain began, not just a light rain but a torrential downpour like I had never seen before, except perhaps in a big thunderstorm in southern Ontario. Soon the village was a mass of mud with streams pouring down the steps from one terrace level to the next. This usually lasted until late in the evening. Then the sky cleared, and this was repeated the next day.

The Philippines lies in the most active area of the earth for tropical cyclones known as typhoons. An average of twenty-one cross some part of the country every year, wreaking havoc on cities and country areas alike. Strong winds tear off roofs and blow down buildings and trees. Torrential rains leave behind floods that destroy infrastructures and crops. In the ten years from 1961 to 1970, the Philippines lost 43 percent of its gross national product and 3,200 lives to typhoons.

During the summer of 1967, we had several bad storms with lots of rain and wind, but in October the strongest typhoon that anybody could remember swept across northern Luzon. It registered center winds of 155 miles per hour (250 kilometers) when it was four hundred miles out at sea but was considerably lessened by the land and mountains before it reached us in the evening. However, all night the winds got progressively worse. The tin walls of our house banged in and out as the wind struck them, and a loose piece of the new roof on our storage room flapped until we were afraid it would rip off.

I didn't sleep all night. Just as I would be nearly asleep, a strong gust would awaken me again. In the morning, we saw that a large piece of the thatched roof had blown off the house next door and was scattered around the yard. Further investigation showed that four other houses lost their roofs, many trees and branches had blown down, and a flying galvanized iron roof had destroyed the bamboo pipe that brought water from the fields.

I put on my raincoat (my umbrella was useless in the wind) and went out to view the damage. A tree to which the guy wires for our two-way radio antenna were attached had come down over the trail, but the antenna was still standing. A number of frightened village women gathered in Bugati's house next door, since some native houses were swaying badly in the wind.

By noon the wind had calmed considerably, but then in the afternoon it picked up again and was almost as strong as during the night. Several people came to our house, since they felt safer in a Western-style house than in their native houses. We cooked rice and offered our neighbors, Adela and her children, a spot on our floor for the night, which they accepted.

Later in the evening, Marcello told us of the damage in several nearby villages. Seven houses were destroyed, and one man fell over a cliff and drowned in the water at the bottom. Many trees were either blown down or stripped of their leaves, including a large patch of banana plants just outside our village. We shared some of our clothing with one woman, who lost her house and everything she owned.

By 8:00 p.m., the wind had calmed, except for the occasional gust, but the rain continued for another day or so. Reports came of many landslides, one of which killed a family in the Ifugao village of Hapao when their house was buried. Over one hundred people were killed in northern Luzon, and eighty landslides closed the road from Baguio to Bontoc.

The day following the storm, everyone was out cleaning up the mess, except our *mumbaki* neighbor. He resumed a *baki* that had been in progress before the storm interrupted it.

Life must go on.

Our Ifugao house

Ifugao women harvesting rice

Chapter 14
Revenge Killings
1967

In the not-too-distant past, Ifugaos were headhunters. Since wars between the various cultural communities in the northern mountains were frequent, warriors brought home their enemies' heads, usually cut off with special axes carried for such a purpose.

These activities are now past, curtailed by the Americans in the early twentieth century. However, revenge killing with its elaborate rituals was still practiced in the 1960s. In December 1967, a killing took place in Amganad.

Tuginayu and Malyano were third cousins. They quarreled over the ownership of a field. Malyano said he had inherited half the field and wanted his share. Tuginayu was in his uncle's house when Malyano came in with a gun and shot him in the back. He died instantly. Malyano fled to the protection of his family. The police came but were not able to find him.

Tuginayu's family took his body to his house, still wearing the clothes that he died in, and placed him on a bamboo mat. At each corner of the mat, they planted a roanoh stalk standing upright in the ground. Roanoh is a ceremonial plant with bright red leaves. The family had killed several pigs under the house, and a *baki* was in progress near the body. The *mumbaki* stopped chanting and buried two eggs in a hole at the side of the yard. He placed rocks on the eggs and filled in the hole before planting the roanoh sticks that he had taken from near the body.

Several men then lifted the body, placed it on a wooden slab, and leaned it against the house post. The *mumbaki* stood before the body and shouted very loudly to Manahaut, the god of war, to take the killer.

The women from Tuginayu's family stood in front of the body with sticks from a weaving frame about two feet long. They pushed the sticks back and forth, pleading with Tuginayo's spirit to help them revenge his death. They shook his head or pushed on his forehead as they chanted. This went on for some time.

On the third day after the death, a *himong* took place. This is a ritualistic dance during which a person is selected to revenge the death of the relative.

Male relatives and friends of the deceased came from many areas of Amganad and even farther away. They arrived about 9:00 a.m., dancing across the terraces at a very slow pace, accompanied by the rhythmic beat of the *bangibang* that each dancer carried. A *bangibang* is a piece of hard wood about three feet long with a bamboo handle fastened in the middle. It was carried in the left hand and tapped briskly with a stick held in the right hand.

The dancers wore red, black, and white g-strings with long-tailed betel nut bags fastened at their backs. They threw red blankets over their right shoulders and tied them behind. They wore feather-like headdresses made from ten-inch bands of *upa*, the white inner bark of the betel-nut tree. They inserted red roanoh leaves into these headdresses, and they wore white bands around their arms and legs.

Two or three leaders of each group carried spears and backpacks made from deerskin blackened from the smoke of house fires. During the dance, the dancers staged mock battles, pretending to spear each other. They did this to please their god Manahaut.

At noon, the *mumbakis* and about two hundred of Tuginayu's male relatives gathered at the top of a hill near the home of the deceased. They started a fire and hung a large new blanket on poles.

We asked if we could go up to see what was happening. Since this was a confidential gathering that only the relatives were allowed to attend, the family discussed it. Finally, they said that since we didn't understand anyway, it was okay for us to watch.

A group of men speared a pig and killed it with a sharp stick. Then several *mumbakis* put their spears into the pig, and the chief *mumbaki* fell on the pig to drink its blood, which he washed down with rice wine. Several men pulled him off the pig, and then they cut it up and gave chunks to representatives of each geographical area present.

Next, the male relatives gathered in a tight circle around the chief *mumbaki* who cut the head off a chicken and let it fall. The headless chicken ran for several seconds before it collapsed. The man in front of whom the chicken died was chosen to revenge Tuginayo's death. He was required to kill either Malyano or one of his male relatives. We were cautioned not to tell anyone who had been chosen, since if any of Malyano's relatives found out, the chosen one's life would be in danger.

After the ceremonies were completed, the dancers formed into four long lines and proceeded to Tuginayo's house where they left their hats before going home. His relatives placed his body on a stretcher and carried it over the mountain to a certain cave. They placed him sitting up so his spirit could see the murderer's house. They also put several red-and-white hats outside the cave so people passing by would know that a murdered person was buried there.

Most of the women relatives wore pieces of grass or leaves in their hair. This was to keep the spirits from spitting on them and making them sick, since the spirits had been aroused by all the shouting and crying for three days.

In cases where the murderer wasn't known because the death happened at night or nobody was around, the family of the deceased patiently bided their time until the perpetrator got drunk and bragged about his dark deed. Then a *himong* would be held.

After observing the practices of the *himong,* we understood why the Ifugao people were fearful. The system of revenge perpetuated fear, since almost every family had someone who had killed someone, so they were all candidates for revenge.

Only men were killed, so the women sat on the terraces at night to prevent their neighbors from stealing water when the springs high in the mountains ran low and the rice fields were short of water.

Only intermarriage between the two families could break the revenge cycle. If that happened, a truce was held.

We longed for the day when God's Word would be translated and the true spirit of His forgiveness could change the culture and bring peace.

Ifugao men dressed for the revenge ceremony

Shirley visting with a neighbor and her grandson

Chapter 15
Medical Work
1967

Although a clinic and a hospital operated in Banaue, it took an hour-and-a-half to walk there. So except for emergencies or major medical needs, the people of Amganad had no medical help.

Knowing this, Anne stocked up on basic medical supplies when we were in Manila. People soon began coming to our house so she could bandage cuts, give medicine for skin diseases, worms, upset stomachs, headaches, fever, and tuberculosis (TB). Since TB is prevalent in the Philippines, a number of our neighbors had active cases. Streptomycin shots were the treatment of the day, but most would not take the long trip to the clinic to get them. So Anne was happy to give them their shots.

We also cared for many babies and even managed to deliver one or two. The birthing process was a natural thing there, and unless a mother had a problem, she or her family did not call us.

An Embarrassing Moment

One day we received a package from Anne's mother containing a can of shrimp. For lunch, I cooked rice and made curried shrimp to go over it.

Soon after this, a neighbor came to our door, saying that his wife had been in labor for three days, and asked if we would help her. We thought we might have to persuade him to take her to the clinic, so we set out to see her. When we reached their house, she was squatting in the back corner and holding on to a post. All her family members had left her alone and were sitting under the house next door, waiting for the birth.

We climbed the ladder to the house, and just as we entered, the baby boy decided to come on his own. Anne caught him and handed him to me so she could run back home and get the kit she kept prepared with a sterile bamboo for cutting the cord and a bulb for suctioning out the infant's airway.

As I knelt on the dirty floor holding the baby, who was still attached to his mother since the placenta hadn't been delivered yet, I suddenly felt the effects of the shrimp I had eaten. I prayed that God would help Anne to get back in a hurry, since I didn't want to vomit on this newborn or place him on the cold, hard, dirty floor.

Just as Anne came in, I knew my time had come. I placed him quickly in her hands and headed for the door. As I reached the ladder, the contents of my stomach came up and fell to the ground six feet below. All the people who were sitting under the house laughed because they thought I couldn't stand to see a baby born.

This was my most embarrassing moment during my time in Ifugao. After that, I didn't eat shrimp or any other shellfish for twenty-five years.

Medical Crisis

In October of our first year in Amganad, our neighbor, Bakwit, had a baby boy and named him Cornelius. From the beginning, he was only able to nurse on one side and didn't make any sound. Something was definitely wrong with him, so we arranged to fly him and his mother to Manila with us at Christmas. Since she didn't speak anything but Ifugao, we took Mary, a high-school girl who knew English, to act as interpreter.

By now Cornelius was two months old. He was admitted to the charity ward at a hospital near our guesthouse. The Episcopal Church had founded St. Luke's as a mission hospital, and the staff often cared for people from the cultural communities in the north free of charge.

By the time we arrived at the hospital, Cornelius had pneumonia, so he was given oxygen and started on penicillin. After a couple of days, the doctors put a tube down his throat to see what was causing his problems. They found a large cyst nearly completely covering his vocal chords and affecting his breathing.

As they began surgery to remove the cyst, Cornelius went into heart failure and nearly died. They performed an emergency tracheotomy, which needed to be suctioned out frequently so he could breathe. Nursing care for such patients was limited, so Anne spent nights with them to help with the suctioning.

After several days, the surgery was performed. Anne taught Bakwit how to suction out the tracheotomy. She was quick to learn and did a good job. Even I learned to do it. After a week or so in the hospital with nothing to do but care for her baby, Bakwit needed to have a break. I stayed with Cornelius while Anne took Bakwit and Mary to see a movie. Bakwit couldn't understand the language, since it was in English, but she was amazed at her first-time experience.

Bakwit experienced many "firsts" on that trip. The day we arrived at the hospital, we had to go to the third floor. We pushed the button for the elevator, and when the door opened, we led Bakwit and the baby into this small "room." The door closed, and the room began to move. Bakwit grabbed me in fright, not knowing why the floor was moving. We learned that we needed to be more sensitive to things that were new to her and warn her ahead of time.

When Cornelius was released from the hospital, we all returned to the SIL guesthouse to get much-needed rest. Christmas dinner was the traditional turkey with all the trimmings. Twenty-eight SIL adult members were at that dinner plus fourteen children. Following dinner, we sang carols and exchanged gifts.

My fears of being lonely at my first Christmas away from home were not well founded. The day after Christmas, a group of us went to see "Holiday on Ice" at the coliseum in a shopping district close to us. We took our Ifugao girl, Mary, with us and enjoyed her amazement. She had never before seen ice, skating, the colorful costumes, or the lights.

Cornelius recovered well from his surgery and grew up to be a strong and healthy Ifugao man. We were also happy that medicine and prayer healed him, since his family thought he had an evil spirit and had planned to do a sacrifice for him. They were ashamed to spend so much money for the pigs though, since we were paying for his care. We were grateful to God for the opportunity to help save his life.

Physical Puzzles

Our health was generally good since going to Ifugao country. At times Anne had bouts of amoeba, which is very common in the tropics, and I occasionally had bacillary. But these infections cleared up with the right medicines.

During my second year in Ifugao, I began to lose weight. I didn't mind, since I had gained quite a bit and was happy to get back to my normal weight. But when I had lost ten pounds and often felt tired and coughed a lot, I began to wonder if something else was wrong. So I saw the doctor at the Banaue clinic, and he took a chest x-ray. Their equipment was old and didn't produce a very clear negative. He could see something but thought it looked like emphysema. Emphysema? I hardly knew what that was. So I was afraid that my old enemy tuberculosis had finally caught up with me, especially since many of our neighbors had it.

We were going to Manila soon, so I booked a chest x-ray at St. Luke's Hospital. The report came back, "Nothing," just an old scar, probably from childhood pneumonia.

I went back to Ifugao with thanks to God and the realization that my weight loss was probably from an excessive amount of exercise. We could never go anyplace without hiking up and down mountain trails. The cough may have been irritation from the smoke that was always in the air from cooking fires.

Although I continued coughing, I was thankful for the report that nothing was wrong.

Chapter 16
Experiences with Spirits
1967

Spain colonized the Philippines in the mid–1500s and brought Catholicism. Huge Spanish churches were built throughout the country, especially along the seacoasts of Luzon and through the Visayas. Eventually, priests and lay brothers traveled into the mountains of Luzon and built small chapels in many villages.

Priests arranged to have one such chapel built in Amganad near the school. A catechist came once a month for a service and to baptize babies. He encouraged the people to register as Catholics. Many would say they were Christians, although the kind of Christianity they practiced was syncretistic. They attended the services when the catechist came, but in the meantime, they followed their own superstitious ways of sacrificing to the spirits and their ancestors.

After World War II, God challenged a number of American former servicemen and women, who had fought in the Philippines and Japan, to take the gospel to the people of those countries. In 1947, the Far Eastern Gospel Crusade, whose name was changed to SEND International in 1981, was founded and began work in the Philippines. Members of that mission established the Good News Hospital and Clinic in Banaue, Ifugao, and started a church there. Beside the doctors and nurses assigned to the hospital, Wayne and Doris Eames, Gundy and Fay Habich, Virgil and Annette Ball, Rae Long, and Janet Davis worked throughout Ifugao in a church-planting ministry.

By the time we arrived, a small service was held each Sunday in the school at Amganad. At first Donato, a believer from the Banaue church, came to preach. Later, Marcello Kabigat, who came to know the Lord through the FEGC work and attended Bible school in Manila, became the pastor. Not many people attended, and those who did were mostly children. In our village, only Hilda and Catalina professed to be believers.

We attended the service each week, although at first we were unable to understand what was said. Marcello had studied in Manila and used either the Tagalog or English Bible, although he preached in Ifugao. Even though missionary work had gone on for twenty years, the church was weak because no Scriptures were available in the local language.

Len and Doreen Newell of SIL had begun translation work in Batad in the late 1950s. By our arrival in 1967, they had translated and printed a number of New Testament books. The Batad dialect was different from that spoken in Banaue, so these published portions were of little use to the Banaue and Amganad churches.

Hilda Ambugawon was a shining light for the gospel in Amganad. Although only seventeen, she had had a genuine experience with the Lord and was eager to share the gospel with her people, especially the children. When Janet Davis went on furlough in 1968, Hilda took over her daily vacation Bible school classes and taught over six hundred children each week in various villages during the summer school break in April and May.

The Problem Surfaced

In the spring of that year, we heard that Hilda was having problems with evil spirits. In April when she returned home from Kiangan where she was a student at Ifugao Academy, she told us that for some time an evil spirit had visited her. It masqueraded as the spirit of one of her classmates, who had died the year before. This Ilokano young man had said he wanted to marry her, but she was not interested in him.

Because Ifugaos believe that the spirits of the dead come back to cause problems for those left behind, her classmates believed that this was who was tormenting her. At school she would go into a trance, and her fellow students would ask this spirit to tell the future for them. This always happened at dusk. Hilda was very upset about this but had no control over it, and nobody at school could help her.

How to Deal with Evil Spirits

One evening when school was over and Hilda had returned to Huyuk for summer vacation, she came to our house with a look of fear in her eyes. "It's coming," she said. "I have a tingling feeling in my feet, and it's climbing up my body. When it gets to my head, I go to sleep, and the spirit takes over. Help me!"

We rushed her into our bedroom. We laid her on one of our beds and sat beside her. In just a few minutes, she began to shake, her body thrashing back and forth. Then she talked in Ilokano, which we couldn't understand. Realizing that this was an evil spirit from Satan and not the spirit of her classmate, we challenged it, saying, "We know you aren't that boy's spirit, but you're an evil spirit."

"Oh," he said in English. "You've found me out."

We asked for his name, since some elderly missionary friends in Manila, who had much experience with dealing with this kind of thing, had told us that if we could get his name, we could cast him out.

But he wouldn't tell us his name, saying, "If you know my name, you will kill me."

Hilda went into a frenzy when we quoted Scripture verses, such as, "In whom we have redemption through his blood, the forgiveness of sins, according to the riches of his grace" (Ephesians 1:7 KJV). "Through God we shall do valiantly; for he it is that shall tread down our enemies" (Psalm 108:13). "And they overcame him by the blood of the Lamb, and by the word of their testimony" (Revelation 12:11). We sang hymns with the same result, especially those about the blood of Christ:

> What can wash away my sin? Nothing but the blood of Jesus.
> What can make me whole again? Nothing but the blood of Jesus.
> Oh, precious is the flow that makes me white as snow;
> No other fount I know, nothing but the blood of Jesus.
> —Robert Lowry (1826–1899)

We held her down, since we were afraid she would injure herself with the violence. Eventually, the spirit left her saying, "I'm going now, but I'll be back."

Immediately, Hilda lay quietly and became herself. She had no recollection of what had happened. She was exhausted and fearful, so we prayed with her, and soon she went home.

A few days later, Hilda had a second visitation similar to the first. Anne and I had no previous experience with anything like this, so we took her to visit two elders of the Banaue church and FEGC missionary Wayne Eames. This church was responsible for the work in Amganad. The elders felt that until this problem could be cleared up, Hilda shouldn't teach. We thought that was exactly what Satan wanted, so we asked the elders to let her go ahead with her teaching. They granted our request and promised to stand behind her.

In the evening after we had returned from Banaue, Hilda came to us again, saying the spirit was coming. We rushed her up the long hill to the road and along to Janet's house, which was empty, away from the unbelievers in the village. As we neared the house, the spirit took control of her. She stopped walking and refused to go further. We dragged her kicking and screaming to the porch of the house. On the door Janet had pasted a large poster that said, "The blood of Jesus Christ cleanses us from all sin" (1 John

1:7 KJV). When she saw that poster, she froze, and we had to drag her inside the house.

We finally got her onto the couch where she sat stiffly. We had sent a neighbor's boy across the terraces to Banaue to ask Wayne and some elders to come quickly to Janet's house. They soon arrived, and we all sat in a semicircle around Hilda. I was sitting on the couch beside her with my knees against hers. As the men read Scripture and we sang hymns, she became abnormally stiff.

The spirit spoke several times. Once he said to me, "I hate you. You are always talking. Hilda is mine, and I will have her. She is the last obstacle in the way to keep me from having all of Amganad!" Two people who had said they were following the Lord had recently turned their backs on Him.

The spirit added, "I'll make Hilda sick, so she won't be able to walk or teach. I've already made her sick." She had just recovered from a severe boil on her knee that had put her in bed for several days.

Usually, Hilda was violent during these sessions, but this night she sat quietly. The spirit said, "You're all my enemies. I don't belong in this house because it belongs to Janet. She's my enemy too, and I've hated her for years!"

At one stage, she swung at me twice as if to hit me, but neither time could she strike me, even though I was sitting right beside her. I was very aware of the restraining presence of the Holy Spirit as we six believers surrounded Hilda and prayed for her.

After three hours, the spirit left her, saying he would be back again. We returned to Amganad, and for the next few days covered Hilda with our prayers. Soon she got another boil on her knee, so we prayed and treated her. She was scheduled to begin teaching daily vacation Bible school the following week. We believed this was another attack from the evil one. Remembering Job, I wondered if boils were Satan's specialty.

This was a very difficult time for me. I was always exhausted after one of these sessions and couldn't sleep for several days. We were not afraid for ourselves, since we knew that God would protect us. We prayed that He would keep us from being discouraged. Amganad was known as being one of the most pagan places in the north, and Satan doesn't give up his territory easily.

Hilda Gets Free

Later in the year, I took Hilda to Manila with me to talk with our seasoned missionary friends. She told them that before she was born, her father had made a sacrifice and dedicated her to the spirits.

"You need to reject that," one man said, "and give your life completely to Christ."

She did so, saying, "Satan, you can't have me! I belong to Jesus now." After that, her problems diminished until eventually she was free from the evil spirit completely.

A few years later, she married a local Christian young man, and together they became strong leaders in the Amganad church. Hilda had an especially fruitful ministry among the women until her death from cancer in 2006.

But our experiences with Hilda are ones I'll never forget.

Hilda, daughter Helen and husband Hukita

Weaving on a backstrap loom

Chapter 17
Rainy Season and a New Job
1968–1969

The rainy season in Ifugao began in late May and lasted until November. This wasn't just a little rain from time to time but torrential downpours every day. Usually, it began in the early afternoon when big black clouds gathered over the mountains. Soon the rain came down heavily, and those outside ran for cover or they would be drenched in seconds.

The square native houses in Amganad were all built up about five feet on posts made from tree trunks. The roofs were mostly thatch, overhanging the houses by about three feet.

Every house had a stack of umbrellas by the door, since nobody went anyplace without one, especially during the rainy season. Some were black and large, some were of beautiful designs, some of plain solid colors. We soon learned that umbrellas were essentials of life. We preferred the fold-up kind, since we could easily slip them into our bags when not needed.

Problems with the Rain

During the first rainy season in Amganad, Anne and I had a difficult time getting around. Because the temperature was hot and the ground was muddy from the rain, we wore flip-flops. But climbing our long hill in flip-flops became a problem. The steps that had been cut in the trail just before we arrived in March of 1967 soon washed out when the rains began. Our feet often slipped out of our flip-flops when hiking uphill on a muddy trail. We had good sneakers, but if we hiked in them, we had to wash them before we wore them again, and they didn't get dry very fast in the hot, humid weather. What to do?

Then we had an idea. Anne asked her mother to buy us each a pair of spiked golf shoes. When these arrived, we used them exclusively for hiking the muddy trails and no longer had problems with slipping and sliding up and down the mountains. Since we didn't wear them inside, we didn't worry about them being covered in mud. When they eventually dried, we brushed the mud off the outside and had them ready for the next trip. Another advantage of those shoes was that the pain I had in my knees from walking down steep trails in the dry season disappeared when the rains began. It took me a while to realize that the shoes had taken the strain off my knees when going down, and I wasn't developing arthritis after all.

I loved the rain. Every year during the hot, dry summer, I longed for the rain to begin. It not only cooled the atmosphere, but it also made the vegetation green and clean from dust. Eventually, mold became a problem, though. Leather shoes or purses soon grew coats of gray.

Drying clothes was also a problem. Our house wasn't big enough to hang our clothes after they were washed, but fortunately the mornings, except during typhoons, were dry and sunny, so if our helper, Eleina, got the laundry done early enough, the sun would dry it before the rain started. We kept an eye on the clouds and often made a run for the clothesline to rescue the laundry from a second washing.

When the first rains began in May, the clouds usually spawned violent thunderstorms that roared through the mountains before dumping their sodden loads. On occasion, lightning would strike the betel-nut palms that grew over the mountainsides. Fortunately, we didn't have any problem with our house or the antenna for our two-way radio, which was strung between a high steel pole and a nearby tree.

And Then the Typhoons Came

As the season progressed into June and July, typhoons became part of the weather pattern. We listened to the radio every morning, especially to the weather report. When a typhoon was heading toward the Philippines, we stayed home, especially if it were heading in our direction. Most of them did come our way during the months from June to September. Later in the season, they moved further south and crossed southern Luzon or the northern Visayas.

Because the roofs of most of the native houses were made of grass thatch, the strong winds did much damage to them. Our metal roof was never damaged, although sometimes we wondered if it would fly off as sometimes happened to such roofs. The trees suffered though, as did the roads. Landslides came down over the mountain roads, blocking the traffic and sometimes burying vehicles and people.

On our second summer in Ifugao, friends invited us to spend a week of vacation in Baguio. We took the bus on the all-day trip through the mountains to the Philippine summer capitol.

We stayed at the Lutheran guesthouse where we did our own cooking. Because Baguio's altitude is 5,000 feet, many things grow there that don't do well in the hot lowlands. It had a great farmers' market with vegetables and fruit grown nearby. I especially enjoyed having many things to cook that we didn't have in Amganad. And being on vacation, I could cook to my heart's content.

The Overseas Christian Servicemen's Center, a mission that ministers to US servicemen stationed overseas, was having a conference at Camp John Hay, the rest and recreation base in Baguio. We went to several of their meetings, enjoyed the spiritual fellowship, and got to know some Christian airmen and navy men who were there.

Mary and Marilyn, the nurses from the Good News Clinic, were also in Baguio, so we had some good times with them. We hiked on trails around Camp John Hay and went out to good restaurants in the city.

Near the time when our week was up, a typhoon blew through, inundating the city and closing the roads with landslides. We were unable to get home on the bus. Our time at the Lutheran guesthouse was up, so Marilyn and Mary invited us to stay with them until we could get home. They were vacationing in the home of a missionary couple, who were on furlough. This couple rented out their house to other missionaries, who wanted a break in Baguio. It was a lovely place, and we enjoyed the luxury of a modern city home with Western appliances, hot water, and a gorgeous view of the mountains.

The weather didn't clear for a whole week. Finally, the sun came out, but the roads were still closed with slides, so we contacted Dave Steiger, the Mission Aviation Fellowship pilot stationed in Baguio, to see if he could fly us home. He was skeptical, since it was still quite windy, but he finally decided we could go. We took a taxi to the Baguio airport and boarded the MAF Cessna single-engine plane for a half-hour flight to the Banaue airstrip.

The airstrip had been built a half-hour drive outside of Banaue on a mountainside. It was very hard to find enough level space for an airstrip in those mountains. This one had a straight-up mountainside at one end and a 1,000-foot drop off at the other. In the middle was a "dog leg" curve.

Because of the winds, our trip was bumpy. As we approached the end of the strip, we dropped into an air pocket, which forced us below the level of the runway. Dave deftly got the nose of the plane up, so we didn't crash into the mountainside but had to abort the landing and come around again. This time we made it safely to the top. We all sat and shook for a few minutes, thanking God that we had missed the mountain.

From that day on for a number of years, I was nervous flying, even in the big jets that took us across the Pacific. It wasn't until a few years later and several cross-Pacific flights that I took a tranquilizer before flying and was cured of that fear. Since then I've had no problem.

Literacy Workshop

By the fall of 1968, our language learning and analysis had reached the point where we were ready to begin some real work. Because literacy was to be my part of the task, I signed up to go to Manila in October to attend a primer writing workshop with Dr. Sarah Gudschinsky, a well-known SIL literacy specialist and professor. I returned afterwards minimally prepared to begin work on a primer for Amganad Ifugao. I would use it to teach the many adults who didn't know how to read. The young people who had been to school had learned there, but most of the older folks were illiterate. We wanted them to be able to read Ifugao for the day when the New Testament would be translated into their language.

SIL Philippines required language workers to take a written and oral language test after a couple of years of language learning. On November 25, 1968, Anne and I caught the 6:00 a.m. bus to Bontoc, where we met Laurie Reid, who with his wife Dawn, were translating for the Central Bontoc people. They lived in a village a three-hour hike from the town center, so Laurie had to come to town to meet us. I was worried about this test, since I felt my language learning had been so poor, but I did pass and was cleared to become a senior member of the branch, allowing me to vote and to begin preparing the Amganad Ifugao primer.

Visitors

From time to time during our nearly two years in Amganad, we had people from overseas or from Manila come to visit us. Since the Banaue area is well known internationally for the beauty of the rice terraces, many tourists visited the town as well.

In early December, Tim and Lucille Diller and baby David arrived. Tim was a Fulbright linguistic scholar doing research in the central Philippines for his PhD at the University of California, Los Angeles (UCLA). He and Lucille were interested in becoming members of the Philippines branch so wanted to visit a language project while they were in the country.

Since the Fulbright scholars were visiting Banaue, they visited us while they were there. I met them when they got off the bus in Banaue, and nurse Mary drove us back to Bokoh. Mary Pattaweg, one of our Ifugao neighbors, carried two-month-old David down the hill. We enjoyed them very much, taking them on hikes over the rice terraces and introducing them to many of our friends and neighbors. They stayed for two days before returning to Manila.

This year we would be at the Nasuli center for Christmas, but before leaving, we needed to give our annual gifts to the local officials to thank them for services rendered. I made tea loaves filled with mincemeat for the mayor, postmaster, the Catholic priest, and the sisters at the convent in Banaue. This gave us an opportunity to build good relations with these influential people and to let them know we appreciated all they did for us. The Catholics ran the high school in town where the teens from our village attended, as well as a small clinic.

Branch Conference at Nasuli

After our public relations trip was finished, we packed up to go to Manila where we caught the plane for Nasuli.

Every two years, SIL Philippines held a branch-wide conference at Nasuli. Since the last one had been held just before we arrived in the Philippines, the 1968 conference was our first. On December 21, we flew from Manila to Cagayan de Oro, where the SIL plane picked us up and flew us to Nasuli. The Philippine Airlines plane no longer flew into Malaybalay after a serious accident two years before.

I had been looking forward to the conference. It would be a chance to get to know numerous branch members that I hadn't met yet. It would also be an opportunity to learn more about the inner workings of the branch.

The residents of Nasuli fit all of us from the north into their extra beds and added cots and sleeping bags, especially for the children. Hazel Wrigglesworth and Jean Shand invited us to stay with them. They were translators for the Ilianen Manobo people of central Mindanao.

Hazel was the first Philippines branch person I had met. She was a graduate of London Bible Institute and came by to visit the first summer I worked in the LBI office. I had coffee with her in the dining hall. Later, when I was doing partnership development and raising support, Hazel was on furlough and living at her cousin's place near Brantford, Ontario. I spent a night with her, since I was speaking in the area. We have been good friends since that time. Now I would get to know her American coworker, Jean Shand.

Hazel and Jean lived on the main plaza at Nasuli near the meeting hall where the conference sessions were held. They had a lovely little house made of *lakap*, split bamboo woven into large mat-like pieces. Two were put together, one on top of the other, to make siding that was fastened to the framework of the house. A plywood lining finished the inside walls and ceiling. Since Hazel and Jean had brought many of their cherished possessions from home, they had made a very comfortable, cozy home. We felt privileged to stay there.

The conference started out with three days of spiritual emphasis with a special speaker, Dr. Harold Fife. We enjoyed singing Christmas carols, having times of fellowship, and sharing meals in various homes. Norm and Doris Abrams, George and Alda Fletcher, Shirley Abbott and Pat Hartung, Morrie and Shirley Cottle, and several others invited us to their homes. At the Christmas Day service, we sang carols and were blessed by Dr. Fife's message. We had brought Christmas gifts for Hazel and Jean and several others that we had become friends with during our time at Nasuli in 1967.

After Christmas, the business meetings began. We elected new directors and a new executive committee to take care of the branch business. Tom Lyman, who had served as interim director since the Troyers had returned to the States the year before, was elected director and Morrie Cottle was elected as associate director. Many other items of business were taken care of over the next week until the agenda was completed and the meetings adjourned.

Following conference, we stayed at Nasuli to have interviews with the director concerning our work and any matters that we wanted to talk to him about. During my session, I mentioned that I was not happy with my ability to learn Ifugao and that the isolation I felt was very difficult for me. I told him that Les Troyer had agreed that my time in Ifugao would be tentative. If after two years I still felt I would be happier doing something else, he would consider it.

This was news to Tom. He was not happy with the idea of my leaving Amganad but said he would keep his eyes open for a support role if something should come up. In the meantime, I agreed to return to Amganad and continue work on the primer I had begun following the Gudschinsky workshop.

A New Job

On January 6, Anne and I returned to Manila. After some shopping in the city to stock up for the next few months, we rode to Amganad with Virgil Ball of FEGC in his car and arrived home on January 9 at 9:00 p.m. This was the first time we had gone to Amganad overland. The road was long, and we were very tired.

Two days later, my life took an unexpected turn. I received a message on the morning radio sked from Director Tom Lyman in Nasuli.

" SIL Amganad from SIL Manila. Over."

"SIL Amganad. Over."

"I have a message for you from Tom Lyman in Nasuli. 'Please plan to be back at Nasuli in a week's time. Dick and Marlene Luartes are leaving for a five-month furlough in early March, and we want you to take over the publications department for them. Over.'"

Help! Take over for Dick and Marlene Luartes? Although I was looking for a support job and the publications department was my number one choice of places to work, I hadn't considered this.

Dick managed all the publishing that was done for the branch, and Marlene was the publications bookkeeper. The publications department not only printed and distributed all of the Scripture and literacy materials produced by our translators but also took care of prayer letters, office forms, publicity materials, stationery, and jobs for other missions, schools, and government officials. In addition to the eleven national workers employed at the print shop, two SIL members were assigned there. Pat Cochran worked in the darkroom making negatives and printing plates for the offset press, and Frances Weathermon worked in production.

How could I manage all that? It's true I had experience in publishing from my graduate degree program and my job at LCBM, but I had never managed anything, certainly not all those people. However, God gave me peace, and I knew that He would help me with whatever I needed to do. Besides, it was only for five months, since Dick and Marlene were planning a short furlough.

The packing began. The message from Tom had arrived on Saturday. By Wednesday, I was packed and ready to go, but I had to take care of many logistics concerning travel and shipping. I scheduled a flight to go to Manila from Bagabag on Thursday, but I had too much baggage. How could I get my extra baggage there? In the middle of making travel arrangements, finding out what I needed for living at Nasuli, and getting my baggage to Manila, our radio stopped working. We had to hike to Banaue to use the radio there, which took almost a whole day. But by Monday, January 20, all of the details for moving were taken care of, and I arrived by plane at Nasuli.

Dick and Marlene and their four children rented a large house across the main plaza from Hazel Wrigglesworth. It belonged to Burt and Glenna Clark, who were on furlough. Since they had room for me as well, I was to stay with the Luartes family for a month until they left and then continue to rent the house from the Clarks until the Luartes returned.

Immediately, I began training for this job. I needed to know the staff and to gain their confidence. Caesar Taga was head of the production department and operated the offset press. He had worked for SIL since 1957

91

under several managers. He was a fine Christian and enthusiastic about the work we were doing. On my way through Bagabag, one SIL member said to me, "You will have lots of trouble with Sar' Taga. He doesn't like working for women."

I prayed about how to approach him and asked the Lord for wisdom in how to get his confidence. On my first day as his supervisor, I said, "We have a big job to do, and this is new to me. You are well experienced, and I am going to count on you to help me out. I don't know many things, so I'll be depending on you."

He accepted this with good grace, and I never had one moment of trouble with him. He was completely supportive, and we worked together in complete harmony.

The learning curve was very steep, and the time was short. Marlene operated a complicated finance system, keeping track of time worked on each job in ten-minute increments. At the end of the month, she calculated the charges by adding up all the times recorded by the workers and converting time into money. These amounts were then entered into ledgers, and the monthly amounts entered into a work-in-progress account. When the job was done, the total from the WIP account was charged to the person or organization that would pay for the job. We had subsidizers who paid for Scripture publishing, so bills needed to be sent to the States to them. This was before the days of computers, so all of the work was done by hand. I had an adding machine, a pen, a pencil, and a large eraser.

Marlene decided we didn't have time for me to learn how to run the system and to learn Dick's job too, so she said I should just keep the records, and she would do all of the charging when she returned. I thought and prayed about that but decided if I were to be responsible for this publishing operation, I needed to know it all. So we worked on it together in January, and I processed the charges in February by myself while Marlene was home packing. She was available to answer questions if I had any, which I did. When it was time to process the charges in March, the Luartes had returned to the States, so except for a bit of guidance from the branch finance manager, I was able to complete the work by myself. Looking back later, I realized that God had definitely guided me to learn how to do the finances for the department.

We worked long hours in publications, beginning at 7:00 a.m. and closing at 4:30 p.m., with an hour off for lunch and a 15-minute coffee break in the morning. I loved my job, and I enjoyed working with the national staff. They were supportive and worked very hard.

After Dick and Marlene left for home, I had their big house all to myself. It was the first time in my life I had lived alone. I found it lonely at first but soon adjusted, realizing that my neighbors next door could hear me if I called. Gordon and Thelma Svelmoe lived on one side and Tom and Pat Mac-Leod on the other. They were all translators so were not there much of the time, but the houses were all close together.

I felt safe on the center, where members were like family.

Christmas at Nasuli

Ifugao rice terraces

Ifugao village

Chapter 18
Sammy, the Cat
1969

Not long after I was on my own, I decided to get a cat. The Luartes had left me Princess, but she had many bad habits that I couldn't cure her of, so we parted ways. I missed Patty, who had become a wonderful pet in Amganad, and I thought another cat would be good company.

Translators Barb Blackburn and Betty McLachlin had a mother cat with four or five kittens. Since they were about to leave for furlough, I took a beautiful gray-and-white six-week-old male that I called Sammy. Sammy and I had many adventures, especially during his growing-up months.

The house had no screens, so I slept under a mosquito net because of geckos, the little lizards that lived on the walls, under the pictures, and anyplace they could hide. We coexisted with them since they ate bugs, and they really weren't a problem. However, sometimes their suction-cup feet were faulty, and they would drop off the ceiling onto whatever was underneath them. I didn't want them on my bed, hence the mosquito net. I didn't bother to tuck it in, though, since at that time of year, we had no mosquitoes.

On the first Saturday morning we lived together, at 5:00 a.m., Sammy climbed up on the foot of my bed and got under the netting. Starting at the foot, he ran as fast as he could and jumped on my face. Fortunately, he didn't have his claws out. To be wakened at that hour on my day off by a ball of fur in my face was not the way I wanted to start my weekend. I tossed him out and went back to sleep. At 6:30 he knocked over my metal wastepaper basket. I wondered what I'd done to have taken in a rambunctious kitten as a housemate. I soon learned I would never have a dull moment with that cat.

The curtains in the living room hung on each side of the big window. Sammy frequently used curtains for climbing and had to be hauled down.

I soon discovered that he had a sweet tooth. Since I was only two minutes from the office, I usually went home for coffee breaks. I often placed a cookie or two on a side table by the couch as I drank my coffee and read my current book. If I didn't watch carefully, Sammy ate my second cookie while I had my nose in my book.

He not only was very active, but he used me for a scratching post. I was covered with cat scratches for some time until he outgrew the need to climb all over me with his claws out.

On Sundays we had church in the meeting hall with men on the center taking turns preaching. After church some adults went to one of the homes for Bible study, but first we had a time of coffee and cookies or cake, which were provided by class members.

One week Vivian Forsberg and I decided to make a jelly roll. We baked it on Saturday night, and I rolled it in a tea towel and left in on my counter. When I got up in the morning, I found the tea towel pushed back and the end eaten off the roll. I didn't need to wonder what had happened to it. Since only the end was unwrapped, I cut off the eaten part, and everybody enjoyed the rest. I didn't tell them they were sharing it with my cat.

Sammy grew to be a large cat weighing eight pounds when fully grown. He lived on rice and mackerel, which was the standard cat food at Nasuli. I liked freshly cooked rice and mackerel myself, so whenever I cooked for Sammy, I had a meal before mixing it all together so he wouldn't just eat the fish and leave the rice behind. He also liked to kill and sometimes eat lizards, although he didn't always eat them but rather left them under my bed. I often smelled a dead lizard and had to get the broom.

The partitions in the house didn't go right to the ceiling but were cut off straight across about seven feet up. The ceiling was lined with plywood following the curve of the roof, leaving space above the partition. We had trouble with bats at Nasuli, and they often flew in the open windows and swooped back and forth in the open space near the ceiling.

Sammy would sit on top of the partition and swat at them as they flew by, often killing them. When he tried to eat bats, they didn't sit well on his stomach. One day I watched him working on a bat he had knocked down. First he chewed a bit then ran to his rice bowl and ate a bit then went back to the bat and worked on it some more then back to the rice bowl. After three or four rounds of this, he deposited the contents of his stomach in a corner.

April and May are the hot months in the Philippines. After lunch I liked to lie on my bed for a while before going back to work, since the 90-degree F. (32 C.) temperature sapped my strength. By this time, Sammy was full grown, but now he decided that instead of being a cat, he would like to be a fur collar. Rarely did I lie down to sleep when I didn't wake up with Sammy sprawled over my neck.

He also liked to sleep on the front porch, but instead of lying curled up as most cats do, I would find him lying on his back with his back feet spread out and a front paw covering his eyes.

Yes, life with Sammy had no dull moments.

Chapter 19
Changed Plans
1969

The first translation team had arrived in the Philippines in 1953. It included Dick and Kay Pittman, who headed up the advance, and thirteen other couples and singles known as the "First Wave." This team and growing numbers in the next sixteen years had fanned over the island nation and were busily translating the Scriptures into hitherto unwritten languages. As Scripture portions were completed, they were typed up, checked by a consultant, and submitted to the publications department for printing.

Dick Luartes had worked in Guatemala before going to the Philippines. Under the tutelage of Walt Agee, the publications manager there, Dick learned how to set up an offset-printing operation. He had brought his knowledge to Nasuli and developed a functional setup for making negatives and plates for the offset press.

Now in 1969, as translators were completing more and more Scripture portions and literacy materials, we were outgrowing our facilities. Dick had researched the cost to increase the size of our building, to purchase larger and faster equipment, and to hire more workers. Before he left for furlough, he presented a proposal to the executive committee for this increase in our next budget. After a long discussion, the executive committee decided that the cost was too great and we should search for a better solution to our production problems.

Publishing in Manila

About that time, the Far East Broadcasting Company opened Marshburn Press, a new, large, well-equipped print shop at their headquarters on Karuhatan Street in Valenzuela, just north of Manila. Since they were looking for work, they offered to take over our printing on an experimental basis. This meant our book publishing would need to move from Nasuli to Manila, and the one in charge would serve as a liaison between SIL and FEBC.

When the executive committee agreed to follow this plan and informed Dick Luartes, he decided not to return to the Philippines, preferring to work in a print shop, not an office. So the committee asked if I would stay on as manager of the publications department and oversee the move from Nasuli to Manila. I agreed. It would be several months before the move could take place in November 1969, so I continued working at Nasuli until that time.

A Visit with Shirley Abbott

In the Philippines, Holy Thursday and Good Friday are both national holidays, so the print shop was closed. Shirley Abbott, who was translating the New Testament for the Ata Manobo people, invited me to spend Easter weekend at her place in Mansalinao, a twenty-minute flight from Nasuli in the Helio Courier aircraft. We flew out on Thursday morning, landing on the tiny airstrip close to the village. Since no road led to Mansalinao, the people had little contact with the outside world. The married women didn't wear tops, especially when working in the fields. The climate was very hot, since Mansalinao was just a bit above sea level and much closer to the equator than Ifugao.

Shirley's house was made of split-bamboo walling and a split-palm floor. It was put down in strips about one-half inch wide with one-quarter inch spaces between to let the air circulate and to provide places to sweep down the dirt. The floor was bouncy and took some getting used to since I felt as if I would break through with each step.

The houses were built five or six feet off the ground. Some were ten or twelve feet up, with only poles with notches to put feet in for ladders. Going up was hard enough, but going down was harder.

On Thursday afternoon, we went fishing with half of the village. Mansalinao is on a large river, which was quite shallow because of a drought. I learned about a new way of fishing. The fishermen built a large triangular-shaped framework of poles in the middle of the river with the open part facing upstream. They lined it all around with branches and leaves and placed their traps inside the "v" mouths facing upstream. Then they went up river and lashed bamboo poles together to make one pole as long as the river was wide. They dragged this pole down the river, yelling and screaming to frighten the fish toward the traps. People stood on either side of the traps toward the shore, poking with white bamboo poles to keep the fish from going by and channeling them into the traps. The fishermen wore little homemade goggles of wood and glass to see the fish under the water. Of course, we had to go out and help, so we were wet to our hips by the time the traps were full.

On Friday, Shirley and I hiked an hour downstream to the place where a new airstrip was being laid out. The river had changed course and cut off the present strip, making it too short. We had to wade through the river six times on our way to the new airstrip.

The whole village gradually moved to the new location. We counted over fifty houses either finished or being built on both sides of the airstrip.

People were relocating there not only from Mansalinao but also from several other villages to be close to the airstrip.

On Thursday night, a number of people gathered at Shirley's house to have a dance. The Ata dance is quite different from the Ifugao dance, being much more animated and rhythmic.

They wanted me to do an Ifugao dance, but I said I couldn't because they didn't have any gongs. They got out a kerosene five-gallon can, and Shirley beat the rhythm for me. Ifugaos would have thought I danced like a child, but the Manobos were satisfied. Then they wanted me to do an Ata dance too, so I followed one of the girls around. The footwork was quite simple, and I thought I did quite well, but they all laughed and laughed, meaning, I presume, that it wasn't quite right. I was happy to be the entertainment for the evening. The Ata dance was done to the plucking of a bamboo two-stringed instrument similar to a guitar.

The temperature was very hot, well over 100 degrees F. (C. 38), so we didn't do much all weekend. It was a very restful time and good to see some of the cultural differences between the Ata and the Ifugaos with whom I had lived.

Chapter 20
Life at Nasuli
1969

For some time, Anne's parents had planned to visit her. I was disappointed that I was at Nasuli and wouldn't have an opportunity to meet them. However, in late April we closed the publications department for a week so all the staff could take their vacations at the same time. Fortunately, this coincided with the Wests' visit to Ifugao, so I traveled north to join them. I was also looking forward to seeing my friends in Amganad again.

One day before my planned trip to Ifugao, Hazel Wrigglesworth received a cable, saying her twin sister had passed away. The director asked me to go to Manila with her the next day to help her catch her plane to Canada. I had only half an hour to pack before flying to Cagayan de Oro on our SIL plane to catch the Philippine Airlines flight.

The weather was bad, and our pilot said he didn't think we could get to Cagayan. God knew we needed to get there, though. When we got off the ground, the valley opened down the center like a tunnel with clouds to the ground on both sides, and we landed safely at Cagayan. The PAL plane was full, though, so we found a hotel after making reservations for the 8:30 flight the next morning, which was to arrive in Manila at noon.

Hazel's flight to Toronto left at 5:00 p.m. It was a great rush for her to get her shots, to get paper work from the travel agent, and to get her hair done. I left her at the beauty shop and went to the SIL guesthouse to iron her traveling suit. We arrived at the airport at 4:20 p.m.—just in time to get her bags checked in.

Back to Amganad

Since my trip to Manila was advanced by a day, I had extra time to spend there before traveling to Bagabag with Len and Doreen Newell in their Jeep. Anne and her parents, who had been in the Philippines for nearly a month, were in Bagabag, so we rented a jeepney to take us to Amganad.

The plan was to have a community feast that week to thank the residents of the area for their friendship and care of us while living in their community. We bought two pigs in Bagabag, which we took with us, one on top of the jeepney and the other on the floor at the back between the seats. I sat with my feet on the pig, since I had no other place to put them.

The feast took place the day after we arrived. We cooked a sack of rice, two pigs, and noodles and fed around two hundred people.

101

One pig was gutted, stuffed with onions, garlic, and ginger, placed on a bamboo spit, and cooked over an open fire to make *lechon*, a favorite dish in the Philippines, especially the skin, which becomes very crispy. Men took turns turning the pig over the fire by hand for five hours.

Our neighbors did all the work for this feast, as they were happy to have the food and celebration. They danced to the gongs, told stories, sang songs, and made speeches. It was all great fun. After more than a month in the Philippines, Anne's parents went home with a good picture of her life here.

ৡৣৡ

Nasuli is almost ten miles (sixteen kilometers) from the nearest town, Malaybalay, the capital of Bukidnon Province. Farms and small villages are scattered along the road from Malaybalay to Nasuli, but for the most part, we only got to know the people who worked on the center. The only vehicles at Nasuli then were a couple of vans and an ancient gray carryall named "Hercules."

We had to make our own social lives, most of which revolved around eating. Because I lived in the biggest house at Nasuli and I enjoyed cooking, I often had people over for meals or for an evening of playing games. My dining room table was six-and-a-half feet long and could easily seat ten or even twelve people.

In June of that year, we had ten single women living at Nasuli, and we often got together, sometimes for Sunday night suppers or during the evenings. Not a lot of special food items were available in the Philippines at that time, so when we got packages from home with special treats, we shared them with our friends. One Sunday night, ten of us ate salads, muffins, cheese, nuts, fudge, cake, and coffee—not a very nutritious meal but one that everyone enjoyed.

We had a small grocery store, known as the "commissary," at Nasuli where we could buy most of the nonperishable food items we needed. Once or twice a week, the buyer went to Malaybalay to buy fresh fruits, vegetables, and meat from the market. A few people could sign up to go along, if space was available in the vehicle. This was a nice outing that I enjoyed from time to time.

I also enjoyed visiting the nearest translation project at Caburacanan where Mary Jane Gardner and Ursula Post were the translators. Since the village was not on a road, they had to fly there. On the weekend of June 14, Philippine Independence Day, Til Kohley, who worked in the finance office, and I flew to Caburacanan to spend four days with Mary Jane and Urs.

The flight was only fifteen minutes from Nasuli, but the area was quite isolated. The house was away from the main village so was quiet and restful. We spent much of the time reading, sleeping, eating, doing jigsaw puzzles, visiting in the village, and walking by the large river that curled its way through the mountains. It was a special treat to get away from our work for a short time.

Down to Davao City

Davao City is located on the south coast of Mindanao. One Friday Til Kohley needed to have her eyes checked and to get new glasses. The optometrist was in Davao, so Til made arrangements to fly there, and Joanne Cochran, wife of Pat, who worked with me in publications, and I went along to shop.

It was now June, and the rainy season had started. Usually, the rains came in the afternoons, leaving the mornings clear for flying. However, that day we woke up to rain in the morning and heavy clouds low over the mountains. By 10:30 a.m., we were able to get over the first ridge and into the mountains in southern Mindanao. We flew through several rainstorms, but by keeping low in the valleys, our pilot, George Fletcher, was able to fly us to the coastal plain where the sun was shining.

The airport in Davao is over six miles (ten kilometers) out of the city, so we caught a jeepney and rode to the eye doctor's office. Joanne and I went shopping while Til and George saw the doctor. We planned to meet for lunch at the Insular Hotel, a beautiful, modern establishment known for its spectacular setting on the ocean, with rolling lawns, tropical flowers, palm trees, and a swimming pool. For those of us who lived at rustic Nasuli, it was a special treat to have a delicious lunch at the Insular.

By two-thirty p.m., we were back at the airport ready to return to Nasuli. A call to the radio operator there confirmed that the weather hadn't improved; they were closed in with rain. Were we stuck in Davao overnight? If so, we would have to find a local hotel, since we couldn't afford to stay at the Insular. George flew up and took a look at the weather. It didn't look good, but George's many years of flying in mountainous terrain and bad weather gave him confidence that we might get through. He found holes in the clouds all the way until we finally crossed the last ridge into our valley and found a space where we could see the ground. That was the only hole in the whole valley. Five minutes after we landed safely at Nasuli, the pass closed in, and it poured. Much prayer went up during a flight like that. I enjoyed flying in small aircraft if the weather were good, but during rainy season, I preferred to keep my feet on the ground.

About that time, I received information that Tim and Lucille Diller and baby David were planning a trip to Nasuli. Tim was working on the Waray Waray language in Tacloban on the island of Leyte, collecting information for his PhD dissertation. Since the Dillers were planning to become Wycliffe translators and were interested in joining the Philippines branch, they wanted to see Nasuli. I knew them already from their visit with us in Amganad and had plenty of space in my big house, so I invited them to stay with me. We had a lovely three days together as they toured the center, swam in our natural pool, and got acquainted with the operations and people there.

As the rainy season continued, the roads and walking paths at Nasuli became more and more muddy. Some of the driving roads had a bit of gravel, but the rain was so heavy that the stones washed out, and big puddles covered the roads.

On one of my trips to town, I bought a pair of rubber boots. They came in not just standard black but in an assortment of bright colors, such as red, blue, green, and yellow. I chose a blue pair and looked forward to keeping my feet dry. It took a while before I could wear them comfortably though, since they rubbed on my ankles and gave me blisters.

One day in mid-August, I got word that the owners of the house I was living in had sold it, and the new owners were returning to the Philippines in just a couple of weeks. Burt and Glenna Clark had decided not to return to the Philippines and had sold their house to Elmer and Bev Wolfenden. Elmer had been working on a PhD in linguistics at the University of Hawaii. It was now time for them to return to the Philippines and begin a new translation project. That left me out of a place to live. Bev said I could move into the extra bedroom on the ground floor and board with them.

When Til Kohley heard that I was losing my house, she offered me hers. She was tired of living by herself and didn't like to cook so was planning to move in with Mary Jane Gardner and Ursula Post, who lived next door to her. Mary Jane and Urs had come back from Caburacanan, so Mary Jane could fill in as the radio operator for a few months. Urs loved to cook and was happy to have Til live with them. That solved my problem.

Til, Mary Jane, and Urs helped me move. Within an hour, I had all my personal things moved to Til's house, and while in a mess, I was in by suppertime. I'd discovered before and had it reconfirmed: People in SIL had no time to think about things. They just up and did them.

I didn't know how Sammy would like this move, but I brought him with me. He inspected his new home, poking his nose into every nook and cranny and then went to the door with a loud "meow" to get out. When I made him stay inside, he curled up by the refrigerator and went to sleep. Later, he found the little cat door that Til had installed for her cat and disappeared into the night. Fortunately, he did learn how to come back in, since his food dish was inside.

Moving to Manila

By now I knew I would be moving to Manila toward the end of the year, since the executive committee had decided to transfer our publishing to the Far East Broadcasting Company's Marshburn Press. I had been assigned to serve as publications coordinator, liaising with FEBC. They would be printing all our books, both vernacular (Scripture and literacy) and linguistic (dictionaries, linguistic articles, etc.).

I went to Manila for a week in August to consult with the management at the press and to shop. Two typhoons had recently gone through, and it was still raining. I got a sample of what life would be like during rainy season in the future. Many of the city streets were flooded and impassable. I saw people wading up to their knees through muddy, garbage-filled water.

Translator Betty McLachlin's Death

Barbara Blackburn and Betty McLachlin had returned home in May for a year of furlough. During the summer, Betty and her parents from Toronto, Ontario, took a long road trip across Canada and the United States. While Betty was sleeping in the backseat of the family car as they drove across Arizona, they had an accident, and Betty was killed. Her parents were hospitalized but were not seriously injured.

News of this event was a great shock to all of us! We were very concerned for Barb, who had lost her stepfather just before she left Nasuli. She and Betty were very close, having worked together for more than ten years.

The Betty McLachlin Memorial Fund was set up, and in 1971, using the assets from this fund, an old building on the center was renovated and remodeled into a new study center. It had a library and study rooms for translators to use as office space.

Beekman Translation Workshop

In September John Beekman, Wycliffe's international translation coordinator, arrived at Nasuli for a translation workshop. In 1955 John had received an artificial heart valve, which made a ticking sound as his heart beat. He became known as "The man with the noisy heart."

Many translators arrived at the center for this workshop where John gave lectures and help to those who were having problems with their translations. Those of us who lived at Nasuli took in all the visitors, since we had no guesthouse at that time. Donna Hettick, one of the four who met me at the airport when I first arrived in Manila, stayed in my extra bedroom. Her translation assistant, Denny, stayed in a room downstairs. We ate together, and I enjoyed having "family" again. I had adjusted to living alone but preferred to have a companion. Denny was very helpful, usually doing the dishes and taking out the garbage. I appreciated his help, since I was very busy at work then as more and more Scripture portions were arriving at the print shop for publication.

Until now our teams provided the funds for printing the books they completed. But with rising costs and increased production, these costs had become more than most translators could handle.

I was involved in finding funds to help with production costs. Several Bible societies in the States were becoming increasingly interested in funding our Scripture translations, and eventually The Bible League International and the International Bible Society took on the bulk of funding for Wycliffe Scriptures worldwide.

About halfway through the Beekman workshop, we had a program at which many of the translation assistants performed songs and dances from their cultural communities. We noticed a big difference between those from the north and those from the south.

Hazel Wrigglesworth worked with the Ilianen Manobo people. She had a kulintang, an instrument made up of eight graduated brass gongs placed in a wooden box and supported by two pieces of rope. They are tapped on the tops with wooden batons, each gong making a different tone because of the size. Three Manobo girls played this instrument.

Ginny DeVries, a missionary working on the island of Palawan and sister of Elisabeth Elliot, also attended the workshop, since she was translating the Scriptures for a language group there. Her two sons, one eleven and the other fourteen, accompanied her. One played the violin and the other the trumpet, both on a professional level. We enjoyed and marveled at their expertise.

Sammy Moves On

A few weeks into the workshop, I was chatting with Dick Hohulin, who was staying with his wife Lou in a house at the far end of the center. He said they were having trouble with rats.

"Oh, dear," I said. "What you need is a cat."

"I know," he said, "but we don't have time to go looking for one, and it's only for a short time, so I guess we'll just get a trap."

"How would you like to see if Sammy would take care of your problem? I don't know what kind of ratter he is, since we haven't had any problems here with rats, but sometimes just the smell of a cat in the house will keep rats out."

Dick grinned. "We'd be happy to try him out."

I got together Sammy's food dish and some extra food that I had prepared and sent him home with Dick. That was the last I saw of Sammy. I expected he would return home when the workshop was over, but we must have had a misunderstanding. Dick thought I was giving him away, so when he and Lou left the center at the end of the workshop, they gave him to Filipino friends who lived down the road. I was sad for a while, but in the end it worked out for the best, since I couldn't take Sammy to Manila with me. I would be staying in the guesthouse until I was able to find a place to live, and pets were not allowed there. This way I didn't have the trouble of finding a new home for him.

But I missed my adventurous cat.

Chapter 21
Settling in Manila
1969–1970

By the end of October, it was time to pack for the move to Manila. I not only had to move myself, but I also had to pack up the office. We decided to move all of the book publishing to Marshburn Press, close down the offset printing operation at Nasuli, and leave only a mimeograph to handle office and other in-house jobs. Caesar Taga would become the new Nasuli publications manager.

Moving to New Quarters

I found it difficult to decide what to take from the office. For a couple of weeks, we packed books, files, and office equipment. The workers at Nasuli were a great help. Although a number of them were losing their jobs, other departments at the center hired some of them. Marshburn Press hired Avelina, supervisor of our composition department, and she would go to Manila with me. By mid-November, we were all packed, and everything was shipped to Manila to be set up in my new office there. I flew with my personal belongings on November 15.

I stayed in the Manila guesthouse, sharing a room with five other single women until I could rent an apartment. The director's new secretary, Sheila Brannon, had just arrived that week from the States. She planned to spend two years in the Philippines and would also need a place to live. Since we would both be working in the same office, we decided to share an apartment. We immediately went house hunting.

We had heard of an apartment that was being built belonging to the family of one of SIL's good friends. We decided to check it out first. Furnished apartments were almost impossible to find in Manila, and since neither Sheila nor I had any furniture or appliances, we thought we would have to buy everything. We were happily surprised to find that this place would have basic furnishings. It wasn't finished yet but would be by the end of December. A lot of dust and building debris littered the grounds, but we thought that wouldn't last too long. So we took it, since the rent was within our means.

I ordered my barrels of household equipment that had been stored in Bagabag to be shipped to Manila, ready for the day we could move in to our new home. I was still waiting for the shipment of office equipment and supplies to arrive from Nasuli, so I wasn't able to begin work yet.

In the meantime, I learned another job. Mary Granaas, the guesthouse manager, had returned to California for a time, and her replacement had become too ill to work. So the director asked me to manage the guesthouse for a couple of weeks until this member was well.

What did this job entail? The list was long, and I felt overwhelmed to be taking this on with just two days notice. I had to supervise four women and three men on staff. My duties included planning menus, shopping, supervising the staff, assigning rooms, answering the phone, and making calls. This also meant sending telegrams, filling orders for people who had only radio contact with us, and making appointments for members who would soon arrive in the city.

Fifteen people were staying at the house at that time. I found it difficult to know how to buy food for that many people. However, the cook was excellent, and without her expertise and help, I would have been in great trouble. I did enjoy it though and managed to keep everything together.

Christmas was soon approaching, and many people came in from their village locations to shop or to vacation over the holidays. The house was full, and it kept me busy finding beds for everybody.

On top of housing people who came to the city, two people had surgery. One had had a miscarriage and the other a hysterectomy. The one who had lost her baby was depressed because she felt she was too old to have more than her three children. When I asked her how old she was, I discovered she was only nine months older than I was, and I wasn't yet thirty-three. I told her to stop talking that way, since I didn't consider myself to be that old. While I had told the Lord I was willing to have no husband or children, I hadn't given up the hope that someday I might have both.

Now that I was in Manila on a permanent basis, I needed to find a church to attend. While in the city on short stays, I had attended several different English-speaking churches. Now I decided to go to the Capital City Baptist Church. This Conservative Baptist church had an English service in the morning and a Tagalog service in the afternoon. I would have liked to join the choir, but their practice time was right after the morning service, and I had no way to get home afterwards. The pastor gave good messages, but they were quite basic.

We had a prayer meeting at the guesthouse every Wednesday night, which I attended. This gave me an opportunity to keep up with the needs of my fellow SIL members and to pray for their ministries.

A Trip to Ifugao

By the middle of December, another member took over managing the guesthouse. Then I took a trip to Ifugao to pack up the things I had left there and to ship them to Manila. During the year I had been gone, Anne had continued to learn Ifugao and was now translating the book of Mark. She needed a translation assistant and found that Ongallan, who had helped to repair our house, was available. He turned out to be very clever and continued through the years as her main translation assistant.

Mary Rhea, who had taught at the Nasuli elementary school the previous year, was visiting Anne with the possibility of joining her in the translation work. Louise Sawyer from British Columbia was also there for the same purpose. When I arrived, I made five in Anne's little house, since she also had a house helper who lived there during the week. I'm sure Anne was glad to have my belongings removed to give her more space.

While in Ifugao, I met Hilda's firstborn, Howie. He was five months old and very large for an Ifugao baby. Anne loved children and became like his second mother. The neighbors had given Hilda a hard time, saying she was raising Howie like an American baby. She followed some of Anne's ideas, like keeping him clean, using diapers and rubber pants, burping him, and putting him down on his tummy. None of these things were done in Ifugao. But since he was so big and healthy, Hilda's neighbors changed their minds and said maybe what she was doing was good.

During my stay in Ifugao, Anne and I hiked to Banaue. I saw some changes, including a first-class tourist hotel that had been built on a large terrace below the clinic. We attended the FEGC Christmas party in Banaue that night, so I visited with all the other missionaries I had become friends with during my two years in Ifugao. Mary Anderson, one of the nurses, was returning home to the States soon to get married to a serviceman she met when he helped build the Ifugao water system. We had a bridal shower for her during the time I was there.

Back to Work

I returned to Manila to find that my shipment from Nasuli had arrived. Now I could set up my office and get to work. When I arrived in the Philippines in 1967, the Manila office was located downtown in the department of education building and consisted of just one room. In the meantime, our administration had decided that the headquarters, including the director's office, finance office, and publications should be moved from Nasuli to Manila, which was more central to the whole country.

The director had an office in his house for some time, but now the group rented a larger office in Quezon City on E. Rodriguez Street, a fifteen-minute drive from the guesthouse, depending on the traffic. The director had opened it just before I went to Nasuli and had closed the downtown office. Jean Haggar, the receptionist, was located in the middle of a large open area surrounded by three or four offices with glass walls. Finance was in the first one, and I was in the next one. The director was at the end, and later the associate director of academic affairs moved there too. Eventually, we had three or four national secretaries who had desks in various locations in the office.

It took me some time to get settled, partly because we had no file cabinet for the oversized hanging file folders I had brought from Nasuli that held the publishing information for each language in which we worked. I ordered an eight-foot-long bin with a sliding top, but it took two weeks for a carpenter to construct it and move it into my office. In the meantime, my files sat in piles on bookshelves and on the floor. I had also brought two copies of every book we had published since the beginning of the branch in 1953. These had to be sorted and placed on bookshelves. Eventually, I got everything organized and was ready to begin work.

My first task was to visit Marshburn Press at the compound of the Far East Broadcasting Company in Valenzuela, just north of Manila. This was a 15-mile (25-kilometer) trip through very heavy traffic that usually took me an hour. Since I didn't have a car of my own, I borrowed one for my trips twice a week. I had brought several jobs with me from Nasuli, which were ready to be printed.

I enjoyed getting to know the workers at Marshburn, especially the supervisors of the production department as well as the composition department on the second floor where Avelina was working.

Paul and Diane Estabrooks, former schoolmates from LCBM, had joined FEBC and were stationed at Manila. They had a home on the compound, along with a number of other expatriate missionaries and Filipino workers. They invited me to join them for coffee when I arrived on my trips, so I got to know a number of the people who worked at the radio station as well as the print shop.

Physical Problems

By January 1970 I was still in the guesthouse waiting for our apartment to be completed. At that time, the Hong Kong flu was raging throughout the city and the world. I soon joined the ranks of the sick and spent a week in bed with a high fever, sinus congestion, and a bad cough. Even after the flu symptoms cleared, I still had a sinus infection, and the doctor finally sent me to a specialist to have my sinuses suctioned out. After several weekly treatments at the ear, nose, and throat (ENT) doctor, he sent me to an allergist, since he thought I had more than a sinus infection. After the allergist gave me skin tests to check for allergies, of seventy possibilities I came up with thirty positives, some more severe than others. The allergist gave me shots twice a week for several weeks, then slowly reduced the shots to once a week and eventually once a month for the next year and a half. The shots helped me a great deal.

One thing I was allergic to was dust, which was impossible to avoid in the Philippines. Feathers and tobacco were also on the "bad" list. I made sure not to sleep on a feather pillow and tried to stay away from people who were smoking. That was more difficult, since most Filipinos smoked at that time. I am still violently allergic to black pepper, but my reactions to most other things are now under control.

By mid-January, our apartment was completed enough so that we could move in. Work still needed to be done on the kitchen cupboards, and not all the furniture we needed had been provided, so we had to buy a few things ourselves. It took some time to get settled, but we eventually had a nice place to live. Dr. Bill McCurry, the doctor from the Banaue clinic, and his family left the Philippines at about this time, and I bought a lovely set of Royal Albert English bone china from them. It was a service for twelve, white with a turquoise fine-leaf design around the plates and cups. This set of china served me well for my whole time in the Philippines, and when I left in 2006, I sold it back to one of the McCurry daughters who, with her husband, was now working with SIL in the Philippines.

Travel Plans

In January our executive committee met in Manila for their quarterly meeting. Doris Porter, the committee secretary, was one of the translators for the Tboli people in southern Mindanao. She had spent quite a bit of time at Nasuli during the year I was there, and we had become good friends.

One day she said, "I need to do something special for a break from these intense meetings. Let's go out for a steak dinner." Never one to pass up a good meal, I agreed, and the next day we proceeded to one of Manila's excellent restaurants. While enjoying our steaks, we discussed the possibility of traveling home for furlough together. At that time, our terms were five years, but because I arrived in January and didn't want to go home in the middle of winter after spending a term in the tropics, I had received permission to leave six months early. That put our departure dates at the same time.

We were both interested in traveling home through Asia and Europe. We could visit friends on both those continents as well as seeing the countries through which we would travel. In those days, before e-mail, all travel arrangements had to be made by mail, which was very slow. So we felt we needed to begin working on our trip, even though our departure wouldn't be for another year and a half.

Changes at Home

About this time, I heard about changes at home. A letter from my sister Marj said they were expecting another baby. This would be three new ones since I left home, making four in all. Since she already had three girls, they were hoping for a boy. Nell and Gary had one son born since I left.

A letter from Mom said they needed to move again. The year before, our rented RR5 house had been sold and all the buildings razed to make additional farmland. Mom and Dad had moved up the road to another house, which was vacant for a while following the death of the owner. Now they needed to move from there. Dad finally had decided that it was time for them to buy a house of their own, so they could stay in one place. Now they searched for something they could afford.

Political Riots

In Manila, unrest, especially among the students, had come to a head, and demonstrations and riots against the government were taking place in the streets. A march on the President's palace, which was to have been peaceful, turned violent, resulting in the death of five students. Substantial communist infiltration swept the whole country, but so far our work had not been affected. We were careful to avoid the problem locations if possible and continued as usual.

Blood Donations

In February I made my first blood donation. A seventy-six year old woman had been in one of the big hospitals in Manila for almost two months. She had a double hernia operation but had complications, including pneumonia and a heart attack. Now she was hemorrhaging. The doctor thought she might have an intestinal ulcer and had given her only a 10 percent chance to live. She had A-negative blood, which is rare in the Philippines, since 99 percent of Filipinos have Rh-positive blood. She was half German so probably inherited her blood type from her German father.

Dan Weaver, our associate director, had A-negative blood and had his name on a list of donors at the hospital. They asked him to donate, and he told me about the need, since I am also A-negative. I agreed to donate since they needed six donors. It was a new experience but not an unpleasant one. My hemoglobin was so high that I was able to give a full 500 cc's. Most women, at least in the Philippines, are only able to give 400 cc's. I met the patient's family, who were very grateful for the donation. The American Association maintains a blood-donor list of people with various blood types, so I placed my name on their list. Throughout my years in the Philippines, I was contacted frequently and was able, on most occasions, to donate without any problem.

Work Details

Regarding my work, I not only facilitated the printing of all the Scripture and literacy books, but I also produced the needed publicity materials. Because SIL had a contract with the Philippine government, we were required to give the President a yearly report of our completed work. Writing and designing this 24-page report was part of my assignment. I had to compile the statistics, write the articles, find the pictures, and lay out the booklet. It then went to our director to check and approve it for printing.

I was happy when the work was completed, since it was a heavy weight, and I was unsure of what was needed. My work was not only sent to President Marcos but also to many other government officials, businesses, and Christian organizations.

I enjoyed entertaining new people and often showed them the sights. One of those was the American cemetery, the largest World War II cemetery in the world, containing 17,206 graves laid out in a large circle, and tall limestone piers containing the names of 36,285 missing in action. The US government maintains this cemetery, and it was well worth a visit.

Gradually, we settled into our apartment, and life was becoming normal. Most of the building work was done, but the compound was still very dusty, since it had no grass. In March it became hot and dry because we had had no rain since well before Christmas. This was normal for Manila in those days, and we could expect no rain until late May or June.

The temperature gradually got higher, and the humidity rose until in April and May it was not unusual to have the thermometer read 100 degrees F. (38 degrees C.) with the humidity at 90 percent. The scorching tropical sun burned our skin in a very short time, so we were careful to carry our umbrellas everywhere we went.

One day when I was out, our landlady, Mrs. Panganiban, told Sheila that the priest was coming to bless our house and hers, which was on the other side of our duplex. The priest carried a candle and a container of holy water, which he sprinkled in every room before offering a prayer for the activities that would take place there. After the blessing, we were all invited to a big dinner of delicious Philippine food at the Panganiban's house.

Off to Cool Baguio

Easter always comes in the middle of the hottest time of the year in the Philippines. This was my first hot season in Manila, which was hotter than any of the other places I had been in the summer. Both Amganad and Nasuli were much higher in altitude than Manila, which sits at sea level, so I was still adjusting to the heat.

As Sheila hadn't been out of the city since she arrived in October, I thought it would be good to take her to Baguio, the summer capital, at 5,000 feet where half of Manila, it seems, heads during the summer. We had both Thursday and Friday off work, so we took a bus to Baguio to spend the weekend with Char Houck and Happy Minot, two of our translators who were taking a break and had rented a guest cottage. They had some extra room, so we stayed with them. The contrast in the temperature was unbelievable. I was very cold, but Sheila enjoyed it. She said it was just like northern Michigan.

Good Friday is a very holy day, so everything was closed. We had lunch with Lee and Arlene Ballard, translators for the Ibaloi, who lived in Baguio. We spent the whole afternoon visiting with them. On Saturday we took Char and Happy to Camp John Hay, the American rest and recreation (R & R) air base where we had steaks at the officers club. It was Char's birthday and while this sounds like an expense that might be beyond missionaries, the cost was far less than it would have been at home. Following dinner, we went to see a Philippine dance troupe performing cultural dances wearing beautiful traditional clothing. On Sunday morning, we returned to Camp John Hay to attend a sunrise service. We sang worship songs as the sun rose over the mountains in the distance before leaving for our return bus trip to Manila.

Move to Another Apartment

Another move was scheduled for the near future for Sheila and me. We had not been many months in our apartment but were finding it very dusty from the continuing construction and noisy from the crowded neighborhood. We couldn't sleep before 10:30 at night or after 5:30 in the morning because of the noise. Some young men often used the street as a drag strip, gunning their motorcycles and racing past our house. Crowds of screaming children surrounded us, and we were often awakened in the middle of the night with people yelling at each other. We soon decided we would look for another place.

Faith Academy, the school that our missionary children attended, finished its school year in May. One of our teachers, who lived in an apartment near the guesthouse and commuted every day, moved closer to the school, leaving an apartment available. We looked at it, liked it, and decided to move there. It had three bedrooms and two bathrooms, so we arranged with Audrey Mayer, who came to teach at Faith Academy, to live with us, making the rent less than we had been paying at the Panganiban's place. It wasn't furnished though, so I needed to buy furniture and appliances for the *sala*, dining room, and my bedroom.

The new apartment was right on the main jeepney route to downtown Manila and only about a five-minute walk to the guesthouse. It was on the back of a large compound far from the street and was surrounded by flowers, grass, and a high moss-covered wall.

We thanked God often for this much-improved place to live.

Chapter 22
Earthquakes and Typhoons
1970

Earthquakes are not infrequent in the Philippines, since it sits on the "ring of fire" that surrounds the Pacific Ocean. We felt about eight or nine small tremors every year, but we mostly ignored them, as they didn't do any damage.

Sometimes a big one would shake the country and cause massive damage. One such earthquake shook Manila on April 7, 1970. The city had not had a big one since 1968 when one of a 7.3 magnitude toppled the Ruby Towers apartment building at 4:00 a.m., killing a number of people.

A Big One

We were at the office at 1:30 p.m. when the building shook, and pictures swayed. It intensified to become a 7.2 quake. First, we crawled under our desks and then were told to leave the building. Our office was on the second floor of a three-story building. When we hurried to the door, we discovered the employees from the third floor were racing down the stairs in a panic, screaming and pushing each other to get out. We waited until they had all passed by before leaving the building and going to the parking lot. Fortunately, our building wasn't damaged, but we heard later that the earthquake had killed seventeen people and damaged more than one hundred buildings in Manila.

God was gracious and protected hundreds of children from almost certain death. For some time, increased gas prices had caused unrest, and even though jeepney fares had gone up, the jeepney drivers were not satisfied. That day they had staged another strike, which took almost all the jeepneys off the streets. Schools had closed, since most children had no other means of transportation. When the earthquake was over, we heard that an elementary school had collapsed. Had the children been there, many would have been killed.

The earthquake was followed by more than one thousand aftershocks, mostly small, but some were big enough to send us outside again.

On the following Sunday, I had taken some visiting friends to the Overseas Missionary Fellowship (OMF) guesthouse, which was located in the area where the quake had been the strongest. Just as we were about to sit down for dinner, a magnitude five aftershock shook the house and knocked tiles off the bathroom walls. We raced outside, since it felt as if the house were coming down. No other damage was done to the house, probably because it was a Spanish-era house made of wood, which had more give and sway than newer cement-block buildings.

I'm not sure I will ever get used to earthquakes, even small ones. They overtake you without warning, leaving you vulnerable to collapsing buildings, falling glass, and other building materials.

Dealing with the Heat

Mid-March through mid-June were exceptionally hot months in 1970. It was my first summer in Manila, and I suffered when the temperature went to 100 degrees F. (38 C.), coupled with 90 percent humidity. I was glad we had air-conditioning in the office, so I was always happy to go to work. Although my bedroom had an air-conditioner, I used it as little as possible because of the high cost of electricity. Sometimes I ran it on Sunday afternoons when I took a nap and found lying in a puddle of perspiration wasn't conducive to a good sleep.

By mid-June the rains began, and the temperature dropped considerably, although the humidity got worse. We never made plans for any outdoor activity in the afternoon, since usually by 3:00 p.m., clouds had built up, and rain came down in torrents.

Visitors to Ifugao

I looked forward to July, since I had received a letter from my friend June Fulkerson, saying that she and a fellow teacher, Ruth Spring, were on a sabbatical round-the-world trip and would be arriving on July 2 for a week's visit. I planned to show them around Manila and take them to Ifugao. They arrived from Hong Kong on Thursday afternoon, and we planned to travel to Ifugao on Friday.

However, on Wednesday, a massive heart attack took the life of Milton France, the center superintendent at Bagabag. His funeral was scheduled for Saturday in Manila, so we didn't want to leave until afterwards. Anne and her new partner, Louise Sawyer, came for the funeral, so we all traveled to Bagabag on Sunday and flew on the SIL plane to Banaue on Monday morning.

June and Ruth had traveled through Europe and parts of Asia, but they hadn't been anyplace that rivaled their trip to Amganad. June said later, "I ran my movie camera on the jeepney as we came down the terribly rough road from the airstrip to give people at home a feel for how bumpy it was." We arrived in Amganad at harvest time, which was a special treat for June and Ruth, as they were able to view much of the harvest ceremony.

Anne and Louise had just finished building a new study house on a dry rice terrace close to their house. This gave them an office and a place to work with their language assistants away from interruptions. Anne had completed a primer and was now teaching from three to ten people for two hours, six nights a week. She was eager to have readers for the translated Scripture portions when they were published.

On Thursday my guests and I caught the bus to Bagabag and then flew in the SIL plane to Baguio, where we stayed in a very nice hotel overnight. Usually, we rented a room in a low-class hotel because it was cheap, but I didn't feel I could take my friends there, so we went to the nicest hotel in town. I enjoyed it, and June and Ruth didn't think it was very expensive in comparison to some places they had stayed on their trip. We went to the Camp John Hay officers club for dinner at night and flew back to Manila on Friday morning. After a lengthy visit to the post office to mail six packages of handicrafts they had bought, I took them to the airport in the evening to catch their next flight to Tokyo, which left at 1:45 a.m. Later, June said that their time in the Philippines was the highlight of their almost year-long trip.

I enjoyed my holiday with June and Ruth but was ready to return to work. I'd been busy during the past seven months organizing and coordinating the printing of New Testament books in twelve different languages as well as several primers and a hymnbook.

House Help Needed

When Audrey Mayer came to Manila to live with us, we hired a full-time live-in house helper, since she would have more work with cooking for three people, and the house was quite a bit larger. We were all working full-time and found housework in the heat after a nine-hour day was more than we could cope with. One of our families left for furlough, so we hired their helper, Lena, an eighteen-year-old Filipina, who was an excellent worker and a very good cook. We enjoyed having her live with us and appreciated her joyful spirit. She knew how to make bread and made better meat balls than I did.

On Lena's nineteenth birthday, we told her she could have the day off to celebrate. Birthdays are very important in the Philippines. I did the cooking that day, and while we were doing dishes, Lena arrived home. She immediately offered to finish washing the dishes, but I said, "Oh, no, I have to do them, or I will forget how. Then when I go home to Canada next year, my mother will disown me because I don't know how to work anymore."

Lena laughed and laughed. She thought that was hilarious, since the goal of most Filipinos is to be rich enough not to have to work.

The house girls who worked for all the SIL families in the area got together on Thursday evenings for Bible study. They came to our house for their study that week so they could have a birthday party for Lena afterwards.

As well as working for us, Lena went to school every afternoon to study dressmaking. She was doing very well, and I looked forward to the day she could sew for me, since I had so little time to make clothes. We could buy very little in the stores then, because everyone hired dressmakers to make their clothes. The tropical sun was very hard on clothes, and I never wore anything more than once without washing it. Everything soon became faded and worn-out looking.

కింత

The administration purchased a brand new Toyota Corolla station wagon which I was allowed to drive on my long trips to Marshburn Press twice a week. My joy was short-lived though. When the executive committee decided to let me drive it, the administration agreed but only for the interim. Bing Castillo, our buyer, needed a car for his work. He didn't know how to drive when he was hired, so he took lessons and drove an ancient jeep until he was proficient enough to handle a new car without too many fender benders. In three months, he was rewarded for his fast learning by being presented with the Toyota to drive for work.

Now I was back to riding jeepneys and buses, but I was able to take SIL's ten-passenger Volkswagen van on my trips to Marshburn Press. Audrey bought a VW beetle, so we had a car in the family again, and I got along for the year without buying a car. Furlough was coming up, and if I bought one, I would have to sell it. If I bought a new one, I would lose too much money on it.

Typhoons and Floods

Typhoons, floods, and more floods! I had been through several typhoons every year since I'd come to the Philippines and had driven through quite a few flooded streets. But in September of 1970, I saw my first real flood firsthand. A typhoon crossed Luzon, bringing with it torrential rains and intensifying the monsoon. The rain started on Monday, and by 10:00 a.m. on Tuesday, the water was up to the hubcaps on the cars in our office parking lot. We started home before we couldn't get there. As it was, we had to make many detours to avoid dips in the streets that were full of water. We crossed the bridge over the San Juan River into the suburb where we lived and saw the river was a raging torrent, and that the street running along our side of the river was under water.

The guesthouse was on a knoll higher than the rest of the houses in the area, and our apartment was also high, so we didn't have any problem there. The rain continued all day and all night. By the next morning, water on the streets in the neighborhood of the guesthouse was four feet deep. Cars were almost completely underwater, and our neighbors fled from their homes. Some men found boats, and others made rafts of bamboo poles and banana stumps to rescue those who were trying to find dry spots. Children were especially in danger, since the water was over the heads of most of them. The only dry place in the area was our guesthouse, so our neighbors came there. By noon we had one hundred wet, cold, and hungry people in our house. And still it rained and rained.

Two of our SIL families lived in the low area. Shirley Cottle was home alone with her five children, since Morrie had gone to Bagabag for meetings. At midnight Shirley awoke and felt she should check the downstairs. The water was just beginning to come in the door. She began to roll up the carpet, but before she could finish, the water was two inches deep on the floor. The children woke up and helped get things off the floor. By 2:00 a.m., Shirley called the guesthouse for help, and some men carried everything upstairs, including the freezer. They also got Cottle's car up the hill to the guesthouse. By morning, the water was two inches over Shirley's dining room table.

The water was also over the bridge, so we could not go to work. Later, we learned that a car left in the office parking lot was flooded to its windshield.

More than one hundred neighbors spent the night on floors in our guesthouse. Fortunately, we had plenty of rice, so we fed them by building a fire under a roof in the backyard to cook rice and make coffee. The power was off by this time.

Sheila, my housemate, took care of the refugee children, drying their clothes, changing diapers, playing with them, and comforting those who couldn't find their parents.

Ours was not the only rescue shelter in the area. More than one hundred people gathered in the Catholic church across the street from our apartment. Since the folks at the guesthouse were caring for those who had come, Simon Gato, the vice-governor of Batanes, who was staying at the guesthouse, Shirley Cottle, and I helped at the church. Since we had no fuel, we made up powdered milk and served it to everybody. Some nuns brought bread rolls to add to the drink.

And still it rained and rained. We watched the water rise on the wall of the house across the street. Someone predicted that if the rain would let up a bit, the water would start to go down by 11:00 a.m., since the tide would turn then. That happened, and by 3:00 p.m., the water had gone down by two feet. The following morning the floodwaters were gone.

Complicating life that day was the need to drive to the airport. Til Kohley, who had been staying with us, was leaving for furlough at 5:00 p.m. Many low areas lay between our apartment and the airport, which was 12 ½ miles (20 kilometers) away, so in the late morning, we packed up Audrey's car and headed out. By now I knew my way around many of the back streets of Manila, so we found our way through the floods. Til spent the afternoon at the airport, but she said she'd rather do that than miss her flight.

In the evening, a new member arrived from New Zealand. We drove back to the airport to pick up Lily Sutherland, whose flight was delayed by three-and-a-half hours. We arrived back at the guesthouse at 11:30 p.m. and picked our way among people sleeping on the floor to find the bed reserved for Lily.

After the flood was over, we heard that twenty-one people had been killed, most by drowning or collapsing walls. More than 90 percent of the city had been under water, eight to fourteen feet in places. This was my first flood, but it wasn't the last.

Travel Troubles and Typhoon Yoling

Part of my responsibility as temporary head of the literacy department was to lend assistance to teams who needed writer's workshops. Donna Hettick and Marge Draper had requested help with training teachers in the Sagada school district to prepare reading materials in the local dialect. I was scheduled to lead a three-day writer's workshop in late November.

I planned to take a vacation in Baguio before the workshop began. The Association of Baptists for World Evangelism (ABWE) operated a nice vacation venue called Doane Rest, and we reserved a cottage for a week. I took the plane to Baguio where Donna, Marge, and I enjoyed a week of rest and fun in the cool mountain air. Then Marge returned to Manila for a doctor's appointment, and Donna and I caught a Dangwa bus to Sagada.

When we started out early in the morning, the day was cold and drizzly. Dark clouds hung over the mountains. Soon the wind rose, and the rain blew horizontally. The road rose to 7,400 feet, the highest spot in the Philippine road system, and the temperature dropped dramatically until we shivered in our seats. The bus had no windows, only canvas covers that the conductor pulled down to keep the rain out.

By 10:00 a.m., a fallen tree across the road stopped us. After half an hour's work, the driver, conductor, and some men passengers removed the tree, and we continued on our way. Then at noon a big tree root and great mounds of soil covered the road, blocking our way.

Two hours later, the bus driver turned around and returned to the small town of Abatan to find the local road grader. We waited until 4:00 p.m., when the road grader said he couldn't get through the slide. At 5:00 p.m., the bus driver said he was going to stay all night at Abatan, and we would have to sleep on the bus.

While living in Amganad, I'd often heard of people spending the night on the bus when it couldn't get through the road. This was the first time it had happened to me. The bus was full, so we had no way to lie down. By now my back was very painful, since the wooden seat backs had no padding. Donna and I prayed for the Lord to help us.

We crawled over people in the aisle to get out of the bus and walked to a small restaurant where we ordered rice, fried eggs, and coffee to prepare for a cold, wakeful night.

Just as we were finishing our meal, three tall, Western men walked in and sat down beside us! They were FEGC missionaries who had flown to Banaue the day before but couldn't fly back out because of the storm. So they had taken a bus, hoping to get back to Baguio. Their bus had stopped on the other side of the slide. They walked across the slide and caught a bus returning to Abatan, anticipating that they could hire someone to take them to Baguio.

When we told them our story, one of them said, "You can go with us, if you want to."

We smiled and said, "Of course, we want to! How wonderful!" Anything was better than spending a night in a crowded bus at 7,000 feet and 50 degrees F. (10 degrees C.).

In just a few minutes, an empty truck pulled up to the restaurant. One of the men found out that it was going to Baguio and we could all ride along. The men and baggage rode in the back, and Donna and I rode in the front with the driver.

It was still very cold, since the truck had no side windows. We arrived back in Baguio at 9:30 p.m. after thirteen-and-a-half hours of riding and freezing. I hadn't been warm since I got out of bed. But we were thankful for the ride and to be back in Baguio.

When we left Baguio in the morning, we had checked out of Doane Rest, so we went to the home of Lee and Arlene Ballard, our translators who lived in Baguio. They had a large house and a guest room and were happy to have us stay with them. They also had a television set, and when the late evening news came on, we found out what had been happening in Manila.

Yoling had arrived, the deadliest typhoon to hit Manila since records had been kept starting in 1865. Four hundred and fifty-seven people were killed, 1,756 were injured, and 31,380 houses were destroyed. We later learned that the roof had blown off our radio shack and the *bodega,* the storage house where we kept our extra barrels and suitcases. Water had damaged some things, but I had only a couple of metal barrels stored there, so nothing was damaged, I thought.

Six months later, I was to learn differently when I opened one of my barrels in preparation to store things while I was on furlough. I found that water had gotten in, and everything inside was one big mass of mold.

Faith Academy, our children's school, which sits on a mountain ridge east of Manila, suffered serious damage. About 35 percent of the school was destroyed, including the roofs of the library, the middle school, and the gymnasium. Only one person had a minor injury, thanks to God's protection of students and staff.

When the sun came out after the storm, many people turned pages of library books to dry them out and salvage what could be saved. More than $150,000 in damages caused serious problems for the school, since it had no surplus of money for repairs. Word went out to the home countries of students enrolled at Faith about the need, and God supplied through His people for the reconstruction.

The day following the typhoon, Donna and I tried to send a telegram to the teachers in Sagada to say we couldn't get there, but the wires were down, so they didn't get our message. We tried to call Manila, but 90 percent of the phones were out of service. We tried to contact Manila by shortwave radio the next morning, but the antenna at our radio shack was down, and equipment got wet when the roof blew off. By afternoon the antenna was back up, and we got word that all our people were safe.

The next day, Donna and I took a bus to Sagada, since the road was now open. I talked to the school superintendent, and we decided to reschedule the workshop for sometime in January. I met with the teachers briefly to make plans. I spent a couple of days with Donna in her village before returning to Manila by way of Amganad, where I spent two days with Anne and Louise. The road was very muddy, worse than I had ever seen it when I lived there. According to local wisdom, someone had tried to kill the governor a while back, so he wouldn't allocate any money to fix the road.

Anne had now finished translating the Book of Mark. She had some corrections to make yet but would soon have it ready for printing. In spite of problems, we were encouraged by her progress.

The bus that travelled through the mountains

Chapter 23
A New Guesthouse and a Crash
1971

I spent Christmas 1970 at Nasuli, since we had conference that year. After three weeks of meetings and a great time of socializing with friends, I returned to Manila, looking forward to furlough. Doris Porter and I had decided to travel together through Asia and Europe, taking five or six weeks to visit missionary friends and college classmates along the way. Doris came to Manila after conference, and we made firm plans. We would leave on June 19, expecting to arrive home in late July.

The Sagada workshop, which had to be postponed because of typhoon Yoling, was rescheduled for February. I took the bus to Sagada and stayed with Donna Hettick and Marge Draper at St. Joseph's Convent. This Anglican guesthouse had been home to Filipino nuns before they moved into another building. It was quite comfortable with eight small bedrooms, a kitchen, and dining room.

Marge cooked while Donna and I conducted the workshop. Forty-four teachers attended, and after I lectured for four hours, they produced seven books in three days for use in the adult literacy program. I was amazed at the high quality of their work.

Sagada Caves

On Sunday after the workshop was over, eight teachers, Donna, and I went to the Sagada caves, famous for their burial coffins. After climbing down a long trail to the first cave, we saw stacks of wooden coffins piled one on top of another. Some were quite old, others new. Vandals had pushed some coffins down to the bottom of the cave, knocking off their lids and spilling their bones.

The second cave was very large. Two local men showed the way with lanterns, since it was pitch dark inside. The ceiling must have been one hundred feet high. The ground that descended into the earth was covered with rocks and boulders, which we scrambled over. We saw deep ravines, mountains of rocks, and hoards of bats. At one point, the cave forked. We went one way and later realized one of the men carrying a lantern followed the other fork.

Suddenly, we heard a rockslide coming from the second fork that continued for some seconds. We were afraid we might be trapped and wondered if rocks had buried Alex, the other guide. Our guide raced back to check and found Alex was safe. He had shoved a rock, and it had triggered the rockslide below him. We were all so frightened that nobody wanted to continue, so we returned to the surface. From that day on, I have never entered a natural cave that didn't have stairs and electric lights.

Travel Troubles

I returned to Baguio by myself on the Dangwa bus. It had rained the day before, and the bus got stuck three times on the way. Twice it skidded into the mountainside and once toward the edge of the road, which had a 3,000-foot drop off into the valley below. Although I was sitting by the window, we were close enough to the edge that I couldn't see the road. Many people got off the bus in a hurry, but the row I was sitting in was filled with sacks of rice and other produce going to market in Baguio, so it was difficult to get out. I sat and prayed for safety and trusted God to get us out of the mud hole. With all the men pushing, soon we were on our way again.

By the time I got back to Manila, I had spent four days riding on buses, a total of twenty-six hours, most of them on crooked mountain roads, which tossed me back and forth as the bus rounded the tight curves. I was exhausted!

Travel Plans

As the end of my first term was drawing to a close, plans for my trip with Doris progressed. We decided to spend a few days in Singapore and to travel from there to Bangkok and then to Kathmandu, Nepal. The SIL work in Nepal was at its height then, and we both had friends working there that we wanted to visit. Les Troyer, the director when I first arrived in the Philippines, and his family had transferred to Nepal. Wayne and Marilyn Aeschliman, a former pilot in the Philippines, were there too as were Austin and Margrit Hale.

Jo Shetler was a good friend of the Aeschlimans, so when she heard about our plans, she decided to take some vacation and accompany us on our trip as far as Katmandu.

In March our associate director, Dan Weaver, arrived from a five-week trip to Australia and New Zealand. He gave an enthusiastic report about his travels, during which he recruited more workers for the Philippines. SIL folks in New Zealand wanted him to stay longer, but since he wasn't able to, he promised to send someone later for a speaking tour.

The next day, he called me into his office to talk about my furlough plans. Then he said, "How would you like to spend the last three months of your furlough year in New Zealand, recruiting more workers for the Philippines?"

While speaking was not my favorite activity, it was something I could do, and the opportunity to go to New Zealand appealed to me immensely. We talked about what I would need to do, and eventually I agreed that I would do this.

Dan put me in contact with the director of the Wycliffe office in Auckland. I learned that he would like me to travel with New Zealander Jean Kirton from New Plymouth, who was translating for the Yanula people of Northern Territory, Australia. The New Zealand office would schedule our meetings and provide a car for our travels. I looked forward to this adventure and prepared my talks and slide presentations with this in mind.

A Needed Helper

However, I was concerned about who would do my job while I was gone for a year. I was busy with new books coming from a number of different projects at the same time. Once I had seven books on my desk to prepare for the printer. Then I heard that Jim Musgrove, who had been teaching at Faith Academy, was returning from a year at home and would be willing to take over my work while I was gone. What a relief!

I also needed to arrange for someone to live in my apartment for a year so I didn't need to give it up and store my furniture. Sheila had moved out, and Audrey moved in with Hope White, another Faith teacher, leaving our apartment empty. A new couple coming to teach at Faith Academy agreed to take my apartment, so I was relieved of the need to store my furniture or lend it out.

Hunt for New Headquarters and Guesthouse

At this time, we were still looking for property for a new headquarters. The biggest need was for a larger guesthouse, since the one we had was overflowing. For more than five years, a committee had been searching for property that we could remodel or develop but so far had found nothing suitable. We had been praying, discussing, and looking, but God had not led us to the property He wanted us to have.

Then one day, John Kyle, our director of public affairs, was talking to his neighbor.

"I know of a property for sale in Horseshoe Village on Big Horseshoe Drive," the neighbor said.

"I know where that is," John said. "It's not far from our present guesthouse and close to Cubao."

John, Morrie Cottle, and Dan Weaver looked at the lot and found it had been abandoned for some time. The grounds were lush with weeds, the fence along the street was broken down, and only a pile of rubble remained where a former house had stood. A newer house stood at the top of the broken driveway, and at the left was an old storage building.

After the beautifully landscaped properties the men had looked at, this one didn't look like much. But it had the right amount of space, and the location was perfect. It was on the jeepney line to Cubao, where transportation could be found for any area of Metro Manila. Later, we found that Magnolia Dairy was planning to build a new plant just one block away, a big selling point for anyone staying at the guesthouse, since Magnolia was adding a delightful ice cream parlor.

Soon our leaders decided to purchase the lot at #12 Big Horseshoe Drive. They asked Jack and Chic Ruth, who had been members of the Papua New Guinea branch, to make plans for the new guesthouse. As an architect, Jack set up his table in one end of my office and began drawing plans for the building.

I have always been interested in buildings and plans. Had God not called me into journalism and Scripture publishing, I might have become an architect myself. I enjoyed looking over Jack's shoulder as he designed the new guesthouse.

Two large narra trees spread their shady branches over the central part of the lot. Unfortunately, they were in the way of the building Jack was designing, so he planned to have them removed.

"Jack," I complained, "you can't cut down those trees. We need every bit of shade we can get in this hot country."

Jack considered what I'd said and redesigned the house to fit around the trees. Instead of one long building, he made two units with a breezeway between. One was set off a bit further north than the other, allowing the trees to snuggle up to the house on both sides.

The guesthouse was to be constructed while I was on furlough. I was sorry about that, since I like nothing better than watching buildings go up. The house at the end of the driveway was to be renovated and made available for the director's family, while an el on one end was large enough for a small two-bedroom apartment.

A Terrible Accident and Answered Prayers

Arriving at work one morning, I was greeted with, "Jo Shetler is in the hospital at Clark Airbase!"

"She is? Why?" I asked.

"She was in a helicopter crash."

"Oh, no! Was she badly hurt?"

"We don't know yet."

Later, we learned the details that sent us all to our knees in prayer for Jo and the Balangaos and thanks to God for her safety. But she still needed much prayer.

For some time, Dr. Robespierre ("Robbie") Lim, a Filipino doctor under the auspices of the Catholic Mission, planned to build a small hospital at Natunin to serve the Balangao people. This made Jo very happy, since she spent much of her time helping her neighbors with their medical needs. A hospital less than an hour away would allow her to spend more time at translation. By now a number of believers among the Balangaos needed God's Word in their own language, and Jo was eager to finish the New Testament.

Dr. Lim had arranged for the US Air Force to bring a load of building materials to Natunin in one of their Jolly Green Giant helicopters. SIL pilot Bill Powell went along to show the way, and Jo was the interpreter for the pilots. Doming, Jo's Balangao brother, was returning from school. Doming, Dr. Lim, and Jo were riding in the back with more than ten tons of bagged cement, kegs of nails, and wooden boxes of windowpanes. Bill was on a jump seat between the pilot and copilot.

They circled the landing spot in the late afternoon—a basketball court on a flattened knoll in the village of Natunin. The helicopter suddenly started losing power and was coming down too soon, first clipping off betel-nut palms. Flailing rotors whirled full blast, the helicopter violently plunged into a deep ravine, coming to an almost upside-down position. Bags of cement, boxes of glass, and kegs of nails burst open and buried the passengers.

Fire started at the rotor blades, and gushing fuel threatened an explosion. The pilots had escaped, and they screamed at the people, "Run! It's going to explode!" But when the Balangaos, who were watching the arrival of the materials for their much-anticipated hospital, learned that Jo, Doming, and Dr. Lim hadn't gotten out yet, they grabbed anything they could—rice pots, plastic pails, and basins. Then scooping up mud and water from the rice fields, they put the flames out.

With the fire gone, they climbed into the nearly upside-down helicopter searching for Jo, Doming, and Dr. Lim. Then they heard a small sound. Digging through broken bags of cement, they located Jo upside down, buried, and gasping for air. Her eyes were filled with cement, and she had a broken collarbone, broken ribs, a collapsed lung, and a gash on her head.

Her Balangao friends dug her out, carried her, and laid her on the rough wooden floor in a nearby building. She was covered with cement soaked with blood flowing from her head wound.

Realizing her eyes were the most important, Jo instructed her friends to force her swollen eyes open and to pour water into them to clear out the cement. The pain was excruciating, since the caustic lime in the cement had eaten into her eyes. All night long, they poured water in her eyes. Someone sewed up the gash on her head. And they prayed. Someone ran back to Botac, where Ama and Tekla lived, with the news. The two friends ran up the mountain, came hurriedly, and spent the night caring for her, comforting her, and praying for her. They told her that Doming was okay.

For some time, Jo had been praying that the Balangao Christians would learn to pray. They had only recently learned they could talk to the Creator God. Now they would venture to thank Him at meal times but were too ashamed to bring other matters to Him. She had asked people at home to pray that the believers would learn how to pray. She would lie awake at night, praying that God would teach them how to pray for everything.

One night she had prayed, "God, I don't care what you have to do. Make these people pray!" As she lay on that hard floor, the pain in her eyes was so intense she could hardly think of anything else. Then she heard Balangaos all around praying for her with intensity, really praying. "God, don't let her die! The Book's not done yet!"

Later, Jo said, "It was the worst and best night of my life all wrapped up in one. The worst pain I'd ever known was eclipsed by moments of indescribable awe over their prayers. Only God could weave such extremes."

In the morning, Jo learned that Dr. Lim had not survived the crash. She mourned for him because he had been a good doctor and a good friend, but he did not know the Lord personally. Just two days before the accident, Jo had asked him what he'd answer God when He asked him why he didn't believe what He had written in His Book.

Dr. Lim countered that with, "God won't ask that. He'll just ask if I was kind to my neighbors."

The next morning when they reached Clark Airbase with the news, another helicopter came to evacuate them all. Jo was in the hospital there for two days and then was transferred to a hospital in Manila. X-rays showed that the break in her right collarbone spread the bones an inch apart, so a pin was inserted. It protruded an inch out of her shoulder and had a cork on the end. Her parents were visiting from California so were able to stay with her in the hospital.

After many weeks of mending, Jo returned to Balangao to continue her translation of the Scriptures. She was amazed to find the believers still praying about everything—big or small. Finally, her prayers for them were answered. Earnest prayer about everything was part of their lives now.

They were not the same after the crash. And neither was Jo.

Chapter 24
Travel through Asia and Europe
1971

The day had finally come. Doris Porter, Jo Shetler, and I left for our trip on June 19. Jo had recovered from her accident enough to travel with us, even though she still had the pin in her shoulder and one arm in a sling.

Singapore, Bangkok, and Kathmandu

We arrived in Singapore late in the evening and went to a hotel, where we stayed for two days. We shopped, rode a bus all around the city, walked through the downtown area, and enjoyed the Chinese and Malay cultures. The first evening, we ate in the Chinese restaurant in the hotel. The food was delicious, but Jo had a hard time eating. She is right-handed, but because of her injury, she had to use her left hand. We were given chopsticks to eat with, not an easy feat, if you aren't used to them, especially using your left hand.

From Singapore we flew to Bangkok where we stayed in a Christian guesthouse for two days and from there flew to Kathmandu, Nepal, for two days. We stayed with Wayne and Marilyn Aeschliman.

We enjoyed visiting with the Les and Maddy Troyer and touring around Kathmandu with Maddy. I found this was a good place to buy gems for a reasonable price. I purchased some smoky topaz and garnet stones for eight dollars. We saw the king arriving from a trip to Russia, escorted by red-jacketed horsemen.

Wayne asked if we would like to fly in the SIL single-engine plane into the Himalayas, which towered over the city. Of course, we would. The weather had been cloudy, so we hadn't been able to see much of the high mountains. We flew up to 16,000 feet and had a good view of the snow-capped peaks. We were too far from Mt. Everest to see it, but we did see two other mountains that were 26,000 feet. On the way back down, we passed an area of rice terraces that looked very much like those in the Philippines, but the houses were made of red brick with stone or wooden roofs.

India, Kuwait, and Athens

Doris and I said good-bye to our friends and to Jo, who was staying a few more days, and caught a Nepali Airlines flight to New Delhi, India, late in the afternoon of June 26. In New Delhi, my friend Marilyn Searle met us and took us to her house for dinner. After eating, her husband Howard drove us to the Jan Path Hotel, where we stayed during our time in Delhi.

Mary Granaas had spent a number of years working in India and had arranged for us to attend church with her friends, Paul and Annie Pillau. They picked us up from the hotel in a taxi and took us to Sunday school. Doris spoke to the children about the Tboli, for whom she was translating the New Testament. During the church service, we both spoke about our work. Since nobody spoke English, we had an interpreter, a first for me. After church, Paul and Annie took us to the Imperial Hotel for an Indian dinner. I asked them to order a meal for me that wasn't too hot. Paul agreed, saying several were very mild. I was certainly glad I didn't have a hot one, since the mild one was almost more than I could handle.

One of the things we wanted to see in India was the Taj Mahal. Since it's only a three-hour train ride south of New Delhi, we went that way so we could see the countryside. We also saw the Red Fort and visited shops where workers were making marble inlay and silver filigree jewelry. We also watched people weaving. A short twenty-minute flight took us back to New Delhi. On the following day, a tour of the city finished our time there.

We caught a flight for Athens at 10:20 p.m. We were scheduled to stop at Karachi, Kuwait, and Beirut, but at Kuwait we had to leave the plane. About two minutes after we touched down, the lights went off, and a steward came racing down the aisle, ordering everybody off at once. We were quickly herded into the airport where we finally received an explanation. When the airport hooked up their power system to the aircraft, it shorted out the electrical system in the plane. The power to run the emergency light was from the battery that started the engines, so we had to get out in a hurry. We waited in Kuwait for two-and-a-half hours while the repair was made before flying on to Beruit and finally to Athens. For breakfast on the plane, we were served peaches. What a treat! It was the first peach I had seen in five years.

KLM provided a ride for us to our Athens hotel where we deposited our bags and set out to explore the area. We had some difficulty, since the street signs were in the Greek alphabet, which I don't know at all. Doris had studied some Greek years before but had forgotten most of what she knew. We walked in circles but finally found our way back to the hotel, after eating lunch in a small restaurant not far away.

When I was on staff at LCBM, we had a student from Greece, Emmanuel Smpraos. He had completed his studies, returned to Athens, and was now pastoring a church. I called him for a short phone visit, and he offered to take us to the Acropolis. We were happy to have a local guide tell us what we were seeing. We also went to Mars Hill. From there we could see the reconstructed marketplace. We drove to see the Olympic stadium, the royal palace, the university, the parliament buildings, the temple of Zeus, and Hadrian's Gate.

The following day was July 1, Canada Day. When we arrived at the hotel restaurant for breakfast, we were surprised to find little Canadian flags flying at every table. We spent the day walking around Athens, and in the evening we went to a Sound and Light show.

Doris had just finished translating 1 Corinthians before leaving for our trip, so she wanted to take a trip to Corinth, which isn't far from Athens. We got tickets for a bus tour and set off the next day along the Adriatic Sea with a stop at Alexis. At the Corinthian Canal, which joins the Adriatic Sea to the west and the Ionian Sea to the east, we were able to see both ends. The canal is 3,281 feet (one kilometer) long from sea to sea, cut out of solid marble straight down for more than 100 feet.

In Old Corinth we walked through the marketplace and stood on the platform from which the apostle Paul preached to the Corinthians.

Rome, Austria, Germany, Switzerland

Following our stay in Athens, we caught the plane to Rome, where we exchanged our money into lire. Twenty dollars gave us 10,000 lire, not exactly easy to work with. We found our hotel and looked up the address of the car rental company that we had contacted from Manila. From here we planned to drive ourselves through the rest of Europe.

Doris had a friend living in Rome, who came to our hotel and drove us to pick up the car. We had asked for a Volkswagon, but we got an Autobianche instead. It was a small white car that we could hardly get our suitcases into. We drove back to the hotel and Bobby, Doris' friend, took us on a tour past the forum and the coliseum to the Mamertine Dungeon, where it is believed that Paul was imprisoned and where he wrote several letters and books.

We were glad to have our own car, since we wanted to see all we could. We found, though, that Rome wasn't easy to get around in, since it has many one-way streets. Moreover, the street signs were on the ends of buildings. If there wasn't a handy building, there was no sign. We did manage to see many things that were on our list—the coliseum, the forum, the Appian Way to the catacombs, the church of St. Sebastian, and the Trevi Fountain. We spent one morning at the Vatican, including St. Peter's Basilica, the Vatican art galleries and museum, and the Sistine Chapel.

After walking miles through the Vatican, we found our car and the Autostrada and set out for a two-week excursion through Europe. Halfway to Florence, we stopped for gas and were told that the car needed to have the oil changed, since it was very low and dirty. So much for that car rental company! We weren't through with our car woes yet.

In Florence we joined the crowd admiring Michael Angelo's statue of David. In Venice we walked through the city and rode a waterbus to San Marcos Square to feed the pigeons.

In Wiener Neustadt, Austria, we spent two days with Neil and Carolyn Rempel, Bible college classmates who worked with the Greater Europe Mission. They took us through a castle and on a tour of the Vienna Opera House.

In Germany we spent two days at the Wycliffe headquarters in Holzhausen, where the summer SIL school was about to begin. Then on to Switzerland where we stayed at the Swiss Wycliffe headquarters in the mountains near Bern. It was heavenly to wake in the morning after a restful night under a down-filled duvet to the clinking sound of cowbells as cows chomped their breakfast in the field across the road.

We spent a day visiting Thun Castle and riding a cable car from Grindelwald to the village of First at the top of the mountain. These towering Alps far outmeasured our 9,000-foot mountains in the Philippines.

From Switzerland we crossed into France near Geneva and proceeded to Bourg to spend two days with Enid Skuce, a friend from the summer I worked on staff at Muskoka Baptist Conference.

Paris, Netherlands, London

Paris was next. After touring through the palace at Versailles on the way, we found a hotel and saw all the usual tourist sights—the Arc de Triumph, the Louvre to see the Mona Lisa and Venus de Milo, the Tuileries, Notre Dame, and the Eiffel Tower.

In Paris we turned in our car and collected what we had spent on it. During our two- week trip, it had needed an oil change, a new muffler, and a fuse to make the instrument panel work. On our way to turn it in, we stopped for a stoplight at a big intersection. The engine stalled and wouldn't start. Two policemen stopped all the traffic and pushed us through the intersection to get it started again. Needless to say, we didn't recommend that car rental company to our friends.

Our flight from Paris took us to Amsterdam, where Terry and Judy Schram lived. These Wycliffe members were manning the Netherlands office. We slept on the floor of the office and enjoyed a tour around Amsterdam, out to the polders where the Zuiderzee had been dammed up and the water pumped out to make new farmland. We toured yet another castle and feasted on an Indonesian dinner, the first rice we'd had since leaving Asia.

Helen Trip had been in my class at LBI and was now working as a missionary in south Holland near the spot where the Netherlands, Belgium, and Germany meet. We took a train to visit her for a day and to hear about her work.

From Amsterdam we flew to London where we caught a bus to Merstham to spend a couple of days at the Wycliffe United Kingdom headquarters and the SIL school. We attended a few classes, met a number of friends who were on staff, and got to know Eunice Diment, who was considering joining the Philippines branch as a translator.

Back in London, we found our hotel and called Linda Miller who had worked with me at LCBM. We arranged to meet her the next morning at Victoria Station. She took us on a tour around London for a day before traveling with us by train to her home in Eastbourne, Sussex. She lived with her parents, but they didn't have space for us, so she had made reservations not far away at Beech Lawn, a guesthouse for lady missionaries and full-time Christian workers.

Linda took us to church at the Brethren Assembly where she attended, our first church service since the one at which we spoke in India. In the evening, we returned for the evening service, after which I showed my Philippine slides and talked about our work to a group of young people.

One of my goals for our time at Eastbourne was to travel to Rye to visit the birthplace of my paternal grandmother. We took the train in the morning and spent the day exploring this quaint seaside town with its cobblestone streets and hanging flowerpots. We ate our sack lunches on a bench in the cemetery at the church, which dated from the early one thousands and listened to the chimes of the oldest working clock in England. I was frustrated as I walked among the tombstones, since I was sure that some of my ancestors were buried there. I had no way of knowing which ones though, since I didn't know any family names on my grandmother's side. We ended our time in Rye by finding a pie shop and enjoying coffee and pie before returning by train to Eastbourne.

After traveling to London by train, we spent most of another day in the British Museum. Our trip home was on the Royal Dutch Airlines (KLM), so we had to fly back to Amsterdam to pick up our flight for New York. We were delayed four hours so didn't arrive until 12:30 a. m. Our plans were to spend the night with Joe and Doreen McCauley in Manhattan, where Dr. McCauley was president of a Bible college. Since it was too late to call the McCauleys, we spent the night in a hotel near the airport and caught a taxi to Manhattan the next day. Late in the afternoon, I returned to the airport for my flight to Toronto and home.

I cried when we flew over Lake Ontario. I was in Canada again, my first glimpse of my homeland in four-and-a-half years.

Chapter 25
Canada and New Zealand Speaking Tour
1971–1972

Wycliffe has a policy that for every year members have spent on the field, they may take one month of personal time during furlough for vacation and interaction with supporters, friends, and family. The remainder of the furlough time must be spent either in study programs or working in Wycliffe assignments in the home country.

I had used more than a month on my trip home so had three months left for personal time. My first activity was to join my parents in a camping trip from Ontario to visit my sister Marj, Vic, and their family in Saskatchewan. It was a precious time to meet my new nieces and nephew. Marj had three babies while I was away—Ruth, Jane, and Paul. Along with Ann, their family was now complete.

Reverse Culture Shock

Many things had changed at home since I left in 1967. My parents had moved from the RR5 house and were now living in a small house in Port Stanley overlooking Lake Erie. It was a great house for them, but it wasn't home for me.

London College of Bible and Missions, where I had studied, worked, and had many friends, had joined with Toronto Bible College and moved to Toronto. Many of my friends had moved with it.

Faith Baptist Church in St. Thomas, where I grew up and where my parents attended, had built another building and moved from the familiar one on Churchill Crescent.

Prices of many things had gone up, and I was used to the inexpensive cost of most things in the Philippines.

I felt lost and out of place much of the time. I felt, too, that most people didn't really want to hear anything about my time in the Philippines. It was so different from their experiences that people couldn't understand what I was talking about. I felt as if I would like to sit in a corner and cry.

What's wrong with me? I thought. *I don't usually feel this way! I'm an extrovert and usually get on fine with people.* It took more than a month to realize that I was suffering from reverse culture shock. When I went to the Philippines, we were given information about culture shock and how we would feel suddenly moved from our own familiar cultures to ones that were totally different. Nobody warned me that the same thing could happen on returning home. Once I knew what the problem was, I soon recovered and felt myself again.

After our trip to Saskatchewan, I spent the remainder of August, September, and October traveling around southwestern Ontario, speaking at churches and presenting the work of Bible translation to many different groups. When November came, it was time to begin my Wycliffe assignment until my furlough was completed.

Wycliffe Canada Office

Wycliffe Canada board meetings were scheduled for November. Since I was to work in the Canadian headquarters office in Calgary, Alberta, until it was time to fly to New Zealand in the spring, the director, Howard Klassen, asked me to take minutes at the board meetings. They were to be held at Winnipeg Bible College at Steinbach, Manitoba. I flew to Winnipeg and drove to Steinbach with some board members. For three days, we spent twenty-seven hours in meetings, handling the business of Wycliffe Canada. Then after a day spent with friends in Winnipeg, we drove to Portage la Prairie to pick up Howard's wife Bea and proceeded on to Calgary.

The Klassens had invited me to stay with them during my time in Calgary. Bea was in the early stages of Amyotrophic Lateral Sclerosis (ALS) but was still able to live a normal life.

During my four months working in the Calgary office, I served as secretary to the director. I enjoyed my work and got to know many Wycliffe members who worked there or who dropped in from time to time. Our office was on the second floor of a building on Bowness Road in northwest Calgary. The days were so short in the winter that sometimes I didn't see the sun from Sunday afternoon until Saturday morning if I didn't go outside during lunch hour, which I rarely did. Every morning on the way to work, Howard and I drove to the main post office in downtown Calgary to pick up the mail. It always amazed me to see a lineup of parked cars with their engines running and nobody inside. It was too cold to stop the engines and get them running again. I decided these Westerners were exceptionally honest, or someone would drive off with one of those cars.

I flew home to Ontario for Christmas and then returned to Calgary to a new home. Bea's health was beginning to deteriorate, and she felt she could no longer handle a boarder. I moved in with Garnet and Barbara Holteen and their five children, ages five to eleven. Garnet was the finance manager at the Wycliffe office. In addition to the Holteen family, Barbara's brother-in-law also stayed with them. Vi Reimer, who was working in the office, also needed a place to stay, so she moved in to share my room. That made ten people in a four-bedroom house. To top it off, we shared the extra space with Flossie, the Holteens' standard poodle. Close fellowship was the order of the day, but it was only for two months, so we managed.

During my time in Calgary, I stocked up on small appliances and other household equipment that I could use in Manila. I packed two barrels to ship back to the Philippines with things I needed in the city. Many appliances were not available there, and if they were, they tended to cost double. I also had to apply for my visa for returning to the Philippines. This took some time, since another mail strike delayed my passport.

Stop at International Headquarters

By February 26, I had my tickets and plane reservations for my return to the Philippines via a three-month visit to New Zealand. I spent a week in Los Angeles on the way, staying with Tom and Elnore Lyman and visiting the new Wycliffe International headquarters in Huntington Beach.

While there, I went to the Wycliffe Associates office in Orange County and met with Bernie May, who was heading up that work. Bernie asked me if I needed anything special that Wycliffe Associates could help me with. I mentioned that I was in need of a car for my work when I returned to Manila. I had hoped that God would provide funding while I was on furlough, but almost nothing had come in. Bernie said he would send out a third-party letter to my supporters, telling them of my need. I was grateful for the help, but I must admit I was skeptical. What a surprise when I arrived back in Manila three months later to find that half of the amount I needed for a new vehicle had come in.

On to New Zealand

My flight to New Zealand was uneventful. We stopped in Honolulu and arrived in Auckland a day later because we crossed the international dateline. In Auckland, Al Williams, the New Zealand Wycliffe director, met me and took me to the center where I stayed for a few days before moving to the home of one of the board members. Jean Kirton, who was a translator with the Australian Aborigines branch of Wycliffe in Northern Territory, was arriving the following week. We would travel together and share the speaking tour. Jean was from New Plymouth, New Zealand, on the West coast of North Island.

Some orientation to the New Zealand way of life and applying for a New Zealand driver's license took up my time until we were ready to leave for

Gisborne, our first stop. Driving on the left side of the road took a few days of adjustment, but I didn't have too much trouble. Right turns were the biggest challenge.

I discovered that many things in New Zealand were left-handed or upside down, according to North American standards. Pedestrians walked on the left side of the sidewalk, and the telephone dial had the small numbers at the bottom and the big ones at the top, light switches were off in the "up" position and on in the "down" position. Eating is basically left-handed as food is pushed on the back of the fork that is held in the left hand and then lifted to the mouth, not an easy feat for one who is right-handed. I learned to eat that way though, since we stayed with families as we traveled throughout the country, and many had children who were learning to eat properly. When they are young, they eat like we do with a spoon or fork in the right hand, but by the time they are five or six, they transition to adult ways. I was embarrassed to be eating like the little children, so I decided this was one more new thing I could learn, even though my hosts often told me it was fine for me to eat the North American way.

When we left Auckland, we received an itinerary that contained the cities where we were to minister, the dates we were to be there, and the name and address of a host in each place. Actual meetings had been left up to the host to arrange for us. We didn't know how many meetings we would have in each place until we arrived. This was frustrating for me, since I always like to know everything ahead of time, but God knew better. By the time we had traveled from Auckland on the North Island to Dunedin on South Island and stayed in nine cities over a period of ten weeks, I had spoken ninety-nine times to about four thousand people. If I had known our schedule would be that heavy, I might have been tempted to skip the whole thing.

At Easter we were in New Plymouth, Jean's hometown, and we were the missionary speakers at a children's camp. Following that, we crossed the straits between North and South Islands from Wellington to Picton and then traveled down the east coast to Blenheim before going on to Christ Church, Timaru, and Dunedin. After Christ Church, we drove to Mt. Cook, New Zealand's highest mountain, for a week's break and stayed in a cottage at the Hermitage. We had planned to do some hiking on the mountain, since there are many good hiking trails, but the day we arrived a foot of snow arrived also. Since we were not prepared to hike in the snow, we spent most of our time in the cabin reading and playing games.

Toward the end of our trip, Jean had to return to Auckland to teach a course at a Bible college there, and school was beginning before our speaking tour finished. Jean flew back to Auckland, and I continued driving to

Timaru and Dunedin by myself. There I ran into a fair bit of snow, and it was cold, especially in the mornings. Since the car I was driving came from Auckland, which is semitropical, it didn't have a heater. On my return trip, I took along a hot-water bottle and managed to keep one hand warm by placing it on my lap and driving with the other. I lodged with people we had stayed with on the way south, catching a ferry at Littleton, just across the mountain ridge from Christ Church, for the trip to Wellington. That ferry usually sailed overnight, but the day I needed to go, it went during the day. I enjoyed a nine-hour sail up the east coast of South Island close enough to the shore to have a good view of the scenery.

Arriving back in Auckland, I debriefed, said good-bye to everybody, and caught the plane to Manila. I changed aircraft in Sydney and stopping briefly in Port Moresby, Papua New Guinea. Many of the women deplaned and went to the ladies' room to remove warm underclothing, since we were now in the tropics.

When I arrived in Auckland at the beginning of my tour there, I met Darlene Bee who had just finished teaching at that year's session of SIL. She invited me to stop in Papua New Guinea on my way back to the Philippines and visit her and her coworker, Vida Chenowith at Ukarumpa, the SIL headquarters. I was considering making that stop, but when Darlene flew back to Ukarumpa from Auckland, the SIL plane she was flying in from Lae to Ukarumpa crashed, and she was killed.

This was a great loss to the Papua New Guinea branch and was the first fatality that SIL had suffered in one of their planes.

Mt. Cook and the cottages where we stayed

Chapter 26
Buildings, Awards, and Celebrations
1972–1973

It was good to be back in Manila. One of the first things I did was to find my umbrella, since June is the beginning of the rainy season. Before many days had gone by, the first typhoon of the season roared through, taking out our electricity. The lines were destroyed and had to be rewired. Authorities estimated that it would be a month before power was restored. This was disastrous in the city where so many things depended on electricity to operate.

New Guesthouse

While I was in Canada, the new guesthouse, popularly known as the "Manila House," was completed on the new property we had purchased on Horseshoe Drive. Workers had landscaped it beautifully, repaired the swimming pool, and remodeled the existing house. It now had two apartments—one large four-bedroom unit and a smaller one with two bedrooms.

When Til Kohley moved from Nasuli to Manila to work in the finance office, she and I agreed to share the small apartment. She had my furniture moved there, so I was able to move right in when I returned.

Back to Work

Jim Musgrove had done a fine job with managing the publications department while I was gone, but a great load of work waited to be done. Quite a few people had gone on furlough so not enough were left to do all the jobs. Those of us who were there doubled up and took care of the essentials. Some new jobs were added to my publications work. We were developing a publicity department, and the director asked me to head it up as well as the branch literacy program, since I was appointed as chair of the literacy committee. I also became chair of the Manila property committee to determine the next step in developing our new headquarters' property. As head of the literacy committee, I also served on the technical studies committee that made long-range plans for the academic work of the branch.

Since I had received half the funds needed for a car, I soon ordered a Toyota Corona station wagon. I needed room to bring books back and forth from the printer, since they didn't have delivery service. This car would take three months to arrive from Japan.

Typhoons Again

Then the rains struck again. The year 1972 has long been remembered as one of calamity. In July two typhoons slowly moved through the Pacific northeast of Luzon and caused an intensification of the southwest monsoon—rainy winds that caused daily downpours for three weeks. The rivers were unable to carry away the excess water, and the land flooded.

Before long, hundreds of square miles of rice-growing countryside were deeply under water. People fled from their homes and crowded for shelter. Food supplies dwindled to almost nothing. And still it rained. Poisonous snakes were flushed out of hiding, and at least five people died of cobra bites. Bridges collapsed, washing away people in raging rivers, and floodwaters washed away roads. People grew hungry. Violence occurred as starving people searched for food.

Even Manila did not escape. More than 90 percent of the city was under water, and many lost their homes and possessions. The majority of the city streets became impassable as great potholes appeared in the pavement, and then the pavement disappeared until many streets became dirt. Schools were closed for three weeks because half of the public vehicles that transported the more than one million students to schools were broken down. Water rose on the street in front of our office building to a depth of four feet, but no damage was done, since we were located on the second floor.

Serious illnesses caused great concern as epidemics of cholera and intestinal disorders took lives throughout the flooded areas. Massive relief operations helped to provide food, clothing, and medicine for people who were suffering.

In the middle of all the rain, we had two new families arrive to work with us in Manila. One was Gerry and Carol Brock, who were from my home church in London, Ontario. When I was there, I had dinner with them and talked about the need for teachers at Faith Academy. Gerry was a teacher and Carol a nurse. They had been interested in the school since the typhoon in 1970 that did so much damage there. Now they had resigned from their jobs in Canada and come to work at Faith. I enjoyed spending time with them and their two children.

Resources for the Blind

Arthur and Inez Lown arrived to take over the management of the guesthouse. Mary Granaas had finally retired, now that she was sixty-nine years old. Inez would be the new manager, and Arthur would work as Manila center superintendent, responsible for the physical plant and the national workers. Although Arthur was totally blind, one would never know this. He took your arm if you were walking with him, but otherwise he was very independent. He soon learned his way around Manila with the help of a city map that he "Braillized" by running a small spoked wheel over the back of the streets, thus producing raised dots on the front of the map. He was soon taking off in a taxi by himself to shop for various equipment and supplies needed for his job.

Arthur had a PhD in special education and had been director of the Atlanta Public School services for blind students for some time. His skills and interests soon caused him to delve into the needs of the blind in the Philippines. He eventually developed an organization called Resources for the Blind, which produced Braille Scriptures for blind Filipinos in their own languages. They also taped Scriptures in several Filipino languages and mailed the cassettes to a mailing list that soon reached twelve thousand names.

Today Resources for the Blind has a well-trained staff of thirty Filipino specialists, providing a full spectrum of services to blind persons nationwide. They removed the obstacles that prevent blind Filipinos from reaching the fullest potential that God has for them. This involves them in counseling, rehabilitation, education, and training. They are also actively involved in preventing blindness and in restoring sight whenever possible.

While Arthur was developing Resources for the Blind, Inez continued as the efficient manager of the Manila guesthouse. Their three children grew up in Manila and attended Faith Academy. After more than twenty years of service in Manila, the Lowns retired and returned to the United States.

Martial Law

Martial law! The words themselves caused ripples of fear. I had read about what happens when martial law is declared. I envisioned mass assassinations and bloodshed on the streets.

For some time now, we had been hearing rumors of unrest throughout the Philippines. Communist influences had entered the country, and disruptive activities caused fear among the residents. In early September of 1972, time bombs exploded in several department stores, government buildings, and airplanes. The government blamed the bombings on the communist New Peoples' Army, which in turn blamed them on the President, saying he wanted to declare marshal law so he could stay in power and avoid the upcoming election. We were without water for two days when a bomb blew up the water main that ran behind our property. This was the beginning of big troubles in the Philippines that would affect our work in the future.

On September 21, 1972, Defense Secretary Juan Ponce Enrile was traveling in a motorcade in Manila when his car was attacked in an assassination attempt. Fortunately, as a safety precaution, he was riding in a car following his. The next day President Ferdinand Marcos declared martial law, which put the military in charge of the country. We had no radio communications, no newspapers, our pilots couldn't fly our planes, and most stores had to close their doors. Everyone was afraid. We didn't know for sure if we would be safe or if we would experience bloodshed.

As it turned out, after several days of uncertainty, our lives returned to normal. Curfew was enforced from midnight to 4:00 a.m., but that was a problem for us only when we had to meet a late-arriving plane. The international airport was on the south side of Manila, a good hour's drive from our center, so if a plane arrived after 11:00 p.m., we couldn't get back home before curfew. We could obtain a pass from the airport, but that meant we had to make a special trip ahead of time to pick it up.

The President launched a campaign of national reform starting with the arrest of more than two hundred people—government officials and others in high places accused of corruption and subversion. Only security guards, police, and military were allowed to carry guns outside of their homes. The military collected more than five thousand guns during the first week of martial law.

My New Car

About this time, I received word that my new car had arrived at the docks from Japan. It took our administrative officer, Peter Torres, several weeks to accumulate all of the paperwork to process it through customs. The day Peter drove it home, I was surprised to see a turquoise-green station wagon when I had ordered one in light blue. I was happy with the color though and thought it was even nicer than the one I ordered. It was a great relief to finally have transportation of my own—a brand new Toyota Corona station wagon that would serve me well for eight years. By this time, all of the money, except $230, had come in to pay for it. By Christmas I was debt free. I had worried about driving a new car on the pothole-filled streets of Manila, since the heavy rains from June to August had made the streets nearly impassable. However, instead of just patching the holes, this year they had rebuilt many streets and paved them with concrete instead of asphalt, so they were in better shape than I had ever seen them.

In January 1973, I had the privilege of welcoming Eileen Curry to the Philippines. I lived at Johnny and Eileen Curry's house when I was teaching in St. Catherine's in 1957. Since then, Eileen had become a widow. While on furlough, I visited her when speaking nearby. She had rented the main part of the house and was now living in the apartment at the back where Alice Andres and I had lived.

I had shared with her a story about one of our Wycliffe members working in Peru. She was a widow too who decided to give her retirement years to the ministry of Bible translation. Her specialty was cooking and entertaining, so for many years she ran the guesthouse at the SIL center in Peru. I suggested to Eileen that she might like to spend a few years using her skills overseas in service to the Lord. God used that story, and within the year she had applied to Wycliffe to work in the nursery at Nasuli, taking care of young children so mothers would have time to work on their language projects or in the offices.

Eileen loved small children and spent several years caring for them. The youngsters called an adult *aunt* or *uncle* as a sign of respect. Eileen got double respect as she became known as "Aunt Grandma Curry."

Publication Work Growing

My work at the office continued to grow. New translation teams arrived regularly, and those who had been working for years were now producing many books to be printed. Almost every week, I received forms to be processed for a new book of Scripture or a new literacy book.

The staff at Marshburn Press kept busy turning out our books. I made two trips a week to the print shop to check on jobs that were in process and to pick up those that were finished. I appreciated my station wagon with room for cartons of new books ready for shipping to the various language projects throughout the country. In the first nine months of its life, I transported 19,700 new books from Marshburn Press to the SIL center.

In addition to making sure the books kept moving, I was responsible for the production of our publicity materials. I wrote and prepared for printing a monthly newsletter that was sent to a mailing list for information and prayer. I was happy to learn that Peggy Pittman was soon to be assigned to Manila to help with this project as well as other publicity materials.

Not long after I returned from furlough in June of 1972, the Manila property committee, which I headed up, decided how we should develop the remaining space on our Horseshoe Drive property. The guesthouse was completed and functioning well, and the existing house had been remodeled into two apartments. The director's family occupied the large one, and Til Kohley and I occupied the smaller one.

New Office Building

For almost five years, we had been operating our office from the second floor of the Permaline Building. Now we planned to build an office building on our property. Although the old storage building by the gate was still useful, space was available at the top of the driveway for a 30-foot by 60-foot building. The plan was to locate the office on the main floor, build two apartments above the office, and build a book depository below the office, as well as some storage space.

My days were filled with office work, processing books that arrived at my office for printing, and taking them to the printer. In the evenings, Til and I worked on plans for the new office building. I had always been interested in designing houses and buildings as a hobby. Now I could design something that would actually be built. When we were satisfied with our design, we took it to the administration, which approved it. Then our design went to an architect, who made professional plans for the contractor.

Ron and Willie Grable left their assignments at Nasuli and moved to Manila so Ron could manage and supervise the building project. Willie became secretary to the director. By March of 1974, we moved our office from the Permaline building to the new office at #12 Horseshoe Drive, San Juan.

The property sloped uphill from the street, so the ground floor of the upper end of the office building was slightly underground. Three small rooms there contained books that were printed but not yet distributed. When I brought them back from the printer, I placed those that the teams in the field didn't need yet on shelves in the book depository. The rest of the ground floor space contained barrels, boxes, and suitcases belonging to our teams who worked in remote areas of Luzon.

Vietcong Captured SIL Member

One of the privileges of owning a car was the opportunity to drive people to places they needed to go. In March 1973, I had one of those opportunities.

In 1968, the war in Vietnam was at its peak. On January 30, the Vietcong captured Wycliffe translator Hank Blood during the Tet Offensive. Taken with Hank was Christian and Missionary Alliance missionary Betty Olson and Mike Benge, a USAID worker. They were marched north toward Hanoi.

Vange Blood, Hank's wife, returned to the States for a while and then came to the Philippines where she continued to work on the Vietnamese language that she and Hank had been studying. She heard nothing about Hank, but after several years, she received a report from Hanoi that he had died in October of 1972. In early March of 1973, a batch of Americans were released from prison in Hanoi and flown to Clark Air Force Base just north of Manila. Mike Benge was among the released prisoners. Vange made arrangements with the US Air Force to see Mike so she could get more information about Hank's death.

On the morning of March 6, I drove Vange to the base, where we spent four-and-a- half hours with Mike. We learned that both Hank and Betty died after seven months of being marched around the country, Hank of pneumonia and Betty of dysentery. Mike spent his first year in Hanoi in solitary confinement. Although we found it difficult to hear the details of their march, Hank and Betty's deaths, and Mike's confinement, Vange was relieved to know that Hank was with the Lord and didn't suffer for five years in prison.

New Publication Equipment

As our teams produced more Scripture portions for publication, we knew we needed better equipment than typewriters to prepare them for the printer. In 1973 Carl DuBois, translator for the Sarangani Manobo of Mindanao, became familiar with a piece of equipment while on furlough. The Friden Justowriter produced punched paper tape similar to a teletype tape. The phototypesetter at Marshburn Press could read this tape and produce photocopy ready to be made into pages for printing. At Carl's recommendation, we purchased a Justowriter, and the branch purchased a similar Flexowriter for use in the finance office. Until then our finance office staff prepared all of the financial entries by hand.

We were delighted with the Justowriter, since we could now make corrections easily. Several translators bought their own units to use in their translation work.

SIL's Twentieth Anniversary Celebration

By April 1973, SIL had been working in the Philippines for twenty years. The advisory committee—a group of Filipino government, business, and Christian friends— sponsored an anniversary luncheon in the Maharlika Room at Malacañang, the President's palace. A number of high government officials, members of the Linguistic Society of the Philippines, representatives from the Asia Foundation, embassies of countries from which SIL members had come, and a number of other Filipino friends packed out the room. Television and radio stations carried the program live, and several Manila newspapers carried it on their front pages.

President Marcos addressed the assembly and conferred SIL the presidential citation "in recognition of the practical and humanitarian acts of mercy that have characterized the work of the members of SIL from the beginning of the project in 1953." He also presented Director Morrie Cottle with the presidential merit medal for his leadership in promoting the work of SIL.

Apart from the directors, the executive committee, and two of our linguistics PhD's, Peggy Pitman and I were the only people from the office to be invited. We were honored in order to write up the proceedings for our publicity publications. I enjoyed the luncheon and program and had the opportunity to shake the President's hand.

Visit to Ifugao

In May of 1973 I needed a vacation. At our conference the previous Christmas, Dan Weaver was elected director, and Morrie Cottle and his family left the apartment next to us to return to the States for furlough. Since Dan and Marilou Weaver preferred to live in the Philippine community, Gerry and Carol Brock moved into the director's apartment. Gerry was teaching in the middle school at Faith Academy, and Carol worked on the nursing staff. Carol's mother, Alice Carey, came from London, Ontario, to spend several months with them. Since I didn't want to travel by myself, and it was school vacation at Faith, I invited them to accompany me to Ifugao to visit Anne West and my friends in the village there.

On Saturday we drove my car over rough roads 180 miles (290 kilometers) to Bagabag, a nine-and-a-half hour trip. On Sunday afternoon a group of us went for a walk near the river, two miles from the center. I took five children in my car halfway, since it was such a long walk. We arrived long before the others. Just as we arrived at the river, a big thunderstorm arrived too. The walkers saw it coming and turned back, leaving me with five small children in the middle of nowhere. We found shelter in a fisherman's grass hut. I thought it would be a quickly passing storm, but the rain didn't slow down for an hour. We had just left the hut to head back when the rain came again, drenching us all. We had to cross a small river and climb up a steep bank to the trail. The river was no longer the same shape or size as when we crossed it on the way, and we couldn't find the trail we had come on. Fortunately, the river was still crossable, so we waded through and found another trail that took us in the right direction.

Soon we met Gerry and Joe France coming to look for us. They had walked up and down the riverbank through the storm but couldn't find us. We were covered with mud, but the children decided that since they had all been to jungle camp except Stevie France who wasn't born yet, we could survive. I found out later that Stevie was terrified of thunderstorms. Along with the others, he bravely kept going and didn't let on he was afraid.

On Tuesday morning, we left Bagabag, and two hours later arrived at Bokoh at the end of the trail to Huyuk where Anne was waiting for us. We spent the day and night with Anne in the village. The next day we went to Banaue where we had lunch at the youth hostel and then went swimming in the hotel swimming pool. On Thursday we visited several small villages in Amganad, stopping to chat with people we knew. Brenda and Brian enjoyed playing with the children, even though they couldn't understand a word they were saying.

One of the highlights of the trip was seeing my namesake, three-year-old Funnell Ongallan. Anne's translation assistant, Ongallan, and his wife, Gela, had a boy not long after I left Ifugao. They wanted to name him after me, but since the baby was a boy, they couldn't call him Shirley. So they called him Funnell instead. He was a delightful child, bubbling with personality.

On our way home, we drove by way of Baguio where we spent a couple of days shopping and celebrating Carol and Gerry's eleventh wedding anniversary with a steak dinner at the officers club at Camp John Hay.

By July of 1973, the office building plans that Til and I had prepared were properly drawn by an architect, and we were ready to find a contractor. Following the declaration of martial law, prices increased very rapidly, and we had trouble finding a company that would do the work for the amount of money that we had to spend. Eventually, we did hire a company to do the work, but Ron Grable, who had now moved to Manila from Nasuli, bought all of the materials. Since we had many contacts in the city, he was able to shop for good prices. The contractor promised to have the building done in seven months, so we anticipated moving into our new office sometime in early 1974.

SIL Given the Magsaysay Award

"I have an exciting announcement to make," said Director Dan Weaver. "SIL Philippines has won the Ramon Magsaysay Award for international understanding for 1973."

Gasps of unbelief rose from the office staff members. The prestigious Ramon Magsaysay Award is the Asian equivalent to the Nobel Peace Prize and is presented every August 30 to worthy recipients in several categories.

157

This award was given in memory of former president Ramon Magsaysay who was killed in an airplane crash on the way from Cebu City to Manila in 1957.

In 1952, when Wycliffe member, Dick Pittman, was anticipating the beginning of work in the Philippines, Ramon Magsaysay, then secretary of national defense, issued the invitation for SIL to begin work in his country. He was elected president in 1953 and was a close friend of the SIL early members who arrived that year. This made the award especially precious, especially to those members who had known Magsaysay personally.

August 30 was an exciting day for all of us. In our best finery, we proceeded to the auditorium where the awards were presented. Dr. Richard Pittman came from the States to accept the award on behalf of SIL Philippines and gave a speech about the work we were involved in. After the program, buffet tables overflowed with Filipino delicacies. The award was accompanied with a check for ten thousand dollars, which was put to good use in our work.

New Office Building

By October construction was well underway on the new office building. The upper end of the building was about thirty feet from our living-room window, so we had a front-row seat. We also had all the dust and dirt from a construction site. We received an education on how to build a cement building in the Philippines. Piles of sand and gravel filled every bare spot. Most of the work was done by hand. A small cement mixer stood on the driveway. The workers poured mixed cement into a box with two handles on each end, and two men carried it up to the construction site. Since no wheelbarrows were available, everything was done with manpower. This slowed the work and frustrated the Westerners who were watching, but eventually, the building was completed. The heavy rains almost every day for the early part of the job also slowed the work. In October, two typhoons went by close to Manila, giving us heavy rains and wind for two or three days each.

When the framework was finished, and it was time to work inside, I took many trips through the building to see what was happening and if they were following the plans. I was especially interested when they came to the inside work on the second floor where the apartments were located. I was aware that Filipino kitchens were different from our Western kitchens. Since these were to be occupied by our members, I wanted to be sure that our Western standards were followed. One thing I insisted on was that the upper cupboards be low enough to reach the shelves. In most local kitchens, the bottom shelf began at about the height of my head. In order to reach the second and third shelves, you had to stand on a stool. This left wasted space between the cupboard and the counter top. Ron Grable and the workers were tired of my interference, but in the end, the work was done correctly. By March 1974, the first floor was completed, and we were ready to move the office from the Permaline building to our new facility.

That fall a worldwide gasoline shortage slowed us to a crawl. Most of the stations where we bought gas posted signs, "No gas." Eventually, we had rationing, which meant we could only buy during certain hours of the day. Each station received a predetermined amount, and when it was gone, no one could buy gas until the next delivery. Many stations saved gas for their regular customers, so if you hadn't built a relationship with a gas station in advance, chances were you couldn't find any at all. We usually bought from the same station, so most of the time we could get some gas. The amount allowed was two gallons at a time with a maximum of forty gallons a month.

National Writers Workshop

In October, a National Writers workshop was in process at Bagabag, and I was scheduled to spend the last week helping to print the books the writers produced. I was unable to drive my car because of the gas shortage, so I flew on Philippine Airlines, which was now servicing the Bagabag airport. I printed two hundred copies each of seven books on the mimeograph and bound them, ready to send home with the participants who came from five language groups. Our mimeograph machine was hand operated. After I had turned the handle from 8:00 a.m. to 8:30 p.m., Monday to Saturday, I had a very sore right arm. We finished by 11:00 p.m. on Saturday, in time for me to catch the plane to Manila on Monday.

Besides writing materials in their own languages to be used in literacy programs at home, the workshop participants learned other things to help in their daily lives. They grew vegetables using compost to show how much better they grow, raised rabbits, budded and grafted fruit trees, and took a number of interesting field trips in the area to get information to write about. During the workshop, Anne West conducted a Bible study, and two of the participants became Christians before they went home.

Christmas in 1973

Christmas in 1973 was one of the best I had experienced in the Philippines. By now I was accustomed to no snow and enjoyed the many different activities surrounding the season. It started with a performance of the Vienna Boys Choir at the Cultural Center. The Sunday before Christmas, I attended the dedication of the son of Bing Castillo, our SIL buyer. After the church service, we enjoyed a Chinese dinner together provided by the Castillo family. This custom is a holdover from the Catholic baptismal party.

On Christmas Eve, Peter Torres, our Filipino manager of services, invited me to share in their "Media Noche" (middle of the night). It is the custom to have a meal at midnight, after which the children open their gifts. Char Houck, Happy Minot, and I spent the evening visiting with Peter and his wife Loida before dinner. Then we had the fun of watching the children open their presents. Excitement kept them awake. Many families attended a church service before dinner. The President removed the curfew for Christmas Eve so everyone could enjoy their Christmas traditions.

On Christmas Day, I invited the twelve single women, who were in the guesthouse or living in Manila, for Christmas dinner at my house. We had turkey and all the trimmings, including a plum pudding that Jill Bembrick from Australia had received in the mail. Eileen Curry made a sauce for the pudding, and we treated our American friends, most of whom had never had Christmas pudding before. I brought an artificial Christmas tree from home when I returned in 1972, which helped with the festive atmosphere, along with garlands and candles. We exchanged small gifts and enjoyed the holiday atmosphere.

The day after Christmas, I traveled to Baguio to attend the first Asian Student Missionary Convention. Over eight hundred students attended from fourteen different Asian countries. We had a booth to publicize the work of Bible translation at this first Asian "Urbana."

At New Year's in the Philippines, everyone sets off firecrackers in the evening and past midnight. With martial law in effect, the President had banned private fireworks, but instead the government provided a wonderful display from two barges on Manila Bay. Again curfew was lifted so everyone could attend.

We watched from 10:00 p.m. until midnight, when we left and went to A&W for an early morning snack before going home. The fireworks lasted until 1:00 a.m.

Chapter 27
First New Testament
1974–1975

In late January of 1974, Til Kohley and I made a trip to Hong Kong. It was my first time there, and I looked forward to seeing the Crown Colony. She had received a free trip from the travel agency that took care of all SIL travel and offered to split the ticket with me. That made it inexpensive enough for me to afford.

Each year our executive committee approved an expenditure of branch funds for equipment that we needed for our work. Often such equipment was not available in the Philippines or was very expensive. So the main reason for our trip was to bring back approved items for the office and our centers. We spent several days shopping for this equipment as well as for ourselves.

We also enjoyed sightseeing in Kowloon and on Hong Kong Island. One day we took a bus trip to the border of China and looked across.

Literacy Projects Funded

After returning from Hong Kong, I spent a week with Pete Fast from the Wycliffe office in Calgary, working on a method of funding our literacy projects. The Canadian International Development Agency (CIDA), an arm of the Canadian government, funds projects around the world to assist third-world countries in education and other aspects of development. We prepared a request for $63,500 to fund our literacy and national training programs.

Pete and I took our project to the Canadian embassy and presented it personally to the ambassador. He was enthusiastic about the request and felt there shouldn't be any problem with the grant. He said he would send it to Ottawa immediately. We did receive the grant, which made a great difference in our literacy program. For a number of years, we continued to receive funding from CIDA, for which we thanked God.

Publications Moved to Horseshoe Village

In March we moved the publications office to the Horseshoe Village location. The move went more smoothly than I expected, and soon we were settled. I enjoyed walking next door to work instead of driving across town. We were short of office space though, since the new building was only phase one. It would be two more years before we had the funds to build phase two.

In the meantime, the executive committee voted to take the apartment where Til and I were living to augment the office. We were given the privilege of living in one of the new apartments still under construction above the office.

Gerry and Carol Brock also had a move in store. The director's apartment was once more needed for the director, so the executive committee assigned the second new apartment to them. About this time, Gerry received word from home that his mother was seriously ill in the hospital and not expected to live. In just two days, the Brocks packed up their belongings and headed for Canada to spend time with her. When they returned, they moved into the new apartment next door to us.

Vietnam Branch Evacuated

The Vietnam War was escalating across the South China Sea. In 1974 the Vietnam branch of SIL evacuated and came to the Philippines. Some members went home for furlough, others transferred to various branches, but many continued to do their translation work in the Philippines, mostly at Nasuli.

Some of their support workers helped us in the publications department, especially with typesetting Scripture on the Justowriter. They brought at least one New Testament from Vietnam that was ready for typesetting. Unfortunately, the numerous diacritics used in Vietnamese languages couldn't be typed on the Justowriter.

So a woman came from the States to type that one New Testament, using a special typewriter that contained all of the diacritics needed. After many weeks of hard work, the New Testament was ready for printing and arrived on my desk. I carefully transported it to Marshburn Press, realizing that this photo-ready copy represented many dedicated years of work by the translators, their language assistants, and the typist.

New Datapoint Computer

About this time, SIL's international publishing office in Dallas, Texas, informed me about a new system they were using for preparing Scripture for printing—a Datapoint computer. It placed the Scripture on a cassette tape, which could then be processed through the typesetter at the printer.

I had been planning to take a three-month furlough in the summer of 1975, since my mother hadn't been well, and I wanted to spend time with her. The director asked me to also make a trip to Dallas to see if we might want to install the new computer system in the Philippines.

Life continued to be busy. Til and I moved into the apartment on the second floor of the new office building and enjoyed decorating and getting settled.

The rainy season came again with a vengeance, putting much of Manila under water for days at a time. People living near the rivers lost their homes, and a number lost their lives.

Completed books of Scripture continued to pour onto my desk, waiting for me to take them to Marshburn Press for printing.

Death of Translator Happy Minot

The first week of September 1974, brought sadness to all of us. Char Houck and Happy Minot were translators for the Botolan Sambal people of Zambales. Early in the year, Happy had a routine physical, and the doctor found a tumor on an ovary and fluid on her lungs. He thought it was likely cancer, so she and Char went to the States immediately for further diagnosis and treatment. Chemotherapy was not as common then as it is now, and by the first week of September, Char sent us a cable saying that Happy had passed to her heavenly home.

This was a very sad time for Char, since they had lived and worked together for seventeen years. The New Testament, 80 percent completed, was now left in Char's hands to finish. A memorial service was held at the SIL Sunday evening service following Happy's death, remembering her life and work. She was only forty-four years old.

Literacy Writers Workshop Again

In December of 1974, I spent two weeks at Bagabag at another literacy writers workshop, helping to print the books that the workshop participants produced. We printed 2,400 books, each from sixty to ninety pages in ten different languages. Then I drove to Manila to clear my desk.

Christmas in Bagabag in 1974

In returning to Bagabag for Christmas, I drove my car with four passengers on a 188-mile (302 kilometers) trip, which took eight hours. We passed road builders in several places, but we were able to get through the construction sites and arrived safely and exhausted.

I always enjoyed being in Bagabag for Christmas. The whole center got together for a Christmas service of carol singing and reading the Christmas story from Matthew and Luke. I took a turkey along, so we had a traditional Christmas dinner for ten people, mostly single women who worked in Bagabag or used Bagabag as their retreat center when needing a break from the rigors of village living. After dinner, we sang Christmas carols and exchanged small gifts. Then I relaxed for a few days before driving back to Manila.

First New Testament Printed—Mansaka

Reports came to my office that the first New Testament translated by SIL members in the Philippines would soon be ready for printing. Gordon and Thelma Svelmoe, translators for the Mansaka of southeastern Mindanao, had worked for twenty-one years to bring the New Testament to this stage.

Gordon was in the first group to arrive in the Philippines in 1953. He had met Thelma in the States and married her in Manila. Together they had served God and the Mansakas, bringing the Scriptures to a people steeped in animism.

I received the tapes for the Mansaka New Testament from Nasuli. These were processed through the phototypesetter at Marshburn Press where four thousand copies were printed. The completed book arrived from the printer in the summer of 1975, while I was in Canada, a small, black, hardcover volume with the title on the spine in gold lettering.

The months flew by as I prepared for my second furlough. At first I planned to leave the office in the hands of Dely Velasco, my secretary. Then Peter and Chris Green arrived to begin their first term as translators for the Aborlan Tagbanwa people who lived on the western coast of Palawan Island. Peter agreed to fill in for me while I was gone, so I trained him to do my job.

Second Furlough

In early April, I left for home. My parents met me at the Toronto airport and drove me to my brother Art and Bonnie's house in West Hill, the east end of Toronto where they had purchased a new home since my last time there.

A friend from their church had recently bought a new car but had kept his old one. He agreed to let me drive the old car while I was in Canada, a wonderful help for getting around to visit my supporters and friends.

People in Canada were going through the change to the metric system that year. Only the school children, who were learning it from the beginning, had any idea how to handle the change. And that didn't happen overnight. I noticed that kilometer signs had been installed along the highways at the appropriate locations to mark the distances in round numbers. Eventually, after quite a few months, the mile signs were removed. At first the containers were the same size, only the labels listed the amounts in metric. Eventually, the sizes of the containers were changed so the amounts were even. Milk containers changed from quarts to liters. Gas was sold in liters instead of gallons. Shops sold cloth material by the meter instead of by the yard. Land was measured in hectares instead of acres. Temperature was measured in Celsius instead of Fahrenheit.

This was all a very big adjustment, especially for older people. In some parts of the country, especially in British Columbia, the changes were never accepted. To this day, most fresh food is still sold using the English measurements in advertisements and on signs in the stores, although the official labels are in metric.

Most of my time was spent in Ontario, except for a trip to Syracuse, New York, to visit the Robert Laubachs and other friends from church and school. I also flew to Dallas for my first visit to the new international linguistic center, located just outside of Duncanville, a southwest suburb of Dallas. The staff introduced me to the new computerized typesetting system that the printing arts department was recommending to the fields for preparing Scripture for printing.

The month was May, and roses were in full bloom, a gorgeous sight. During that trip, I participated in my first Texas barbecue on the center when many neighbors from the surrounding community came to be introduced to the work of SIL around the world. I went back home excited about the technology I'd seen. I was ready to return to the Philippines with a report to our executive committee and a recommendation that we purchase one or two of the Datapoint units for our work.

Translator Doreen Newell Died

One day on my way back to the Philippines I was at the new Wycliffe USA headquarters in Huntington Beach, California. While there, an announcement came over the intercom that Doreen Newell had passed away. She had been fighting leukemia for nine years and had suffered immensely for a year before her death. She and Len had returned to Calgary where he was serving as director for Wycliffe Canada and completing work on the Batad Ifugao New Testament. He found someone in Calgary to typeset it and then sent the typeset copy to Manila for printing. This was the second New Testament to be completed in the Philippines.

On my return to the office in Manila, I found that Peter Green had done a good job, and everything was in order. Rainy season had begun while I was gone, cooling the temperature but raising the humidity into the 90 percent range.

A few days after arriving, I drove to downtown Manila to shop. While there, the rain began. In twenty minutes, the water was over my hubcaps and soon lapped on the bottom of my car. Fortunately, aerodynamic design in cars didn't arrive until the 1990s, so my 1972 Toyota was still high at the front. I was able to drive through deep water and arrived home safely. The rain had washed out part of the back wall that surrounded our property, requiring us to rebuild it.

When I arrived in the Philippines in 1967, Anne and I went right to Ifugao after orientation, so I didn't have an opportunity to study the national language, Tagalog. Now that I was living in Manila where Tagalog is the language spoken by everyone, I wanted to learn, at least a little to communicate better. Most people who have been to school speak English quite well, so I could get along without knowing Tagalog.

Elmer Wolfenden, our linguistics coordinator, returned from furlough and agreed to run a Tagalog course for six of us who were working in Manila. It was a conversational course, so Elmer found a Filipina who drilled us on our conversational skills. The class was held three nights a week, and Elmer expected us to study at least an hour a day outside of class. I found it difficult working all day and then going to class and studying in the evening. Elmer was only available for five months, so I thought I might be able to survive for that long.

Move to Union Church

Not long after returning from furlough, I decided to change churches. I had been attending a Filipino Baptist church previously. The pastor preached a strong evangelistic sermon, and I enjoyed his fervor. However, I felt that I would like more in-depth teaching.

Over the years, I had occasionally attended Union Church of Manila, an interdenominational, international church that ministered primarily to expatriates. Many business and diplomatic families lived in Makati near their offices and embassies. Union Church was located in the business district, about seven miles (twelve kilometers) from our center in San Juan. Every week a vehicle went from SIL with people who either attended regularly or were staying at the guesthouse. I joined this group and soon came to enjoy this unique church. The congregation numbered about 350 at that time, mostly expatriates, and they had recently opened a new church building on the edge of the Makati commercial center. It was a beautiful round building with the ceiling of the sanctuary rising to a point in the center like a huge upside-down flower. A large bronze cross hung from the center of the ceiling over the front of the platform. The seats were in a semicircle, which brought everyone close to the front. Several rows of steps surrounded the front of the platform and became risers for the choir.

I missed singing in a choir. The Baptist church had a good one, but their practice time didn't work for me, so I couldn't join them. I thought that after attending Union Church for a while and when I felt more at home there and got to know a few people, I would join their choir. In the meantime, I enjoyed the excellent preaching of a new pastor who had arrived in 1975.

By now we were three years into martial law. In many ways, it didn't affect us at all. We adjusted to small things like curfew and went on with our lives and work. I was especially busy at the end of 1975 after returning from furlough. On top of my regular work as publications coordinator, I was appointed office manager and was still in charge of the literacy department. This meant making budgets for each of these departments on top of the regular work. It wasn't long before I felt the need of a break.

On the three-year anniversary of martial law, President Marcos declared a one-day holiday. Since it was a Friday, I packed my car with Faith Academy students who were off school for a week and headed to Bagabag.

A typhoon had just gone through, leaving many large puddles of muddy water on the road. One puddle had a rock in the middle, hidden by the mud. It was too high for my car, so when I drove through the puddle, we hung up and were unable to move. Some people along the road pushed us out so we could continue on our way.

One of my reasons for going to Bagabag was to see a new house that Anne West, Marge Draper, and Judy Wallace were having built. Judy had joined Marge in the Northern Kankanay project when Donna Hettick left. Marge and Judy were working near Sagada, across the mountains from Ifugao. Like Anne when they came to the center, they had to stay in the guesthouse or rent a space in the house of someone who was away. The three women decided to build a house that would be home for all of them when they came to Bagabag. It had two stories, with five small bedrooms upstairs and one downstairs to accommodate their language helpers and their house helper as well as themselves.

By now, Helen Madrid had joined Anne in Amganad. Helen was one of the first Filipinos to study linguistics in our new Summer Linguistics Training Course at Bagabag. She joined Anne in the translation project and remained until the New Testament was completed in 1980.

Help for Char Houck

Char Houck returned to the Philippines at the end of her furlough, following the death or her coworker, Happy Minot. She found life difficult for some time, being responsible for the translation project on her own, as well as many visits from neighbors. In November of 1975, my work had slowed a bit, so I spent a week helping Char with things that she needed to have done. She had moved to a new house when she returned from furlough, and it was my first time to visit her there.

Botolan is located on the west coast of Luzon, a four-hour drive from Manila. The speakers of Botolan Sambal lived inland as well as along the coast. Those who lived inland were Negritos—short, dark-skinned people who earned their living by hunting and gathering from the forests. The coastal Sambalis were city dwellers, many of them educated. They spoke the same language, but there were some dialectical differences.

Char and Happy had begun their work in the mountains. After a few years, they realized that the dialect they were learning and using for translation was not accepted by the lowland, more educated people. So Char and Happy moved to the town of Botolan for the remainder of their work.

Char was working on 1 and 2 Corinthians, Galatians, and Philippians, getting them ready to be checked by a consultant at a workshop the following January. So she could concentrate on her translation work, I did odd jobs, cooked, and mended. I also sorted through Happy's letters and an eighteen-year accumulation of her things. In addition, I helped Char in the translation, checking the English back translation of 1 Corinthians. I used the RSV, several other versions, and the exegesis, checking to be sure she had included everything. I enjoyed that work, since it was the first real translation job I had done.

John and Carolyn Miller Released from Vietcong Prison

Back in Manila, I had the privilege of being at the center when John and Carolyn Miller arrived from Vietnam. John and Carolyn were translators who were working in a minority language during the war. The Vietcong overran their village and took them and their six-year-old daughter, LuAnn, into captivity. Their three older children were in school and were evacuated with the other SIL members. The Millers were held for eight months, the last three in Hanoi. It wasn't until they were released and their plane stopped in Laos that missionaries there told them that their three older children were safe and in the States with their grandparents.

The Vietcong had treated John, Carolyn, and LuAnn quite well. Except for being very thin, they seemed to be in good health. However, their New Testament manuscript, which they kept with them the whole time, was confiscated a week before they were released. An archived copy was available, but they had made revisions that were not in the archived copy. We prayed fervently that God would return the manuscript to them so it could be published.

The Millers flew to Nasuli along with other Vietnam branch people. Most of the other Vietnam members were already at Nasuli. They all had two days together with the Millers to hear their story, pray for them, and love them. When they returned to Manila, they spoke at a meeting at our guesthouse that was attended by more than one hundred people. It was so good to hear how God had taken care of them and answered our prayers.[1]

Visit to Translators in Zamboanga

After Audrey Mayer finished teaching at Faith Academy, she returned to Nasuli and teamed up with her former partner, Rosemary Rodda, to begin a new translation project in Zamboanga City. The people who live in Zamboanga speak Chavacano, a Spanish creole language that had no Scriptures.

Zamboanga is a beautiful coastal city, filled with flowers, especially orchids, located at the southwest tip of Mindanao. Audrey and Ro rented a small house on the outskirts of the city and began language learning in preparation for translating the New Testament.

They invited me to spend Christmas with them in 1975. Since I needed to be at Nasuli for a workshop soon after New Year's, this invitation was convenient. I flew from Manila to Zamboanga just before Christmas.

Christmas Day was filled with activities. In the morning, we drove into the country to attend a Sunday school program at a small Christian and Missionary Alliance church. From there we went to the home of Mrs. Rivera, a

---

[1] For the complete story of the Millers' captivity, see Carolyn's book: Miller, Carolyn Payne. *Captured: A Mother's True Story of Her Family's Imprisonment by the Vietcong*. Chappaqua, NY: Christian Herald Books, 1977.

close friend of Ro and Audrey's. She and her two daughters had prepared an elaborate dinner consisting of chicken cooked in coconut milk; *pancit*, a mixture of fine rice noodles, shrimp, and vegetables; pork and chicken cooked with vinegar and soy sauce; macaroni salad; and a big punch bowl of *buko* salad, a mixture of immature coconut and various tropical fruits. Dessert was Spanish cream and marble cake. We went home loaded down with food, enough for two more meals.

It was the custom in the Philippines for carolers to arrive at your gate for nine nights before Christmas, singing a few carols and asking for money. Most of them were children, but some church groups raised funds for projects this way. Audrey and Ro gave the children candy instead of money. Many of the carols are English, and the children don't know what they are singing. Sometimes they get the words wrong, causing smiles among English-speaking listeners.

The day after Christmas, we went shopping in downtown Zamboanga, weaving among the great crowds of people. This is the place to buy *batik*, hand-dyed material from Indonesia. I bought two pieces to be made into dresses by my dressmaker in Manila. Many tourists frequent Zamboanga for the materials, shells, and pearls they can buy on the streets.

New Year's Eve in the Philippines is very loud with firecrackers of all sorts, skyrockets, and bamboo cannons. I was familiar with the first two in Manila but not the cannons. To make these, a section of bamboo is cut with the cross membrane left intact. Kerosene is inserted and lit so the bamboo explodes, making a very loud, deep bang.

Insurgent activity had been going on in the area of Zamboanga for some time, and when I heard the bamboo cannons, I thought it was bombing. Ro and Audrey assured me it was quite safe, and the noise was from the neighbors celebrating New Year's.

Eunice Diment Kidnapped

When I arrived at work on February 28, 1976, one of my coworkers greeted me with, "Did you hear the news? Eunice Diment has been kidnapped!"

This was the beginning of three weeks of high stress as we waited for news. Eunice, a translator from England and her American coworker, Jo Ann Gault, lived on the island of Panigayan, southwest of Zamboanga City. They were translating the Scriptures into the language of the Bangingi Samal people. Eunice and their landlord were on their way in a small boat to the island of Basilan, twenty minutes away, when another boat pulled alongside and ordered Eunice into their boat at gunpoint. Her landlord requested to go too, since he felt responsible for her.

When Jo Ann heard what had happened, she sent a radio message to Nasuli and then crossed to Basilan to stay with American friends for safety. SIL's southern associate director, Seymour Ashley, flew to Zamboanga to inform the authorities. The suspects were a group of rebels who had been responsible for a number of kidnappings and other terrorism in the area. Soon the British embassy was informed, and the BBC spread the news in Britain.

Colonel Cirilo Bueno Jr. of the Philippine Constabulary, Southwest Command, coordinated the negotiations between the government and the kidnappers. Seymour kept all SIL members informed, and we spent much time in prayer for Eunice's safety and ultimate release. After three weeks of hard work by the government negotiators, the rebels released Eunice unharmed. To express our gratitude to God for Eunice's safe return and to express our thanks to the government officials and military officers who succeeded in effecting her release, SIL hosted a reception at the guesthouse in Manila before her departure for England. She personally thanked those who were instrumental in her freedom.

Summer Linguistic Training Course

When the dust had settled, it was March and would soon be summer vacation time for schools. Graduations took place in late March, so students could be out of school during April and May, the two hottest months of the year, returning to school in early June.

Several years earlier, when Morrie Cottle was our director, the administration became increasingly interested in training Filipinos in linguistics and Bible translation. We began a summer course at Bagabag called the Summer Linguistic Training Course (SLTC). Two of the first students to complete the course were Helen Madrid and Rudy Barlaan. Helen joined Anne West in the Amganad Ifugao work, and Rudy joined Dick Roe in Dibagat to co-translate the Isneg New Testament.

Dick Roe was a linguist to the core and led the SLTC program. After several years, he felt that if the program were going to grow, it needed to be accredited so the students could receive degrees for their work. He and others began consulting with the department of education about the possibility of using teachers' camp, the department's vacation normal school facilities in Baguio. Dick wanted an expanded program at which the students could earn master of arts degrees in education with a concentration in functional literacy. A memorandum of understanding was signed with the department of education in October of 1975, giving us a ten-year mandate to train Filipino linguists and Bible translators. In April of 1976, staff at the first summer at the Baguio Vacation Normal School (BVNS) campus in Baguio welcomed twenty-three students to the new course.

Setting up the BVNS school was no small task. We had to transport library books, teaching supplies, and household equipment from Manila. The staff was assigned one of the cottages at teachers' camp where they would live for the summer. The first summer the teaching staff consisted of Dick Roe, Elmer Wolfenden, Dick Elkins, Jean Shand, Ron Morren, and Anne West.

Since none of these people owned a vehicle, they asked me to fill my car with supplies and drive to Baguio to help set up for the summer. Betty Elkins was the office manager and librarian, so she and Dick went with me. We loaded my station wagon to the roof with all the things they needed for the summer.

I stayed for three days and helped to set up the cottage. Baguio, at 5,000 feet altitude, is a glorious place in April, cold at night and usually sunny in the daytime. It is known as the City of Pines because of the many pine trees that cover the mountains.

We found several restaurants that we liked. One was Mario's in downtown Baguio, another the officers club at Camp John Hay, the US military R&R base.

Baguio market was also a special treat, since it was loaded with fresh vegetables and fruits of all sorts that are grown in the neighboring mountain communities. April was strawberry season, so I took orders from people in Manila and transported many pounds of that juicy fruit back to the lowlands.

After three days of hard work and cool breezes in the summer capital, I returned to Manila and my job in the heat of the hottest months of the year. I looked forward to a return trip to help close up the cottage, pack up my station wagon, and return everything to Manila for storage. Another few days of cool weather was a longed-for treat each year.

Because I had one of the few vehicles on the center, two trips every summer became my assignment. For ten years, I enjoyed helping to set up and take down the BVNS school facility. Each year some of the staff changed. Dick Roe was always there. Dick and Betty Elkins also spent all their summers in Baguio during those ten years, and we all became wonderful friends, friendships that lasted until the end of our lives. The last summer, when the contract was completed and other arrangements were made for training Filipino linguists, the staff presented me with a thank-you certificate for my twenty trips to Baguio.

That summer I made a second trip to Hong Kong. Char Houck, Doris Porter, Hazel Wrigglesworth, and I spent three days shopping and sightseeing in the Crown Colony. We found a very inexpensive package, consisting of two nights and three days in a first-class hotel, breakfasts, and a tour of Hong Kong Island. It was sweater-wearing cool in Hong Kong, a treat after the scorching-hot days of Manila. A friend of Char's, who was a missionary there, drove us through the New Territories to the China border where we looked across into Communist China. I bought a new wristwatch for myself, but we had a long list of things to buy for other people in Manila. Cameras, typewriters, and other electronic equipment were much cheaper there than in the Philippines. We returned home loaded down with equipment, mostly for other people and the branch.

Another Typhoon

The rainy season began early in 1976, with a very wet, moderate-sized typhoon. The winds were only 53 miles an hour (85 kilometers), but the rain inundated Manila and much of central Luzon. Six hours after it hit Manila, the city was under water. It rained for nine days, causing the rivers in central Luzon to flood to a depth of thirty feet in some places. In the mountains, landslides took out villages and destroyed roads. More than one hundred people were killed.

Bagabag, our northern center, was cut off from southern Luzon, the source of supplies and fuel. Cooking gas began to run low, and wood was unavailable, since Bagabag is located in the middle of a valley of rice fields. Eventually, fuel arrived by air, but many people in the area suffered shortages for some time.

My health since going to the Philippines had been exceptionally good. I rarely got the intestinal diseases that affected so many foreigners. But after the typhoon, I came down with bacillary, fungus, and yeast and was not able to digest my food. I suffered for a week before going to the doctor. Six kinds of medicine later, I recovered nicely and learned that it's a good idea to go to the doctor early rather than later.

*Checking blueprints for new office building
with Carol Brock's mother, Alice*

BVNS graduates

Chapter 28
Changes and Catastrophes
1976–1977

Nineteen seventy-six was a year of change and catastrophe for us and for others in SIL. In June the king of Nepal closed the SIL work there. He gave members until the end of August to pack up and be out of the country. For two months, the Nepal branch members worked day and night to complete translation projects and get them printed so that every language group in which they were working would have at least one book of Scripture available.

Our Philippine Branch Director Dan Weaver and the Asia Area Director Bus Dawson went to Nepal to help make decisions. Some Nepal members decided to work in the Philippines, some in other branches, and some would go home.

Fire in the FEBC Print Shop

On Sunday morning, July 10, I was sitting in my kitchen eating breakfast and listening to the 7:30 news on the radio. "Fire destroyed the print shop of the Far East Broadcasting Company," said the announcer. He was in the middle of the next news item before it registered what he had said. *But that's where we have our printing done!* I thought.

The news was too terrible to believe, and I actually forgot what I had heard until several hours later. While sitting in church, I saw a man from FEBC walk in. When I talked with him, I found out it was true. He said that the whole second floor of the print shop, containing the composition department, office, files, records, camera, and plate-making departments, as well as the phototypesetter, were completely destroyed. The estimated damage was over half a million dollars.

We had seventeen books in process, and nine were completely lost. One of them was the Vietnamese New Testament that had been hand typed on a special typewriter by the volunteer who had come from the States just to do that job. The print shop had no backup, since this was before the days of handy copy machines or computers. We were able to salvage plates for some books and finished copies for some others.

The following months were difficult for the print shop staff and for me as we tried to redo the work that was lost. Fortunately, the presses were saved and were soon back in working condition. With the help of another printer who provided the photo and plate-making work, books were soon rolling off the presses again, provided the copy was photo ready. Reconstruction of the building progressed quickly and was completed by September.

A Visit to the MacLeods

Kathy Novak, a single young woman from Hawaii, came to Manila for the summer to type the Umiray Dumagat New Testament for printing. Tom and Pat MacLeod lived on the east coast of Luzon and translated for the Umiray Dumagat people, who are nomadic Negritos. After Tom and Pat moved to their area, many Dumagats settled around them, making it possible for Tom and Pat to learn their language and translate the New Testament.

In July when Faith Academy began a new school year, Tom and Pat brought their four children to Manila. They met Kathy and invited us to visit them. Since Kathy was here for a limited time, I thought she ought to see where the MacLeods lived, so we returned with them to their home on the beach. I drove two-thirds of the way and left my car at the home of Tom and Pat's friends because the road was too bad for a regular car. We rode the rest of the way with the MacLeods in their jeep.

Their house was on a point right on the beach with tall coconut palms and other large shady trees all around it. On one side of the point, a coral reef came to the shore, and on the other side of the point was a long sandy beach. It was an ideal place for a holiday.

The first day we were there, Tom's language helper brought us a large lobster that he had just hauled in from his net. Pat cooked it for lunch, a wonderful treat right out of the ocean. However, my stomach didn't enjoy it much, and soon I felt nauseated. Remembering the problem I had with shrimp while in Ifugao, I wondered if I were allergic to shellfish. Pat found some medicine for upset stomach, which I took, and by suppertime I felt better.

On the second day we were there, Tom took us in his *banca* (a 30-foot canoe with outriggers) fifteen miles up the coast to visit with Perry and Pat Macabuhay, a young Filipino couple who had just begun their training program for work among the Dumagats. They were living in a Dumagat house consisting of poles and a palm-leaf roof. Some houses have a bit of siding but not much. Pat and Perry were living in this house until they could build a house of their own. We went swimming and walked on the lovely beach before returning to Tom and Pat's home.

176

The next day Kathy and I caught the bus back to the place we had left my car. The bus trip was a cultural experience that Kathy wouldn't soon forget. The conductor and several other men dumped a load of loose coconuts through the back window of the bus onto the backseat. When all the coconuts were in, they reached to the top of the back window and filled two seats and the floor under four more seats. The aisles were filled with sacks of green bananas level with the seats, so to reach the seats, riders had to climb over the bananas. Chickens roosted under our seat, and two tubs of fresh-caught fish were tied in the doorway. Fortunately, we were in the first seat by the door so didn't have to walk on the bananas.

A week after we returned from visiting the MacLeods, Kathy had an epileptic seizure in a bathroom at the guesthouse. We didn't know she had epilepsy, since she didn't tell us. It had been eight years since she'd had a seizure, and the doctor told her she had probably outgrown it.

A doctor staying in the guesthouse knew what to do. Since Kathy was badly dehydrated from having diarrhea for several days, the doctor felt she should go to the hospital. She was admitted for two-and-a-half days, two days of which she had no recollection later. After returning to the guesthouse, she didn't know anyone for a while. Then she couldn't remember things she was told. On Sunday night I invited her for dinner at my house on Tuesday. By Monday night she didn't remember my invitation. The doctor put her back on the medication she had not had to take for three years, and soon she was normal again.

We had now been occupying our new office for two years. The branch was growing quickly with many new translators and support workers arriving regularly. We had already felt the pinch for space, so early in the year, work began on phase two of the office building. This would double our office space and add storage and five more apartments. The deadline for completion was December 1976. This time I didn't have any responsibility for the structure and could only watch and grumble when they didn't do what I thought should be done. As I feared, the kitchens in the apartments were built with high cupboards.

Adventure in the Rain

Many of my adventures in Manila had to do with rain. One afternoon in August, Lou Hohulin, head of our linguistics department, needed to attend a meeting of the Linguistics Society of the Philippines that was to be held at the Philippine Normal College (PNC) in downtown Manila. She asked me to accompany her. Normally, I would have taken her in my car, but it was in the shop being serviced that day, so we took off in a taxi. It was a bright, sunny day, and neither of us remembered to take our umbrellas.

About 4:00 o'clock, I noticed that the sky had darkened, and soon it began to rain. By 6:30 when we were ready to go home, it was pouring. We went outside to the curb to hail a taxi, since you can't call one by telephone in the Philippines. In about five minutes, we were drenched to the skin. Everyone from the meeting was trying to get a taxi at the same time, and we were not aggressive enough to be successful.

Finally, we went back inside the school, found a telephone, and called the guesthouse to see if anybody could pick us up. The only man in the house who could drive was John Rollo who worked at Nasuli and didn't know his way around Manila at all. Arthur Lown was also there, but he was blind. Together they decided to see if they could get a taxi near the guesthouse and come for us. Although John didn't know where the Philippine Normal College was, he thought the taxi driver would know, so that was a better idea than his trying to find it himself. They waited forty-five minutes and finally flagged down a taxi. By then the streets were flooded, so flooded that water came inside the car, and John and Arthur got their feet wet. About halfway to their destination, the flooding was more than the taxi could handle, and it stopped running in the middle of a deep pool.

When John and Arthur left the taxi, they were stranded some way from the school where we were waiting. They walked in our direction under a large umbrella, Arthur holding John's arm to help him over the curbs. Arthur had learned his way around Manila quite well by this time and was sure he could find PNC. As they walked in the pounding rain, he kept saying to John, "Do you see a bridge with a high metal top?"

Peering through the rain, John answered, "No, I don't."

Arthur kept asking, and finally John said, "I see the bridge ahead of us now."

"Good!" said Arthur. "We're on the right street."

Not long after, we saw the two of them arriving on foot as wet as we were. Now four of us were stranded downtown in the rain! About a half block from our location stood the Hilton Hotel. We searched our pockets and purses to see if we had enough money for two rooms at the Hilton if we couldn't get home. We did but hoped we wouldn't have to take such drastic measures.

Shortly, we noticed that people were arriving at the Hai Alai a half block up the street. People gamble on a fast ball game played in a big arena. We walked that way quickly and were able to get a taxi, which was delivering gamblers to the Hai Alai.

The taxi driver was very resourceful and knew where the worst flooding was likely to be. He took an extremely roundabout way and delivered us at the guesthouse door at 10:00 p.m. By now we were all tired, hungry, and wet, which made us giddy. We weren't sure what the taxi driver thought of us, since we laughed all the way home.

I learned a lesson that day. I needed another umbrella. I always carried one in my car. Now I needed a small fold-up model to fit in my purse.

A Dangerous Weekend

In late August I experienced one of the most dangerous weekends of my life. Kathy Novak had been typing the Umiray Dumagat New Testament for two months and now needed to return to her job in Hawaii. Before she left, I decided to take her to Amganad to visit Anne and see where I had lived and worked for two years.

I drove to Bagabag where we planned to leave the car, since finally, after many years of negotiating, the government was rebuilding and paving the road from Bagabag to Banaue. But I was told I wouldn't be able to get my car through.

Judy Wallace drove us to Lagawe, about halfway, where we could get a bus for Amganad. The road was nearly finished to Lagawe, so we sailed along on relatively smooth pavement, except for a short strip where the road was very narrow, hugging the mountainside. I commented, when we drove past this spot, that I couldn't imagine how they would ever widen that place, since the mountain went straight up.

We arrived in Lagawe at 9:30 a.m. Judy let us off and returned to Bagabag, while Kathy and I sat on a pile of rocks under a big tree waiting for a bus or jeepney to come through from Banaue. About forty-five other people were waiting there as well. At 10:50 a.m., a small jeepney came, and the stampede started. We didn't even try to get on. It had been raining, and no vehicles were getting through, the jeepney driver said. A bulldozer had pushed him through. So we sat until 1:30 p.m. and then decided to go back to Bagabag, since it was getting too late to expect another vehicle that day. In just a few minutes, a jeepney came that was going to Bagabag, so we got on.

Just outside of Lagawe, we came to a bridge over the river. I noticed that two huge landslides had occurred right in the spot where I had wondered how they could widen the road. While we had been waiting in Lagawe, the builders had dynamited the side of the mountain to begin widening the road. Now we were stuck between the muddy road to Banaue and the blasted road back to Bagabag. We had taken a quick look at the hotel in Lagawe and decided there was no way we were going to stay there if we could help it.

A bulldozer was working on the first pile of rocks, but about fifteen minutes after our arrival, the bulldozer broke down. The workmen said there was little possibility of the slide being cleared that day. We climbed over the slides to see if we could find a bus on the other side that might be turning around to return to Bagabag.

It was a frightening experience to climb over a new slide, carrying our suitcases, since the rocks were loose. I felt as if we might roll down the mountainside any minute—and we might have. We made it across without a mishap and found a bus on the other side that was planning to turn around and return to Bagabag. Several buses stood there, but this was the only one with enough gas to get back. However, our chosen bus had no tread on its tires, so the driver had a difficult time turning around on the uphill muddy road. After he made several tries with much grunting and groaning and spinning of tires, he finally got the bus headed in the right direction. We all climbed aboard with sighs of relief, thinking we were clear for a smooth trip to Bagabag.

Just as we were about to start, we heard the loud rumble of an explosion ahead of us. We saw rocks flying in every direction. The workers had blasted another spot in front of us, and now we were trapped between two slides. I couldn't believe it. They must have seen us coming.

Kathy was quite frightened with the blasting. A loud rumbling in the mountain sounded as if it were coming down on our heads. She got out of the bus and ran around to the side away from the mountain. When the noise stopped and the rocks settled down, she and the bus conductor walked up to the spot where they had been blasting to see the damage. Since not too many rocks landed on the road, they started throwing them off. The spot was on a corner, and soon the two of them disappeared out of sight.

Suddenly, a slide came down right where they had been standing. I thought Kathy might have been under it, but nobody seemed too excited, so I decided she must have moved farther away. A bulldozer around the corner cleared the rocks in about fifteen minutes, so the bus could go through. Just as we got to the place where the slide had been, the bus got stuck. There we sat with loose rocks over our heads, waiting for the bulldozer to push us up the hill.

When we finally got around the corner, I saw Kathy standing on the side of the road. The bus driver wouldn't stop on the hill to let her on because it would get stuck again, so he kept on going. The conductor called to her to hurry up the hill on foot. She ran uphill as fast as she could, thinking the bus was leaving her behind. When the bus got to a level place, it stopped to let her climb aboard.

Finally, we were on the new concrete road on our way to Bagabag. The only thing I could think of that could happen now would be for the bus to run out of gas or break down. About halfway home, we were rounding a slight curve when the driver ran his right front wheel off the pavement into the thick mire of the shoulder. The bus went down with a loud bang, and I thought we were going to tip over. A man who was standing in the doorway was thrown out against the mountainside and injured his foot.

Now we had to wait for someone to get us out of the ditch. Workers found a jeep and a cable that they hooked together. But when the jeep started up, the cable broke. Finally, a truck with a full load of gravel came by with enough power to pull us out. Nothing was broken on the bus, so we all got back on board and proceeded to Bagabag.

When we came to the long driveway into the SIL center, the bus turned in and drove us right to our gate. By now it was 7:10 p.m. and dark. Kathy and I were very hungry, since we had little for lunch. A hot bowl of soup and homemade bread looked very good when we straggled into the house where we had been staying.

I had complained a short time before this weekend that life in Manila was very quiet, and I never had anything interesting to write home about. This weekend had enough excitement to last for several letters.

Office Building Finished

Work on phase two of the office progressed quickly, and the building was finished ahead of time. By late November we were able to move in. This addition to the building provided space for the library and a conference room as well as new offices for the director, assistant director, and the director's secretary. Additional storage space on the ground floor made room for a new book depository and a new *bodega* for storing members' barrels and boxes. The area occupied by storage before was now converted to office space for the academic affairs department. Five new apartments on the second and third floors provided additional housing for staff members who were assigned to the Manila office.

This increased our Manila center housing from two apartments to seven. The two bachelor apartments on the third floor each consisted of one large room, a kitchen, and a bathroom. Tall bookcases made room dividers, so the residents were able to have separate bedrooms and living areas.

Since I was now the office manager as well as publications coordinator, I was responsible for the move and for finishing details. I shopped for material for drapes for all the windows and arranged with a drapery maker to sew them. Several people helped me hang them when they were finished.

Another Literacy Writers Workshop

When the office move was completed, I traveled to Bagabag to assist in another national writers workshop. People from several language groups in northern Luzon created reading books for the literacy programs among their people. I mimeographed these materials so the workshop participants could take finished copies with them when they went home. In two weeks, we printed twenty-three volumes of two hundred copies each. This was literally a night-and-day job. One day I worked for eighteen hours. My shortest workday was thirteen hours.

Branch Conference at Nasuli

When the workshop was over, I was exhausted but had no time to relax. After returning to Manila, I had only five days before leaving for Nasuli to attend our biennial conference. I had to clear my desk of all that had accumulated while I was gone, finish my Christmas shopping, wrap my gifts, make cookies and candy to give to our national staff, and pack to go to Nasuli. I arrived the day conference began.

I loved conference. For the first three days, we enjoyed a time of spiritual emphasis with a special speaker, Pastor Dick Woodward from Virginia Beach Community Chapel. Business consisted of elections for the director and the executive committee and other items that needed input from the whole branch.

On the first day of meetings, Director Dan Weaver made a surprising announcement. He had received a cable from Len Newell, who was working in Calgary as the Wycliffe Canada director, announcing that he was engaged to marry Johanna Schipper.

Soon after Doreen's death in 1975, Johanna had begun working as Len's secretary. She was from St. Thomas, although I didn't know her, since she was much younger than I was. When she became a member of Wycliffe, she had attended jungle camp in Mexico as I had. On her return home, the *St.*

Thomas Times Journal had interviewed her and ran an article, with her picture, about her experiences. My mother saw it and mailed it to me, wondering if I knew her. The article said she was a graduate of the business college. Since we were desperate for secretarial help in our office, I wrote to her, asking if she would be interested in working in the Philippines. She responded that she wasn't interested in the Philippines at all. She was then assigned to work in the Calgary office.

Len's cable indicated that they would be married soon and would be returning to the Philippines in April of 1977. I expected him to bring the typeset copy of the Batad Ifugao New Testament when he came, since a typesetter in Canada had prepared it for printing.

We broke in the middle of our meetings for Christmas. Anne West and I were staying with Audrey Mayer and her Australian coworker, Rosemary Rodda. We enjoyed a restful day, opened our gifts, and had dinner with John and Claudia Rollo with their two small children.

In the evening, we had a center-wide carol sing. During the week following Christmas, a fifty-voice choir sang a cantata called, "Alleluia." We practiced every spare minute after we arrived at Nasuli and enjoyed sharing this glorious Christmas music with the other branch members.

New Equipment for Typesetting

After returning to Manila, I was back to work again. About the middle of January, a man from the printing arts department in Dallas arrived to discuss the possibility of our purchasing computers for our typesetting needs. This was the equipment I had gone to Dallas to see when I was home in 1975.

As a result of his visit, we ordered two units that would arrive in about two months. This meant that I would need to take some training to operate the equipment. The training was being offered in Papua New Guinea and in Dallas. The director decided that I should plan to spend part of my next furlough in 1979 at Dallas to take the training course that the department there offered.

From time to time, major fires destroyed large areas of Manila, usually squatter villages where hundreds of people lost their homes. This year the domestic airport burned down. The fire began in a restaurant and spread via the ceiling throughout the whole structure. Because we had curfew and only three or four other airports in the country had lights, no night flights were scheduled. It was out of control by the time workers discovered the fire.

Flights were operated out of a nearby restaurant and a golf-driving range for almost two years until a new airport terminal could be constructed.

Visit from Frank Robbins, SIL Vice President

By the middle of February, we were well settled in our new office, so we scheduled the official opening to coincide with a visit from Frank Robbins, SIL International's executive vice president, and his wife Ethel. A number of activities kept us busy for the week they were in the Philippines.

This began with a reception to introduce them to the office staff. Ethel was the speaker at a ladies' salad luncheon around the swimming pool. Director Dan Weaver and his wife, Marilou, joined the Robbins on a visit to the President's palace, Malacañang, to greet President Marcos. On the last evening, we hosted a large reception at the guesthouse in honor of the Robbins to which we invited many government officials and other important people. At the same time, we had the dedication and official opening of the new office. Doña Josefa Marcos, President Marcos's eighty-four-year-old mother, cut the ribbon.

Those of us involved in the planning and preparation of these activities were exhausted when they were over. Following the office dedication, eight of us women decided that, since we were all dressed up and it was still early, we would finish the evening by climbing into the SIL van and driving downtown to the best hotel there for coffee.

I enjoyed such activities, but all this with work on top made me want to sleep for a week. Instead, I took a vacation in Baguio with Marge Moran, Doris Porter, and Til Kohley. We stayed in a guesthouse operated by another mission and relaxed in the cool mountain air.

While in Baguio, Doris and Til took Marge and me out for a steak dinner to celebrate our birthdays. Marge's is March 5 and mine is March 6. After returning to Manila, friends and office staff celebrated my birthday on five separate occasions. I have other friends whose birthdays are in March, and since going out for dinner was the usual celebration, we began to call March "Fat Month."

Chapter 29
New Testament Dedications
1977–1978

New Testaments were being finished, and my work was increasing as I took them to the printer and kept track of the processing of each one. Tom and Pat MacLeod's Umiray Dumaget and Len Newell's Batad Ifugao New Testaments were both submitted for printing in March of 1977. At the same time, Scripture portions and literacy materials produced by teams in northern Luzon were increasing. Some members were discontented at the length of time it took for Marshburn Press to print them.

We decided that we should set up a publications department at Bagabag to print small volumes. I went to Bagabag to work with the people there to find space and to organize the paperwork for whenever a job came in for printing.

All the books would still come across my desk in Manila, since I did the branch records' keeping. Then I would send the forms back to Bagabag, giving permission and instructions for them to proceed with the jobs.

By early June, the first copies of the Batad Ifugao New Testament and the Umiray Dumaget New Testament arrived from the printer. I was excited to be the first person to hold a New Testament translated by one of our teams. I had missed that privilege with the Mansaka New Testament, since I was on furlough when it arrived.

Batad Ifugao New Testament Dedication

The alarm clock went off. It was 3:30 a.m., June 12, 1977. The long-awaited day had come, the dedication day for the Batad Ifugao New Testament.

I had traveled in my car to Bagabag the day before, and now we were up and ready to make an early start to the mountains. About thirty of us climbed into two jeepneys and were off by 4:15 a.m. The sun came up as we climbed higher and higher. By 7:30 we had reached the end of the first leg of our journey and the end of the ride. Now we had to climb by foot over a mountain pass, up for an hour and down for an hour. I hadn't realized what eight years of sitting at a desk at sea level could do to one's ability to climb mountains. I used to climb this mountain when I lived in Ifugao without any trouble at all.

After numerous stops to rest, we arrived in the Batad Valley at the home of Len and Jo Newell, just in time for the program to start. Ifugaos had come from many miles and mountains away, some hiking as long as two or three days to get to Batad. When they had all assembled, about eight hundred were in attendance.

The program lasted for more than three hours. We all sang and praised God for His goodness in allowing Len and his late wife, Doreen, to complete the translation of the New Testament. A time of prayer dedicated the Book to God. The doctor from the clinic in Banaue gave a special message.

For part of the service, I sat in the sun under my umbrella but soon had to find a shady place. Afterwards, we climbed up the mountain to the little chapel that the Ifugaos had built and dedicated to Doreen's memory. I was very hungry, since all I'd had to eat that day was a hard-boiled egg and half a cup of coffee just before we began the climb up the mountain into Batad. Women served a lunch of boiled pork and a bit of rice, using sections of banana stalk for plates. It tasted wonderful, but the crowd of eight hundred people was bigger than the cooks had anticipated, so each meal was rationed.

In the afternoon during a baptismal service, eighteen more Ifugaos rose from the waters to stand with the nearly two thousand who had already confessed Christ. In the evening, a testimony meeting lasted nearly all night when people from the various Ifugao villages told of God's working in their lives. It was a joyful time for everyone, and I felt privileged to have had a part in the printing of this New Testament.

Those of us who came from Bagabag returned in the late afternoon. The climb back over the mountain was almost too much for me. We stopped at the hotel in Banaue for a meal before proceeding to Bagabag. While waiting for the cook to prepare our food, I fell sound asleep.

The road to this day had been a long and discouraging one for Len and Doreen Newell. For sixteen years, they lived and worked with the Batad Ifugao people before seeing even one come to know Christ. Then the Word they were translating touched Len's three helpers, and they gave their hearts to the Lord. They became evangelists to their own people, taking home copies of the work they had done during the day and reading it to their families and neighbors by the light of their small fires.

Len had talked with many of these people about the gospel and their need of salvation, but while they thought it might be true for other people, they didn't think it was true for Ifugaos, who were steeped in the animistic religion of their ancestors.

Now the people heard the words of Jesus in their own language. One Ifugao priest said to Len with amazement in his eyes, "It was just as though God was talking to us!"

"He was," Len answered. "You see, what was read is God's Word. He now speaks to you because He speaks your language through what is written in Ifugao."

Soon a group of believers wanted to be baptized. Who would do the baptizing? Len didn't want to be the one, since he felt it shouldn't be a foreigner but one of their own people. Then he had an idea. The church was growing among the Balangao people where Jo Shetler was translating the Scripture. Perhaps some of their elders would be willing to travel over the mountains to Batad to baptize these new believers. Balangaos and Ifugaos had been enemies in the past. This would be a wonderful witness to the reconciling love of Christ.

The Balangaos agreed, and although they couldn't speak Ifugao, they could speak the trade language, Ilokano, as could many of the Ifugaos. In this way, the new Ifugao believers were baptized, and the Ifugao church was born.

The translation progressed, and as the New Testament books were completed, they were printed, several in a volume, so the Scripture would be available for the believers to read. Ilat, one of Len's translation helpers, became a book distributer, carrying copies to many villages of the Batad area, reading to people as he went, selling books, and talking to people about Jesus, his life, death, resurrection, and their need for Him.

Len spent five years in Canada. Then following Doreen's death from leukemia that she struggled against for nine years and his marriage to Jo, he returned with the manuscript of the New Testament ready for printing. When he left, there were three churches in the Batad Valley. Now thirty-five churches with two thousand believers lived throughout the language area. People from the Ayangan Valley could also understand the Batad New Testament, so the translation spread God's Word far beyond the original area for which it was prepared. By 2007, there were 125 registered churches.

The believers, realizing that they had only one-third of God's Word in their language, requested a translator to translate the Old Testament. Unable to find a missionary to do this, they decided to do it themselves. A Bible training center was established. Under the supervision of Helen Madrid of the Translators Association of the Philippines and Trevor Douglas of World

Team (formerly Regions Beyond Missionary Union), the complete Bible was published and dedicated in October 2010.

While living in Canada, Len was diagnosed with esophageal cancer, and he soon became very ill. The family gathered around his bed, held his hands, and sang hymns.

Suddenly, Len looked up at the ceiling and exclaimed in awe, "Oh, man!" He told the family that he saw heaven's gates with Jesus standing there waiting for him, surrounded by a crowd of people he knew. He started naming some of them and then was gone.

Len didn't live to see the publication of the complete Bible, but God gave him great joy in knowing that many thousands of his beloved Ifugaos had given their lives to Christ.

Umiray Dumaget New Testament Dedication

The Umiray Dumaget New Testament was also dedicated in June of 1977. Two weeks before the dedication, Tom and Pat MacLeod flew home to Calgary, Alberta, where Tom entered the hospital with a severe liver ailment. Three days before he left, I brought him a copy of the printed New Testament as it arrived from the printer. This book was the culmination of fifteen years of work by the MacLeods, work that was their life. On June 3, Tom went into the presence of his Lord. We were sorrowful to lose him but rejoiced in the knowledge that he had already heard "well done" from God.

I had planned to attend the dedication for the Umiray Dumaget New Testament, but bad weather prevented our plane from reaching the village where the dedication was held. A solid wall of black clouds forced us to return to Manila.

The books had already been delivered, and the speaker, photographer, and a number of other visitors had flown in the day before, so the program went on, except the master of ceremonies and the program were with us. Filipinos are very adjustable, so the program went on without us.

Computer Training

In addition to my trip to Batad for the New Testament dedication, I spent three weeks that June participating in an intensive training course for the new computerized text-editing system that we had just purchased to assist in the production of the many Scripture portions, New Testaments, and literacy books that we were producing each year. Paul Griffiths from Dallas arrived with the computers and helped to get them up and running.

This was my first experience with a computer. The training I received, along with Ken Zook, our radio technician, was enough for me to use the system but also enough for me to realize I needed much more training. Paul's time was limited, so he left us to figure out many procedures on our own.

Fortunately, Ken was a genius when it came to computers. Without him, I would have been in serious trouble. With Ken as a consultant, I was able to typeset two New Testaments in the next two years before going home for furlough and enrolling in the training program offered in Dallas.

One of the advantages of living in Manila was the opportunity to attend many international cultural presentations at prices we could afford. A beautiful cultural center was the venue for concerts, ballets, and dramas often presented by visiting performers. In August of 1977, President and Mrs. Marcos sponsored a benefit concert to raise funds for a new sports center soon to be built. The guest performers were the famous American pianist, Van Cliburn, Dame Margo Fonteyn, a British ballet dancer, and Rudolph Nureyev, a Russian ballet dancer. They were all world-famous performers in their fields. I was able to get tickets for $6.80 in the top balcony and accompanied a group of us from SIL to the concert.

This was a gala affair. As we arrived at the center, each woman was presented with a long-stemmed red rose. A small orchestra played in the lobby as the crowd gathered. Flowers were everywhere. Great baskets of red roses, white carnations, and sampaguita (jasmine), the national flower of the Philippines, stood along the front of the stage, on the floor of the theater near the front, and fastened on the balcony rails. These flowers, added to the red roses throughout the audience, made it a very colorful scene.

President and Mrs. Marcos were there, as were many of their wealthy friends. The most expensive seats cost $1,360. Since the theater seated five thousand people, many millions of pesos were raised that night for the sports arena. We were grateful that inexpensive seats allowed people who couldn't afford much to attend.

In addition to professional cultural performances, we usually attended the senior class play at Faith Academy. I was always amazed to see what a professional performance those high-school students presented. Faith also had an excellent choral group called "The Madrigals and Guys," who put on an annual concert for families and friends. We loved to attend those concerts also.

When SIL was asked to leave Nepal and a number of their members came to the Philippines until they could decide what to do next, we hoped that some would join our team. Some did. Heather Kilgour was one who transferred to the Philippines branch. She had only been in Nepal for one year so hadn't yet become involved in a translation project there. She worked in our Manila office for some time. We became good friends, and when Til informed me that she wanted to live by herself when she returned from furlough, I asked Heather if she would like to join me in my apartment over the office. She was from Australia, so we had much to learn about and from each other. We had much in common though, since we both came from a farming background. Her father grew peanuts in Queensland.

Choir Ministry

Heather and I attended the same church, and we both liked to sing, so when we were invited to join the choir at Union Church in June of 1978, we did so gladly.

From then, every Wednesday evening for the next twenty-eight years, I spent from one to three hours in the choir room at Union Church of Manila at choir practice. Heather and I left work promptly at 5:00 p.m. to get to the church by 5:45 p.m. We packed a lunch and ate our supper in the car on the way. In the early years, choir practice was just one hour. When it was over, we rushed the almost eight miles (twelve kilometers) back across town to SIL in time for the weekly prayer meeting.

The choir director at that time was David Yap, a fine Chinese musician. He directed not only our choir but another called Chorale Philippines made up of members from a number of different church choirs. He invited us to join Chorale Philippines for a concert to be held in October at the Cultural Center at which we would sing the "Brahms German Requiem" with the Philippine philharmonic orchestra. For this we rehearsed three hours every Sunday afternoon and then practiced a half-hour every day at home. Our next-door neighbor had a piano, and Heather played quite well, so we often sang in our spare time. I thoroughly enjoyed learning this difficult but beautiful music. I also learned a bit of German. A German speaker tutored us so our pronunciation would be correct. The concert was sung to a sold-out crowd on two nights in October and was probably the most exciting thing I had ever done.

Publishing in Bagabag

During that year, I made several flights to Bagabag to care for publications business. Our teams continued to increase and to produce literacy and

Scripture publications. The Marshburn Press staff was not able to keep up with our demands, so we decided to buy a tabletop offset press and set up a print shop at Bagabag. With the press came a plate maker to provide paper plates for printing. I made one trip to Bagabag for the dedication of the new department and another to train Helena Oderkirk to prepare materials to be printed on the new press.

While at Bagabag, I made a side trip to visit Dick and Ruth Gieser who were translating for one of the Kalinga dialects. They were leaving for furlough soon and asked me to take pictures for them to be used during their speaking engagements at home. I flew to their place, a half-hour trip from Bagabag.

The Kalingas grow coffee. It was an education for me to see how they processed coffee beans for sale. I learned that coffee, which grows best in the mountains, takes a whole year to mature. It produces ripe berries at the same time as it puts out flowers for the next crop. The beans were spread on the ground and left to dry in the sun before being roasted. I enjoyed Kalinga coffee, which had a strong, nutty flavor.

While at Bagabag, I stayed at the Kafi House. The translators for the Northern Kankanay who lived in Bogang near Sagada were my prayer partners. During the years, several women had come and gone. Now the team consisted of Doris Porter, Marge Moran, and Judy Wallace. Marge Draper was now stationed in Bagabag, working as the radio operator. Anne West and Helen Madrid worked with the Amganad Ifugao people. The house they built together at Bagabag was very practical with five bedrooms upstairs and one downstairs as well as a room for the house helper. But rarely was everybody there at the same time, so I usually was able to join whoever was home when I needed a bed in Bagabag. They called it the Kafi House – "Ka" from Kankanay and "fi" from the first two letters of Ifugao spelled backwards to make it pronounceable. Marge Draper was the permanent resident for many years as she continued to serve as the radio operator in Bagabag. I often joined them for Christmas and always had a delightful time.

Visits to Translators

I also made several trips to visit Marge Moran, Judy Wallace, and Doris Porter at Bogang. Sagada, where I had conducted the writers workshop a number of years earlier, was their market town. Heather and I took a trip over Easter in 1978 to visit Doris. Judy and Marge were both away at the time. We drove to Bagabag where we spent the night, then drove to Banaue where we stopped to have coffee with Janet Davis, who was still living on the road south of town. Continuing on to Bontoc for several more hours, we stopped to have lunch with Keith and Kathy Benn, who were translators for the Central Bontoc people. They were also Australians, who were quite new in their assignment. Kathy's parents were visiting them, so all the Australians had a good time together.

We continued on to Sagada, arriving at 4:15 p.m. Doris met us at the post office and guided us down a very narrow road for about one mile (two kilometers) to a spot where I could leave the car. From there, we hiked over the rice terraces for half an hour to Bogang.

Trips to visit our translators in their villages were always special treats to me. I loved getting out of Manila and enjoying the fresh air and the pine trees that grew in the mountains of northern Luzon. Our weekend with Doris was especially relaxing as we hiked around the village of Bogang and over the rice terraces. This was a very dry year. We watched as people worked to channel what little water there was into their rice fields.

We decided to return to Manila by way of Baguio instead of returning to Bagabag. We should have been able to get home in twelve hours, but partway down Mountain Trail on the way to Baguio, the muffler fell off my car, no doubt from driving on one of the worst roads in the world. A kind Filipino stopped and offered to fix it for us. Unfortunately, he had only American nuts to replace the one that had fallen off, and I had a Japanese car. The threading was different. After two-and-a-half hours, our angel of rescue wired the muffler and tail pipe back into place so we could get home. We arrived safely at 12:20 in the morning, tired, nineteen hours after getting out of bed.

Heather and I made another trip that April. The President declared a five-day weekend to accommodate people who needed to travel to their home places to vote in elections. We decided to visit three of our translation teams who worked along the west coast of Luzon. We visited Char Houck in Botolan, spending two days with her before driving an hour north to Candelaria, where Hella Goschnick was translating for the Tina Sambal people with two young Filipinas. After one day in Candelaria, we proceeded to Bolinao on the northern tip of the Lingayan peninsula. Gary and Diane Persons had just begun translation work among the Bolinao people. We spent the weekend with them before returning home. On the way to Bolinao, we needed to pass through the town of Alaminos. As we approached the town, we could see great billows of smoke arising ahead. Five or six blocks of the center of town were on fire. Our highway ran right through the fire area, so we had to find a detour among the fire engines and crowds of people with their personal belongings attempting to escape the fire.

In June of 1978 I joined Union Church of Manila. Many people attended the church, but few became members because they were not expecting to be in Manila very long. Those assigned to embassies and business people usually moved on after two or three years. I wanted to be more involved in the church and its ministry so signed up, along with Heather, to take the new member classes. I became an associate member, which gave me all the privileges of a full member, except that I was still able to retain my membership in my home church in London, Ontario.

Later, I served on the nominating committee and as a deacon. One of the special privileges of being a deacon was to serve communion to my fellow worshippers. I became more aware of the meaning of this ordinance by actively participating as a server.

Seeing Mt. Mayon

Because my work schedule was so heavy, I realized that I needed to take a break whenever I could. In November of 1978, I fulfilled a dream I'd had for some time. Mt. Mayon, an active volcano, sits on the southern tip of Luzon near the city of Legazpi. It is the world's most perfect cone and the most active volcano in the Philippines, having erupted forty-nine times in four hundred years. In 1814, the town of Cagsawa was completely buried. Today only the church's bell tower is visible rising above the surface under which the town lies. In May of 1978, Mt. Mayon erupted again, sending lava cascading down its sides.

Mayon is a popular photo for postcards as are the ruins of Cagsawa. When I could take a break from work, I organized a trip to Legazpi. Heather, Marji Cook, who also worked in our office, Alice Davis, and Elizabeth Smith squeezed into my car for the twelve-hour trip. Alice and Elizabeth came from Nepal with Heather when the SIL work closed. We had all become good friends during their time in Manila and looked forward to an adventure together.

We left at 7:00 a.m., driving south on the highway that began at Aparri on the north coast of Luzon and ran all the way to Davao on the south coast of Mindanao. Ferries connected the islands of Luzon and Samar, and Cebu and Mindanao in two places. This road was still under construction in 1978, so we drove through some rough patches as we wound our way through the mountains south of Manila. Part of our trip took us along the ocean where we enjoyed the sight of palm trees and sandy beaches. By 7:00 p.m., we arrived in Legazpi and found the hotel we were to stay in.

Mt. Mayon's eruption the previous summer had calmed down so that now all we could see was a small plume of steam rising from the top of the cone. We drove partway up the eastern slope to the Philippine Institute of Volcanology and Seismology (PHIVOLCS) station, where we had a tour and could see the seismograph in operation. Then we drove farther north to Tiwi, the location of the large geothermal plant that provided electricity for much of southern Luzon. Our trip back to Legazpi took us past Cagsawa, the site of the buried town.

On our return trip to Manila, we had a broken fan belt in Naga City so were delayed on our arrival home. I was beginning to think that I should plan for car trouble in every long trip I took, since it always seemed to happen.

ফ৯ফ৯

Western Bukidnon Manobo New Testament Dedication

In early December of 1978, I received from the printer in Manila the sixth New Testament to be completed in the Philippines and arranged for its shipment to Mindanao. Dick and Betty Elkins were the translators of this New Testament.

The little wooden church at Barandias was gaily decorated for the Christmas program. Palm fronds framed the doorway, and colored streamers twirled in the breeze. After the morning rain, the sun streamed through the gaps in the walls, lighting the dark interior.

Wooden benches were filled with Western Bukidnon Manobo people— some mothers with their babies, young girls in brightly colored dresses, dozens of children, and a sprinkling of older men and women. Those who couldn't find places on the benches sat on the cement floor or crowded around outside to see and hear what they could.

The Christmas program was the biggest annual event for the Barandias church. Many who did not ordinarily worship there gathered for the two-hour program. Friday, December 22, was no exception, with about two hundred people present.

But this year's program was special. On a table at the front of the church were two piles of brand new books—the *Western Bukidnon Manobo New*

Testament. The first fifty copies had arrived from Manila just in time for the Christmas program.

Amid the noise of babies crying, conversations, and people pushing their way inside, Christmas hymns and special musical items were followed by the Christmas story read from the new book by Mecaria Kinumpas, a former lay pastor of the church who had helped check the translated New Testament.

The present lay pastor, Catalino Libo, led the service, and his son, Winifredo, trained in literacy by SIL members George and Valery Hires, told the Christmas story using flash cards. A spokesman from a related language group, Tigwa Manobo, asked for prayer, and then Dick Elkins, translator for the Western Bukidnon Manobo, dedicated the new books to God.

Dick and his wife, Betty, first started working among the Manobo people in 1953 and were delighted to find that their first language assistant was a believer. Dick said that when he told him why they had come to the Philippines, the man wept and said, "For fifteen years, I have prayed that my people might have the Word of God in their own language, and now you have come. This is the hand of God."

Dick also paid tribute to his main language assistant, Rosito Lumansay, now confined to bed in the last stages of terminal cancer: "He was a marvelous help to us—faithful and sharp. I just cannot express my thanks enough to the Lord for Rosito and for what he has meant to us." Rosito could no longer talk, but when Dick handed him a copy of *The New Way* (the New Testament), he nodded a "thank you," put his arm around it, and just held it against his chest for a while.

The translation job wasn't always easy. When Rosito committed his life to Christ, his family disowned him. They had the pagan priest come to sacrifice to appease angry spirits. Another man, Siblian, lost his whole rice crop in 1985, staying out of his fields in order to work on the Gospel of Mark with Dick.

And during the revision process, Dick and Betty wrote, "The opposition has been very strong, and week after week, almost, something comes up to distract us, to make us anxious, and to turn our minds from our work. It is encouraging to know that what we're doing is so important to God that Satan has expended this much effort to oppose us."

But it was worth it all, and Dick said, "It was a marvelous experience for me to look out on that group of people [at the dedication], to speak to them in Manobo, and to tell them why we had come."

Iney Piyano summed it up like this: "How happy I am and how grateful we are for the Book. We had many gods—the baliti trees, graves of dead people, stones, and waterfalls, but now, praise God, our American brother and sister came and brought God's Word."

Following dedicatory prayers, copies of the New Testament were given to the ten Manobos who had helped in the checking work. The director of a local Bible Institute gave a message, stressing the importance of God's Word and the greatness of His love in sending the "Word made flesh"—His own Son.

That Sunday, Christmas Eve, an unsolicited testimony from Men-Irning gave Dick and Betty one of the finest Christmas presents they would ever receive. He said, "Long ago we never dreamed that the Word of God would be translated into our language, but now we have the Book. God acted long ago so that our American brother and sister would come translate for us. They became tools in the hands of God, and now the Word is like a shining star for us."

Then came Christmas. The wind blew as usual, ladies went to the water to wash as usual, men plowed, and to the small community around Barandias, it might have been any other day of the year—but not for Dick and Betty Elkins, the Manobo church, or the hundreds who prayed and helped. The day not only marked the birth of their Savior but also the first Christmas when the entire New Testament could be held and read by Western Bukidnon Manobo believers.

Although I wasn't able to attend this dedication, I gave thanks to God for allowing me to have a part in getting His Word into the hands of these believers.

Chapter 30
Furlough and Medical Problems
1979

Christmas for us in Manila was a special time. We enjoyed the decorations, attended the *Nutcracker* ballet at the culture center, celebrated with our office staff at the annual party, and stuffed ourselves at the SIL turkey dinner at the guesthouse on Christmas Eve. Following dinner, we went to church for the Christmas Eve candlelight service. Then everyone proceeded to the parking lot, carrying lit candles and singing "Silent Night." The staff had lined the sidewalks around the church with luminaries—brown paper bags with sand in the bottom holding lit candles.

Following the service, I invited all of the SIL singles to come to my apartment for cookies and eggnog and to exchange gifts.

Since they had no family, an older couple from the church invited me for dinner on Christmas Day. They lived in a beautiful mansion in the upper-class part of the city, and they had arranged gorgeous decorations from many parts of the world throughout their home.

Planning for Furlough

By February of 1979, I started planning for my next furlough that was due in May. I flew to Nasuli for a two-week furlough workshop, at which I prepared messages, slide presentations, a photo album, and other materials for use when speaking to my supporting churches at home. I found this workshop especially beneficial, since I didn't have time when I was working to prepare the things I would need on furlough.

By now my car was showing its age. The hot, humid, somewhat salty air of Manila was hard on the body, which had rust in many places. Repairs were costing more than I wished to pay. Since several people were interested in buying it, I decided to sell it before leaving for home. I would order a new one when I returned the following year. I had my parents looking for a car for me while on furlough, since I would need one to get around. I also made plans to spend three months in Dallas to take the training course for the computer system that we had put in two years previously.

Preparations for furlough included training someone to do my job while I was gone. Gary and Diane Persons had recently begun their work in Bolinao, so Gary agreed to come to Manila for the six months I planned to be away to fill in for me. He and Diane would come to Manila a month or so before I left, so we could have a good length of training time and he would feel comfortable with the job details.

In March I had another new experience. As I celebrated my forty-second birthday, I went to the circus for the first time in my life. A large international circus set up at our coliseum, so some of my friends and I went. We saw tightrope walking done on stilts, trapeze artists, balancing acts, jugglers, a lion tamer, and some really good clowns. Heather had been to many circuses in Australia, but she said this was the best she had ever seen. We attended a matinee performance with twenty-five thousand other people. One night the Filipino house helpers from our guesthouse went together. They were so excited, they couldn't eat their popcorn.

The weeks flew by quickly. The Persons arrived, and Gary was busy learning my job. He learned quickly and was soon able to handle most of the work. This gave me time to prepare for my trip. I was planning to leave on May 22. Heather was staying in the apartment with a new worker, who was attending language school. I needed to get some new clothes made, since everything I had was either worn out or too short, now that skirt lengths had gotten longer again.

Family Visits

On my way home, I stopped in Calgary for a few days and took the bus to Gull Lake to see Marj and her family. They were in the process of building a large cedar log house that came in a package from British Columbia. Every piece was numbered and stored in a warehouse in Gull Lake until the foundation was completed and the builders could put it together. In May the foundation was under construction on a knoll overlooking the Trans-Canada highway four miles (6 kilometers) from town. I looked forward to seeing the house when it was completed. It would have a large living room, dining room, kitchen, family room, laundry room, and five bedrooms. The four Sawatsky children were growing and looked forward to relocating to the country. As one said, "What's the point in being a farmer's kid if you have to live in town?"

While I was in Gull Lake, Marj and I planned for Mom and Dad's fiftieth wedding anniversary that we would celebrate in July. Their anniversary was May 18, but it was still quite cold in Ontario that early. Since their house wasn't very large, we wanted to have the celebration outside on the lawn. Marj planned to drive to Ontario with her four children to attend the party. Vic would stay home to take care of the farm.

I flew home from Regina and began making arrangements for the anniversary. I needed a car to drive. I found that Mom had been saving money for me during my last term and had a thousand dollars in the bank. A lady from my parents' church gave me another thousand, so I was able to buy a 1976 Pontiac Duster. These gifts were a surprise to me. God knew that I couldn't afford to make car payments while on furlough and that I needed a new car when I returned to the Philippines. The sale of this car and my old one would give me a good down payment when I returned to Manila.

The anniversary celebration went very well. The weather was perfect—warm and sunny but not too hot. Marj and her brood arrived in her Volkswagen Beetle and were a big help with the final decorations and last-minute cooking and serving. I had baked cookies for several weeks. My sister, Nell, her husband, Gary, and their two boys arrived from Quebec and Art and Bonnie from Toronto.

On the day of the celebration, seventy people gathered on the lawn. It was to be come-and-go, but many people stayed most of the afternoon. We welcomed friends and relatives that I hadn't seen for years. We went to a studio and had a family picture taken. The evening before the celebration, we went out for dinner together to a good restaurant in Talbotville, three miles from St. Thomas. Mom and Dad were happy, and we had a wonderful family time together.

For the rest of the summer, I had meetings that kept me occupied until it was time to go to Dallas in late August. Carol Heim, who had worked in our publicity department in Manila as a short-term assistant, returned home that year also. She lived in Berwick, Pennsylvania, not far from Wilkes-Barre. Her parents had come to visit her while she was in Manila, and I had taken them all to Ifugao to visit Anne and Helen. Carol had decided to become a full member of Wycliffe and needed to attend the linguistic training course, so we arranged to travel to Dallas together.

In August I drove to Berwick and spent a day with Carol and her folks before leaving for Waxhaw, North Carolina, not far from Charlotte, where we planned to spend a couple of days visiting former Philippine branch members that we knew. Waxhaw is the location of Wycliffe's Jungle Aviation and Radio Service (JAARS) center, the headquarters for the aviation, radio, and computer operations.

Carol had friends in Charlotte, so our plan was to drive from Berwick to their place and spend the night with them. It was a long day's drive, especially for Carol, since she had never driven a standard-shift car before and found it stressful. She was brave though and took her turn helping with the driving. We arrived just in time for dinner at her friends' house.

199

While we were waiting for dinner to be served, I felt a strange fluttering in my chest. It lasted for only a few minutes and then stopped. I thought nothing of it, guessing I was just tired after our long drive. We went on to the JAARS center the next day and enjoyed our visit with friends there. Our trip across the south to Dallas was uneventful.

Typesetting Training

The SIL International Linguistics Center had been built on one-hundred acres of land that was purchased in 1971. It is located on the southwest corner of Dallas adjacent to Duncanville. This is the headquarters of SIL International and now houses the Graduate Institute of Linguistics as well as office space for partner organizations. In 1979 the printing arts department (PAD) was situated in two houses across the street in a housing development known as Sunset Acres.

This was to be my workplace for the coming months. Walt Agee was the director of PAD at that time. I had met him in 1975 when I made the trip to investigate the new typesetting system. Ted Goller conducted my typesetting training. He had been working in Scripture typesetting for a number of years. When he retired in 2006, he had the distinction of having been involved with typesetting 175 New Testaments and Bibles, more than anyone else in the world.

It was late when we arrived on the center, so I stayed overnight in the dormitory until I could find out where I would be living. Mary Dobson was a retired missionary from India, who had a two-bedroom apartment in Duncanville. She had agreed to take me in for the four months I planned to be there. Mary was in her sixties and had a daughter and two grandchildren living in Duncanville. We all became good friends, and since I didn't know many people in Duncanville when I arrived, I appreciated being taken in as one of their family.

Mary attended the Duncanville Presbyterian Church. I went with her the first Sunday and enjoyed an excellent sermon and good singing, so I decided to attend there regularly. A number of Wycliffe members were in the congregation. The choir was off for the summer, but I was invited to join them when they resumed in two weeks. Because I had missed the Union Church choir since arriving home, I decided to do that and found it to be a worshipful experience. The pastor's wife led an excellent Bible study before the morning service, which I also attended.

My typesetting course was mind stretching, but because I had already used the program for two years, I knew quite a bit of the contents already. Ted was a hard taskmaster, but I appreciated his insistence on excellence, and I learned quickly. At the end of one month, I had completed the material and now needed practice. Soon I was working on real material, a New Testament from Africa, which was encouraging. I loved the work and felt useful as I went to work every day.

A Surprise Wedding

In September I missed June Fulkerson's wedding. June had spent a year in Kenya teaching at a girls' school under the auspices of the Canadian University Services Overseas (CUSO). She returned home and went back to work in London, Ontario. Her parents had both passed away by this time, and she lived alone in the family home that my father had helped build.

One day she received a phone call from Alberta. Her brother Irwin lived in Calgary, but the call wasn't from him. It was from Howard Spencer, the airman she had been engaged to during World War II. After Howard was discharged from the air force following the war, he returned to Saskatchewan to the farm, where he married and had two children. They were both grown now, and his wife had died some time before.

One day he was in Calgary to buy parts for his tractor. He was paging through the phone book, looking for a phone number, when he spotted the name *Fulkerson*. He thought of June and wondered what had become of her. On a whim, he called the number and discovered it belonged to June's brother. Upon learning that she had never married, he got her phone number and contacted her.

June was now sixty-one years old, but the sound of Howard's voice on the phone brought back memories of years ago when she had planned to marry him. Many phone calls later, June flew to Calgary, where she met Howard for the first time in almost forty years. She returned to Ontario wearing an engagement ring.

Howard and June were married in London in September 1979 and moved to Calgary, where they bought a small house, just right for the two of them. I was sorry to miss their wedding, but I visited them many times through the years when I would come there on furlough. Their story inspired me, and I've shared it with many people.

Medical Problems

I hadn't been feeling as well as usual that fall and wondered if something was wrong with me. I had a physical with my doctor in London when I got home from the Philippines in the spring. He said he didn't find anything wrong. I had lost five pounds, but he didn't worry about that. I did though, since I had never been able to lose weight without working at it very hard.

201

I noticed during September and early October that my emotions were a bit on edge. I often felt like crying when I didn't have anything to cry about. I felt shaky, needing to hold onto the handrail when I went downstairs. I even had difficulty putting on nail polish.

Finally, I decided to see the doctor at the center. He was an elderly, retired doctor who volunteered his time to care for SIL members who lived and worked there. After talking with me, he decided that I was probably beginning menopause and recommended hormone replacement therapy. I didn't want to do that so thought I'd see if I could survive without it.

Nadine Lyman, who had worked for a number of years at Nasuli as the director's secretary, wanted a change of jobs. She had agreed to take over the management of the publications department at Nasuli when she returned from furlough, so she had come to Dallas to train for typesetting. We were both returning at about the same time so needed to get our visas. The closest Philippine embassy was in Houston. In mid-October we drove there for a couple of days to get our visas. We discovered that we needed to have physicals by a Filipino doctor who was connected to the embassy. Fortunately, he was able to do it that day, which meant we only needed to spend two nights in Houston.

When the doctor examined me, he said, "Your heart beat is too fast, your blood pressure is too high, I hear a heart murmur, and you seem to have an enlarged thyroid. I suggest you see your doctor when you return to Dallas." This surprised me. I didn't have a doctor in Dallas other than the one I had seen on the center, and I didn't have much faith in him.

We returned to Dallas, and I asked if anyone knew of a family practice doctor who might be able to take a new patient in a hurry. Someone suggested Dr. Don Christiansen in Duncanville. When I checked with him in the morning, he was able to see me that day. As I sat in his office, he talked to me a bit and then said, "Hold out your hands." I did so, and he laid a file folder on them. It jumped up and down from the tremor.

"I suspect you have a thyroid problem. We'll do some blood work to check it out."

That night after dinner, I was sitting in my usual chair watching TV when I felt the flutter in my chest that I had felt that day in Charlotte. This time it didn't stop. By 9:00 p.m., I said to Mary, "I think we should go to emergency at the hospital. I'd like to know what's going on, and I won't sleep feeling like this."

At the hospital, I said to the woman at the desk in emergency, "I'm not sure, but I think there might be something wrong with my heart. Could I get it checked out?" She calmly pointed to a chair and asked me to sit there. In a few minutes, a doctor appeared and took my pulse. His eyebrows went up, and he moved very fast.

In no time, I was on a stretcher and then in a bed with a monitor attached. My heart was beating more than two hundred beats a minute. He asked me some questions, and I told him what Dr. Christiansen had said that morning. He called him, but it was too soon to have results from the blood test. I was given some medication and admitted to the Duncanville hospital.

The next day I had a visit from an internist who said that my blood work showed that I had a hyperthyroid condition with normal for the blood test being three to eleven, and my reading was twenty-one. He also said that the mortality rate for a thyroid crisis, which I had had, was 50 percent without rapid treatment. I would need to stay in the hospital until the medication lowered my vital signs enough to make it safe for me to walk around. That took thirteen days.

I felt good most of the time, so I had a somewhat boring rest in the hospital. Since I didn't know many people in the area and those I did know were working, I had few visitors. I spent most of my days reading books or watching television.

When I finally was released, I had an appointment to go to the Methodist Central Hospital in downtown Dallas to drink ten millicuries of radioactive iodine, which would destroy much of my thyroid function, requiring me to take thyroid medication for the rest of my life. The doctor at the nuclear medicine department assured me that nobody ever has any reaction to this treatment.

Now he couldn't say that any more, since it made me high, as if I were drunk. I went to work in the afternoon but found everything funny. When someone told a joke at lunchtime, I laughed so hard, I cried. I couldn't stop talking, and I ended up almost hysterical. The drug reaction wore off by mid-afternoon, for which I was very thankful.

I was required to remain in Dallas for two months for follow-up to be sure that the radioactive iodine had done its job. I had planned to return to the Philippines in late November by way of Australia where Heather and I would have a holiday together. That had to be cancelled. Then I heard that she had been asked to teach at the SIL school there in December, so our holiday would have been cancelled anyway.

My parents were planning to go to Marj and Vic's house for Christmas, so I decided to join them and leave for the Philippines after the holidays. I sold my car to the son of the director of the childcare center and caught a flight to Regina via Chicago. I arrived on the Saturday before Christmas without my suitcase, which didn't arrive until Monday on the bus. Fortunately, Marj's oldest daughter, Ann, had a dress that fit me, so I didn't have to go to church on Sunday in my traveling clothes.

Marj and Vic had just moved into their new house two weeks earlier. It was beautiful, and they were quite well settled, in spite of the short time they had to get everything arranged for visitors. We enjoyed our time together, the last I would see them for another four years. I flew to Los Angeles and left from there for the Philippines on January 12, 1980.

Chapter 31
The Tenth New Testament
1980–1982

Anne West stayed with me in Manila while we typeset the Amganad Ifugao New Testament, and she also studied Tagalog. One day she received word from home that her mother had cancer, and the doctors did not expect her to live very long. Anne packed up immediately and flew to Tucson, Arizona, where her parents lived.

Again I had no roommate for a while, but pilot Bob Griffin's daughter, Becky, now in Manila, needed a place to stay, so she moved into Anne's room. I enjoyed having her and her cat. The cat didn't like me at first, spitting at me when I tried to pick her up, but she adjusted and soon jumped up on my lap without being asked.

Anne's mother's cancer progressed rapidly, taking her life on December 31, 1980. Anne returned to the Philippines the second week of January. Her father talked of going with her but felt he wouldn't have anything to do, since Anne would be busy working, so he decided to come for the New Testament dedication instead.

Amganad New Testament Dedication

We had finished our part on the Amganad New Testament in the fall, and we sent it to the printer. Anne set the dedication for March 14, 1981. When Anne and I first went to Amganad in 1967, the area had almost no believers. Now fourteen years later, a growing congregation numbered about one hundred people. Scattered throughout the mountains of the area, forty more churches had sprung up as small Scripture portions became available in the language that communicated to the people.

I attended the dedication of the New Testament with great joy. I drove to Ifugao, accompanied by Hugh and Joan Barrie from the Philadelphia area. They had come to Manila for Hugh to set up the computer system for the Central Bank of the Philippines. They had worked as volunteers at the Wycliffe center in Colombia, South America, previously, so Joan came to our office to see if she could help. I needed a typist at that time, so she typed Scriptures.

The New Testament was a lovely black-and-gold, hardcovered book of over one thousand pages. We had typeset it in a large font to help those who had poor eyesight, were just learning to read, or who had only candles to read by at night. The New York International Bible Society provided the major part of the funds for publishing. The rest came from memorial gifts for Anne's mother.

The dedication program was held on Saturday morning. It consisted of special numbers by church choirs, greetings from local officials, testimonies from Ifugao Christians, presentation of copies to those who had assisted in the translation, a prayer of dedication, and an inspiring message by Frank Allen, field chairman for the Far Eastern Gospel Crusade, the church-planting mission working in Ifugao. The service lasted three hours.

When I listened to the testimonies from vibrant Ifugao Christians and saw the hundreds of believers eager to buy New Testaments, tears ran down my cheeks as I thanked God for the part I had played in making this possible.

The day was hot and sunny, so people crowded under the white nylon tarp that shaded the seating area. I sat under my umbrella for part of the time, but eventually, even that wasn't enough, so I found a spot in a shelter that had been built to one side. After the program, the Amganad church members served a lunch of rice, pork, and cabbage to over seven hundred people.

Then came time to buy the available copies. We could get only two hundred copies from the print shop in time for the dedication. Within half an hour, they were all gone, and many people cried for more. We sent them later. The book sold for $1.30, about one-fourth the printing cost. But by subsidizing them, they were cheap enough for anyone to afford one.

The night before the New Testament dedication, a new Ifugao hymnbook, prepared by Janet Davis of FEGC, was also dedicated, and over five hundred copies were sold that weekend.

The Amganad Ifugao New Testament was the tenth that SIL completed in the Philippines. The eleventh came off the press the end of April, and eight more were in various stages of publication.

I thanked God for giving me a job I enjoyed and could do well. But sometimes when the work piled up or I was too tired, I felt that a translator's job was more important. All I did was look at a computer all day.

So it was good for me to attend as many dedications as I could. Then I realized that my part in getting God's Word into the hands of those who had never heard was essential. Only then could they come to know and love Him.

This Book is important to His people everywhere.

Chapter 32
More Dedications
1982–1983

I have always loved cats. We had several when I was growing up, and I preferred to play with them rather than with dolls. I hadn't had a cat since I left Nasuli in 1969. I was too busy at work to miss one, but when Becky Griffin came to live with me and brought her cat, I realized how much I missed having one. However, the group's watchdog killed it, which made us both very sad.

When Anne came back from her mother's funeral, she moved back in with me, and Becky stayed with the Rollos, who were now working in Manila and had an extra bedroom.

On a trip to Bagabag in March, I discovered that a family there had a kitten to give away, so I decided to become a cat owner again. She was a six-week-old calico with markings very similar to Patty, the cat Anne and I had in Ifugao. I called her Patty II. She was still a kitten and quite rambunctious, but as she grew up, she became a beautiful cat. When she was six months old, we had a woman from Ifugao and one of her children staying with us while her husband was in the hospital. We were unable to keep Patty in the house, since the children were in and out, often leaving the door open.

Before long we had a batch of kittens on the way. Patty had three fat, healthy kittens, which we managed to give away, two to some friends and one to a couple in Bagabag. Since we didn't have any neighbors in the city clamoring for cats to keep the rats down, I soon took Patty to the vet down the street to be spayed. Forcing down antibiotic tablets, applying ointment to the wound, and keeping a bandage on the incision so she wouldn't lick off the ointment was almost impossible. I wrapped her in a towel like a straight jacket. Anne held her down while I applied the medicine. The surgery hardly slowed her down at all, except that her jumping up on things was a bit slower than usual.

Vacation Travels

I was entitled to a month of vacation each year but never took it all at one time. I needed breaks from the stress of work more often so usually went away for a week at a time. In May of 1981, Marge Moran, Judy Wallace, and I explored parts of northern Luzon. I had never been to the north coast of Luzon, so I picked up Marge and Judy at Bagabag, and we drove north to Tuguegarao and then south of the city a short distance to the town of Enrile.

Chuck and Mickey Richards lived there, translating the New Testament for the Itawes people. They were not with SIL but attended our workshops, and our consultants checked their work. They eventually checked for many of our translators in return. We got to know them, as they spent time at Bagabag and stayed at our guesthouse in Manila. They had often invited me to visit them in Enrile, so Marge, Judy, and I decided this would be a good opportunity to see where they lived and to meet some of the people with whom they worked.

When we arrived in the late afternoon, Chuck and Mickey greeted us. They lived in a lovely house in the middle of town. Our two days with them was interesting, informative, and fun as we shared many stories from our past.

From Enrile, we drove north and then west to spend two days with Claudia Whittle and Ruth Lusted, who lived at Pamplona on the north coast, very close to the ocean. They were translating for the Atta, a Negrito group, who had settled in the Pamplona area. We spent two nights with Claudia and Ruth, enjoying the cool breezes from the ocean. In the morning, we went to the beach for a swim but soon had to return home when a ferocious thunderstorm came up.

From Pamplona we drove across northern Luzon where the road runs along the ocean, sometimes high above the water, sometimes closer to the beach. All day we enjoyed gorgeous views across the South China Sea. By late afternoon, we had rounded the tip of Luzon and were heading south down the west coast, arriving in the city of Laoag, where we spent the night in a hotel.

The next morning we set off early to continue our trip. A few miles from Laoag, we stopped at a restaurant along the highway for breakfast. A fisherman had just arrived from spending the night in his fishing boat on the sea. He had delivered freshly caught lapu-lapu, one of the most delicious fish to be had in that part of the world. We waited for the cook to prepare it for us and enjoyed freshly cooked rice and lapu-lapu, which fortified us for our trip down the west cost of Luzon.

Since this was summer, many flowers were in full bloom. Someone had planted bougainvillea bushes on both sides of the highway. Their brilliant rose-and-white blossoms were feasts of color as we drove between them for many miles.

Later in the day, we arrived at Vigan City, an historic Hispanic city dating from the sixteenth century. The city has many ancient buildings erected by the Spaniards when they controlled the Philippines. We spent the rest of the day exploring the numerous old buildings set on cobblestone streets and enjoying the flowering gardens that surrounded many houses. We stayed overnight in a hotel that dated from a previous century. We thought the air-conditioner must have been almost as old as the building, since it rattled and banged its way through the night.

From Vigan we drove to Baguio, where I dropped off Marge and Judy so they could catch a bus to Sagada and home to Bogang. In Baguio I spent a night with the staff at teachers' camp, since the summer course was just completed. Betty and Dick Elkins returned to Manila with me, along with all the books and supplies that had been used during the summer.

By August, Anne had completed her Tagalog studies. Now she was helping Char Houck complete her New Testament. This task would take about two years. I was, once again, without a housemate.

Margaret Blowers, a new secretary for the director's office, arrived from Australia about this time. After getting to know her a bit, I invited her to live with me with the hope that she would stay for some time, since she was a full member on a four-year term. I was used to Australian ways, since I'd lived with Heather Kilgour for some time and felt we would get along fine.

Choir Joys

The choir at Union Church was still a big part of my life. When Heather and I first joined, the choir had about fifteen members. Now it had grown to thirty-five. In September we participated in a choir festival and had to learn five numbers by heart as our entry. For some time before the festival, we practiced almost every evening. It was a noncompetitive festival, so there was no judging, but we felt it went well. The Manila Symphony Association televised it for use on their TV program later.

By early October, we began practicing for our Christmas concert, which was to be a full evening concert. On top of the concert practice, we had to learn music for the Sunday services when we sang four numbers—an introit, a call to prayer, an anthem, and a benediction. Every Wednesday I left work at 4:30 p.m. to drive to Makati, where the church is located. We had a light supper and then practiced until 9:00 o'clock. I usually arrived home by 9:30, a quick trip for the eight miles (twelve kilometers), since by then the rush hour traffic had finished for the day.

More About Blood Donations

A few years after coming to Manila, I began donating blood. Since Filipino blood is more than 99 percent Rh-positive, there is little call for Rh-negative blood. Because it only keeps for less than a month, the blood banks in the Philippines didn't store Rh-negative blood, so when it was needed, usually for a foreigner or a Filipino with mixed blood, a call went out for a donor. The American Association maintained a list of Rh-negative blood donors, who could be contacted when blood was needed. My blood is A-negative, so I placed my name on their list. As a project one year, students at Faith Academy surveyed the missionary community and collected names of people with Rh-negative blood types for an additional list of people who could be called on when needed.

The first time I was called, I didn't know what to expect, since I had never donated blood before. After checking my hemoglobin to be sure I wasn't anemic, I lay on a recliner, and a nurse inserted a needle into the vein on my inner right elbow. This was nothing new, since I had blood drawn regularly for my thyroid checks, and I have a very good vein there. The nurse sat beside me and talked to me while the blood flowed from my arm into a plastic bag that contained 50 ccs. of anticoagulant. In about ten minutes, the bag was full. The nurse removed the needle and gave me a glass of juice and some cookies. After consuming these, I was free to go. I felt nothing.

I didn't know how often I would be called to donate blood and didn't think to keep track of the amount I gave over the years. I guess it would be at least twenty times or more, probably in the neighborhood of two to three gallons.

I only had trouble once. I was at work late one morning when I received a call to go to a nearby hospital. Since it was nearly lunchtime, I said I would eat my lunch and then go. When the donation was completed and I was ready to leave, I suddenly felt faint. I sat down on a bench and got my head down, kneeling with my forehead on the floor.

The next thing I knew, I was lying on a bed with someone holding a vile-smelling bottle near my nose. I had passed right out. I stayed there for a few minutes and then was able to stand up. I was afraid to drive home, since I didn't know what had caused me to faint and didn't want it to happen again in the middle of Manila's heavy traffic. So I called the office, and Norm Purvis, one of our associate directors, agreed to come. He took a taxi to the hospital, so he could drive my car home.

Since I never felt faint again after giving blood, I decided that, since I had just eaten lunch, my blood was all in my stomach digesting my food.

When the extraction lowered my blood volume, I didn't have enough to give adequate flow to my brain, thus causing me to pass out. After that I was always careful to donate blood before eating, not after.

Sarangani Blaan New Testament Dedication

By November of 1981, we had completed and dedicated New Testaments for twelve language groups in the Philippines. The twelfth was the Sarangani Blaan, translated by Barbara Blackburn and Mary Rhea.

The Blaan live in southern Mindanao, several hours from General Santos City. On the day of the dedication, more than one thousand Blaans came from the mountains around, over wet and muddy trails, and some over eighteen river crossings, to witness the four-hour dedication program. Blaan believers gave testimonies, local speakers told of the value of the Scriptures in their language, choirs sang, and people bought copies of the newly printed New Testament. The local women wrapped eight hundred servings of rice in banana leaves to feed the crowd. It was an exciting time as people finally held copies of God's Word in their hands in the language dear to their hearts. But thousands of Blaans couldn't read. Literacy programs were in process, but much work still needed to be done.

Six more New Testaments were in process by early 1982. I found my time occupied keeping up with the work, not just typesetting New Testaments and following them through the printing process but also managing the record keeping of all the materials that were printed at both Nasuli and Bagabag.

After Christmas 1981, I took another break and flew to Singapore with Hazel Wrigglesworth to shop and sightsee. We found a special package that included accommodations in a good hotel and breakfast for a reasonable price. Like Hong Kong, Singapore is a duty-free city, so we had a long list of things to buy for ourselves and for others in the Philippines. We attended the Wesley Methodist Church on Sunday, a large evangelical congregation near our hotel. We went with Jackie Maier, the Wycliffe representative in Singapore at the time. She introduced us to a group of her friends and took us for lunch to a Singaporean fast-food place, where I ate a number of dishes that were new to me.

While in Singapore, we met with a young Singaporean couple, Michael and Soo Jong Wee, who had visited us in Manila several times. They took us around, first to the Jurong Bird Park, which contains birds from all over the world. We went to a Chinese noodle house for lunch and to their apartment in the evening. They had only been married a few months and didn't have much furniture in their tenth floor apartment. But it was wonderful to see where they lived and to visit with them again.

Furlough Workshop and Conference

Furlough was coming up in 1983, so I attended the annual furlough workshop at Nasuli to prepare for it. I had taken the workshop before my 1978 furlough but felt it would be good to have a refresher and to have time to prepare materials for presentation when at home. I also enjoyed getting updated on what was new in the church world at home as well as having a good break from the Manila office.

Conference took us all to Nasuli again in June of 1982. Anne and I stayed with Hazel in her guest room on the ground floor. We elected Dave Ohlson as our new director, since Len and Jo Newell were planning a furlough that year. They now had two children of their own and were in the process of adopting Lisa, a Filipina baby they had brought home when she was only a few weeks old. The process of adopting was lengthy, and they were hoping their furlough would not be delayed.

While at conference, we sixty-four single women had a picnic after church on Sunday. It was potluck except for the dessert that consisted of two big birthday cakes to celebrate two of our number who had birthdays that week.

June is the beginning of rainy season, and although it was very hot that year, one day it rained so hard that everyone who spoke from the floor had to go to the front to use the microphone since the roof of the meeting hall was galvanized iron and nobody could be heard.

David Cummings, the new president of WBT International, was the spiritual emphasis speaker that conference. His messages were exactly what we all needed. His wife, Ruth, came with him, and we enjoyed getting to know her.

Conference wasn't all meetings. We had many fun times as well, including a hilarious skit night, and a cantata put together by one of our musical ladies. It consisted of a collection of praise hymns; psalms; special numbers by a small ensemble of three guitars, two flutes, and the piano; and two numbers by the children's choir. The adult choir consisted of forty-five of us. On Sunday afternoon, four of the children were baptized in the natural pool, and in the evening, we all participated in a communion service.

My job during conference was to take minutes of the business meetings for three days. At other times, as I listened and participated in the discussions, I also embroidered a tablecloth. It had been the custom for people to do handwork during the meetings. I had hooked a rug, embroidered a pillowcase, and embroidered a set of napkins at earlier times. At each conference, someone was assigned as a reporter to produce a conference newspaper when it was over. A poll was taken, and a list of the handwork completed during conference was always listed. The most memorable production was by Carl DuBois, who each conference wove a hammock, strung across the front row of benches.

Back in Manila, I enjoyed the single adults group at church. We had regular social activities, which were especially good for many whose work brought them to Manila for short times. Some were lonely and needed the fellowship of a group of Christians with whom to associate. This was an international group with members coming from Japan, Indonesia, England, Korea, Australia, the US, Canada, and the Philippines.

One meeting was at the Metropolitan Club in Makati where we gathered for dinner, a meeting, and a swim in their Olympic-sized swimming pool. The club set up a buffet just for our group of nineteen, consisting of salads, beans, carrots, rice, mashed potatoes, fish, roast beef, and a dessert tray of brownies, cookies, and custard. One of the men was leaving the Philippines, so we had a farewell cake for him. I became good friends with several of these international business and diplomatic people.

Handicrafts for Sale

Folks in many of the language groups in the Philippines where our teams were working produced beautiful handicrafts of various descriptions. People who visited us and stayed in the guesthouse often commented on samples they saw. They wanted to know how they could purchase them. I decided to set up a display case of the various popular crafts and make them available for purchase. I commissioned one of the men in the workshop to build a display cabinet with locks where I could place the weavings, beadwork, and shell work that our teams provided for me.

In no time, I had a thriving business. I sold the materials for the prices set by the creators. I had Tboli bead necklaces, Ifugao placemats and bookmarks, Northern Kankanay handbags, shell dolls from the Calamian Tagbanwa, marble carvings from Romblon, and various other small items. I only handled items from language groups with whom our translators were working.

Sometimes keeping track of the things for sale and ordering new stock kept me busy in my spare time. I enjoyed doing this, since it gave a sales outlet for people who didn't have a good source for marketing their handicrafts.

Balangao New Testament Dedication

The fourteenth New Testament had arrived from the printer, the Balangao translated by Jo Shetler and her Balangao translation partners. A few years previously, Australian Robyn Terry had joined Jo to head up the literacy program, since thousands of Balangaos didn't know how to read. Jo and Robyn were excited to see the New Testament finally available and joined Balangao church leaders to plan a dedication program to present to the Balangao churches.

Since I hadn't been back to Natunin since my first month in the Philippines in 1967, I decided to attend the dedication. I drove to Bagabag and then on to Banaue, since Janet Davis needed a ride from Manila and I needed a new stock of Ifugao weavings for the display case. We stopped at Hilda's house, since she was providing the weavings I bought for sale. It was good to see her again and her children, who were growing quickly. She had a new baby girl not long before.

The next day, a Saturday, we flew into Balangao, a twenty-minute flight from Bagabag. It had rained hard the night before, and the trail from the airstrip to the church where the dedication was to be held, was muddy and slippery. The hike took a half hour, and the next day my knees let me know that I was out of shape. Balangao men carried our baggage down the trail and sometimes helped us when the trail was exceptionally slippery.

Because the church wasn't big enough to hold all the people, the service was held on a hillside below the church where men had cut seats in the ground to make an amphitheater. They built a canopy of palm leaves, blankets, and tarps over the area as a rain and sun protection for the more than one thousand people who came. Although it was the rainy season, people prayed for good weather. God answered, and the sun shone all day.

Some of the program was planned and written out, but the rest was held freestyle. Anyone could talk, and everyone was invited to sing, and sing they did. Some groups of women sang songs they had written about the New Testament and the dedication celebration, and some sang impromptu songs about the eighty-two American visitors. Each village had prepared its own presentation, and all of the visitors were individually introduced.

Those who had participated in the translation of the New Testament were presented with New Testaments. Many people told stories about the struggles they had gone through. They also told how God had changed their lives when they were able to read parts of the New Testament, as individual books were printed and made available to them. Their appreciation for God's Word and for Jo and her partners was evident on their faces and in their voices.

Even though I couldn't understand most of what was said, since it was in Balangao, I was overjoyed to see how God had used His Word in their lives. And now they had the whole New Testament in one book to read and study. I remembered those days fifteen years before when I spent my first two weeks in the Philippines among these precious people. I realized that God had done a mighty work here and was continuing to bless the lives of the Balangaos.

The program began at 10:30 a.m. and was still going three hours later. Because the planes had to ferry many people out in the afternoon, some had to leave early. I was scheduled on the 1:30 flight so missed lunch. I was disappointed, since I was looking forward to the delicious Balangao rice. The local people prepared rice and pork for the crowd. I was there for the best part, though and thanked God for the opportunity to attend. Many Bibles were sold, and the celebration continued through the weekend with native dancing, storytelling, and a mini-Bible conference on Sunday.

The hard part for Jo and Robyn followed the celebrations—closing up their house and moving all their belongings out as they prepared to leave for furlough and to other assignments. Tears were shed as they said good-bye to their Balangao family and friends, sisters and brothers in Christ.

When I returned to Manila, I continued working on the Botolan Sambal New Testament. Char Houck, with Anne's help, had finished the revision, and I was now typesetting the text. Char was in the process of proofreading the typeset copy. In another month, it would be completed and ready to go to the printer.

About this time, I received a letter from home saying that my sister, Nell, and her husband, Gary, were moving to Calgary. After their first church at Courtwright, they had ministered for a short time in Brampton, Ontario, and then had moved to Lachute and Dalesville, two small towns in western Quebec. Gary preached at both churches, which were just a few miles apart, but they lived in the parsonage next to the Dalesville church.

215

Now they had received a call to Killarney Baptist Church in Calgary, a big change for them—from country living to city living. I would be thankful for that move during my next furlough when I worked in the Wycliffe office in Calgary and stayed with them.

Chapter 33
Off–Center Housing
1983–1985

A major change was soon to take place in my life. Since we had completed the construction on the first phase of our office-apartment building in 1974, I had been living in one of the apartments on the second floor.

Now with the growth in the branch, the administration decided that short-term assistants needed short-term housing. However, almost no furnished apartments were available in Manila. The leaders felt that people coming for two years or less shouldn't have to buy appliances and furniture. So from now on, the apartments on the center would be reserved for short-termers. That meant when I returned from furlough in 1983, I would have to find a place to live off-center.

Marjorie (Marji) Cook was living in a small apartment not far away. Her landlady had just increased the rent to an exorbitant amount, so she considered moving. Three other single women needed housing too. So we decided that if we could find a house large enough for five people, we could all live together. We started house hunting.

We discovered interesting aspects about renting a house in Manila. Some were in bad shape, needing paint and repairs, and some had no light fixtures. When we asked the real-estate agent why anyone would rent a place in such bad shape, she said that nobody fixed up their houses before they rented them. New renters might like something different, and they would have to paint all over again. So we had to use our imaginations to see what houses could be like.

Unfortunately, we didn't find a big house we could afford, but after looking for four months, we found a duplex under construction. It was to be completed by April 1.

April! Who wants to move in April? It's the hottest month of the year. But move we did. It was Easter weekend, and we had a couple of extra days off work to get settled. The temperature was in the mid-90s F. (mid-30s C.), with not a cloud in the sky. We survived, but moving in April wasn't something I wanted to do every year.

We ended up with a lovely, new three-bedroom house with a garage, a small front yard and backyard, and lots of room for plants. Marji was an orchid fancier. We had space for her collection on the side of the house and in a tree in the backyard. Bronwyn Madder, an Australian with another mission who had just arrived to work in the Philippines, agreed to move in with us to fill the third bedroom.

When the house was being built, the workmen had lived in our side of the duplex. Unfortunately, they didn't clean it before they left. So we had to scrub the kitchen counters, the bathrooms, and the hardwood floors. We worked for weeks trying to get everything into shape in the extreme heat of summer.

Botolan Sambal New Testament Dedication

While we were house hunting, a number of other activities kept me busy. In February, Char Houck's Botolan Sambal New Testament came off the press. Botolan was not far from Manila, about a four-hour drive on a good highway. Seventy-five people from Manila attended the dedication, which was held in two parts. On Saturday afternoon, we drove to the program to be held in the town of Botolan. Since Char had become good friends with the mayor, he invited visitors to a dinner at his home.

Unfortunately, I was not able to attend the dinner or the dedication celebration either. On my way to Botolan, I became sick with stomach flu. We discovered on arrival that three others had the same thing. So we set up a mini-hospital in Char's house and went to bed, much to the disappointment of everyone, especially the other three sick women. They had to return that evening on the bus right after the program. About fifteen hundred people attended the program, which lasted four-and-a-half hours.

I planned to stay over the weekend to attend the second celebration, which was to be held in the mountains, an hour's drive away. By Sunday morning, I felt fine, so Char and I took off in her jeep to drive to the town of Maguisguis. The road crossed four rivers without bridges. Fortunately, the water was low enough for us to drive through without being washed away.

Five hundred people attended the second program, which lasted three-and-a-half hours. To see the enthusiasm with which these people received the Word in their own language made the long hours I had spent at my computer preparing it for the printer worthwhile.

Char and I drove back to Botolan through the four rivers when the program was finished and arrived at our beds by midnight. She was exhausted when the weekend was over. She was sixty-five at the time but had a great amount of energy and spirit, which never left her until she went to her heavenly home at the age of ninety-six.

Someone to Take Care of My Job

Later in February, I flew to Cagayan de Oro on Philippine Airlines. Then the pilot of our SIL plane picked me up and took me to Nasuli for the furlough workshop that was held there.

I was scheduled to fly home on May 13 for six months. While at Nasuli, I talked with Nadine Lyman, who was managing the publications department there, and discovered that she would be happy to take care of my job in Manila. She also agreed to live in our house to help with the rent while I was gone. The plan was for her to move to Manila in April so I could train her for my job before I left. She stayed in the guesthouse and then moved into our apartment in May after I left.

A number of other extracurricular activities kept me busy outside of office hours. Our church choir had a picnic at a beautiful beach a two-hour drive from Manila. Our office staff held a picnic one afternoon at the center with all the usual games and good food. A week before I left, Elna Singma, one of our Scripture typists, got married in a lovely church wedding. Audrey Mayer and Marge Moran arrived from furlough with a new teacher for Faith Academy. We all went on a sunset cruise on Manila Bay, ending by sailing along the waterfront to see the city lights and enjoying a steak dinner at a fine restaurant. I made a trip to Baguio to buy gifts to give to my supporters and friends at home.

Dengue Fever

One week before leaving, I came down with dengue fever. This is a tropical disease carried by a striped-legged, day-biting mosquito. Five days of high fever and three days of an unbearably itchy rash laid me low. How could I pack feeling like this?

I took aspirin to bring down the fever (something I learned later is very dangerous since dengue reduces your platelets) enough to crawl out of bed, pack a box or two, and crawl back in again. I didn't think I'd ever be ready to go. The worst part was the itching. It felt as if a thousand mosquitos were biting me. By the time I had to leave, I was well enough to travel, although my rash wasn't completely gone yet.

Off for Furlough

I was eager to see my parents. My mother had a slight stroke two days before Christmas, and although she seemed to be doing well, it worried me. I flew to Toronto and then on home to Port Stanley to begin my furlough.

One week to get over jet lag and repack, and I drove off with my parents to visit Marj and family in Saskatchewan. Ann, their oldest daughter, was graduating from high school, and it was a special privilege to attend.

After the festivities and a short visit, we put my parents on a plane for home, and I drove Dad's new car to Calgary, where I planned to work at the Wycliffe office for the summer. I looked forward to spending a whole summer with Nell and Gary in their new home, which was across the city, twelve-and-a-half miles (twenty kilometers) from the office.

I worked in the publicity office with Grace Rau on the development of a new Wycliffe Associates magazine. We had it ready for the printer by the end of the summer. Grace would continue with it after I left with the help of her husband, Larry, who worked in the finance office. I also did some editorial work on *Word Alive*, Wycliffe Canada's award-winning magazine, as well as evaluating the Wycliffe literature on the shelf, looking for gaps that needed to be filled.

Up in the Mountains

Although I would have been happy to use Dad's old car, he insisted I take his new one to Calgary, leaving him with the old one. I learned my way around Calgary and had a great time traveling to the Rockies with Nell, Gary, and Chris, who was then about ten-years-old.

One Saturday we drove to Castle Mountain, formerly called Mt. Eisenhower from 1946 to 1979, halfway between Banff and Lake Louise. From the Trans-Canada Highway, Castle Mountain looked impenetrable, but a trail ran around the eastern end and up the back, which was long but not too steep.

We ate our lunch and set off just after 12:00 p.m. to climb high enough to look out over the valley below and take pictures. However, because the terrain was heavily forested, we were not able to see much for a long time. We met people coming down, and we asked them how far it was before we would have a good view. They all said, "Oh, keep on going to the top. The view from there is gorgeous."

So we kept on climbing until finally about mid-afternoon, we reached Rockbound Lake, high on the back flank of Castle Mountain. It nestled against the peak that continued to rise straight up above the lake. Only one-third of the lakeshore was accessible, since the rest was bounded by rock, rising hundreds of feet toward the top of the mountain.

On our way up, we stopped at a couple of small streams to drink from the cool mountain spring water. We also enjoyed gazing at meadows of alpine wildflowers, most of which I had never seen before. At the lake's edge, we rested, ate apples we had carried in our pockets, and then began our return trek to the bottom of the mountain.

I thought climbing up was difficult, but going back down was much worse. My knees hurt, and my toes, pressing on the front of my sneakers, soon caused considerable pain. It was 7:00 p.m. by the time we reached our car. We collapsed, grateful for a place to rest our sore feet. We had been on the trail for seven hours. We were ready for a good meal too, so we headed for the town of Banff and an excellent restaurant that Gary knew about.

It was mid-summer, and tourists packed the town, so we had to park some way from the restaurant. When we crawled out of the car, we had all stiffened up so we could hardly walk across the street, except for young Chris. After dinner we went for a short walk down the street, when who should I meet but a friend from Singapore? She had worked in our office in Manila before returning to Singapore to work in the Wycliffe office there. We were both shocked to find each other so far from home. She had come to Canada for a vacation and to visit a friend, who was a student in Vancouver.

Following my summer in Calgary, I returned to Ontario to visit with my supporters in the area. I made a trip to Syracuse, New York, where I stayed with Gordon and Bernina Danielson. Bob and Fran Laubach invited me for dinner one evening, and we feasted on a delicious roast lamb that Fran had prepared.

Halfway through dinner, I felt a severe pain in my right back. I'd never had pain like that before. Fran thought I might be having a gallbladder attack, so she and Bob rushed me off to the hospital emergency room to see if anything could be done. The doctor ordered x-rays and blood work, but they came back negative.

After several hours, I felt a little better so was able to get back to the Danielson's house and into bed. I told the hospital that I would pay for the treatment, but they didn't know how to find out what the cost was, so they said they would send me a bill. That was the last I heard of it, since no bill arrived in my mail. It took four days before the pain subsided, and I could go on my way, feeling normal again.

Back to Manila

I returned to Manila in October and found that Nadine had done a fine job at the office. I had a New Testament in process and due in January, as well as a number of literacy books and Scripture portions.

Soon it would be Christmas with all of the many extra activities associated with the season. Before long I was heavily into extra practices, as our choir prepared to sing John W. Peterson's cantata *Christmas Is Love*. Then in December I attended our choir Christmas party, *Holiday on Ice* at the coliseum, and the Philippine Ballet Company's annual Christmas presentation. It was usually *The Nutcracker* but this year had been changed to *Peter Pan.*

One Sunday afternoon, our pastor and his wife hosted the whole congregation at an open house at the manse, an annual come-and-go affair with carol singing and wonderful food. In the evening, our eighty-five voice children's choir performed their annual concert, a singing Christmas tree, and a playlet. Then we had our office Christmas party at the SIL guesthouse, where we had entertainment by the office staff, gift exchanges, and more great food.

After all the pre-Christmas activities, I needed a break, so I decided to go to Bagabag for Christmas, since Anne West and Judy Wallace would be there. Most of my friends from Manila were going away.

On the day before Christmas, I had an invitation to a wedding at Botolan where Char Houck lived. Josie Fabra, Char's co-translator for the New Testament, was getting married on December 24. Anne and I drove to Botolan on the 23rd, since the wedding was at 8:30 a.m. After the wedding, we left for Bagabag, a seven-hour drive from Botolan. We arrived well into the evening, ready for bed.

Since we arrived in Bagabag so late the night before, we drove to Banaue to have Christmas dinner at the first-class hotel there. The drive was only one-and-a- half hours, the food was delicious, and we arrived home in the evening much more rested than if we had cooked a big dinner ourselves.

ॐॐ

Over the past year, the political and economic situation in Manila and all over the Philippines had been deteriorating. The peso was devaluated, and prices for many items doubled. From time to time, groups of people took to the streets demonstrating against rising prices and poor security. We were not affected much by this, except for the higher prices and shortages in the stores. Unless people were violent, the demonstrations were usually not even mentioned in the news.

ॐॐ

After returning from furlough, I spent quite a bit of my off-work time getting our apartment into better shape. I needed a new refrigerator and stove, which I was able to buy with a generous gift from my church at home. New drapes and bedspreads made my bedroom a more pleasant place.

A Fine House Helper

After arranging for the upgrade in our home, we set about finding someone to work for us who could live in. We had someone coming occasionally to clean, but the dust and pollution were so bad that we needed more cleaning than we could manage on our own and work full-time too.

Finally, we found Tilde, short for Matilde. Filipinos often abbreviate names from the end instead of the beginning as we do in the West. Tilde was a fifty-three-year-old single woman who had worked in Manila for twelve years. She came from the Batanes Islands, the farthermost northern islands of the Philippines. She had been working for a Japanese woman, who treated her like a nonperson, so she finally quit her job. We found her through Ginny Larson, our translator in the Batanes.

Since we had a room with a bathroom especially built for a house helper, she had her own quarters and seemed very happy with us. We were relieved to have our home taken care of too. In a week, she had it looking wonderful. Eventually, we planned to work her into some cooking along with the cleaning.

In March of 1984, Marji decided to move from our place and find one of her own, so that left just Bronwyn and me. Since the peso had been greatly devalued by this time, the extra rent was no problem for us. We decided not to look for another housemate. Instead, we would use the extra room as a guest room. Bronwyn's mission had no guesthouse, so we were able to house her friends when they came to the city.

Pursued by a Collection Agency

In June, I received a bill from the Syracuse hospital for the treatment I had there the previous September. A letter accompanied a bill from a collection agency stating that if I didn't pay this immediately, they would take it to a lawyer and sue me.

I was confused, since this was the first notice I had received. Then I looked at the address on the bill. I had given the receptionist at the hospital my parents' address, Box 287, Port Stanley, Ontario, Canada. The address on the bill was Box 287, Ontario, CA 99999. The collector had been looking all over California for me for several months. I think the zip was a default put in by the post office's computer, since it didn't find the address in Ontario, California. That was the only time in my life that I have been chased by a collection agency.

223

A Typesetter for Publications

While I was home in 1983, the Philippines branch decided to buy a typesetter. We had been having our work done at FEBC, but after the fire, their work had decreased, and finally they closed their print shop. We moved our printing to Shangkuan Printers, run by a wealthy Chinese family. They were not able to do typesetting for us, so we needed to do our own.

One of my first jobs was to learn to run the Graphic Systems Incorporated (GSI) phototypesetter that was installed in our office. The director moved from his spacious office into a smaller space, and the computer department took over that room. A small restroom was attached to this room, which was ideal for the processor that developed the photo paper on which the typeset material came out of the typesetter.

It made a big difference to my work not to drive 25 miles (40 kilometers) round trip to Marshburn Press to get our typesetting done. Shangkuan Printers was much closer, still within the city limits.

Northern Kankanay New Testament

The first New Testament I had to process in 1984 was the Northern Kankanay. A number of my friends had worked on this New Testament, and I felt privileged to complete the work. Donna Hettick and Carolyn Kent had begun the work. Then Marge Draper had worked there for a while. Doris Porter, Judy Wallace, and Marge Moran completed the translation before Doris moved into administrative work. Now Marge and Judy finished the revision.

When they were satisfied that their work was done, they sent a typewritten copy to Bagabag, where a Filipino typist typed it into the Datapoint computer to produce a cassette tape. When finished, the typist made a printout and sent it to Marge and Judy for proofreading. The printout went back to the typist to make the corrections onto the tape. When Marge and Judy were satisfied there were no more errors and the book was approved for publication by the translation department, I made a printout, book by book, of the whole New Testament.

On this printout, I marked off the lines that would fit on each printed page, inserting codes that would leave space for pictures and codes that would insert the book name, chapter number, and page number at the top of each page. I marked the places where footnotes would be inserted. Then I edited all of these codes into the tapes. Finally, I made a new printout to see that everything looked right. Then I was ready to typeset.

I placed the finished tape into the computer attached to the typesetter, and the typesetting process began. The type fonts in the typesetter were on little pieces of negative mounted on a drum that spun at high speed.

When the computer told the typesetter which letter to set, the drum lined that letter up in front of a lens. A light flashed and exposed the character onto photo paper, which line by line was fed into a light proof cassette on the right side of the typesetter. This cassette held fifteen pages at a time. When it was full, I removed it and developed it through a print processor, just like photographs are developed, first through a developer tank, a fixer, a water bath, and through a dryer.

The copy came out the other end of the processor, a long strip eight inches wide and 175 inches long. I cut the pages apart, and when a whole book was completed, it went one more time to Marge and Judy for another proofreading.

At this stage, we should have had very few changes, but we found some. I typed these on the computer, printed them out, proofread them, made any further corrections, and then put them through the typesetter. I then pasted these corrections into the original pages.

The Kankanay New Testament had maps, a concordance, and a glossary of terms. I typeset all of this material, going through the same procedure as the Scripture. When everything was completed, including the title page and the text for the cover, it was ready to go to the printer.

I could prepare a New Testament for the printer in about a month if I had nothing else to do. But I always had many other jobs in the office, so sometimes it took me more than two months. I enjoyed the New Testament processing more than my other office work, and sometimes letters and reports stacked up.

In 1984 I processed four New Testaments. The Northern Kankanay was our nineteenth New Testament to be published in the Philippines.

The Chinese Cemetery

Even though I had been living in Manila for fifteen years, I hadn't yet visited certain places. One of these was the Chinese cemetery.

Char Houck was in town for a break, so she and I visited this tourist attraction located in Santa Cruz, a part of Manila. It is the second oldest cemetery in Manila, built in the mid-1800s during the Spanish rule as a burial place for Chinese residents who could not be buried in Catholic cemeteries. It not only is the burial place for many wealthy Chinese Filipinos, but it also was the execution ground for many during the Japanese occupation of World War II.

When we arrived at the gates, we hired a guide to take us around and explain what we were seeing. The cemetery was like a small town with streets lined with marble mausoleums. Many were very luxurious with electricity, air-conditioning, running water, rest rooms, kitchens, dining rooms, and lounge areas. Paintings or photographs of the deceased hung on the walls. The bodies were interred in tombs in the center of the mausoleums. Most of the people buried here were Buddhists who revered their ancestors, so those Chinese who can afford it bury their loved ones in great luxury. These mausoleums then become worship centers for their descendants.

We visited inside several tombs as we walked through streets of burial places, each more opulent than the one before it. We learned that every week, people bring offerings of food to the cemetery for their ancestors. They eat what they brought the week before, leaving the new offering for the deceased.

I found this place interesting but also sad as I thought of the millions of poor people in the Philippines who have little to eat and only makeshift places to live.

Canadian Thanksgiving

Canadian Thanksgiving was always an enjoyable day for me. Since many Canadian missionaries worked in Manila, we got together for a Thanksgiving dinner and program. Grandma's Inn, a restaurant not far from where we lived, served a roast turkey dinner every Friday night. We gathered in that restaurant on the Friday closest to Canadian Thanksgiving for a delicious traditional turkey dinner, which was very hard to find in the Philippines. After our usual meals of rice, fish, chicken, or pork, it was wonderful to feast on soup, salad, roast turkey, dressing, mashed potatoes, gravy, mixed vegetables, cranberry sauce, hot rolls, and blueberry cheesecake.

We had a private room so were able to have a short program following the dinner. Everyone's nametag had a number on it. Several numbers were drawn during the program, and people who had those numbers on their nametags were interviewed. Since we all worked with various missions, I didn't know many people. During the program, I discovered that I had been in the Philippines longer than anyone else. Only three of the fifty people present had been there as long as fifteen years.

Seventieth Anniversary of Union Church

In October of 1984, the Union Church of Manila celebrated its seventieth anniversary. The choir sang a special rendition of "The Lord's Prayer," accompanied by a children's deaf choir, which signed the anthem. After the service, we enjoyed a reception in the fellowship hall with a big cake and coffee. At 12:30 p.m., ninety people, since that was all the restaurant would hold, went to the German Club across the street from the church for a dinner together. Since they had been in the church for a long time, four people told what the church had meant to them in their spiritual walk.

November of 1984 brought another change in my life. Bronwyn's mission asked her to move to a new housing development so she and a couple could begin Bible studies among the residents. That left me on my own again, since Marji had already moved to her own place.

A new office secretary was arriving the end of the month, but until I had met her, I didn't want to commit to living with her. Doris Porter would be returning from furlough in April 1985, and she had agreed to move in then.

Sometimes I thought I should stay by myself and not always have different women living with me. But the cost of rent was prohibitive, and I, being an extrovert, needed people around me. So I preferred to continue adjusting to the ebb and flow of housemates to living by myself.

Christmas in Sagada

That Christmas my prayer partners, Marge Moran and Judy Wallace, invited me to spend the holiday with them at their home in Sagada. They had moved there from the village of Bogang, after they had completed the New Testament translation work. Life was easier in town, so they rented an apartment while they revised and prepared the Northern Kankanay New Testament for printing.

I drove to Bagabag two days before Christmas to pick up Marge Draper and Juana Banawe. Marge Moran and Judy Wallace had invited Marge Draper to spend Christmas with them too, and Juana's family lived in Bogang, so she was going home.

On the day before Christmas, we left in the morning for Sagada. We stopped to have coffee with Janet Davis near Banaue and then began the climb to the top of the pass on Mt. Pulis.

A few miles out of Banaue, the narrow road made it difficult to pass another vehicle. As we rounded a bend, a bus blocked our way, since it had stopped beside the mountain. We wondered why the bus was not moving and saw the conductor slowly creep out from along the side of the bus.

I got out of the car and walked over to him. "Why are you so frightened?" I asked.

Shaking, he said, "A group of New People's Army (NPA) guerrillas attacked us and shot a woman in the bus!"

"What are you going to do?"

"We're afraid to go ahead for fear the NPA might come again!"

"What about the woman who was shot?" I asked. "Is she bleeding?"

"Yes."

"You need to go, so she can get to the hospital in Bontoc."

"Will you stay with us?"

"Yes, we'll stay behind you."

I presumed he thought that if we were attacked, the NPA would go for the carload of *Americano* women. Perhaps they were attacked in the first place because he was wearing camouflage clothing, very popular for macho young men. They may have thought he was part of the army, since he as conductor was hanging onto the outside of the bus. The woman who was hit was against the window in the back row.

The bus started up and moved slowly up the mountain, so slowly I thought we would never get to the top. Finally, we reached a clearing at Mt. Polis where the bus pulled over and stopped. I went to see how the injured woman was and found her bleeding profusely in the back seat of the bus.

"Can't you drive faster?" I asked the bus driver.

"No, that's the best I can do in the mountains."

"If some of your passengers will carry her, I'll take her in my car so she can get to the hospital sooner."

Someone gave us a couple of towels so we bound up the woman's wounds and lay her prone on the backseat of my car. Juana squeezed in with her, and we were on our way.

The road was very rough, and I had to make a decision: *Should I drive slowly so the bumps don't hurt her so much? Or should I drive faster so she won't bleed to death before we get to the hospital?* I chose the latter and took off as fast as my Toyota could manage the rough road.

We arrived in Bontoc about an hour later and deposited our rider in the emergency department of the hospital. Then we drove to a school where the patient's sister was a student. With Juana's help, we located the sister and took her to the hospital. Since we could do nothing more, we went on our way to Sagada, arriving about two in the afternoon.

Since this was Christmas Eve, we enjoyed a delicious dinner of roast chicken and mountain-grown vegetables that Marge and Judy had prepared. Then we opened the small gifts we exchanged. It is traditional for people to come visiting on Christmas Day, so we thought it might be difficult to cook a big meal with visitors in the house.

Later in the evening, we attended a community Christmas program at the basketball court in the middle of town with dancing, skits, and songs. Afterwards, we went to the Anglican church, the only church in town, where they performed a pageant telling the Christmas story. We planned to attend midnight mass, but they held it at 10:30 p.m. instead of 11:30 p.m. as advertised, so we missed it. We did get up early and attended the 8:00 a.m. service before enjoying a waffle breakfast at home.

The day after Christmas, we hiked to the village of Bogang where Marge and Judy had lived when working on the translation. Their Igorot (what the people called themselves) sister made a big dinner for us. We had brought along gifts for many of the people in the village and enjoyed visiting their homes to deliver them. In the afternoon, we hiked forty-five minutes back up the trail to the spot where we had left the car and returned to Sagada.

Instead of going back to Bagabag from Sagada, we took Mountain Trail, seven hours south to Baguio, to spend a few days in the summer capital. Darwin Bayani, who was our graphic artist in Manila, was marrying Nanette at an outdoor wedding on the weekend. I was a sponsor so was part of the wedding party. The wedding was held on the grounds of the Campus Crusade Seminary. It was a beautiful wedding, but the air was chilly, since it was winter. While winter in Manila at sea level may mean a low of 75 F. (23 C.), at 5,000 feet the temperatures ranged from 58 F. to 75 F. (14 C. to 23 C.).

We returned to Manila on New Year's Eve in time for the usual noise and smoke of millions of fireworks. We went to the midnight communion service at church, followed by snacks at one of the big hotels afterwards.

By the end of the first week of January 1985, I had a new part-time housemate. Kathy Bosscher, the Asia area literacy consultant for SIL, needed a place to stay when in Manila. When she was away, Doris and I could use her room as a guest room. Kathy was a joy to have around, but we didn't see much of her, since she traveled a great deal.

Northern Kankanay New Testament Dedication

In February I made another trip to Sagada, this time for the dedication of the Northern Kankanay New Testament. The Episcopal church and other Christians planned a grand celebration in town.

Mission work began in Sagada during the first decade of the twentieth century when Father John Staunton, an American Episcopal missionary, founded a church there. He was a man of great vision. Through his influence, Sagada, perched at more than 5,000 feet on top of a mountain, became a model town with paved streets, electricity, and telephones. A beautiful stone church was built in the middle of town, and several Western-style houses became homes for the Stauntons and several other American missionaries assigned to work.

Almost all of the people in Sagada became Episcopalians. Most of the children learned some English in school, since the teachers used that language. The older people who had not been to school could not understand it. Eventually, the American missionaries left Sagada, and local people became priests and lay workers in the church. While Northern Kankanay was used in the homes and community, English remained the language of the church.

Father Richard Abellon, the parish priest in 1965, recognized the need for the Scriptures in Northern Kankanay and invited an SIL team to begin work in his language. And so twenty years after its beginning and almost eighty years after the church was founded, the New Testament was finally finished.

On January 30, two days before the scheduled date of the dedication, Don Leonard, an SIL member whose job was to distribute literature in a language area just south of Sagada, arrived. He brought a projector, a large screen, and a sound system to show a series of films on the Gospel of Luke. One of the priests read portions from the Gospel of Luke in Northern Kankanay to narrate the films.

The hillsides surrounding the basketball court were crowded with about fifteen hundred very attentive viewers. They sat on cement seats or on the ground for more than three hours to see the eight reels that were shown. A second showing the next night drew about one thousand people. Following the films, a woman that Marge didn't know came to her and, holding on to her hand, said, "It was wonderful! It was just as if we were right there."

The actual dedication service was held on the evening of February 1 at the basketball court in front of the church and attended by two thousand people. The Episcopal bishop of Northern Luzon led the audience in dedicating the New Testament to the Lord. All those who had had a part in the translation, including the local team from Sagada and the village of Bogang where the translation was done, were called to the front and recognized. Local people and SIL directors gave speeches.

After the dedication, more than six hundred copies were sold. Thanks to the International Bible Society that paid for the publishing costs, the Northern Kankanay New Testament could be sold for the equivalent of

$1.00. Following the service, the school children and some of the civic groups sang songs and danced until 11:00 p.m.

The dedication service was in the evening, so in the afternoon, some of us who had arrived earlier, went hiking to see the famous Sagada burial caves. A local man accompanied us, showing us the location where coffins filled with bones were piled high one on top of another. Some had toppled down, and bones were spilling out. Then we hiked across the rice terraces to the village where Marge and Judy had lived previously, where we rested for a half hour before hiking back to Sagada. The whole trip took us three-and-a-half hours, too long for some of us who were not very fit.

After the dedication, I returned to Manila and began typesetting the next New Testament.

Doris Porter returned from furlough and moved into our apartment. It was good to have a new housemate. Now permanently assigned to Manila, she was working as chairman of the literacy and literature in use department.

Kathy Bosscher, who still shared the apartment, was away on trips to parts of Asia much of the time, and I had been alone except for her brief returns home. Now I hoped we could settle down for a while to a more normal home life.

In May of 1985, when the temperature in Manila was at its hottest, I took another short vacation. Doris and I made arrangements to meet Marge Moran and Judy Wallace at a resort hotel in the mountains of Mountain Province that none of us had ever stayed at before.

Doris and I drove to Baguio, leaving early in the morning. We had lunch with Betty Elkins and Jo Shetler, staff members at BVNS, our summer linguistics course that was then in session. Then we began our trip north up Mountain Trail to Mt. Data, a four-hour drive from Baguio, where we had reservations at the Mt. Data Lodge for two days.

Marge and Judy left Sagada on the morning bus to Baguio and met us at Mt. Data. Marge Draper also joined our party, coming on the bus from Bagabag. They were all there before we arrived at 4:30 in the afternoon.

The road from Baguio to Mt. Data was in very poor shape, since an earthquake in the area recently had caused many landslides. It rained most of the day as well, and since the road is nothing but switchbacks the whole way, climbing to 7,400 feet, we drove through rain, fog, and mud all day.

The hotel was beautiful, with a large fieldstone fireplace, a dining room overlooking the forest, and many well-kept flower gardens, all in full bloom. In the evening, we sat by the fire and caught up with each other's activities.

Mt. Data sits at an elevation of 7,200 feet, so we were happy for the fire to keep warm. We didn't have a thermometer but guessed the temperature was about 50 F. (10 C.), quite a contrast from Manila where the temperature had been running in the 90s F. (32 C.) for some time.

After breakfast the next morning, we hired a couple of guides and went for a hike. Mt. Data Lodge is situated on a high plateau where local people grow vegetables that are shipped to Baguio and on to the lowlands. Potatoes and cabbages are the main crops.

We hiked for four hours, climbing to over 8,000 feet to the edge of the plateau where the mountains drop off for thousands of feet, and we could see for miles in the distance. We also saw several waterfalls dropping over the cliff. Our guides told us that the headwaters for two large rivers rise here and run to the ocean, one to the Pacific and the other to the South China Sea. Mt. Data is like the continental divide in North America.

After our hike, we rested in the afternoon, reading and visiting. Only three other women were guests in the hotel and one Japanese man, who worked on the radio, so we had most of the hotel to ourselves.

The next day we returned to Baguio for a day and then back to Manila. I was glad for my sturdy Toyota that took us over rough roads with no problems.

Dictionary Workshop

A week after returning to Manila, I was off again, this time to Bagabag to attend a dictionary workshop. Translators gathered for instructions on how to prepare and keyboard dictionaries for publication. Since I needed to know this so I could help in the publication of dictionaries, I attended two of the three weeks of the workshop and began to keyboard dictionary entries for one of our teams.

I also had a chance to catch up with Heather Kilgour, her partner Gail Hendrickson, and their language helper Blissy, who were attending the workshop. When it was over, they rode back to Manila with me. Gail and Heather had begun translation work on an island in the Visayas with the Bantoanon people. I planned to visit them when I needed another break from my work.

Since our work in the Philippines continued to expand, the Manila office became too crowded. I was the office manager in charge of facilities and realized that we needed to renovate our office in order to make more room, especially for the computer department that was growing rapidly.

The apartment in the house at the end of the driveway, which we had designated for the director, was no longer needed for that purpose, since our present director preferred to live in the community. We moved the library to that apartment, leaving room for expansion inside the office. The conference room moved to the space that had been occupied by the library, and the computer department took over the space where the conference room had been. Since I was responsible for managing all these renovations, I kept busy until they were completed.

The rains had begun now, so the temperature had gone down by ten degrees from the high 90s to the high 80s, which made moving and carrying a bit easier.

Two Typhoons

With the rainy season came typhoons, two in a row in June that year, which caused severe flooding in the city. The first one started on a Wednesday evening just as Doris and I were leaving the church after choir practice. By the time we got to within three miles (five kilometers) of home, the streets were so badly flooded that we wondered if we would make it. It continued to rain until Saturday morning.

By Friday noon, we sent our office staff home, since we were afraid they wouldn't get there if they didn't go then. Some hadn't been able to get to work that day at all. In a thirty-two hour period from Thursday morning to Friday afternoon, we had sixteen inches of rain. The Pasig River that runs through the middle of Manila overflowed its banks by fifteen feet, and 60 percent of Manila was under water. Fortunately, it was high where we lived, so we were safe.

Seventy-nine people lost their lives either to drowning or electrocution. Electrocution was common during flooding, since people would try to use electric appliances standing in waist-deep water, or sometimes the wiring in their houses was substandard.

და

In 1985, our pastor, Dr. Alex Aronis, his wife, Carol, and their children returned to the States. Everyone in the church was sad to see them go, since we had enjoyed his preaching and grown spiritually under Alex's ministry. The attendance had increased considerably since FEBC radio aired the morning services. Many local people heard the programs and began attending the church. However, two of the Aronis's four children were now in college in the States, and they felt they needed to be closer to them.

In June we called the Rev. Darrell Johnson from Los Angeles to be our pastor. He and his family would move to Manila in September to begin their ministry with us. They were young with two preschool children, and we looked forward to having a full-time pastor again.

Dedication of the Amganad Church

By now, the Amganad church had had the New Testament in their own language for five years, eighteen years since Anne and I had first begun work there. The congregation had left the school and built a small church building several years before but had outgrown it. Now they had built a larger church to hold all the people who were attending.

In November of 1985, Judy McGinnis, our director's secretary, and I drove to Amganad to attend the dedication of the new church building. It was more than double the size of the old one, seating about three hundred people. We estimated the crowd at the dedication service numbered between four and five hundred people, many from other churches in the area.

It was special for me to be there to see all those people. I thought back to the time when Anne and I had first arrived in Amganad. I thought then that it would certainly take a miracle for God to do anything in that place because the spirit worship was so strong. And now to see almost every person in our village believing brought tears to my eyes.

Janet Davis directed a cantata of well-known hymns sung in Ifugao, performed by a choir of thirty-five, mostly young people. After the morning service and the special dedication service, the women served a beautiful lunch of carabao (water buffalo), pork, rice, and *pancit*, a popular noodle dish. After lunch there was more singing.

Judy and I returned to Manila with rejoicing, having seen that God was working mightily in Ifugao.

❧

Christmas of 1985 was a special time for me. Our choir sang two concerts, each one different. That meant many evenings of practice, beginning in October. On December 15, we joined the children in the singing Christmas tree. This tree-shaped structure at the front of the church had rows rising higher and higher. Although the top held only two people, the whole singing tree held sixty adults or ninety children. My spot in the tree was on the third row from the top, about twenty-five feet from the platform. I had a wonderful view. The church was packed for the performance.

On Christmas Eve, the chancel choir sang Vivaldi's *Gloria*, accompanied by a five-piece string ensemble. Almost one thousand people crowded into our five hundred seat church and fellowship hall. It was my first but not the last time to sing *Gloria*. It was difficult but glorious music, which I delighted to learn.

For Christmas Day, Doris and I invited eight other single SIL women to join us for dinner. We bought a turkey and served a traditional dinner for ten. We had a delightful time together, sharing good food and a feeling of family. I discovered early in my time in the Philippines that since I was far from my own family during the holidays, the best way to keep from feeling sorry for myself was to entertain others in the same situation and create my own "family."

Soon Christmas was over, the decorations were packed up, and the smoke from the New Year's Eve firecrackers had dissipated. It was time to return to work.

The Binukid New Testament files had arrived on my desk just before Christmas. Mary Jane Gardner and Ursula Post, the translators, were eagerly awaiting a copy from the typesetter to proofread.

Sometime toward the end of November, we heard that the town of San Juan where we lived was going to pave our street with cement. It was asphalt and full of potholes, so we were delighted to get this news. While asphalt is cheaper and easier to lay than cement, the heavy rains and tremendous amount of traffic made it a poor choice for paving material. Also, the city never had enough money to keep asphalt in good repair.

Soon the work began, and the city informed us that we would not be able to get our cars out after a certain date, so we should park them some place other than at home if we wished to use them during the construction. Some people we knew, who lived about three blocks away on a side street, offered to let me park my car at their place where it would be safe inside their walls. It was an easy walk for us, so we thanked them and moved the car to their yard.

We had to adjust to getting up a bit earlier in the morning in order to get to work on time, since the walk added to our commute.

Chapter 34
Death and Revolution
1986

On January 22, 1986, I set out from our house to pick up my car for the fifteen-minute trip to work. As I walked down the street, I noticed a woman coming toward me. The figure looked familiar. When she got close enough to recognize her, I realized it was RuthAnn Price, one of our associate directors. *What is RuthAnn doing in our neighborhood the first thing in the morning?* I wondered. *She lives just a half-block from the office.*

Then it dawned on me. She must have bad news. The directors always delivered bad news in person. I felt my stomach tie in a knot, and I stood still, letting her reach me.

"Shirley, I'm so sorry to tell you this." She put her arms around me and hugged me close.

I felt the tears come. It had to be about one of my parents. "Is it my mother?"

"No, it's your father. Your sister called this morning, saying he passed away yesterday."

By this time, my tears were flowing. "I can't believe it! My mom hasn't been well, but I thought my dad was doing okay."

RuthAnn's eyes filled with tears. "I'm so sorry. What can I do for you? Make phone calls?"

"That's nice of you. But I'll call my sister to get the details."

I had thought I might hear this news about Mom, since she had not been well after her stroke. I knew that Dad had heart problems because he suffered from angina occasionally and carried medication for it. But he never said anything about it or complained, so we tended to forget about it.

When I called my sister Marj, she told me that Mom and Dad were on their way to St. Thomas to go shopping. He went ahead to get the car out of the garage, as was his custom. They didn't have an automatic garage-door opener, so he had to lift the door up on its spring.

Mom noticed when she came out that the car was in the driveway, but the garage door was still open. She wondered why he hadn't closed the door until she noticed that he was in the car with his head down on the steering wheel. He was breathing heavily, and she realized something was very wrong.

She hurried across the street and called their neighbor, who was a nurse, to come. By the time they got back, he was gone. He had succumbed to a massive coronary.

I discussed with Marj whether I should go home for the memorial service and to help Mom. It was the dead of winter, and at that time I didn't own any winter clothes, my last several furloughs having been in the summer. A trip from the Philippines, especially one on short notice, was very expensive, and while I had enough support to live on, I didn't have much extra for airfare.

But the biggest factor against my going then was that I was in the middle of typesetting the Binukid New Testament, and Mary Jane Gardner and Ursula Post were planning to be in Manila specifically to proofread. I felt unhappy about causing a delay in their New Testament production, even though I knew they would understand.

The deciding factor was that Mom could not live by herself in their house in Port Stanley. It was at the top of a long hill, and the shops and post office were at the bottom of the hill. Since she could no longer drive the car and because of arthritis was not able to walk the hill, she would be trapped in her house. Someone would have to help her move.

Since both Marj and Nell were working and had families to care for, we decided that we would wait until April when I would have finished the Binukid New Testament, and the weather would be warmer. Marj would take Mom home with her to Saskatchewan until then, and I would fly to Calgary to take Mom back to Ontario to pack up the house and get it ready for selling. Marj hoped to find a place in Gull Lake for Mom to live so she would be close to family.

My director gave me permission to take the remaining two weeks of my vacation for that year and two weeks of compassionate leave and fly to Calgary on March 31. If I needed more time, I could take it, but I should get back in May, since I had responsibilities for our biennial conference at the end of the month.

The People Power Revolution

Before that trip home following my father's death, I lived through the Philippine revolution.

For some months, the peace-and-order situation in the Philippines had been bad. Increasingly, through the years of martial law that President Ferdinand Marcos had declared in 1972, the citizens had become more disgruntled with their lives. As foreigners, we were unaware of much that was happening behind the scenes. We didn't know about the Marcos's corruption, since most of the news was censored. We didn't know that the President had maltreated and imprisoned many opposition leaders.

Then we learned that Marcos had imprisoned his chief rival, former senator Benigno (Ninoy) Aquino, after martial law was declared. In 1980 Aquino had suffered a heart attack in prison and was allowed to go to the United States, where he lived with his family in self-exile for three years.

In February 1983, he returned to his homeland to do what he could to give peace and stability to the Philippines. As he stepped from his aircraft at Manila International Airport, a round of gunfire ended his life. Marcos was blamed for this, even though Rolando Galman was officially blamed for the shooting and was killed on the spot.

This was a turning point for the Filipino people. Anti-Marcos groups began to rally and riot. Cory Aquino, Ninoy's widow, entered politics and ran against Marcos in the snap elections of 1986. Although Marcos was declared the winner, widespread reports told of his tampering with the results in his favor. At this point, the people had had enough, and the revolution began.

Radio Veritas, a Catholic radio station, took up the people's cause. Huge gatherings began near Ortigas Avenue on Epifanio de los Santos Avenue (EDSA), the main highway circling Manila. Two of Marcos' henchmen, Defense Minister Juan Ponce Enrile and Deputy Chief of Staff of the Armed Forces Fidel Ramos, turned against him and joined the people. Cardinal Sin over Radio Veritas encouraged the common people to join the crowd on EDSA. And they did.

By the time the whole thing was over, more than two million people had gathered on that street. Marcos ordered the army to clear the street, and a number of tanks arrived. But the people stood firm and would not move. This was the beginning of the People Power Revolution. Nuns offered sandwiches and flowers to the tank drivers, who would not mow them down. The people wore yellow shirts and waved yellow banners, Cory Aquino's color. They chanted, "Cory, Cory!" After four days, President and Mrs. Marcos gave up and fled to Hawaii, and Corazon Aquino was declared the new president.

EDSA was just a short distance from the SIL center. Since nobody knew what was going to happen, we stayed at home until the situation was settled. We lived with our ears to the radio, but almost all of the reporting was in Tagalog. Since I had studied Tagalog for only a short time, I didn't know much of what was happening until later.

It was a very tense time for us all, and we did a lot of praying during those days for our protection and for God's protection of the millions gathered on EDSA. God answered our prayers and the prayers of many others, since it was virtually a bloodless revolution with few deaths or injuries reported.

The Worst Five Weeks of My Life

On March 31, 1986, I flew from Manila to Hong Kong and spent a day with Terry and Carole Madison, longtime friends who had worked in the Philippines and were now assigned to Hong Kong. From there I flew to Vancouver and on to Calgary to begin the worst five weeks of my life.

After Dad's death, Mom had gone home with Marj to Gull Lake until I arrived. Marj then brought her to Calgary and spent a couple of days with Nell and Gary before Mom and I caught a red-eye flight to Toronto. My brother Art met us at the airport, took us to the airport cafeteria for breakfast, and helped us find the shuttle bus that would take us to St. Thomas.

When we arrived, I called Dave Dadson, Mom and Dad's care deacon from their church, to take us the almost seven miles (eleven kilometers) to Port Stanley and home. I asked him to bring his jumper cables in case the car wouldn't start, since it had been parked for over three months, but they weren't needed. I was glad Dave was with us at Mom's home, however, because I couldn't find where to turn on the water, and Mom didn't know either. We followed the pipe around from the water heater and finally found the right place.

Marj had told me that she had had a very difficult time with Mom while she stayed with her. Since her stroke, Mom had been gradually losing her ability to cope with life. Dad covered for her, so we were not aware of her real state until he was gone. Her short-term memory and ability to concentrate were poor, but she was adamant that she could live on her own in a retirement apartment in town. With no family nearby, we felt that this was unrealistic, but she was sure that her friends would take care of her. I tried to impress on her that friends were wonderful to have but for the long term, she needed family nearby.

I did a few experiments when we first arrived at home to see how she could function with cooking and taking care of herself. I bought fish and chips in town when we arrived on the bus, so we would have lunch prepared when we got home. While I took my suitcase to the bedroom, she turned on the oven and placed the fish, cardboard box and all, on a rack to keep warm. We would have had a fire if I had not rescued it. By 5:30, she said it was time to get supper. She decided to have fried onions and boiled potatoes. I said that was fine since we'd had fish for lunch and didn't need any meat. She forgot the onions and let them burn. She was able to rescue enough for us to eat by 7:30.

The next day I made an appointment for her to see her doctor. He checked her over and said she was okay but definitely showed signs of senile dementia and should not live alone.

Art and his wife Bonnie came the next day from Toronto, and we visited several retirement places in St. Thomas that had openings. We felt she would be better in Gull Lake where Marj could keep an eye on her, but all she could think of was how hard life was there when she was a girl. We tried to persuade her that with modern conveniences in homes now, life was the same there as in Ontario, but we couldn't persuade her.

My main priority was to dispose of all the needless things that had collected in the house, to decide what furniture to keep and what to sell, and to get the house ready for the market. Mom was a collector. Her main theme in life was, "Keep everything, since it might come in handy some day." This was probably a leftover from having lived through the Great Depression. We gave the three-foot stack of *Reader's Digest* to a neighbor, and I surreptitiously disposed of many magazines and other printed pieces that I found stacked in various places around the house.

As the days went by, I realized that in spite of Mom's resistance, we could not leave her in Ontario on her own. It upset me a great deal to see how unhappy she was at the thought of leaving this place where she had spent the entire fifty-seven years of her married life and returning to Saskatchewan where she had spent a very difficult ten years in her youth. However, after many discussions with Art and my sisters, we decided that this was the only thing we could do. Marj began looking for a place in Gull Lake where she could live. We thought she might be able to live on her own if someone could check on her every day.

The town of Gull Lake had built a number of nice small apartments for seniors with private entrances. The rent depended on one's income. One was available at that time, so Marj put a reserve on it. With that in mind, it was easier for me to see what to keep and what to put in the auction sale.

Mom was not able to make decisions easily. When I asked her which of the twenty-five drinking glasses she would like to take, she wanted them all. So eventually, I decided and packed up what I thought she would need. Her furniture was old and large, so except for a few small pieces that would fit in Marj's big van, we decided to sell the furniture and appliances and buy new pieces that would fit in her apartment in Saskatchewan.

Mom had many personal things she wanted to take. She had always loved greeting cards and kept most of what she received over the years. I suggested that she keep just a few. For three days, she sat by the fireplace and read her cards, occasionally throwing one into the fire and putting those she wanted to keep in a stack. When the stack grew too high, I got rid of a bunch of them when she was out of the room. Eventually, we got the pile small enough.

Toward the end of April, Marj arrived in her big Ford van from Saskatchewan. We loaded it up with all the things that were to go, including Mom's favorite rocking chair, small pieces of furniture, and her personal things. The auction rooms picked up the rest of the furniture, and we listed the house with a realtor.

After we put Mom on the plane for Calgary, Marj and I drove the three days to Gull Lake with the load of Mom's things. When we got there, we went shopping for a bedroom suite, a sofa, and a chair. Marj donated a small kitchen table and chairs so we were able to furnish her apartment before she arrived with Nell and Gary. I was able to see her set up in her little apartment. We made sure she had a good microwave and encouraged her to use it, since she often forgot to turn off the stove, while the microwave shut itself off.

I went back to the Philippines the beginning of May, leaving Mom in God's hands and feeling we had done the best we could for her. I had shed quite a few tears during those days in Port Stanley, missing my father, feeling sad about Mom's condition, and struggling to do what needed to be done in spite of her opposition. I was happy to return to my work and life in Manila.

Letters from Marj and Mom herself indicated that she didn't settle well into her apartment, complaining constantly about all the things she didn't have from her house in Ontario and missing her friends. It was a difficult time for Marj, as she was responsible for her care. I felt guilty that I had to leave it all for her, but there wasn't much I could do if I had stayed, and nobody could do my job in Manila.

Chapter 35
My Twentieth Anniversary
1987

Conference that year was one of the best I ever attended. I didn't have much responsibility, so it was a relaxing time. Anne West and I stayed together and enjoyed getting caught up with our news.

Anne had joined Ginny Larson and Rosemary Thomson in a new translation project on Orchid Island off the southeast coast of Taiwan, but they were still in the Philippines waiting for their visas. Since SIL had no other work in Taiwan, the Yami team was still part of the Philippines branch. The Yami language is closely related to Ivatan, for which Ginny had completed the New Testament. Anne spent one-and-a-half years on Orchid Island to help get the work started there.

Soon after returning to Manila from conference, I learned that I had to return to Nasuli in June for six weeks to take over the management of the publications department. John Bailey, who had been in charge, had to return to the States to care for his son who had been injured in an accident. A new manager was arriving in August, but I needed to fill in until she arrived.

It was a busy time to be away from my office, but I managed by flying back to Manila once for a few days to care for urgent business. Marti Binder arrived the second week of August, so I spent the rest of the month training her to do the work at Nasuli before returning to my job in Manila.

Doris Porter and I had been looking for another housemate, since we had three bedrooms, and a third person would help with the rent. In September, Betty Eastman arrived from Waxhaw, North Carolina, to work in the office. She had lost her husband five years before and decided she would like another field assignment. She and her husband had been translators in Peru. She moved in with us in late September. We enjoyed her very much, and we have been good friends since. It was great to have our house full again.

A Wet Year

That year was especially wet with a large typhoon north of us. A high-pressure area prevented it from moving on, and heavy rains inundated us for several weeks. Flooding put a good part of Manila under water. More than twenty people were either drowned, electrocuted, or had walls fall on them.

243

We were fortunate to be on high ground, so our house didn't flood, but our street flooded at both ends. The worst flood occurred one day when we were at work, but by the time we got home, one end had drained enough for us to get through. Schools were closed for several days. Even the presidential palace was flooded. Government officials got around on rafts and boats. The road to Faith Academy was neck deep in one place, preventing school buses from getting through. One of the teachers reported that her family had twenty-three inches in their house. Fortunately, they lived in a two-story house so carried many things upstairs.

Mold soon took over, and until the sun came out, life was miserable.

❧❧

Our choir director, Carminda Regala, was diagnosed with rheumatoid arthritis, which made it difficult for her to direct or to play the piano. We were sorry to lose her but were happy to welcome Lois Shellrude as our new director.

Lois and her husband were Christian and Missionary Alliance missionaries from the States. Her husband served as a professor at the Alliance Biblical Seminary in Quezon City. As Lois was a trained musician and choir director, she took over with great enthusiasm. We sang a Christmas concert that year, and in February performed a concert of spirituals, many familiar ones set to new and difficult arrangements.

❧❧

I sat on the porch of a little wooden house in the village of Caburacanan in the mountains of Bukidnon, watching the brilliant stars, when I saw, for the first time, a satellite wending its way across the cloudless sky. The year was 1969, and I was visiting Mary Jane Gardner and Ursula Post in their village home. They had gone there in 1963 to translate the New Testament for the Binukid-speaking people. I often thought of that peaceful visit through the years as I prayed for Mary Jane and Urs. They faced many struggles in the task God called them to do.

By 1977, the peace-and-order situation in Caburacanan had deteriorated to the place where the local military commander asked Mary Jane and Urs to evacuate for their own safety. So they moved permanently to Nasuli and continued to translate there. Since Binukid is spoken not only by the mountaineers of Bukidnon but also by the lowlanders around Nasuli, they found adequate language help to complete the New Testament.

However, they discovered that the dialect was not quite the same. The translation they had done in the mountains used a "hillbilly" dialect that was not acceptable to the educated people of the lowlands. So in 1983, Urs began the enormous task of redoing the whole New Testament to make it acceptable both to the lowlanders and the mountain people.

Johnny Dumala, a Baptist pastor, worked with Urs on the project. He spent countless hours checking her work and helping her to make the necessary changes. When the work was only partly completed, Johnny and his wife were in a serious motorcycle accident and nearly lost their lives. But God was good, and they both recovered.

Finally, the work was done, and the New Testament came to Manila in January of 1986 for typesetting and printing. This is the one I was working on when I received word of my father's death. Since Binukid is widely spoken among many Christians and churches, anticipation for the New Testament was high.

In early July, Johnny Dumala came to Manila. One of Urs's supporting churches in the States had paid his way to the itinerant evangelists conference in Amsterdam sponsored by the Billy Graham Association. The day before he left, I received the first copy of the Binukid New Testament from the printer and gave it to Johnny. Can you imagine his delight that he was able to take along on his trip God's Word in his very own language?

Binukid New Testament Dedication

In September I flew to Mindanao to attend the dedication of the Binukid New Testament. I always felt privileged to attend such dedications. I had a real part in each completed New Testament because of the many hours I spent preparing it for printing.

The dedication was held on Saturday in the gymnasium of a college in Malaybalay, the provincial capital. It consisted of three hours of singing, speeches, messages, and a special prayer, dedicating the Book to God. This was followed by food for everyone. On Tuesday, a second service was held out in the mountains, where many of the people lived.

A Visit to Tablas

I took one more break that year before Christmas. Helena Oderkirk and I flew to Tablas, an island in the Visayas, to spend a few days with Heather Kilgour and her partner, Gail Hendrickson. They had begun translating for the Bantoanon people a couple of years earlier, and I had wanted to visit them for some time. They lived in Calatrava on the northern coast of the island. We took a jeepney from the airport up the east coast of the island to Heather and Gail's home, where we spent a lovely three days.

The second day we were there, Heather and Gail took us on a jeepney to Odiongan, a major city on the southwest corner of the island. We enjoyed shopping for marble, which is plentiful there, and poking through the shops. In the afternoon, we noticed that very dark clouds were forming, so we immediately found a jeepney to take us home and climbed in.

Soon it began to rain, and we had another adventure with the weather. It rained so hard that we could hardly see ten feet ahead of us. The jeepney driver kept on, though, until we came to a raging torrent sweeping over the road. Our friends told us that this torrent usually was a small stream that trickled down from the mountains across the road and over a cliff into the ocean below.

The driver pulled up to a house, and we got out and went inside. The woman who lived there gave us all bottles of Coco Cola, and we stood under the eaves of her house to keep dry. We were stranded. Not surprisingly, another jeepney, headed south, was stranded on the other side also.

Soon the rain stopped, but the water still raged across the road. Both jeepneys turned around to return to their place of origin, threatening to leave us on the wrong side of the water.

Heather and Gail talked to some men on our jeepney, and they also wanted to return to Calatrava. They said they were strong enough to escort us through the stream. So they took our arms and walked us through the water. The current was so strong that I couldn't keep my feet on the ground. Helena was wearing sandals, one of which washed off and made its way to the ocean below. When she realized she had only one sandal, she removed the other one and sent it over the cliff to follow its mate. With great relief, we climbed into the jeepney and returned to Calatrava.

৯৽৽

Christmas that year was exceptionally busy. I was involved from September in practices until our big concert on December 14. We also sang special music at two services each Sunday during December and two Christmas Eve services. Since our congregation had grown to eight hundred people and the church only seated five hundred, we now had two morning services.

On Christmas Day, Doris Porter, Betty Eastman, and I had some of the single women in for dinner, making twelve of us. We enjoyed playing with a six-month-old baby, the newly adopted son of Judy McGinnis, our director's secretary. We had a great time of fun and fellowship.

Twenty-Year Anniversary

January 2, 1987, was the twenty-year anniversary of my arrival in the Philippines. Looking back, I could hardly believe I had been there for so long. The years had flown by with great speed. On March 6, 1987, I would be fifty years old! Perhaps this was the first time that I said, "At the way time is flying, I'll be eighty before I know it."

When I first moved to our town house, Marji Cook had been my house-mate. Of course, I took my cat, Patty II, along since she had become an important part of my life. Marji was also a cat lover so was happy to have her.

Al and Natalie Earp were going on furlough about that time, and Natalie asked if we would take care of their Siamese cat for them. We agreed that since it would only be for a few months, we would become a two-cat family.

Unfortunately, Patty had a different idea. Our house soon became a den of howling, screeching fur balls. We couldn't keep the cats separated, and since we couldn't give away Natalie's cat because we'd promised to take care of her, I reluctantly agreed to give Patty away.

Len and Jo Newell and their three children lived across the street from the SIL center. The children had been begging for a cat, so when Jo heard I was planning to give Patty away, she gladly took her.

One day several months later, I met Cheryl, the oldest of the Newell children.

"How is Patty doing at your house?" I asked.

"Oh, we don't have her any more. She wasn't compatible with our family, so we took her to the vet and had her sent to kitty heaven."

I was a bit shocked to hear this, but I had given her away, so I couldn't complain. I didn't think any more about it.

Now, three years later, I stood in the driveway near the back of our house when I noticed a cat crawling under the gate. She marched down the drive toward me with her tail standing high. When she reached me, she rubbed my legs as if to say, "Hi, please feed me."

I could hardly believe my eyes. It was Patty! Even though she was dirty and scraggly, the markings were exactly the same, and she certainly knew me.

Patty II had come home. Where had she been for the past three years? Had the vet taken the Newells' money for euthanasia and then dropped her off someplace in the city? Three years was a long time to wander the streets of Manila, but many cats spend their whole lives living out of garbage cans.

247

The Earps had long since returned from furlough and collected their cat, and Marji had moved to an apartment of her own, so I was happy to have Patty back. I fed her and cleaned her up. But I noticed that she looked bloated and wondered if she had worms. So I took her to the vet.

The vet remembered me, and she remembered Patty. I said I thought the cat must be full of worms because she had been wandering for three years. The vet looked a bit sheepish but checked her out.

The diagnosis was worms and a possible liver problem. I took the medicine and returned home. Even though I faithfully gave her the worm medicine, her bloating didn't get better; in fact, she seemed to be getting worse. Otherwise, she was her usual happy self.

Some four weeks later, Patty presented me with three fat, healthy kittens. I was amazed. Not only had the Newells paid the vet to have her euthanized, I had paid for her to be spayed.

I got a new vet!

Chapter 36
My 1987 Furlough
1987

New Testaments continued to arrive on my desk for typesetting. In March of 1987, the twenty-fifth New Testament came in ready to be printed.

This was the Central Sinama New Testament, translated by Kemp and Anne Pallesen from New Zealand. Every page of this book had a border around it. This meant special processing. We printed the border first then typeset the text and pasted it inside the border. The New Testament was beautiful when finished.

Reprint of the Amganad Ifugao New Testament

That year we did our first reprint for the Amganad Ifugao New Testament. Hilda Gotia and Helen Madrid had translated four hundred and ten pages of Old Testament portions that we added to the New Testament. Three thousand copies of the New Testament had been sold, so more were needed.

It was time for furlough again. I had planned to go home in May but was delayed until July. Nadine Lyman, who was planning to do my job when I was gone, was in the States awaiting back surgery. The doctor told her she had to lose thirty pounds before he would operate, so that meant she wouldn't be available to fill in for me.

Darrel Eppler, our publications general manager, was returning in early July and would take over for me when he came. I made my reservations to leave on June 29. Then I attended a furlough workshop at Nasuli to prepare for meetings I would hold while at home.

Hollywood Came to Our Community

That May Hollywood came to San Juan with the making of a movie set in Vietnam, starring actor Chuck Norris. The movie company moved into our neighborhood, one block from our house, with fifteen big trailer vans. It was messy and noisy with firecrackers going off to sound like bombs, and hundreds of people milling about. They used an old abandoned house on the corner that was built during the Spanish days before the turn of the century. They ate their lunches from fast-food containers and threw them on the sidewalks. They had a very loud generator to make their electricity, which they parked just beyond our house.

A number of movies set in Vietnam were shot in the Philippines, since the country has jungle like Vietnam, and the people look similar. Because Vietnam was communist, the movie company was not able to shoot films there.

Apocalypse Now was the most famous movie that I am aware of that was made in the Philippines. Some of our friends from Ifugao were hired for walk-on parts and were very well paid.

My 1987 Furlough

Now that my mother had moved to Saskatchewan, and we had no family home in Port Stanley, I needed a place to stay in London while on furlough. During my 1983 furlough, the missionary committee at my home church, Wortley Baptist in London, asked me how I felt about my relationship with the church.

"I appreciate the wonderful support I've received since I first went to the Philippines," I said, "but I feel like I don't know many people anymore."

The church had grown, and many of my friends were now working in other parts of the country. It seemed like a different place from when I left in 1967.

"On your next furlough, why don't you stay in London for a while, attend the church regularly, and get involved in the life of the church? Then you can get to know us again," the committee chair said.

"I would love to do that, but I would have to find something to do all week. Wycliffe requires us to spend part of our furloughs involved in the mission—taking a study program or working in one of the offices or at one of the SIL schools."

"Perhaps we could find a job for you at the church."

"That would be great, but I would have to get permission from Wycliffe to do so."

We left it at that. But as I thought about the possibility, I felt it would be good to become involved with my main supporting church so they could get to know me better.

I asked Wycliffe's permission to work at Wortley Baptist during my next furlough, and this was granted.

Now it was time to make plans for spending part of my furlough in London. I would take the summer for vacation and to connect with other supporters then begin work at Wortley the end of August.

Carroll McKay was the church secretary. Her assistant helped her with the multitudinous tasks required to keep a large church's office functioning.

About this time, Carroll's assistant had a disabled baby and had to resign from her job.

The church asked if I would like to join Carroll in the office. This was exactly what I liked to do, so I quickly accepted. Carroll and I had been good friends for many years, and I looked forward to working with her. But where would I live?

The church put out a request for someone to take me in for the fall. I expected to be there only until Christmas, so I didn't want to set up an apartment for myself.

A former missionary with a house in London informed me that she took in boarders. She had an extra room, and I could stay with her. I had known her for many years, and I accepted with thankfulness.

The last few weeks in Manila were busy ones. I needed to do myriads of things—shop; get clothes made; visit the hairdresser, the doctor, the dentist; make lists of things to take home; make lists of things to bring back from home; write last-minute letters; pack up my room to allow someone else to live in it while I was gone; and pack for the trip.

And then I also had final work in the office as well. Since Darrel wasn't arriving until two days after I left, I had to write detailed instructions for every part of my job; finish the final details on two New Testaments and get them to the printer; work on other parts of my job that had piled up on my desk; and work on the 1987–1988 budget, which was due on August 1 and was too big a job to leave for someone new.

Finally, my departure date arrived, and I flew out of Manila to Hong Kong where I spent one night. From Hong Kong, I flew to Vancouver and on to Calgary where Nell and Gary met me. I spent five days with them before traveling on to Gull Lake to see Marj, her family, and Mom. I spent the remainder of July with them.

I was glad to see Mom in her apartment but realized that she would not be able to stay on her own much longer.

Marj had put her name on the waiting list at the special care home in Gull Lake. This was a nice assisted-living facility where she would have good care. It would relieve Marj of the responsibility of checking on her every day to be sure she was safe and eating well. Marj was still working as a regional health nurse, traveling to the homes of seniors to assist them so they could stay in their own homes. Mom's name had come up once at the special care home, but she had refused to move there, saying, "People just go there to die," which, of course, is true.

Toward the end of July, it was time for me to go to Ontario. Since Mom hadn't been back since she left, she could go with me and visit her old friends. We flew to Toronto, and Art and Bonnie met us. Art loaned me his car so we could get around until I was able to buy one for myself, and we drove to Port Stanley where we stayed with Hazel Gordon.

Curt and Hazel had been good friends of our family, having lived next to us on the Lake Road where I was born. Curt had passed away about the same time as Dad, so Hazel was alone now. Some years before, both Curt and Hazel had become Christians, which made the bond of friendship even stronger, so we enjoyed our time with Hazel.

I took Mom around to visit many people she wanted to see. We drove to our former street where we discovered that the new owners of Mom and Dad's house had remodeled it considerably, adding an addition on the front and changing the outer finish. Mom didn't like it much.

After our time in Port Stanley, we drove to Toronto to Art's house. Bonnie took me to Simcoe to pick up a car I had bought, a 1986 Chevette, which would serve me for the few months I would be in Ontario. We put Mom on the plane for Saskatoon where her granddaughter, Jane, met her and took her back to Gull Lake.

Meanwhile, I moved to my friend's house. When I walked in, I was shocked to see her housekeeping. Huge piles of magazines, newspapers, books, and papers were stacked everywhere. I had hardly any place to sit and just a path to walk through.

A student was still living in the bedroom I was to have, so the owner gave me her bedroom. I had a hard time getting my suitcases in, and I had no place to put anything. She also had a dog that shed hair on every spot it settled.

My friend did all the cooking with a closed door to the kitchen. She cleared a space on the dining room table for the food and dishes, but she wouldn't let me help with cleaning up or cooking. The kitchen was completely out-of-bounds for everyone. Her mother was also living in her house, but they didn't get on very well together.

I soon realized that my friend was a hoarder, although I'm not sure that the term for such living had been invented yet. I also knew I couldn't live there. Yet I didn't want to hurt her feelings by just moving out.

God solved the problem for me. About two days after my arrival, I came down with a severe sinus infection. I'm not sure if it was caused by an allergy to the dog or the dust, but the dog was a good scapegoat. I needed to find a different place to live and used the dog as my escape.

I began work in the church office the last week of August. Carroll and her twin sister Sharon shared an apartment and had plans for a two-week vacation, so they asked me to house-sit for them while they were gone. That solved my housing problem for the time being and gave me a chance to see if anyone else in the church would have room for me.

I spent one day with Carroll in the office before she left and then had the whole job to myself. Fortunately, it was summer, and I didn't have much to do apart from answering the phone, getting out the church bulletin, and sending out an all-church mailing.

During this time, Pete and Isabel Plewes, an older couple in the church, told me they would be happy to have me live with them for the rest of my time in London. They had a lovely home just out of town at Pond Mills. Their property ran to the pond where they had a dock and a rowboat. They also had a dog, but he was a grey poodle called Silky. I didn't have any allergy problems with him, so I moved in to board with them. They treated me like family, so I was happy there. Their daughter was a missionary, so missionaries weren't unusual people to them, and I felt at home.

I enjoyed my work at the church and got to know many people, especially since I answered the phone and interacted with people who came to the office. Carroll was great to work with, and I felt I had made the right decision to spend part of this furlough at Wortley. I joined the church choir and especially enjoyed singing in the Christmas cantata.

For some time, Heather Kilgour and I had talked about the possibility of my going to Australia when she was on furlough. We could have a holiday together and do some touring there. This year our furloughs coincided, so we had made plans for me to fly there on my way back from furlough and spend January traveling about. In October she called to say that Wycliffe had asked her to teach at the Australian SIL school. She wouldn't be finished until the end of January. I changed my plans and scheduled a flight to Melbourne the beginning of February.

The daughter of Beulah Frezell, one of my Bible-college classmates, worked for a travel agent in London, so she made travel arrangements for my trip. She reserved a bus pass for Heather and me that would allow us to travel any place in the country for two weeks. We decided to take the bus from Melbourne where Heather was teaching, up the east coast to her home in Woombye, 62 miles (100 kilometers) north of Brisbane. Then we would spend the remainder of my time driving to places that could be easily reached by car from her home.

I became somewhat impatient with the travel agent because she didn't deliver my tickets when I wanted them. One day near the end of my time at Wortley, the staff had a farewell party for me. They presented me with a new NIV Bible that I wanted as well as the plane tickets for my trip. With my airfare was a bus pass, paid for by the church, which included two weeks of bus travel for both Heather and me. As a Wortley-supported missionary, I had refused to take any pay for my time working in the office. This was their gift as thanks for my work.

When I learned that I would be an extra month in Canada, I contacted the Calgary office to see if they had any work I could do for a month. They informed me that Geert De Koning, who raised funds for international literacy projects, could use some office help.

I decided to keep my car and drive West so I would have a way to get to work in January. But I didn't look forward to driving by myself in December from Ontario to Saskatchewan for Christmas.

One day I was visiting with Helen Deinum, with whom I had grown up at Faith Baptist in St. Thomas. We had been friends since childhood. I suggested that she might like to drive West with me to visit Marj, since they had been good friends too. I didn't imagine she would do it, but shortly I received a phone call, saying she had arranged a week's vacation from her job and planned to join me on the trip.

On December 8, Helen and I loaded our suitcases into my car and set off for Saskatchewan. We prayed for good weather, since we would be driving across 1,800 miles (2,896 kilometers) of the United States and Canada in winter.

God answered those prayers, and the roads were clear the whole way. In Minneapolis it snowed, but the highway was cleared by the time we left in the morning. We stopped the last night in Estevan, Saskatchewan, expecting to arrive at Gull Lake by mid-afternoon. Neither of us slept well that night, so at 4:30 a.m., we decided to get on the road and stop for breakfast wherever we could find it.

It was dark when we left the motel and headed down the main street of Estevan. The town had only one stoplight on the highway which was clear of snow. As I stepped on the brake at the stoplight, nothing happened. We sailed right through the red light as if I hadn't braked at all. I had hit a spot of black ice. Fortunately, at that time of day, no other cars were in sight, so we carried on our trip unscathed.

Marj was glad to see us, especially Helen, since she hadn't seen her for a number of years. Before Marj was married, they had been very close, spending much time together. Helen had married and had two sons, who were both grown now. Her husband had recently left her for someone else, and she was alone. It was good to have this time with her.

At the end of the week, we took Helen to Saskatoon to catch a plane back to London, and I spent the rest of December with Marj and her family at the farm near Gull Lake. After Christmas, I drove to Calgary to spend the month of January with Nell and Gary and to work in the Calgary office.

This was my third time to spend part of my furlough working in Calgary. I knew many of the staff and enjoyed my time with them, doing the work that they assigned me.

Chapter 37
Australian Trip and Losses
1988–1989

At last, the long-anticipated trip to Australia was underway. On February 4, I flew from Calgary to Melbourne with stops in San Francisco, Honolulu, and Auckland. Heather along with Harold and Hazel Parsons met me at the airport. Harold and Hazel had worked at Nasuli as children's home parents for a number of years, so it was good to see them again. Heather had a speaking engagement for the weekend, so I went home with Harold and Hazel until she returned.

In the evening, we visited a camp run by the Brethren to visit the Parsons' son. This was my first time to hear the bellbird, calling from across a beautiful man-made lake on the campground. Its call is like a china bell ringing.

On Sunday morning, I went to church with the Parsons at the Swanson Street Church of Christ. There I met Rosalie Peeler, who had also worked in the Philippines. She came home with us for lunch and then took me for a drive in the Dandenongs, a low range of mountains northeast of Melbourne. The whole area contained upscale homes built on the mountainsides. We stopped at a village called Sassafras to look through the souvenir and craft shops before resting at Miss Marple's Tea Shop, where we enjoyed hot scones, jam, whipped cream, and tea.

On Monday Harold took me to Kangaroo Ground, the Australian headquarters of Wycliffe Australia. We had a tour and met up with Heather, who had returned from her weekend trip. We also saw a number of others who had worked in the Philippines but were now home in Australia—Margaret Blowers, my former housemate; Len Wally; and Jenny and Otto Wischert and their one-week-old baby. We had tea in the afternoon at the home of David and Ruth Cummings. David was the director of Wycliffe Australia, and I had met him on several of his trips to the Philippines.

On Tuesday Heather and I went to Melbourne on the train. We took a tour of the city and stopped at the bus station to pick up our tickets for Canberra, the first stop on our trip north. During the city tour, I learned that the population at that time was three million, and the weather was undependable. Although it was summer, it was quite cool, especially at night. The next day, it could be scorching hot.

After the tour, we caught the train fifty minutes to Nunawading, where Bruce and Judith Grayden lived. Bruce and Judith had been translators for the Southern Kalinga people in the northern Philippines.

257

Our bus trip north left at 6:50 a.m., which meant we had to be up by 4:00 a.m. in order to catch the train into the city and a bus from the train station to the Greyhound station. I learned that buses in Australia are called coaches. Our trip, which lasted for eight-and-a-half hours, took us through dry and desolate countryside, covered with brown grass and gum trees.

From Canberra we took a tour to the Burbong Sheep Station, consisting of 810 hectares and three thousand sheep. We were shown how they sheer the sheep and prepare the wool for shipping, removing the head and leg pieces to go as second class and packing the body separately into bags. Sheep are no longer dipped to remove ticks. Now they are given shots that put medicine into their blood streams, and that keeps the ticks away. We watched a rider and two dogs bring in a flock of sheep from the pasture, had a tour of the house that had been built by the present owner's grandfather, had soft drinks, and were served an Australian barbecue—steak, sausage, fried onions, grilled potatoes, French bread, and oranges for dessert. Along with this went billy tea, which we drank and fed to several kangaroos, who lapped it up with great gusto. We also learned how to throw boomerangs.

Following our trip to Burbong, we took a tour of Canberra. It was built as the capital of Australia and is beautifully laid out. Later, we enjoyed a movie that showed the development of the capital.

On our second day in Canberra, we rented a car and drove to a wild animal farm where we saw numerous kangaroos. They were accustomed to visitors and came to get something to eat. We saw gorgeous birds—cockatoos, budgies, peacocks, and many kinds of parrots. We also saw wombats, koalas, emus, and camels.

From Canberra, we took the bus to Sydney. The countryside was quite different as we drove north. While it had been dry and brown in the south, now it was green and lush with rolling hills and trees. In Sydney we stayed with Heather's friends in north Sydney. We rode the bus to downtown Sydney and toured on foot. One special treat was a tour of the Sydney Opera House, which was fabulous. We also rode to the top of a Sydney Tower to view the city.

On another day, we took a bus tour to the Blue Mountains west of Sydney and to the Jenolan Caves. Unfortunately, the weather was bad that day, and the mountains, especially the Three Sisters, were completely covered in clouds. We did enjoy our trip through the Jenolan Caves, although it wasn't a trip for the infirm. We climbed nine hundred steps, fortunately not all at once. The caves were gorgeous with limestone formations. One of the rooms was huge, called the Cathedral. The guide said that the acoustics are tremendous and invited someone to sing a bit. Nobody did. Our tour through the caves took one-and-a-half hours.

From Sydney we abandoned our bus tour, since we were unable to get a ride during the day. Instead, we took a beautiful new double-decker train to Hamilton. We had morning coffee in the dining car, the first time I had ever eaten in one. At Hamilton we transferred to an old noisy wreck of a train that took us to East Maitland where we got off at 4:00 p.m. Heather had a friend living there, so we stayed with her overnight. The next day we caught the train to Tamworth to visit with more of Heather's friends.

During the time we were traveling around Australia, the Winter Olympics were in session in Calgary. When we stayed with people overnight, we had the chance to watch, since the eyes of the whole country were glued to their televisions during those days. It was intriguing to see the Olympics from an Australian perspective instead of Canadian.

From Tamworth, we got back on the bus for Brisbane, a full day's trip. Neville Southwell, who worked in the Brisbane Wycliffe office, met us. He drove us to the home of Andy and Sherry Gallman. They had worked in the Philippines before going to Australia to serve as the Wycliffe director for the Pacific area. Andy was then on a trip to the Solomon Islands and New Zealand, but Sherry took us in. We did the usual tour of Brisbane to see the special things the city has to offer. Sherry took us to the Gold Coast to Sea World, where we enjoyed the whales, porpoises, seals, and attended a special dolphin show. The following day, we visited the Wycliffe office and then went to the bus station to catch the bus for Nambour and home for Heather.

Heather's eighty-one-year-old father was at the bus station in Nambour to meet us and take us to his home in Woombye, just a few miles away. Again we spent the evening watching the Olympics.

We borrowed Mr. Kilgour's car and spent the next day driving around the countryside, looking at the gorgeous views in the Glasshouse Mountains, along the Sunshine Coast, and through a state park with a lovely waterfall.

We drove to Noosa and caught a bus tour to the colored sands and Fraser Island. Our bus was four-wheel drive, since much of the trip was on the sandy beach. The cliffs along the beach ranged in color from white to pink to orange and deep red. At one spot, we stopped to see the hull of a ship, the *Cherry Venture*, that had run aground and washed ashore. Our bus boarded a ferry for a ten-minute trip to Fraser Island, the largest sand island in the world. Here we saw dingoes on the beach.

We drove inland to the center of the island, where we walked through the rain forest and were treated to a steak-and-salad luncheon. As we returned home, the tide was beginning to come in, so we drove through water part of the way. Stopping at some sand formations, we took pictures and then returned to Noosa. The day was one of beautiful and interesting sights.

Not far from Heather's home is a ginger factory, the largest in the world. We toured the factory, eating vanilla-ginger ice cream and learning how ginger is grown and processed. We also visited a macadamia nut plantation and a pineapple plantation. Here a gift shop is housed in "The Big Pineapple," a thirty-foot high pineapple-shaped building. I had been looking for an opal ring since coming to Australia but hadn't found one I liked. Here in "The Big Pineapple," I found one that was just what I wanted.

On Sunday afternoon, we visited an elderly couple who were Heather's friends. I had wanted to see a kookaburra close up so was delighted to find one sitting on their veranda railing.

Our next adventure was a trip to the outback. We left on the morning of February 29 and drove west to Kingaroy, where Heather's father had owned a peanut farm and where Heather had grown up and gone to high school. The soil was dark red, and the countryside was dotted with peanut silos. We stopped to have lunch with Heather's aunt and uncle, Alice and Bob Kilgour.

On our way, we had had a flat tire, having picked up a nail. Thanks to Heather's dad, who had given us a good tutorial on how to change a tire on his car, we changed it with no problem. We left the tire in Proston for repairs and went on to the Kilgours' house for lunch. We found two of Heather's cousins there also, so she was happy to visit with them. Lunch was roast chicken and pork with plum pudding for dessert.

From Kingaroy we drove on a farm road, only one lane wide, toward Miles to stay with more of Heather's friends, Ted and Betty Little. Their house was almost a mile from the road, a typical Queensland country house—very large, one story with rooms in no kind of arrangement. Most old Queensland houses are built up on posts. Some have the underneath part closed in to make garages and workshops.

The Littles were not at home when we got there, so we waited for twenty minutes before calling their son. He said they had gone to the creek to pull out their boat. Eventually, they arrived. We had planned to spend an hour or so with them, have tea, and then go on to Roma for the night. They told us that heavy rains had left three feet of water on the road beyond Roma, so it was closed. We decided to stay overnight and drive north the next day toward Emerald.

We got up early the next day, and after a breakfast of steak, pineapple, grapes, toast, and honey with coffee, we set out, hoping to get to Emerald. It was raining lightly as we drove through the bush country. Just before Theodora, we had another flat tire. We were able to change the tire before the rain came down much harder.

We stopped in Theodora to get the tire repaired and then continued to Maura where two of Heather's cousins lived. We stopped at the home of one cousin to eat our lunch and to call the Auto Association to check on the state of the road going west. They told us the road was flooded, so we turned back east toward the coast. We arrived safely at Gladstone in very heavy rain and discovered this was the edge of a severe cyclone (known as typhoons or hurricanes in other parts of the world) that had come ashore further north, causing the worst flooding since 1911. We looked for a motel in Gladstone and finally, on the second try, were able to find a room.

The next day we called Heather's father to tell him we were on our way home and set out south toward Nambour. We took some detours to see the views of the countryside, stopped in Bundaberg for lunch at a fish-and-chips restaurant, drove on to Hervey Bay where we stopped to have tea with Heather's aunt and cousin who live there and arrived home at Woombye by 6:30 p.m. It had rained all day but not as hard as the previous day. That was the end of my trip to the Outback. Perhaps I'll manage it on another trip sometime.

My trip was about done. On March 4, Mr. Kilgour drove us to Brisbane to catch my plane for Manila. Heather's furlough wasn't over until May, so she was staying longer with her father.

Back to Work

Back in Manila, life soon returned to normal. At work I had a New Testament to typeset. But while I was gone, one thing had changed. The computer department men had installed a laser printer for printing typeset copy. This meant the end of our big phototypesetter. In some ways I hated to see it go, since we had become good friends, in spite of the work it caused me. The laser printer would make a tremendous difference in the preparation of a New Testament for the printer. I soon learned how it worked and was grateful for it.

This was conference year again, and I looked forward to a trip to Nasuli and the great times we always had when everyone was together. I had to work extra hard to get finished with the New Testament I was working on before leaving.

More changes were coming in our house that year. Anne West was finishing up her time in Taiwan, where she was helping to get the Yami project going, and was returning to the Philippines. Doris Porter was planning to leave later in the year, so Anne would be taking over her job as head of the literacy department. I asked Anne if she would like to live with me again when she arrived, and she readily consented. But Doris wasn't leaving until later, so Anne would stay in my room until she could get a room of her own. My room was quite large, so I borrowed a bed and made space for her. Betty Eastman was planning to leave later in the year also, and we would have plenty of space then.

Heather returned from Australia in May. Her partner, Gail, decided not to return to the project at that point, so Heather now had to decide if she would stay on by herself or if she would wait until she could find someone else to work with her. She eventually decided to continue on by herself.

Conference Again

The speaker at our conference that year was Dr. Stuart Briscoe, the pastor of Elmbrook Church in Brookfield, Wisconsin. He and his wife, Jill, brought a number of excellent messages on the fruits of the Spirit. We had changed our conference time from Christmas to June, and now it was the rainy season. Nasuli didn't have any paved paths, just grass or gravel, so the mud became quite deep when it rained every day. Rubber boots were the footwear of choice for those days.

At every conference, those of us who liked to sing prepared a musical to entertain the group. This year we did Gilbert and Sullivan's *HMS Pinafore*. It was a lot of work, but everyone did well, and the audience enjoyed it. I sang in the chorus so didn't have any speaking parts to learn. My work job at this conference was to prepare the final minutes for printing. Since most of this had to be done when the business meetings were completed, I stayed a few extra days at Nasuli after most of the rest had gone home.

When I returned to Manila, I began work on the Cotabato Manobo New Testament that was translated by Canadians Ross and Ellen Errington and their Manobo co-translators. The Cotabato Manobo people live in the southwest part of Mindanao. While we were working on this New Testament, we heard from Wycliffe International that this would be the three hundredth New Testament to be completed by members of Wycliffe worldwide. We prepared a special dust jacket for it with information about the people and the project.

Cotabato Manobo New Testament Dedication

The dedication of the Cotabato Manobo New Testament was held in January 1989, in three different locations. Three thousand people gathered to celebrate the arrival of "God's Instructions" in their own language. The crowds pulsed with joy and excitement. Never before had so many Manobos gathered together.

Five years before, the work among this group of Manobos was not very exciting. In fact, it was downright depressing. Pressures and influences from the outside world caused them to drift from their cultural moorings and lose self-esteem. The Cotabato Manobos had been forced into the mountains, as their land was slowly taken from them. They had very little, and most eeked out a living by growing small quantities of coffee.

Perhaps the realization of their inability to cope with life as it was unfolding around them caused them to look for alternatives. They found hope in literacy and health education classes. But the Word of God in their own Manobo tongue had the deepest impact on their lives. God spoke their language, bringing hope into their troubled world. It also challenged some of their beliefs and superstitions, which didn't meet their deep needs and longings.

In 1980 the Erringtons were extremely discouraged. They saw very little response to Scripture portions. However, they continued toward the goal God had given them—to provide God's Word in the language of the Cotabato Manobo people. The faith, patience, and work of the Erringtons and members of the Translators Association of the Philippines bore much fruit.

By 1989 fifty literacy teachers had taught over five hundred people to read. Thirty-two indigenous congregations of Cotabato Manobo believers were scattered throughout the mountains. The translated Word had brought new meaning and vitality to their lives and culture.

The Cotabato Manobo New Testament was the twenty-sixth to be completed in the Philippines. Now I was about to begin work on the twenty-seventh, the Ilianen Manobo translated by Hazel Wrigglesworth, from Brantford, Ontario. We not only had a new computer program but also a new laser printer for the typesetting. This equipment reduced the time needed to prepare a New Testament for the printer to about one-third of the time it had taken with the old phototypesetter.

In addition to my work on the New Testaments as they were completed, I often had other typesetting jobs to do as well. Bill and Ruth Atherton had been early members of the branch but had gone back to the States a number of years earlier. Now they returned to Manila so Bill could write a history of the first thirty years of our work in the Philippines from 1953 to 1983. Bill had a master's degree in journalism from Syracuse University so was well qualified for this work. It was a massive undertaking, but now it was completed and edited by Natalie Earp. I was grateful for our new typesetting program and laser printer to assist me in the preparation of this book. Its last page is numbered 602.

Anne West returned from Taiwan to take over as literacy coordinator from Doris Porter. I enjoyed having her live with me again. After Betty Eastman went back to the States, we rented our extra room to Jenny Golden, who was a literacy worker among the Botolan Sambal people. Since she lived only about a four-hour drive from Manila, she came in often and enjoyed having a home in the city to come to instead of always staying in the guesthouse. We enjoyed having her when she came.

Dengue Fever

Everyone living in my house that fall had dengue fever. My fever rose to 104 degrees F. (40 degrees C.), and I had the usual itchy rash, joint pain, and weakness. I called two of my supporting churches in Ontario, asking them to pray for me. During the time of their Sunday morning services, my fever broke, returned to normal, and didn't go up again. God answered their prayers. In nine days, I was completely well and able to return to work, even though it often takes a month to get over dengue fever.

જ્જ

I received a letter from home saying that Mom's name had come up again at the special care home, and this time she would be going there to live. I was grateful to God for this opening, since I worried about her still living on her own, even though Marj checked on her every day. She had a room of her own and took some small pieces of her furniture, so she felt more at home there.

Sorrowful Occasion

In October of 1988, some of Anne's Ifugao friends brought their two-and-a-half year old son to Manila for heart surgery. He recovered well and returned home with an appointment to come back to the heart center each month for a checkup.

In February the father and a daughter brought the boy on the night bus for his regular check. Since the appointment wasn't until 4:00 p.m., they stayed at our house for the day with plans to take the night bus home. When we arrived home from work, they had already returned from the checkup.

The doctor said that the boy's heart was doing well but that he probably had pneumonia. Just as we got home, he was having trouble breathing and had turned quite blue. We hurried them into the car to take them to the hospital, but it was rush hour, and the traffic was very heavy. It took fifteen minutes to reach the hospital, and by the time we arrived, the boy had died. The doctors in emergency worked on him for some time but were not able to resuscitate him.

In the Philippines, it is very expensive to transport a dead body, and the family had no money, so Anne and I decided to drive them home to Ifugao, a six-and-a-half-hour trip. By the time we could get the body released from the morgue, it was 10:45 p.m. We drove to our house, where we got something to eat, and left by 11:30 p.m. The father sat in the backseat of our car holding his son, while we drove all night to his home north of Bagabag, arriving at 6:00 a.m. It was very hard to see the sorrow on the mother's face when she learned that her son had died.

Anne and I drove one-and-a-half hours back to Bagabag, where we found some beds and slept for two-and-a-half hours before driving back to Manila. We arrived home at 6:30 p.m., ready for a good meal and bed.

Translator Dick Roe's Illness and Death

About this time, we received word that translator Dick Roe had been diagnosed with non-Hodgkin's lymphoma. This was a shock to all of us. Dick had been in the branch since 1955 and was now in his late fifties. He, along with Filipino co-translator Rudy Barlaan, had translated the Isnag New Testament.

He was now serving as consultant for the Ibanag New Testament, which was being translated by a group of mother-tongue translators in Tugeugerao. He had served in a number of administrative positions in the branch through the years and was known for his excellent linguistic and language-learning abilities. He had lived at the Manila center and worked in the office on several occasions, so he had become good friends with all of us working there. Being single, he often joined a group of us who enjoyed music as we attended concerts, ballets, and other cultural productions at the cultural center.

Dick went through several rounds of chemotherapy but was able to continue with his work. For almost six years, he struggled with cancer until on July 8, 1995, he passed into the presence of his Lord. Those of us who knew him well were sorrowful at his loss but rejoiced since we knew that the Lord had received him in heaven with the words, "Well done, good and faithful servant."

Ibanag New Testament Dedication

On June 10, 1989, just a short time after Dick's diagnosis with leukemia, I had the privilege of attending the dedication of the Ibanag New Testament and Psalms in Tugeugerao. The Ibanags live in northeastern Luzon, a ten-hour car trip from Manila. They are an educated, sophisticated people with many churches and many believers, but until now, they had no Scriptures in their own language. Because educated Ibanags could do the translation themselves if they were trained to do it, a joint project was worked out between SIL and the Philippine Bible Society to form a committee, which Dick Roe would train and supervise. The Bible society agreed to provide the funds for the project. Because both Catholic and Protestant Christians are among the Ibanags, all of them needing the Scriptures, it was decided that both should be represented on the committee. Dick worked with four Ibanags for six years, training them in translation principles, supervising, and checking their work. Finally, the task was finished.

The dedication program was held in a high-school gymnasium in Tugeugerao, the heart of the Ibanag-speaking area. Hundreds of people came, and after many speeches and joyful praising of God in song, almost one thousand copies were sold that first day. Some bought one copy, some bought four, some bought twenty. One church ordered five thousand. Since only ten thousand had been printed, all had been distributed in just a few years. God used His Word among the Ibanag in a mighty way.

A Trip to Taiwan

In July of 1989, I took the first real vacation I'd had since returning from furlough the year before. Anne West, Barbara Knutsen, the wife of our accounting department manager, and I flew to Taiwan for ten days. While there I was able to visit two families from my church in London, Ontario: Ross and Becky McKay in Taipei and Mark and Anita Cassidy in Taitung, both couples working with The Evangelical Alliance Mission (TEAM).

Our main reason for going to Taiwan was to visit Ginny Larson and Rosemary Thompson on Orchid Island where Anne had worked before returning to Manila. The translation for the Yami was progressing well. While the Yami language is closely related to Ivatan in the Philippines where Ginny had completed her first translation, the culture was a mixture of Chinese, Philippine minority groups, and Japanese who had controlled the island for a number of years.

Orchid Island was a beautiful dot of land, a mountain with a strip of flat land around the edge containing a road and where the people lived in six villages. The Presbyterians worked there for many years as well as the Roman Catholics, so every village had both a Presbyterian and a Roman Catholic church. But without the Scriptures in Yami, the churchgoers didn't have much spiritual life. Ginny was translating the New Testament with two Yami men, and Rosemary was teaching literacy classes.

This was my first trip to Taiwan. While we had a marvelous time, we also learned about the frustrations of being illiterate. The Yami people were not able to read anything, since almost all writing was in Chinese characters, and few people could speak English. I came away with a new appreciation for Ginny and Rosemary. They lived in an isolated place to give the Yami people the Word of God.

The time had come for me to buy a new car. I ordered a Toyota Corona from Japan but had to wait nearly six months for it to arrive. By July of 1989, it was finally delivered, a beautiful blue-gray sedan. This was the first time I had bought a car for use in the Philippines that wasn't a station wagon. By now, I didn't need to carry books to and from the printer so decided to buy a standard sedan. It was wonderful to have a new car again, but since the price was now very expensive, I hoped to make this one last for the rest of my time in the Philippines.

Union Church's Anniversary

In October of 1989, Union Church of Manila celebrated seventy-five years of service to God. We celebrated with a number of special activities. Our choir sang Bach's *Kantata Number Four* in German with the choir of a nearby church, accompanied by the Manila Philharmonic Orchestra.

We held a banquet at a nearby club to which we invited the ambassadors of all the countries from which our members came. I had the privilege of sitting at the same table as the Canadian ambassador. Our new organist played a concert on the organ. On anniversary Sunday, the choir sang several difficult anthems, accompanied by a brass ensemble from one of the universities.

In the afternoon, we had the installation service for a new pastor. Darrell Johnson had returned to the States several months earlier, and we were now installing our interim pastor who had agreed to stay on a full-time basis. We unveiled a new plaque commemorating the pastors from the past twenty-five years. Two other plaques already listed the earlier pastors. The guest speaker for the day was the Rev. Earl Palmer who had been the pastor twenty-five years before and whose name was first on the new plaque. He was now from Seattle, Washington's University Presbyterian Church.

It was a glorious week as we praised God for what He had done through this congregation for seventy-five years. The congregation now numbered more than one thousand people, meeting every Sunday for worship.

New Typesetting Program

With the changes in our typesetting equipment and new computer programs to learn, I needed training so I could understand how to use it all. The International Printing Arts Department in Dallas ran a course for desktop publishing specialists, which I had planned to attend, but it didn't work out for me to go to Dallas. Since a number of us in the Philippines needed to learn how to use the new typesetting program, Ventura Publisher, the Dallas office sent one of their trainers to the Philippines.

In the fall of 1989, Karelin Seitz, the international training manager for desktop publishing, came to Manila for a five-week workshop on the use of Ventura Publisher. This equipped me to be more efficient in the use of this software as I produced camera-ready copy for the printer. I used this program for typesetting New Testaments for the remainder of my time in the Philippines, adjusting to new versions as they became available.

During the years since the Philippine revolution in 1986, unrest increased among members of the Philippine Armed Forces. Seven coup attempts were quashed, but in early December of 1989, the Reform the Armed Forces Movement (RAM), and others loyal to Ferdinand Marcos, launched a more serious coup attempt, which lasted for nearly a week. Ninety-nine people were killed, fifty of them civilians, and five hundred and seventy were injured.

At the request of Mrs. Aquino, the US military put an end to the attempted coup. One of the battle areas was quite close to our house. When the American forces became involved, the US and Canadian embassies asked us to remain indoors for our safety. Threats had been made against Americans, and to Filipinos, everybody with white skin is an *Americano*. We could hear the gunfire and see the planes flying over. At one point, we heard a barrage of gunfire not far from our house.

Anne was away at the time, but Heather was staying in Manila with me. One night when she went upstairs to bed, she found a shell lodged in the floor of her bedroom. It had come through the roof and hit the floor just at the foot of her bed. I have that as a keepsake to this day. For four days, we stayed inside the house, praying for safety for everyone. God took care of us, and nobody we knew was injured, although two of our families had to be evacuated because they were right in the battle area.

My Mother Dies

On December 9, my brother Art called to inform me that Mom was with the Lord. She had been ill for several weeks, and her health had been declining for a number of months. I was sad to know she was gone but was happy to know that her suffering was over and that she was with the Lord.

I decided not to go home for the funeral, since it is very difficult to travel at the Christmas season without having reservations a long time in advance. Winter was not a good time for me to travel either. My family all agreed that I should not come. They made a tape of the funeral service, and it was a blessing to listen to it later.

I would miss my mother, but she had not been herself for a number of years. I felt that I had mourned for her already, since the mother I knew and loved had long since departed.

Percy and Mildred Funnell on their 50th wedding anniversary

Chapter 38
Major Earthquake and a Mountain Eruption
1990–1993

In March of 1990, I experienced the first bout of real physical suffering in my life. Apart from my thyroid problem from which I had no pain, a couple of bouts of dengue fever, which only lasted a few days each time, and bursitis in my shoulder, my health had been exceptionally good.

One Sunday afternoon in March, without any warning, I experienced severe pain down the right side of my back near my spine and down my right arm. The pain increased until I could hardly bear to sit or stand. I dragged myself to work because I was in the middle of typesetting a New Testament that needed to be finished. But finally, I was able to stay out of bed for only four hours a day.

A few trips to the chiropractor did no good, so I finally went to an orthopedic surgeon to see if he could find the root of my problem. An MRI showed that I had two collapsed disks in the base of my neck. The disks pressed into the front of my spinal cord and pinched a nerve. I also had osteoarthritis spurs pressing the back of the spinal cord. An EMG showed definite nerve damage in my right arm. I was hospitalized for three days with my head in traction to see if I could get some relief. Nothing happened, except for a very sore chin. The verdict was surgery.

The day the doctor scheduled surgery, I told him that I had had trouble in my right shoulder with bursitis for about six months. I don't know why I didn't tell him this before. Since I had already had all the usual treatments for bursitis—ultrasound, heat, exercise—the doctor gave me an injection of cortisone into the shoulder joint. Surprisingly, the next day the pain in my back was about 50 percent reduced.

I called the doctor. "Dr. Ver, the pain in my back is about 50 percent less today. The cortisone seemed to help."

"What?" he said with surprise. "That's unusual. I'll cancel the surgery for now and see if the pain will subside."

The pain continued to go away. In about a week, I was pain free except for discomfort in my neck occasionally and intermittent muscular pain on the left side. The doctor decided that the pinched nerve was not from my neck but from my shoulder. When the cortisone took care of the bursitis, the pain went away. I still have two collapsed disks in my neck but have almost no pain so have not had the surgery that was scheduled.

During those two months of pain, many people were praying for me—my family, my SIL family in the Philippines, and my church families at home. God heard all of their prayers and rescued me from unnecessary surgery.

Major 1990 Earthquake

On the afternoon of July 16, 1990, I was typesetting a New Testament when I felt a jerk under my feet. And then another. Soon the whole floor was shaking.

"Earthquake!" shouted Darwin, our graphic artist who was working in the next room. Quickly we headed for the back exit, which led from our office, through the automotive repair shop, and to the front of the building. As we reached the front sidewalk, I could see it rippling like a fast-moving snake. The office building looked as if it was made of rubber instead of concrete. The swimming pool near the guesthouse became a wave tank with waves more than a foot high spilling over the sides. Finally, it stopped.

Later, we heard that the earthquake had registered seven on the Richter scale. Thankfully, none of us was injured, including those who were vacationing in the worst hit city of Baguio. Thankfully, minimal damage was done to our buildings at Bagabag.

For many people though, the earthquake was a major tragedy. The final death tally was 1,521 with major destruction to buildings and infrastructures throughout central Luzon. Baguio, at five thousand feet in the mountains, was completely cut off for three days because of landslides on the major roads. Two hotels, including the Hyatt, collapsed with eighty hotel employees and guests killed.

Hazel Wrigglesworth, Barbara Blackburn, and Mary Rhea were on vacation at a small hotel across the street from the teachers' camp, where we had held our summer linguistic courses for ten years. They escaped from the hotel but slept the night in a car, since the building was not safe to enter.

Darlene Pridmore, our pastor's wife at that time, worked for the United States Agency for International Development. She was in Baguio at a USAID conference at the Nevada Hotel. Since this was the last day of the conference, she skipped the last session and went to the market instead.

She was inside the handicraft market when the quake struck but escaped by climbing over piles of merchandise that were strewn across the aisles. On returning to the hotel, she found it had completely collapsed. Twenty-seven of the people attending the conference had died, and many others were injured.

Later, when telling of her experiences and how God had saved her life, Darlene said that the Baguio market had not collapsed. That market had been funded by USAID. It took many years to complete, and after the construction was half done, nothing more happened for quite a long time. She told us that USAID officials had inspected the construction and stopped the funding because of inadequate earthquake safety measures. When the new building was brought up to standard, the funding began again. She was grateful to the Lord and to the officials who required that high standards be met; otherwise, the market might have collapsed as well.

The airport had major damage, including the runway, so only helicopters were able to land. Since our planes at Bagabag were Helio Couriers, constructed for short takeoffs and landings, our pilots could land on the limited useable places on the airstrip. For several days, they flew in and out of the city, transporting people to hospitals. They picked up our three women who were stranded in Baguio and returned them to Manila.

Reconstruction took many months, since the earthquake destroyed a number of buildings and damaged many roads and bridges. After seeing the damage that occurred, I understood better why our builders put so much rebar in the walls of our office building and guesthouse.

Christmas Open House

At Christmas of 1990, my housemates and I began a tradition that lasted for the remainder of my time in the Philippines: we entertained all of our SIL coworkers at an open house. We decorated our house, made fancy finger sandwiches and elegant desserts, and fixed a special punch. Forty people came to eat, drink, and visit. This was so successful that we continued every year until I left the Philippines. Our open house became one of the highlights of the Christmas season every year.

Tuwali Ifugao New Testament Dedication

Little old Matima in a red handwoven skirt and antique beads actually ran to the podium to receive her own copy of the Tuwali Ifugao New Testament. She held it up in the air, bent over backwards, and whooped for joy! Then she read aloud the verses assigned to her, choking up occasionally. When she was finished, she held up the Book, and whooped for joy again before she ran off.

One thousand and fifty Tuwali Ifugao New Testaments were sold that day. Translators Dick and Lou Hohulin said it called to mind Ephesians 3:20 (NIV), "Now to him who is able to do immeasurably more than all we ask or imagine." Judging by the number of banana stalks cut into twelve-inch lengths and peeled apart into layers for plates, four thousand people ate boiled pig meat and rice at the dedication.

This was the most interest in the Scriptures that the Hohulins had seen in the ten years they'd lived and worked with the Tuwali people.

A form of Christianity had been taught the Tuwali Ifugaos for ninety years, but it hadn't liberated them or changed their belief system because it had been in English. And though many spoke English, it did not touch their hearts. The language of their hearts was Tuwali. It spoke to them deep down inside. That's why Matima jumped and shouted for joy.

Ten years is a remarkably short time to complete a New Testament. Often it takes fifteen to twenty years. The Hohulins did this translation quickly because it was the second Ifugao New Testament that they and Ifugao colleagues had translated. They spent the first twenty years translating the Antipolo Ifugao New Testament. Many from Antipolo were now following Christ. Because the language and cultures of the two Ifugao groups were similar, the Hohulins learned more quickly the second time around.

But that doesn't mean it was easy for them. When they translated the Antipolo New Testament, they saw spiritual fruit right away. But the Tuwali were more sophisticated and harder to reach. Also, while the Antipolo New Testament was translated, the whole Hohulin family lived in the Philippines. During the second translation, their four adult sons stayed behind in the States. And worse, they started having grandchildren that Lou couldn't read stories to and Dick couldn't take fishing. That was a sacrifice for them.

But though the boys were in the States, the second translation was also a family affair. They are a very close family, but they all put aside their desires to be together so Dick and Lou could take the Word of God to another people in the Philippines.

Dick said, "Not only was it a responsibility, but as we invested these thirty years of our lives, we found it was a tremendous privilege to provide God's Word for people previously cut off from a life-changing knowledge of Him. We can't think of a better way to spend thirty years."

It was always a privilege for me to attend New Testament dedications like this one, knowing that along with the Hohulins and their Ifugao assistants, I too had a part in the production of the Tuwali New Testament. From the beginning of December 1990 until it came off the press in May 1991, it was in my hands for typesetting and printing. This was the thirty-first New Testament completed in Philippine languages by SIL members.

I well remember the excitement I felt when I held in my hand the first New Testament in 1975. That excitement hadn't diminished a bit as each New Testament made it possible for other believers to read God's Word in their own language.

Mt. Pinatubo Erupts

In the beginning of June, I took a few days off work, and Diana Stuhr and I drove to Maguisguis in Zambales. Jenny Golden and her coworker, Vangie Lunn, were teaching literacy classes to the Ayta people who lived there. Their home was small, but we found room to sleep for two nights and to visit their village and people. It was hot and sandy, but we enjoyed our time there.

One day we went for a hike outside the village toward Mt. Pinatubo. It was still far in the distance, but we had a good view of the mountain and could see dark grey smoke twirling out of the top. Mt. Pinatubo was a volcano that had been dormant for six hundred years. Recently, it had begun to show some life and was now threatening to become active again.

On the evening of June 16, RuthAnn Price invited Diana and me to her house to play games. At ten o'clock, we went outside to drive home and couldn't believe our eyes. It looked as if we were having a snowstorm. It had been dark and rainy in the afternoon, since a typhoon was in the area.

Mt. Pinatubo had erupted while we were at RuthAnn's house, and the circular winds of the typhoon brought the ash to Manila. My car was covered with a half-inch of fine ash called lahar. Since it was windy and blowing, it was difficult to see our way home. Unfortunately, we had left our windows open, so our house was full of ash from top to bottom. It took the better part of a week to get it all cleaned up.

The airport was closed for ten days, causing much inconvenience to people trying to travel. Anne West was stranded in the States for a week before she could get home from a seminar she had attended.

We were well off in comparison to the people who lived in the area around the mountain. Some places had an accumulation of ten to twenty inches of heavy ash, which brought down houses and destroyed trees and crops. The rice fields looked like beaches, and over 200,000 people were evacuated from the danger area. Rainy season had just begun, and the heavy rains caused mudflows that endangered towns all around for up to 31 miles (50 kilometers). Four SIL teams lived in the area. They were all able to evacuate before the mountain exploded. One family lost their house.

The village of Maguisguis, where we had visited Jenny and Vangie two weeks before, was completely destroyed. They grieved to see the people suffer. It was ten years before the effects of Mt. Pinatubo's eruption were over, and the land was useable again.

New Testaments continued to arrive on my desk for typesetting, and now we needed more people trained to do this job, since I couldn't handle it all. After returning from Bagabag where I attended another workshop in preparation for my next furlough coming in the summer of 1992, I organized a New Testament production workshop in Manila to train more people to handle Ventura Publisher, the program we used for typesetting Scripture. I taught a two-week course to six people. Some of the class participants had experience with Ventura already, having used it for different applications. I conducted a basic Ventura course at the same time. A New Testament was ready just at the time of the workshop, so we used it for practice.

During the two-week period, we typeset the complete Tagbanwa New Testament. This was published with 16 percent of the Old Testament included. In addition to the Tagbanwa, six other New Testaments were coming for production that year.

This was not only furlough year for me but conference year as well. I was scheduled to leave for home on June 30, but conference began on June 8, and I wouldn't get back to Manila until June 25. That left me only four days to finish packing and to take care of any other last-minute details.

That meant I needed to be almost ready to go before flying south. I still had many things to do. Packing was the worst. All those decisions that had to be made kept me awake at night. I wondered: *What do I pack in my barrel? What do I need to take home? What do I need to take to conference? What do I need between now and then? What do I want to throw out or give away?*

And then last-minute work needed to be done in the office—detailed instructions on how to run the office for my replacement, who wasn't arriving until after I left; a final edit and typesetting of the Book of Mark in Palawano if the translator got it back to me in time; typesetting the Book of Mark in Yami of Orchid Island in Taiwan to be done for Ginny Larson who was bringing it on the way to conference; finishing last-minute correspondence; writing a report of my work for the last three months for my supervisor; attending finance-committee meetings that would take a whole day; writing and getting out a newsletter; and a dozen other things that came up every day.

One of the advantages of getting older is the realization that, even though what needs to be done may look impossible, everything will get done on time. God gave me the needed peace in the midst of the rushing around to accomplish it all.

Furlough Again

During furlough, I spent two months in London then traveled around Ontario, New York, Ohio, and Pennsylvania, speaking at meetings and visiting supporters and friends.

By now I had finished the personal time I was allowed and was ready to begin my months of group service for Wycliffe. I had been asked to help in the training office of the printing arts department in Dallas, Texas.

To get there, I drove over 2,485 miles (4,000 kilometers) through New England and down the east coast of the United States as far south as Charleston, South Carolina, and then west through Georgia, Alabama, Mississippi, and Louisiana to Texas. I spent three-and-a-half weeks on the way, visiting friends and sightseeing in Colonial Williamsburg, Virginia, and Charleston.

At the International Linguistics Center near Duncanville, Texas, I stayed with Doris Porter in her mobile home. She was now head of the international ethno-linguistics department. I was glad to see her again, for it had been some years since we lived together in Manila. By the time I arrived in Dallas, I had slept in thirty-one beds. I was glad to settle down for a few months.

My job at the printing arts department was to assist Karelin Seitz with a course that prepared new people to do typesetting in the various countries where we work. It began in January and ran until May. During that time, we trained six new desktop-publishing specialists.

The first eight weeks consisted of classes in which fourteen members took part, followed by nine weeks of internship. Six of the fourteen participated in practical exercises to prepare actual jobs for printing. They prepared several newsletters, prayer cards, an annual report, a form, a calendar, part of a dictionary, the Gospel of Matthew, a primer, and a linguistic paper. They were working with languages from Africa and Mexico, which have much more complicated orthographies than ours in the Philippines. Some of the things they needed to do were new to me also.

These students experienced times when "nothing goes right," along with the satisfaction of seeing jobs completed. And we had a lot of fun along with the work. They used their training in Colombia, Peru, Brazil, Papua New Guinea, and Ethiopia. One couple remained to work in Dallas because of their children's educational needs.

Since I had never been in Texas in the spring before, I had no idea how beautiful it is. Beginning in February, gardens burst into bloom with daffodils, irises, pansies (they bloom all winter long), tulips, azaleas, dogwoods, and redbuds. In April the roadsides and fields are blanketed with wildflowers—Texas bluebonnets, Indian paintbrush, wild primroses, wine cups, lemon mint, and Indian blanket.

Later in April, Doris, April Erbe, and I spent the weekend in Austin to see the wildflowers. We drove backcountry roads, toured through beautiful caves that ran under Interstate 35 north of Austin, visited the National Wildflower Research Center, and then drove fifty miles west to the LBJ Ranch, home of former president Lyndon B. Johnson. Lady Bird Johnson had the roadsides sown with wildflower seeds, so the whole countryside was ablaze with color.

Five More New Testaments Completed

I received a report from the Philippines that since I had left the previous summer, five more New Testaments had been completed.

The Tboli New Testament was a revision of the first edition, which had sold out.

The Tagbanwa New Testament, translated by Peter and Chris Green, was the last one I had typeset before leaving for home. It contained 16 percent of the Old Testament as well as the New.

The Cagayan Agta New Testament, translated by Roy and Georgialee Mayfield, was dedicated in March and was now available for the Agta people, a small nomadic group with very few literates and only a handful of believers.

The Central Bontoc New Testament was dedicated on May 23. Keith and Kathy Benn translated it, and they had worked hard to encourage the local churches to use the Scriptures. They held a number of small dedication programs in outlying villages with the hope that this would increase the distribution and use of God's Word among the Bontocs.

The Central Subanen New Testament, translated by Bob and Felicia Brichoux, was almost ready to be released from the printer.

The United Nations declared 1993 to be the International Year for Indigenous People. We in Wycliffe were especially grateful for this attention to the people with whom we work. Wycliffe prepared a special logo, which we used on our printed material for that year to emphasize the importance of language among indigenous peoples.

God's Word in people's languages brings powerful changes for those who learn to read it and accept its message.

Chapter 39
SIL's Fortieth Anniversary and a Kidnapping
1993–1996

After eleven months in North America, I returned to my job in Manila. Those who had filled in for me while I was gone had done excellent work, but I was happy to take over again.

Unfortunately, the manager of our academic publication department had gone to his home country and was not able to return. This department published dictionaries, grammars, linguistic and anthropology articles, and books. Since we lacked an editor for these materials, the work was light.

The director asked me to take over the management of this department, along with my own job of managing the vernacular materials publishing department. This was to be a temporary assignment, since as soon as we found an editor, the work of the academic publications department would increase to a full-time job.

Fortieth Anniversary of Our Work

This year, 1993, marked forty years of SIL's work among the cultural communities of the Philippines. We planned a number of different activities throughout the year to celebrate this milestone and to further acquaint our friends with our work.

On July 20, we held an open house at the Manila center. We planned for weeks in advance and organized tours and presentations to educate our guests. I was responsible for invitations and nametags. We sent out over one thousand invitations, and more than two hundred people attended the occasion.

The week before the open house, the staff cleaned and arranged the offices, library, conference room, and grounds, during which we enjoyed picnic lunches together.

On the day of the open house, everyone had jobs. Some guided tours, some served refreshments (the ladies baked over three thousand cookies), some did troubleshooting, and some explained the work of their departments.

When it was all over, we went home exhausted but happy, feeling it had been worth the effort. That was confirmed later as those who attended sent notes and made phone calls, complimenting us on an excellent and informative program.

Chuck Walton's Kidnapping

The end of November 1993, was an exceptionally stressful time for those of us working with SIL in the Philippines.

Chuck Walton, and his wife, Janice, had been translating the Scriptures for the Sama Pangutaran people of the southern Philippines for twenty years, and they had just completed the New Testament in that language. They had been living in Philadelphia for several years so Janice could care for her elderly mother. Every year they returned to the Philippines for a few months to check the materials they had worked on.

That fall, Chuck had come alone to complete work on the alphabet. He and Janice planned to return together in March so we could typeset their New Testament for publication.

While Chuck was on the island where they worked, a group of men abducted him. They carried him away in a boat and held him on another island for three weeks. Much prayer went up around the world for his safety and release.

Government negotiators finally secured his release, and he flew back to Manila and home to Philadelphia and Janice. We rejoiced that Christmas as we understood in a new way that Christ came to set the captives free.

Masbatenyo New Testament Dedication

Translators continued to complete New Testaments, and we made them available for more people in the Philippines. February 26, 1994, was a special day for the Masbatenyo people who received the New Testament in their own language for the first time. The translators, Elmer and Bev Wolfenden, saw the culmination of more than twenty years of work. The Masbatenyos live on a group of islands in the north central part of the Philippines. They number about 800,000 people.

Because Masbate was easy to reach by air and the dedication program was set for a Saturday evening, which enabled us to attend without missing work, about fifty members of SIL attended. We filled the only real hotel in town and overflowed into a rooming house nearby.

Matt and Marcia Welser, newly assigned to distribute the Masbatenyo New Testament, made arrangements for us. Jeepneys and tricycles picked us up at the airport and took us to our hotel, a local restaurant prepared a buffet lunch for us, and a printed map showed us the main streets of town and things to see.

In the late afternoon, a great crowd of people paraded through the town to advertise the dedication, which would begin at 6:00 p.m. It was held in the Cultural and Sports Center, a large arena in the middle of town and attended by about eight hundred people.

The program was a model of Christian cooperation led by one of Wolfenden's co-translators. A local committee had prepared the program, which included songs, speeches, community singing, Scripture reading, and prayer.

The music was beautiful—a ladies' trio sung a capella (all three were voice majors in college) representing their churches, a solo by a local school teacher, a lively choreographed presentation by the youth from the Catholic Charismatic Renewal Movement, and three hymns sung by everyone in Masbatenyo.

The main speakers included Dr. Frank Robbins, president of SIL International, who happened to be visiting the Philippines, the general secretary of the Philippine Bible Society, the chairman of the International Bible Society of the Philippines, and the governor of Masbate.

Before, during, and following the program, which concluded at 9:50 p.m., New Testaments were for sale at the back of the hall. Since the International Bible Society graciously paid for the printing, a New Testament could be sold for just $1.85, well within reach of most Masbatenyos.

The Welsers had rented a store across the street from our hotel where the New Testaments were on sale, along with blue-and-white tee shirts advertising the dedication.

As we flew back to Manila on Sunday morning, the flight attendant wanted to know why she had a whole planeload of foreigners. When she heard the reason, she talked to Elmer and Bev Wolfenden about their work among the Masbatenyos. As we landed in Manila, she came on the plane's P.A. system saying, "Congratulations to Dr. Wolfenden for a job well done."

We all felt it was a lovely ending to a lovely weekend where God was glorified. His children in Masbate now had His Word for themselves.

A Visit from a Chinese Delegation

Because our work had become known in many countries of the world, we occasionally hosted delegations of officials who wanted to see what we were doing, especially in literacy. In November of 1994, a group of six came from China, each a high government official in his or her area of the country, arrived to familiarize themselves with the literacy work of SIL in the Philippines.

Since they were still with us at American Thanksgiving time, our director said we should show them what Thanksgiving is all about. He asked for two volunteers to each host one-half of the group with their interpreters for a traditional turkey dinner.

Not many members were comfortable with entertaining people of such high status, so my housemates and I took on the challenge. I certainly knew how to prepare a dinner! Our interaction with our guests at the office had been quite cordial, so we prepared our meal with enthusiasm.

Our guests were two men and a young woman of about thirty years of age. Since she was from an ethnic group in China, she came dressed in a colorful embroidered garment with a bright headdress. Their interpreter was an SIL member from Singapore.

None of our guests had ever seen a roasted turkey, so when I pulled it out of the oven, they asked me to bring it to the living room so they could all take pictures. I held it on a platter to have my picture taken with our dinner.

We had a delightful time of interaction. We explained about Thanksgiving and why we celebrate it. We told the story of the Pilgrims, and we each spoke of one thing for which we were thankful.

After dinner my housemate, Jenny, and the young Chinese woman went upstairs and exchanged clothes. Jenny had a Philippine ethnic costume that fit our guest, and Jenny wore hers. We all took pictures amidst much laughter. When the evening was over, our guests took their leave with more pictures and many thanks for the meal and our hospitality.

As we talked over this occasion, we felt sorry for all the members who were afraid to entertain these wonderful people. We had enjoyed every minute of our evening.

❧❧

This was to be a year for visitors. First Dorothy Woodford's sister, Harriet Hill, visited us from Los Angeles. She brought a suitcase of clothing and other wonderful things from the States that we couldn't get in the Philippines.

Then my sister, Marj, Vic, and their oldest daughter, Ann, came for two weeks. I enjoyed showing them around Manila, taking them to Nasuli, Bagabag, Amganad, and Baguio, and introducing them to my friends and our work.

Both Jenny and Anne had friends visit, and later in the year, three more friends came to visit Dorothy. I enjoyed getting to know these visitors and helping to show them around the city.

Rainy season this year was heavier than usual. From the beginning of May to the end of August, we hardly had a sunny day. Two years before, Diana had given me a rain gauge, which I installed in the middle of our front lawn. During the month of July 1994, Manila had 29.7 inches of rain, almost exactly double that of the year before.

Because of the constant rain and the heavy traffic, the asphalt streets sprouted enormous and multitudinous potholes, some almost big enough to swallow a car. The condition of the streets caused the traffic jams to become much worse than usual. One week it took me one hour and twenty minutes to get to choir practice on Wednesday night, a distance of 7.4 miles (12 kilometers). God was teaching me patience on those long trips.

The traffic in Manila continued to get heavier every year. By now, loud complaints came from all sides, but no matter what the city did to alleviate it, the problem continued to intensify. A new law was put in place in 1995, which prohibited cars with license plates ending in one and two from driving on EDSA, our busiest thoroughfare, on Mondays, three and four were prohibited on Tuesdays, five and six on Wednesdays, seven and eight on Thursdays, and nine and zero on Fridays. The same scheme applied to public transportation vehicles, such as busses, jeepneys, and taxis, but they were not allowed to drive on any street on their days off. This did make some difference, but the frustration of having to drive back streets on your day off and fight all the other cars with the same number as yours, caused more stress than the original traffic.

A popular joke went around Manila at this time: A man was driving down a street when he saw a friend walking on the sidewalk. He pulled over and called out, "Would you like a ride?"

"No, thanks," replied his friend. "I'm in a hurry."

Each year after Mt. Pinatubo erupted in 1991, *lahar* (a geological term meaning ash, sand, rocky boulders, and pumice, mixed with rain water) washed from the sides of the mountain and hurtled down the river channels to bury the countryside during rainy season.

In 1995, we received reports that the devastation was worse than any previous year. The flooding intensified, since the lahar washed down in previous years had filled the river channels, and the water went where it would through villages and towns and over croplands.

When the water receded, it left behind sand deposits to bury buildings. One town had almost completely disappeared with only some rooftops sticking through. The very large, old Spanish church was buried halfway to its roof. Some people lost their lives, and others lost all their possessions, homes, and livelihoods. Workers dredged the rivers and built dykes, but all the work was to no avail.

Evacuation centers were set up, but the food, clothing, and sanitation needs were tremendous. Government agencies, many churches, and Christian organizations did what they could to help, but the needs were overwhelming. Gradually over the years, the lahar became less, but it was ten years before all the lahar was washed down.

Rents began to rise, and we knew that we would need to move when our lease was up in June of 1995. Our landlady increased our rent 10 percent each year, and we had now reached the maximum amount we could afford. We liked our town house in its quiet neighborhood, but we were not sad to leave the obnoxious odors that arose from our landlady's backyard.

She lived on the other side of our duplex and ran a home business. About once a month, her employees conjured up a batch of *bagoong*, a fermented fish paste made from shrimp, other fish parts, and salt. They sold the mixture both locally and exported to Japan.

The odor of the processing was very strong and came in our windows until we could hardly endure it. Many nights I went to bed with a tissue soaked in perfume tucked against my nose.

We liked to walk for exercise and often left our gated community to walk through the streets of New Manila. One of our SIL couples, Winston and Lois Churchill, lived in a compound on Fourth Street, about three blocks from our house. Their spacious apartment was on the third floor of a six-apartment building inside a family compound.

We liked it and told Lois that if an apartment in their building came up for rent, to let us know, since we were interested in moving there. It was closer to the SIL center and had good security, since the landlady who lived at the back of the property with two of her daughters, hired a twenty-four hour gate guard.

In March Lois informed us that the missionary couple, who lived across the hall from them, was leaving, and their place would be for rent. We made arrangements to see it and told the landlady we would take it as soon as it was available. The rent was considerably more reasonable than where we were living, although it had only two bedrooms, and four of us were living at our present house.

By May we moved to our new home. The bedrooms were large, and Jenny and Dorothy divided the master bedroom with a row of high bookshelves, so they each had their own space. Anne and I shared the second bedroom, which was the same size but with a smaller bathroom and closet space. Anne was leaving for furlough in June, so we could manage until then. By the time Anne returned in 1996, both Dorothy and Jenny would be gone, so Anne and I would each have our own room.

The compound was beautiful with many trees and flowers. Three of the other units in our building were soon occupied by SIL families, leaving one apartment on the second floor with a Filipino couple. It took us just ten minutes to walk to the SIL center, which made it very convenient when we didn't want to take the car.

By late in 1995, Claudia Whittle and Ruth Lusted, translators in northern Luzon, had completed their New Testament, and I now had it on my desk for typesetting.

Claudia and Ruth had been working with the Atta people for forty years. The Atta were a Negrito people, one of the earliest people groups of the Philippines. Since they were nomadic, this made work with them difficult and slow.

In the years before this time, the peace and order situation in their province was poor, making it necessary for Claudia and Ruth to live at Bagabag away from the people, except for a few who moved with them.

In spite of many difficulties, quite a few believers were eager to have the New Testament in their own language. We worked through the end of 1995 and into 1996 before completing the typesetting and sending the book to the printer.

On January 10, 1996, I woke up in the morning with pain in my right back just above the waist. I thought I was having a muscle spasm, which I had had previously in that location. By the next morning, the pain was considerably worse, and I noticed a rash on my back. Consultation with one of my coworkers, who is a doctor and happened to be in Manila at that time, confirmed that I had shingles.

Now that is pain, the worst I have ever experienced in my life! It developed into quite a severe case, spreading all around in a two-inch band from the middle front to my backbone. In three weeks I was still in pain and on heavy doses of pain medication. Several nights I walked the floor, unable to lie on my bed. This was before medication specific for shingles had reached the Philippines. I continued to have pain and itching for six months after the onset of the disease, and I hope never to have it again.

When I contracted shingles, I had just begun typesetting the Western Subanon New Testament for Bill and Lee Hall. They had to leave for furlough the beginning of February to attend their daughter's wedding. I wondered how I would finish in time, since I was not able to work for more than two weeks when I was sick.

At that time, Doug Rintoul, head of our computer department in Bagabag, arrived in Manila with his parents who had been visiting over the holidays and were on their way home. Doug agreed to stay in Manila and finish the Subanon typesetting for me. It is wonderful to work with people who are willing to step in where help is needed.

ॐ

In addition to the Western Subanon New Testament, six other New Testaments were completed that year, bringing the total by the end of 1996 to forty-four.

One of those was the Ibatan, translated by Rundell and Judi Maree. July 15–19, 1996, was the celebration of the Coming of the Word of God to Babuyan Island. Rundell and Judi had returned to the island a few days before the dedication and were standing with their Ibatan friends on the grass airstrip to welcome visitors as small single-engine airplanes came in. It took a total of twenty-one flights to ferry in the guests and family members—making Babuyan probably one of the busiest Philippine airstrips outside of Manila that week!

When each airplane landed, village people greeted the visitors. They took group pictures then ushered guests to the shade. They offered them fresh fruit, introduced them to their hosts or hostesses for the week, and guided them up the steep pathway to the village. Delicious meals, special programs, palm leaf shelters, fresh lobster from the nearby ocean, a delightfully decorated stage area, and even a large PA system were some ways the villagers made the celebration special for their guests.

Although Rundell and Judi had helped plan the events, the people of the church and the community carefully assigned and meticulously carried out the work—a testimony to their realization that the coming of the Word of God was worth extra effort.

It was also a time of miracles. The Ibatan people prefaced their guests' confirmations and flight information with the reminder "that July is typhoon season, and Babuyan always is hard hit, so prepare for the possibility that all flights may be cancelled."

God honored their prayers and of others around the world. From the first flight in until the last flight left, the weather held, a miracle that the

Ibatan people, after having lived their entire lives on the island, could hardly believe. God had indeed "stilled the storm" on Babuyan!

On the day of the actual dedication service, the crowd gathered early. Almost everyone sported a Babuyan Bible dedication tee shirt—even the dignitaries on the platform. Many exclaimed over the fact that because of the many guests, it was an international conference. Actually, eight nationalities were represented.

As the guest speakers shared—the vice mayor, the doctor representing the department of rural health, representatives from the department of education, pastors representing neighboring churches, and SIL—each one told of the impact of the Word of God. They recounted the exemplary community spirit witnessed on Babuyan, the faithfulness of the health workers in the clinic, the intense interest in education, the sacrifice made to work at the translation desk rather than at business ventures. Each one attributed these positive influences to the love of God and the coming of His Word to Babuyan.

Truly God had worked a miracle in the hearts and lives of the Ibatan people, and the outside world noticed it. During the celebration, almost three hundred and fifty copies of the New Testament were sold, more than could be expected, since the Ibatans number only one thousand people.

When the excitement of the dedication died down, typhoons returned to batter the island. But the Ibatans now had the Word of God in their own language. They believed that the Word would continue to stir people's hearts and lead them in paths of righteousness. The church was alive and growing. Already the people talked of an annual Bible conference to be held on the reunion of the dedication. The Word of God made a real difference to the Ibatans.

This was the year for our biennial conference again when we all gathered at Nasuli for two weeks of spiritual refreshment, good fellowship, and business meetings. One of the highlights of our time together was a service called the "Celebration of the Word," where we dedicated to God all the materials published in the past two years. This consisted of 117 books and articles, including six complete New Testaments.

May was a busy time at our home in Manila as Anne West returned from a year of furlough in the States. Her sister-in-law accompanied her and visited for two weeks. I always enjoyed meeting people I had heard about for years and to compare my mental image with reality. Maxine was a lovely person, and we all enjoyed her visit very much.

Dorothy Woodford also left us in May for her home in California. She had lived with us for nearly two years while working in the accounting office. She went home with many stories to tell of her time in Manila, one of which was watching the workmen from the center move her piano from our town house to our new third-floor apartment. They didn't have any equipment, just the strength of four small men, who had grown up in the mountains and developed unusual brawn.

Two weeks before leaving, Dorothy presented a beautiful piano concert at our church, along with a lady who played a French horn and another who played a flute. A full-length concert of mostly classical music takes a lot of practicing, so we enjoyed listening every evening for several months to her repertoire on the piano.

Jenny also left in July for a short home leave to take care of medical needs and to visit her family. She returned in September to bring our family back to three, along with twenty-five-year-old Melanie, who cleaned our house and cooked for us. Melanie also went to college full-time and had one more year to finish her degree in commerce so she could get a job in finance. We paid her tuition and gave her room, board, and spending money in return for her excellent work. Another young woman came two days a week to do laundry and ironing for us.

We were grateful for Tess and Melanie's help, because it freed us to spend more time doing the work that God had called us to do.

Chapter 40
Forty-Five Years in the Philippines
1997–1998

By 1997, SIL's work in the Philippines had been underway for forty-five years. As we completed more and more New Testaments and Bibles, we talked about finishing the needed translations. My greatest desire was to stay until the very last group in the Philippines had received the Word of God in its own language.

At every conference, we discussed how we could complete this work. Members had differences of opinion: Should we set a date and work towards that? Or should we set other criteria to know when we would be finished?

I liked the idea of setting a date, since it would give us something concrete to work toward. Many others felt this put too much pressure on the translators and preferred to set trigger points, indicating that when such-and-such occurred, then we should start closing down the work. In the end, the trigger-point people won.

Thoughts of Retirement

In March of 1997, I turned sixty. Although I wasn't ready to retire for some time, I did think about where I should go and what I should do when the time came. My sisters both lived in western Canada, but this tropical transplant didn't want to live in either Calgary or Saskatchewan. The same was true of Ontario, where my brother, Art, and his wife, Bonnie, lived. The winters were much too cold. So I thought about living near the coast in British Columbia, where the winters were mild.

However, I had one problem. I had never even been in British Columbia, except for a trip to the Rockies as a teenager and a few stops in the Vancouver airport on my way to and from the Philippines.

Nell's younger son, Chris, attended the Northwest Baptist College in Langley, BC for one year. He informed me that I would hate it there because it rained all the time. But other people told me the Fraser Valley in BC was beautiful with mountains all around, and I would love living there.

How to know? I decided the only way was to spend a winter there to see for myself. Rain didn't depress me, since I had carried an umbrella my whole time in the Philippines. Could BC be any worse?

As my next furlough was coming up in the summer of 1997, I wrote to Dr. Mike Walrod, who had been a translator for the Ga'dang people in the Philippines. He was the president of the Canada Institute of Linguistics (CanIL), Wycliffe Canada's linguistics training school on the campus of Trinity Western University in Langley, BC. I asked him if he had a job I could do there on my furlough so I could experience a winter in British Columbia. He said he did and that I should plan to come in time for the beginning of the fall semester in September 1997.

Furlough Preparations

Now it was time to prepare. I went to Nasuli in February to attend a furlough workshop in preparation for meetings I would take in Ontario and New York State when I first got home in May. While I felt privileged to be involved in the actual production of Scripture, I sometimes felt far removed from work among the people for whom the Scriptures were being translated. This workshop gave me lots of stories of God's work. A major emphasis was put on relationships with our partners at home, people who prayed for us and helped us financially.

While at Nasuli, I stayed with fellow Canadian, Sharon Dickinson. She had begun her work with Wycliffe in Papua New Guinea but had transferred to the Philippines several years earlier and worked in Manila for some time. We had become good friends then. Now she worked as the librarian at Nasuli and lived in an apartment over the commissary (grocery store).

Her mother had been visiting for some time and was now planning to return home to Brantford, Ontario. We sailed back to Manila on the Super Ferry 9, which had now become my favorite way to travel. It took longer than the plane, two nights and one-and-a-half days compared to one-and-a-half hours on the plane, but it was a wonderfully relaxing trip.

My next big task was to train Robyn Terry from Australia, who had agreed to do my job during the year I planned to be away. I needed to be sure she was adequately prepared.

She came to Manila, where we went over everything she should know. I also taught her how to operate the typesetting program we used for preparing Scripture for printing. She was very sharp so had little difficulty in grasping the work. She also agreed to move into my room at home to help pay the rent while I was gone.

1997 Furlough

This furlough was a time of reuniting with old friends. On the way home, I stopped for three days in Hong Kong to visit Australian friends who were working there. Then I flew on to Calgary to visit Nell and Gary, to take care of business at the Wycliffe office, and to buy a car for my travels across Canada and the United States. I found a pretty blue Chevy Cavalier, which took me many miles across the country on my trip east to visit supporters and other friends.

My first stop was in Gull Lake to spend a few days with Marj, Vic, and their family. Then I drove on to Portage la Prairie, Manitoba, where I visited with Marg and Bruce Schnurr. I hadn't seen them since they left their church in Buckingham, Quebec, and had taken a pastorate in Portage. We enjoyed reminiscing about Bible college days in the 1950s and 1960s.

This was the year of the great flood on the Red River, which was still well above its banks. I drove on to Winnipeg, where I stayed with Winston and Lois Churchill, who were there during their furlough.

I checked the road conditions and found the highway was still flooded south of Winnipeg toward the US border. So I drove southwest to Morden, Manitoba, where I spent a day with Mary Poetker, who had taught at our Nasuli school for several years. From there I could drive straight east along the border and get on the highway going south into North Dakota. While the highway was open, the water hadn't yet receded from the fields on either side of the highway. Fortunately, the road was built high above the adjoining farmland, so driving on it felt like crossing a causeway over an ocean.

Eventually, I reached Fargo and turned east on Highway 94 into Minnesota, away from the river. My destination that day was St. Bonifacius, Minnesota, a short distance west of Minneapolis, to visit Dr. Al and Josie Cramer. Al had been my Old Testament professor at Bible college in London. They had left there in the early sixties, and he was now teaching at Crown College. I had not seen them in more than thirty years so looked forward to a great time of reminiscing about those days when I was a young student, and he had just taken up his first teaching assignment.

Following a day-and-a-half of nonstop talking, I drove on to West Chicago to spend a day with Audrey Mayer. She was working at Wycliffe's North Central Regional office while on furlough. They had a guest room where I stayed.

From there I drove south and east through Indiana to Upland to visit Tim and Lucille Diller. After their visit to the Philippines in 1968, they had decided not to join Wycliffe after all and returned to the States where Tim got a job as head of the computer department at Taylor University. They had graciously supported me financially since their return to the States, but I had not had an opportunity to visit them before this trip. Their family was now grown, and Lucille was teaching at the local elementary school. She asked me to talk to her sixth-grade class about the Philippines. Tim gave me a great tour of the Taylor campus, and I came away feeling that I had a much better picture of their lives than I had before.

I arrived in London, Ontario, just in time for a reunion of graduates from London Bible Institute and London College of Bible and Missions. While the school hadn't existed since 1968, many alumni were eager to be reunited with former classmates. We met in a church in London for Friday evening and all day Saturday. The first evening was unstructured, allowing people to visit. Imagine the sound of two-hundred people all talking at the same time! I saw a number of people I hadn't seen for thirty-seven years.

Following the reunion, I spent six weeks in the East, including a trip to New York State and Pennsylvania, visiting supporting churches and friends.

I visited Joan and Hugh Barrie, who had attended the Amganad Ifugao New Testament dedication with me. They lived in Newtown Square, a suburb of Philadelphia. We walked through beautiful Longwood Gardens and enjoyed a day at the Jersey shore. We picnicked on the beach, shooed off seagulls, and walked the boardwalk at Ocean City, while munching saltwater taffy.

Following a time in Ontario, I drove west to visit my sister Marj and her family on their Saskatchewan farm. One of the pleasures of summer was enjoying delicious fruit—strawberries, raspberries, cherries, nectarines, grapes, pears, peaches, plums, and apples. Few of these were available in the Philippines, and, although I loved the tropical fruit we had in abundance, I missed the fruit with which I had grown up.

After my time at the farm, I drove on to Calgary and spent three weeks visiting Nell and Gary. It was summer sale season, so I stocked up on clothing and other items to take back to the Philippines with me.

Since I didn't need to be at CanIL until early September, I drove to northern California to visit Dorothy Woodford, who had shared my home in Manila for two years when she worked in our accounting office. We made a special trip to Yosemite National Park, which is not far from her home.

When I returned back to Langley, British Columbia, I had put over 8,699 miles (14,000 kilometers) on my car.

Work at the Canada Institute of Linguistics (CanIL)

Since I knew no one at CanIL except two families who both lived in Abbotsford, I asked Mike Walrod if he could find me a place to live while I was in Langley, and he did.

Eileen Meston, a single woman who lived just a few blocks from the campus, was looking for someone to share her house for the year while her housemate was away. Her price was right, so I moved in with her until I returned to the Philippines in May 1998. As a bookkeeper, she worked for Corrections Canada. Her house was in the country with a big backyard and cows and goats over the back fence.

I worked as receptionist at CanIL, answering the telephone, taking care of walk-in traffic, answering questions, buying office and maintenance supplies, filing, distributing office mail and e-mail, and other odd jobs. Since I was new in the area and the school and didn't know many people, it took time before I was efficient at my job, but I learned quickly and enjoyed my work.

I also learned my way around Langley and decided that I could certainly be happy to retire in this area. I especially enjoyed getting to know my Wycliffe coworkers on staff and the students who were taking linguistic courses. At that time, the student body was the largest CanIL had ever had with thirty-seven enrolled, many preparing to become part of the Bible translation ministry.

Eileen attended a small Fellowship Baptist church in Aldergrove, about nine miles (fifteen kilometers) east of Langley. I attended church with her and enjoyed the fellowship very much.

On my first Sunday, I was shocked to see people I knew. Dr. Ken Davis, who had been a professor at LCBM when I worked there, was directing the singing, and his wife Dorothy was playing the piano. After they left London and went to Waterloo, Ontario, to teach at the Lutheran University, I had lost track of them. I had no idea that Ken was now teaching at Trinity Western University.

Before the service began, the assistant pastor shook my hand, welcoming me to the service. I felt that I knew him also. He introduced himself as Fred Davison, and I immediately remembered that he was an alumnus of London Bible Institute. I had met him at alumni meetings when I worked in the alumni office before joining Wycliffe. His daughter, Beth, was wife of the church pastor, Marshall Davis.

To find people I knew from my past in this place where I thought I knew no one was a special blessing from the Lord. Dorothy directed the choir and invited me to join them, which I did. I felt at home at Aldergrove Baptist and knew that God had led me there.

The months flew by quickly, and soon it was December. I flew to Calgary to spend Christmas with Nell and Gary. The weather was beautiful, above freezing and sunny most of the two weeks. Then on New Year's Day, we woke to snow and steadily dropping temperatures. When I left Calgary, the thermometer stood at -18 degrees F. (-28 degrees C.). I was happy to return to BC, where it was much warmer, until the day after I arrived when we had four inches of snow. It only lasted one day, however.

Classes finished at CanIL in early April, and the students scattered to various locations. Those who graduated went on to the work to which God had called them. Others looked for summer work to earn tuition money to continue the following year.

April in BC brought spring and flowers everywhere. I attended a daffodil show where more than four hundred varieties of daffodils were on display. The tulips were just beginning, and the fruit trees had just finished blossoming. Azaleas and early rhododendrons splashed their bright colors in gardens and parks. Many varieties of birds visited our backyard, and a Canada goose daily walked around the Trinity Western University campus.

I planned to return to Manila in early May, but first, I needed a vacation. Mary Stringer from Australia, who had taught literacy during the school year, joined me as we crossed the Straits of Georgia on the ferry to Victoria on Vancouver Island. We visited Bob and Pearl Williams for three days. Bob and Pearl had worked for several years at Nasuli, managing our guesthouse.

From the Williams's home, we drove to the west side of the island to Ucluelet to stay in a guesthouse for Christian workers. It was located on a cove on the Pacific Ocean near Pacific Rim National Park. We had a restful week, watching and listening to a family of loons, writing letters, reading books, walking on the beach, and hiking in the temperate rain forest park.

Mary stayed for a second week, but I needed to pack for my flight to Manila, so I drove to Nanaimo and took the ferry to Vancouver and on to Langley.

CanIL portable office

Chapter 41
More Books Published and Another Dedication
1998–2001

I arrived back in Manila on May 2, 1998, ready to begin my eighth term of service in the Philippines. Robyn Terry had done an excellent job of managing the publications department. So after getting updated on all the things that had taken place during my absence, I soon felt as if I had never been away.

I tackled the first job to be done—preparing the publications budget for the next fiscal year. This was always a big job as we projected what work would be done in the coming twelve months and what it would cost to do it.

Several books were waiting to be typeset when I returned. These included the Book of Jonah in Tagabawa, a language spoken in southern Mindanao, translated by Carl and Lauretta DuBois, and an Old Testament compilation in Itawes of northern Luzon. Chuck and Mickey Richards had translated all the Old Testament portions that are mentioned in the New Testament, amounting to about 25 percent of the Old Testament. The book was 725 pages long.

The third book waiting for me was Genesis 37–50, the story of Joseph in Romblomanon, a language spoken on the island of Romblon in the Visayas, translated by Phyllis Rappa. This was the first book of Scripture to be published in this language.

The fourth book was a sixty-page manual for our e-mail program prepared by Roger Stone, one of our programmers. This was a welcome volume since, until now, we had no written instructions on how to operate the e-mail system, which was quite new at that time.

The fifth book waiting for me was a PhD dissertation by Rudy Barlaan, one of our linguists. Normally the academic publications department produced linguistic material, but at that time we were without a typesetter for that department, so I filled in. This manuscript was two-hundred pages long and was difficult to prepare, since more than one-half was interlinear text material that had to be set up so the English translation of each word was lined up below the word in the original language using tabs.

A month after arriving back in Manila, I sailed on the super ferry to Mindanao to attend our biennial conference at Nasuli. During the "Celebration of the Word," all the materials published during the past two years were presented and dedicated to God. Ninety-six volumes had been prepared, published, and made available for the speakers of thirty-seven language groups.

Sarangani Blaan New Testament Revision Dedication

In 1981, we published the Sarangani Blaan New Testament, translated by Barbara Blackburn and Mary Rhea. They had sold all the copies and now needed a revision. So Barb and Mary, along with their Blaan co-translators, revised the New Testament and added a number of Old Testament portions and psalms. After we published this new book, Barb and Mary scheduled the dedication for June 12, 1999.

Most of the dedications I had attended had been on Luzon, so I looked forward to a trip to southern Mindanao for this occasion. My housemate, Diana Stuhr, also attended and wrote about our experiences:

Excitement was high. The long-prayed-for day had finally arrived. Getting there had taken years of hard labor, setbacks, disappointments, tears, and temptations to quit. Most recently for Barb Blackburn and Mary Rhea and for Ding and Saring Roque, the obstacle of Ding's recent truck accident seemed a hurdle too huge to overcome.

Ding and Saring had worked with Barb and Mary since 1978. The New Testament was dedicated in 1981 and was out of print by 1997. It seemed important to the Blaan team that a revision of the New Testament with added Old Testament portions and psalms would be vital to the blossoming church of committed believers.

So excitement was high as we set off by truck and jeepney for the village of Faku. We had prayed the road would be passable, since several of our group could not have made the trek on foot. It was steep and muddy in places, interrupted twenty times by a winding river. As we arrived at Faku, we realized that God had answered our prayers.

Faku is a beautiful place on top of the world, or so it seems when you're there. The view all around us was impressive. The scene, however, etched in my mind is Ding sitting on a bench obviously in pain but there to greet us. With a weak-sounding voice, he told us that on his way up the mountain the day before, the brakes had gone out of the truck he was riding in, tipping it on its side and bruising him. We listened as he praised God, reminding us that God is the Victor.

The village was already a beehive of activity when we arrived. People came from as far away as twelve hours by foot. Reports came of others who had to turn back because it was not safe to cross the river in their area.

There were happy children everywhere, it seemed. Several fires held brimming pots of delicious meat—pork, beef, and chicken—to delight our taste buds. These pots would feed hundreds of us during the two days we were there as the cooking continued around the clock. Four Faku families gave up their homes to those who came from SIL. They did everything they could at significant sacrifice to themselves to make us feel comfortable and at home during our stay.

The message at the opening service Friday evening set the tone for the whole celebration. Pastor Ernesto preached with passion the message, "Heaven and earth may pass away, but His Word will last forever." Perhaps the most impressive and moving part of the weekend was the thirty believers from various churches who had memorized Scripture and recited it one by one on Friday night and Saturday afternoon. They had learned whole chapters, and most quoted them perfectly without hesitation. Many of them had never been to school. They had learned to read as a result of classes held by the Blaan literacy workers.

On second thought, perhaps the most impressive part of the weekend was the gathering of these thirty-three literacy workers who traveled throughout the mountainous Blaan area teaching classes, bringing the light of Christ to far-flung reaches. Their sacrifice and hard work were bearing fruit, and it was apparent to all as we gathered in Faku to celebrate together.

Ding and Saring Roque were and are the backbones, the foundation stones of the literacy work. They trained these men and women. Ding, the pastor and spiritual advisor of this impressive group, stood at breakfast surrounded by them as they hung on his every word. God said His power is made perfect in weakness. How true it was for us who were privileged to hear Ding preach on Saturday morning. Sometimes with his voice only a hoarse whisper, sometimes with a pause to catch his breath, sometimes with a pause to catch his thoughts, he proclaimed God's power over Satan. He challenged us to live lives of faith, to drink deeply from the Word, to never give up.

Bill Hall, the regional director of SIL, gave his greeting. He said, "Because of Jesus Christ, the world has never been the same. The truths of this sacred Book have changed the world. It is now your Book. Read it often and well. May the Word of Christ dwell in you richly."

Guests from as far away as Michigan and Alaska had come just to attend this celebration. They represented congregations of people who, for years, had backed this project. Betty Cole came to celebrate with Barb. Betty had led Barb to the Lord. How fitting it was that she got a firsthand glimpse of the multiplied fruit of her faithfulness and obedience to the Great Commission.

Plaques were given, history related, tears shed, joys remembered, the gospel preached. Barb preached it as she related the story of Ding's salvation, how it had changed him, and how he's never turned back. Mary preached it as she related Ding's accident. He didn't give up to Satan, and neither can we. Pastor Dekok from Michigan preached it, using Psalm 19 as his text.

I looked up from my place in the crowd to the hills, breathing a prayer of thanks. Not only do they have God's Word, but they also have men and women committed to seeing them learn to read it. Right there, right then, I felt my hands twitching to clap, to give thunderous applause to the God of the impossible.

Following the formal program, Blaans dressed in their traditional costumes, danced Blaan dances and sang Blaan songs. I went home feeling I had been mightily blessed of God for the privilege of attending another Bible dedication, knowing God would use His Word in the lives of the hundreds of Blaan people who now had the privilege of reading it in their own language.

Home for a Wedding

When I received my income tax refund in 1999, I discovered that it was enough for me to buy a round-trip ticket home. I had never taken my annual vacation at home before, but when I received an invitation to my niece Ann Sawatsky's wedding in August, I spent my tax refund on a ticket. This was the first family wedding I had been able to attend since I went to the Philippines in 1967.

The small family affair was held in a little church in a heritage park in Swift Current, Saskatchewan. The church had been built in 1937, and in 1940, the groom's grandparents were the first couple to be married there. Recently, the city had moved the church to Swift Current, and it seemed a fitting location for their grandson Mark's wedding.

The family held the reception on the lawn of the Sawatsky farm. Everything went well except the weather, which was cold and windy. The bride shivered in her wedding gown and finally found a sweater before the reception was over.

For the last of my three-week vacation, I flew to Abbotsford, BC, where I spent a few days with former London friends, Gordon and Anne Bell, and visited with the folks working at CanIL as well as many other friends living in the area.

One day Gordon, Anne, and I caught the ferry to Victoria on Vancouver Island, where we met friends for lunch in Sydney. The day was beautiful, and the restaurant overlooked the water, which glimmered in the sunshine. Hanging baskets of summer flowers adorned the streets and trailed over doorways. We poked through a bookstore before catching the 4:00 o'clock ferry back to Vancouver.

In a few days, I was on a plane to Manila, feeling wonderfully rested, except for the experience of jet lag twice in three weeks.

Typesetting Workshop

Back at work, I looked forward to a month-long workshop to learn the latest state-of-the-art typesetting programs. John and Sharon Edwards came from Dallas to conduct the workshop. This updated me on my typesetting skills and also trained a number of other people, who could assist when the workload became overwhelming.

That November my sister, Nell, and brother-in-law, Gary, came to visit me for a week. This was their first trip to the Philippines, so we traveled around the country, seeing the sights and looking for birds, since they are birders. They were on their way to Australia to look at birds there.

During this time, everyone was concerned about what would happen when the calendar turned over to the year 2000. Would computers, which ruled our lives, adjust to a new millennium? Leaders assured us that all the systems in the Philippines were compliant, but just in case, we stored extra food, water, candles, and batteries.

As it turned out, the calendar rolled over the year, and absolutely nothing happened. We watched the usual fireworks on New Year's Eve and went home to everything as usual.

New Church Building

Things had changed for Union Church, which I had now attended for twenty-five years. We had enjoyed worshipping in a beautiful, round church since 1975. Now the congregation had grown, as had the pastoral staff. We worshiped in two services, one traditional and one contemporary. As I sang in the choir, I enjoyed ministering with my fellow choir members, most of whom were now Filipinos.

Since we were still basically an expatriate church, we were not able to own the property on which the church building stood. The Ayala Corporation, a development company and owner of the land, wanted to develop the lot, since it was on prime property, the city having expanded around us during the years.

Church officials made an agreement with the Ayala Corporation to give up two-thirds of our land so they could build two high-rise office towers. In exchange, they would build us a new church on the last third of the lot. Since we now had many Filipinos attending UCM, the UCM Philippine Foundation was established, which made it possible for UCM to own the property on which the new church would be built. While the Ayala Corporation built the building itself, the cost for completion of the interior and decorations was the church's responsibility.

Dr. Alex Aronis had returned to the church as pastor, so he and his wife, Carol, launched a fund-raising campaign. The goal was forty-five million pesos, but members exceeded this amount and provided sixty-three million pesos, equivalent to almost one-and-a-half million US dollars.

Since the new church would be built on the same location as the old one, a new venue for services had to be found for the two years it would take to raze the old church and build the new one. During this time, worship services were held in the theater of a bank a few blocks away from the church lot.

A high-rise office building across the street from the bank had a vacant seventeenth floor. The owner agreed that the church could use this undeveloped space for offices, a library, Sunday school rooms, and other facilities needed for the administration of a church of over one thousand people.

We watched the new building rise with great anticipation. On several occasions, leaders invited members to take tours through the developing building to see what it would look like when it was completed. Because the lot was only one-third the size of that on which the original church had stood, the new building had to go up.

The sanctuary rose in a circle four stories high to a domed ceiling. Around the back half, rose three stories of offices, Sunday school rooms, a balcony, a boardroom, a babies' room, and a columbarium, with niches for ashes of members who wished to be buried there. Church leaders used the sale of columbarium niches as one way to raise funds for completing the building.

A large fellowship hall and a full-scale kitchen filled the space beneath the sanctuary. The nursery, library, and choir room occupied one level below the fellowship hall. This floor was open in the center, allowing for a two-story recreation gymnasium on the bottom floor, with Sunday school rooms around the outside. Underground parking occupied the bottom floor.

The church was completed and dedicated on December 9, 2001. The building was paid for and has become a witness to God's faithfulness to His children as the congregation continues to grow, numbering over fifteen hundred regular attenders.

I was especially pleased with the choir facilities. Marble floored the practice room, and the cantilevered ceiling made our choir sound like one hundred voices. Since the church was round with no room for a choir loft, the choir sat in the front rows of the congregation and used the five steps to the platform as risers.

By the time we began to worship in the new building, Carminda Regala was once again directing the choir, since her rheumatoid arthritis was in remission. Lois Shellrude had ably directed for several years until her family returned to the States. The choir grew to between thirty and forty singers, several of them semiprofessionals, who lent much to the sound and helped us ordinary singers.

I thanked God often for the privilege of singing in the UCM choir and missed it a great deal when I returned to Canada. During my time in the choir, we made two compact discs, which I continue to enjoy.

In addition to singing in the choir, I had the privilege of serving as a deacon and as a member of the nominating committee.

Tina Sambal New Testament Dedication

In January 2000, the Tina Sambal New Testament was dedicated to God and made available for the Sambal people. This was the forty-fifth New Testament that SIL Philippine members completed.

The Tina Sambal people occupy the province of Zambales along the west coast of Luzon, five hours north of Manila. Many of these people live in five towns dotting the coastal road. So instead of one big dedication, five Bible fiestas were held, one in each town.

Hella Goschnick from Germany and her Filipina partner, Precy Elgincolin, worked for more than twenty-five years to translate the New Testament for their Sambal friends and neighbors. Sotero, Precy's father-in-law, and a team of Sambal speakers had checked every part of the book. Since many of the Sambal people are Roman Catholics, Father Almo, a local priest, also checked the translation, and the bishop placed his imprimatur in the book, saying it was approved for Catholics to use.

Each Bible fiesta began with a parade, leaving the town square and winding through the town to the location of the program. A fife-and-drum band from the elementary school led the parade, followed by everyone who attended the program. Posters designed during a contest in the schools were carried in the parade. Prizes were presented at the programs.

During the week before the fiestas, each elementary and high school held a Bible reading contest. The best readers in three age levels came to the fiestas to read their winning portions and receive their prizes. Interestingly, all the winners were girls.

As a symbol of the acceptance of God's Word in Tina Sambal by all the churches, a Protestant pastor and a Catholic priest placed their hands on a copy of the New Testament during the prayer of dedication.

Some of us who drove to Zambales from Manila stayed overnight at a lovely beach resort. Because it was winter, the night temperatures dipped as low as 68 F. (20 C.), and we were the only people at the resort.

Car Troubles

I enjoyed having a car, not only for the times I needed it for work but also to use as a ministry to other people. Not many single women had vehicles, so I drove people to places they needed to go. I was grateful to God for supplying money for three cars during my time in the Philippines, each of them a new Toyota. But they all got old in time, and occasionally I had car trouble. I was often aware of God's care when these occasions arose.

One time when driving on a somewhat isolated road south of Manila, the top of my radiator split, letting all the water out. We were in the middle of a pineapple plantation with no house in sight. While we tried to decide what to do, a truck came along and stopped. The driver was a mechanic, who had a tube of steel epoxy and several gallons of water. Soon we were on our way again.

Two days later while waiting to find a new top for my radiator, I once more had a problem. The temporary fix didn't hold, and again an overheated engine stopped me in my tracks.

This time I was in the city right across from a radiator shop. Sure enough, the manager said they could replace the top with a copper one, not a plastic one like the original. I went on my way in a taxi to take care of my business. When I returned two hours later, mechanics had fixed the car at a reasonable price, and I was able to drive home.

While my friends and I were on our way back from the Tina Sambal New Testament dedication, we were on the expressway about an hour from Manila. Suddenly, the car in front of us threw a stone that hit our windshield, shattering it into thousands of pieces. I could see through the cracks only enough to get to a service center to call the Philippine Motor Association for a tow. When we got back into the car and closed the door, the whole windshield fell in with glass everywhere. But now I could see, so we cleaned up the glass as best we could, cancelled the tow, and drove home without a windshield. We got lots of attention on the way.

Unfortunately, no windshield was available in Manila that would fit my car, since it was now eleven years old and imported from Japan. A shop that specializes in solving such problems made a windshield for me. It took a week, but the finished product was perfect, and the price was very fair. I praised God that nobody was injured and that we didn't have an accident when the stone hit, since I was driving 62 miles per hour (100 kilometers per hour).

A Visit to the United Arab Emirates

In September of 2000, Anne West was leaving for furlough. Rachel Yogyog, our young Ifugao friend, who had worked for us before graduating from nursing school, was now nursing at the Oasis Hospital operated by the Evangelical Alliance Mission (TEAM) in Al Ain, United Arab Emirates. Nancy Brock, Gerry's sister from London, Ontario, also served there. They had encouraged us to visit them for some time, so Anne flew home by way of Asia and Europe.

I joined her as far as United Arab Emirates, where we spent eight days with Nancy, Rachel, and three other Filipino friends, who all were nurses at the hospital in Al Ain.

This was a trip of a lifetime, as we had many new experiences. We rode on camels into the desert to watch the sun rise over sand dunes, attended an Arab wedding, and visited a village in the mountains where the residents were date farmers. A local family invited us to dinner where we ate delicious middle-eastern food, while sitting on the floor and using our fingers for forks. During our visit, we drank Arabian coffee along with fresh dates. We had arrived at the end of the date harvest, and fresh dates were plentiful. After our visit, Anne proceeded to the States on her furlough, and I returned to my work in Manila.

෨ஒ

During my years in the Union Church choir, I had numerous opportunities to sing music that touched my soul and gave me great enjoyment. I also worked hard as I learned to sing it.

One of those opportunities came in August of 2001 when we were invited to join five other choirs to sing in a gala concert with the Philippine Philharmonic Orchestra to celebrate the fortieth anniversary of the Manila

Electric Company. We sang "Ode to Joy" in German. This is the final movement of Beethoven's *Ninth Symphony*. This challenging music took many long hours of practice, but it went well. I especially enjoyed singing this caliber of music with 150 other good singers. After the anniversary concert, we sang a second concert in a large church to a standing-room-only audience.

Our new church was now completed, and in December we held the official opening and dedication with a day of special services. It concluded with a new musical sung by the chancel choir, the worship team from the contemporary service, and the children's choir. Our director and several choir members arranged the musical and entitled it, "My Utmost for His Highest." It was a day of great rejoicing as we began worship in our new debt-free building.

Four New Testaments Printed

This had been a busy year in the office as well. I typeset and sent four New Testaments to the printer and prepared two others for reprinting. In May when Walt and Virginia Carrell retired, I again became the general manager of the Philippines branch publications department. This was in addition to my work as manager of the Manila publications office.

I also served as chairperson of the Manila center committee, which was responsible for housing and other concerns, and was a member of the crisis management committee. In addition, leaders appointed me as chairperson of the nominating committee in preparation for elections at our next branch conference scheduled for June 2002.

Family for Christmas

After many long hours of work in the office and rehearsals for concerts, I looked forward to Christmas and a break from work.

Nell and Gary were on a birding trip in Vietnam and had arranged to spend Christmas with us in Manila. This was the first time anyone from home had ever come for Christmas. So we invited several SIL people to join us for a delicious dinner with twelve people in all.

Nell and Gary stayed for ten days. We didn't go far out of Manila but did spend one overnight on the island of Corregidor in the mouth of Manila Bay, famous because during World War II, General Douglas McArthur made it his headquarters. We enjoyed the cool ocean breeze and walked around the island, which still had ruins from the war.

Our new church was beautifully decorated for the season, and we enjoyed the special Christmas services. On New Year's Eve, we watched the spectacular fireworks that light up the night sky every year. Our next-door neighbors had an exceptionally good display.

Nell and Gary still talked about the fireworks many years later.

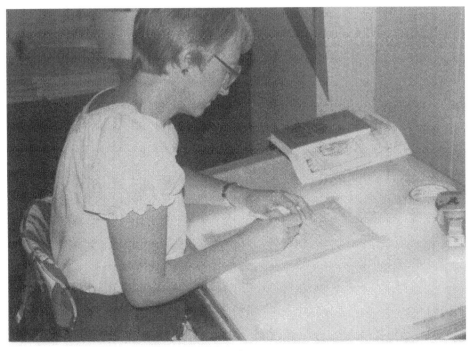

Cutting corrections into typeset copy

*Operating the GSI typesetter
to produce copy for printing
New Testaments*

Chapter 42
Travel Woes and More Dedications
2002–2004

With another term finished, I flew home on July 3 to begin furlough. My trip was an adventure. Travel time from Manila to Abbotsford, BC, where I planned to begin my time at home, should have taken eighteen hours. Instead, it took forty-eight.

Before leaving Manila, I heard on the weather news that a typhoon was approaching Taiwan where I would change planes before flying to Vancouver. I called the airline to ask if it would affect our flight but was assured that it wouldn't.

I arrived in Taipei about 3:00 p.m., expecting a two-hour wait, but when I checked in, the clerk informed me that my Vancouver flight was delayed until 11:00 p.m. I received a ticket for a free meal and permission to wait in the business-class lounge.

When the time came, we found our seats on the plane and waited to depart, but nothing happened. After a while, the pilot announced that the typhoon had closed in, and we would wait to see if a break in the storm would allow our plane to fly out.

By 3:00 a.m., no break had come, so the pilot again announced that we would return to the airport so buses could transport us to the Holiday Inn in downtown Taipei. Too many hours had passed for the crew to continue on the trip without a mandatory rest period, so the passengers would rest also.

My seatmate was a Filipina woman who lived in Montreal. She and her two sisters, who were sitting in the seat behind us, had been visiting their family and were now returning to work. In typical Filipina fashion, they took me in as one of their family, and we stayed together through our long wait. At the Holiday Inn, clerks gave us chits for breakfast and lunch and rooms in which to sleep until 1:00 p.m., when we were to return to the airport. I enjoyed these women, shared a bed with one of them for two hours of sleep, and returned on the bus to continue our flight.

By 2:00 p.m. we were back on the plane ready to leave. The plane taxied to the runway, stopped, and sat there. The pilot came on the intercom and informed us that some passengers had change flights, and their baggage had been off-loaded, which upset the weight balance of the plane. We needed to wait until this could be rectified.

Then another announcement came, saying that we had been sitting with the engines running for so long that we now didn't have enough fuel to take us to Vancouver. We would return to the airport to top up the fuel tanks. Finally, at 5:00 p.m. we took off from Taipei for a normal flight to Vancouver.

Since we were off-schedule on arrival, we joined passengers from all the other flights that normally arrived at that time. The immigration hall at Vancouver International Airport was overflowing. One official informed us that 1,300 people were in the room. It took an hour and a half to get through immigration and customs.

Gordon and Anne Bell were waiting for me when I arrived. When in Taipei, the airline gave every passenger one free phone call. So I had called them to let them know of the delay. It was now afternoon rush hour in Vancouver, and it took another hour-and-a-half to drive from the airport to the Bell's home in Abbotsford, making my trip last for forty-eight hours, a lifetime record for me.

❧

My first task was to buy a car. Anne Bell took me to a car dealer to see what I could find. When I told him what I was looking for and approximately how much money I could spend, he said, "I think I may have just what you need. It came in this morning and hasn't even been cleaned yet."

We walked to the back of the lot where he showed me a beautiful maroon Buick Regal with very low mileage. "An eighty-year-old man owned this car and only drove it around town," he said. "Since it was six years old, he sold it and bought a new one. We have done all the service on it and have the records in our files. It has never been in an accident."

When he quoted the price, I was very surprised, as it was well within my price range. I had never imagined owning a Buick. That seemed way out of my class. But God seemed to have dropped this one here for me, so I agreed to buy it.

Later, when thinking about my trip, I realized that if the typhoon had not delayed my flight, I would have looked for a car the day before. This car had only come in that morning. Once again, God had provided for me. I loved that car. It got good mileage and was very comfortable, so I was sad at the end of my furlough to have to sell it.

My plan for this furlough was to work at CanIL again. I had been in contact with Ross and Ellen Errington, translators for the Cotabato Manobo people of the Philippines. They had purchased a town house in Langley and were now working there and traveling back and forth on occasion to the

Philippines. They had planned a trip for the fall of 2002 and had asked me if I would be willing to stay in their home while they were gone. Although their daughter, Kathy, would be there, she didn't want to stay alone for the three months, so I agreed to stay with her. I visited them in Langley the first week I was home to make final arrangements, since my work at CanIL didn't begin until September, and they would be gone by then.

I spent the remainder of the summer visiting with my sisters, Nell and Gary in Calgary, Alberta, and Marj and Vic in Gull Lake, Saskatchewan. While in Calgary, Nell, Gary, and I drove to Cranbrook, BC, to visit Ruth, Marj's second daughter, who is a veterinarian and was working in a vet clinic there. It was my first time to visit Cranbrook or to drive over Crowsnest Pass, Alberta.

In August, our whole family, including Art and Bonnie from Toronto, gathered at Panorama Mountain Village near Invermere, BC, for a family reunion. It was the first time in ten years that we had all been together. All twenty-two of us had a wonderful time swimming in the hot pools, playing golf, hiking, visiting, and eating.

After the reunion, I drove to Sonora, California, to visit Dorothy Woodford, stopping on the way in Snohomish, Washington, to visit John and Atchie Lawless. She was my friend from graduate school days in Syracuse, New York. By the time my summer travels were over, I had put 3,331 miles (5,362 kilometers) on my car. I was ready to settle down and go to work at CanIL.

Back at CanIL

This time my job was office coordinator and receptionist. This was what I had worked at when I was there in 1997, and I was happy that I could do this job again.

CanIL was still meeting in the portable building but needed more space and a better building, since the portable was in poor shape by this time. A campaign was now in progress to raise funds for a new building. The plans were finished, and the location on the campus of Trinity Western University had been set aside, but adequate funding was still not available. The student body was now the largest in history with 165 students, requiring a larger staff, many with inadequate office space. Three staff members had their desks in the hall. Mine was in the entryway in front of the outside door. While convenient for greeting people who came in, I found it quite uncomfortable when the weather got cold.

My housemates at the Errington's house included Carolyn Finamor from Australia, a graduate student at CanIL, as well as Kathy. She worked at

CanIL as librarian and also took courses at the University of the Fraser Valley to become a certified library technician.

I enjoyed attending Aldergrove Fellowship Baptist Church, which I had attended previously when working at CanIL. I joined the choir again, where I had made a number of good friends.

In November, Lisa, the assistant to the Director of Development, became a Wycliffe member and began preparing for further training and a field assignment in Asia.

I was asked to add her responsibilities to that of mine as receptionist. The Director of Development Dale Schatz was raising funds for the new building, which would cost $3.7 million. One-third of that amount was now in hand, and work was scheduled to begin in May of 2003. Part of my job included keeping the literature and audiovisual materials in stock and packing the development suitcase before Dale went on a fund-raising trip.

Ross and Ellen Errington returned from their trip to the Philippines in December and needed their bedroom, so again I had to move.

Charlotte Landsman, academic affairs assistant at CanIL, had an apartment for rent at her house. Randy and Anita Lebold, CanIL students, had just completed their studies and were moving out at Christmas, so the timing was perfect for me.

I spent Christmas in Calgary with Nell and Gary and New Year's with Marj and Vic. They had recently moved from their big farmhouse to a seniors' condo in Swift Current, leaving the farm for Ann and Mark.

On my return to Langley, I moved into the apartment at the Landsman's house. Although it was farther from work, the traffic flow was in my favor, since I traveled away from Vancouver.

Visits to Family and Supporters

The spring months sped by, and soon it would be time for me to return to the Philippines. I hadn't seen any of my supporters in the East yet, so I needed to make a trip to Ontario and New York State.

Eleanor Toews and I became good friends when she worked in our office in Manila. Now she was in BC. One day I asked if she would like to ride with me to visit my supporters and friends around the United States and Canada. She was enthusiastic, so we made plans to drive around North America.

When classes were finished for the semester the end of March, Eleanor and I set out from Abbotsford and drove to Fresno, California, where we visited friends of hers. From there we drove to Albuquerque to see Dick and Betty Elkins, translators and dear friends from the Philippines. Betty had been diagnosed with terminal cancer, and I was eager to see her. Since some of their family was home, we stayed with their friends, who took us in as if we were family. From Albuquerque, we drove to SIL's International Linguistics Center in Dallas, Texas, to visit friends and coworkers I hadn't seen for some time. From Dallas, we drove to Jackson, Mississippi, to visit Kit Prestridge, who had worked in our finance office in Manila. She took us to a restaurant where, for the first time, I ate frogs' legs and alligator, both quite palatable.

Proceeding east, we reached Helena, Alabama, south of Birmingham, for a weekend with Walt and Virginia Carrell. After retiring from RCA, Walt had served as our publications and computer services general manager for ten years before retiring again. We found no end of things to talk about, enjoyed worshipping at their church, and eating at an interesting restaurant. We ate peanuts as appetizers and tossed the shells on the floor, like the rest of the patrons.

From Birmingham we drove to Waxhaw, North Carolina, a few miles south of Charlotte, the home of JAARS, Wycliffe's aviation, radio, and computer center. Char Houck had retired to Waxhaw many years before, and I hadn't seen her since she left the Philippines.

Char and I had a mutual friend, who lived in Bradenton, Florida, so Char joined us in a trip to visit her, with a stop in Orlando to visit the US headquarters of Wycliffe Bible Translators. From there we drove to Atlanta, to visit Jenny Golden, my former housemate. On her last furlough, she had met Gary Evans, and they were soon married and lived in a suburb of Atlanta. Char and Jenny had worked in the same language group, so Char was eager to see her.

We returned to Waxhaw to deliver Char to her home and then headed north to Lancaster, Pennsylvania, where we spent Easter with Gordon and Bernina Danielson. I hadn't seen them for a number of years. After they left Syracuse, they spent a few years in Akron, Ohio, then retired and moved to Lancaster, which was Bernina's home area. They bought a house in a subdivision on land which had been owned by her grandfather.

Now, however, they were planning to move into a large retirement center on the south side of Lancaster. Their condo was still under construction, but they drove us there to see the grounds and the layout of their apartment. It was very beautiful, and the grounds had large flowerbeds and spreading lawns.

We drove from Lancaster to Newtown Square near Philadelphia to visit Joan Barrie, who was now a widow. She took us to see many tourist attractions in Philadelphia, as well as in Valley Forge and Ocean City, New Jersey.

I shared at a Wycliffe prayer meeting and with a Bible study group of young women at Joan's church.

From Newtown Square, we drove to Syracuse, New York, where we enjoyed the hospitality of Bertha Van Amber, who had been the church secretary when I was a student, and Marion Seymour. I was scheduled to speak in the morning service of my supporting church, South Presbyterian.

When we arrived at the church, we found police cars in the parking lot and tape around the place we planned to park. We had to park down the street and enter the front door. We learned that a shooting had taken place in the parking lot earlier in the morning. The neighborhood had deteriorated considerably since the days when I attended church there.

Eleanor left me in Syracuse and went to visit her daughter, Roxie, who lived near Jamestown, not far from Buffalo. I drove north to Toronto to spend a week with my brother Art and Bonnie. I stopped in Lindsay to visit Enid Skuce, who was retired from many years of missionary service in France. I hadn't seen her since my visit at her home there in 1971.

This was the year the severe acute respiratory syndrome (SARS) virus invaded Canada, and Toronto was the strongest center for the infection. Many people were concerned about my visiting there, but since I didn't have any contact with people who had it, God spared me.

From Toronto I went to London to stay with Ruth Roe, a friend from my church. I visited many people in the area as well as two other supporting churches. During my time in Ontario, I attended the reunion of my Bible college, which is held every other year. I had been to the first one in 1997 and now saw many more classmates who hadn't come before.

I had expected to make the trip back across Canada by myself, but a woman from my church wanted to visit relatives in Kelowna, BC, so she rode with me. I appreciated her company as we drove through Michigan, Wisconsin, Minnesota, and North Dakota before returning to Canada in southern Saskatchewan. We stopped in Swift Current for a night to say good-bye to Marj and Vic and in Calgary to Nell and Gary. We arrived back in Abbotsford on May 29, exactly two months to the day after leaving.

During the two-month trip, I traveled 9,868 miles (15,882 kilometers) and slept in twenty-two different beds.

Back to Manila

I left my car with George Folz, a CanIL board member, and his son, who agreed to sell it for me, and boarded the plane for Manila on June 1.

Two days later, I began work in the office. Jonathan Ford had come from the States especially to man my office while I was gone, but he needed to get home by the middle of June, so I had no time to get over jet lag. Jonathan did a fine job while I was gone, but it took me a week or two to get caught up on what had been done and what needed doing.

I had a great deal of work ahead of me. Three New Testaments came to my desk for typesetting before the end of the year, and several others were nearing completion. The Finallig New Testament translated for a Bontoc language group in the mountains of northern Luzon, came first with a strong deadline. Rundell and Judy Maree had been consultants for this translation. Rundell is a Canadian, but Judi is an American citizen and a Canadian permanent resident. She was required to be back in Canada by the end of August to preserve her residence status. We needed to work night and day to complete the typesetting of the Finallig New Testament before their departure.

Housemate Changes

Again changes took place in my housemates. Anne West had been living with me in Manila for fifteen years. She went to the States in October for a year, and when she returned, she would begin a new assignment in the north.

Sharon Dickinson, our librarian and fellow Canadian, had agreed to share the apartment with me. She had lived there when I was on furlough, so after I returned, we made room for her until Anne's departure in October. Sharon was also due for a five-month furlough later in the year, so once again, I would probably be left alone unless someone else arrived who needed a place to stay temporarily.

In October, before beginning a very busy time at work, I took a short vacation. Heather Kilgour and I found a reasonable tour package to Chiang Mai, Thailand, for five days. We had a wonderful time sightseeing, visiting SIL friends who worked there, eating great Thai food, and Christmas shopping. Our hotel was in the middle of the night market that had everything imaginable for sale, especially beautiful Thai silk garments.

One of the tours we took was to an elephant camp where elephants are trained. We had a half-hour ride on one. I could now say I had ridden on both an elephant and a camel. I returned to Manila refreshed and ready to tackle the tall stack of work waiting for me.

This had been SIL Philippines' fiftieth year. We prepared a number of special publications to celebrate this milestone. The Philippine government honored us by publishing twelve Philippine SIL stamps, featuring weavings or other artifacts from twelve of the language groups where we had done translations.

After Anne and Sharon left for home in October, I learned that Missy Melvin could stay with me for a while. She, Gail Hendrickson, and Steve and Janice Quakenbush had completed the translation of the Agutaynen New Testament and had delivered it to my desk for typesetting. They needed to be on hand for proofreading while I was working on it.

I appreciated Missy's willingness to join me and enjoyed her company during the two months she was there.

At the same time, I inherited another housemate. He was a beautiful but elderly Siamese cat named Kitkit. He belonged to Marji Cook, who left for an extended time in the States, so I agreed to take care of him. I had missed having a cat after the demise of Patty II. I enjoyed several years with a dog but really preferred a cat.

Kitkit was thirteen years old, which is very old for a cat in the tropics, but he had a lot of energy and jumped about, often climbing up on the top shelf of a room divider, on a bookcase, or on a chest of drawers. He was very affectionate and liked to cuddle. Siamese tend to bond with just one person, and Kitkit was no exception. Most of the time, he completely ignored my housemate but insisted on lying on my lap or over my shoulder.

At night he was a nuisance, since he wanted to sleep in the middle of my bed, effectively pushing me out. I made him sleep on the rug by my bed, but some nights it took three or four tries before I could make him leave my bed. He especially liked to sit on my mouse pad or keyboard when I was working on the computer. Occasionally, a paw pressed on a key, providing a line of "cat language" in my work.

I had hoped that the typesetting of the Agutaya New Testament would go smoothly and be finished by the end of December, but unfortunately, we had many problems. This book was a diglot version with two languages, Agutaya and Tagalog. My typesetting program didn't want to do some things I tried to make it do, so the work was delayed. Then Missy and Gail needed to attend meetings in Bagabag for three weeks, so we were further delayed.

I put the book on the shelf until their return and began work on the Mayoyao Ifugao New Testament, since Barbara Hodder, the translator, was waiting. The work progressed quickly with no problems, and in three weeks Barbara and I had completed the whole project.

Gail and Missy returned to Manila, and we picked up the work on the Agutaynen again. Steve Quakenbush had waited for us in Manila. He had translated most of the books from Acts on, but I had to work in order so was not able to work on his section until the first books were done. We finally finished, and both the Agutaynen and Mayoyao Ifugao New Testaments were at the printer by April 2004.

Saddened by Losses

This was another year of sadness for us in the Philippines. Felicia Brichoux, who with her husband, Bob, had worked in the Philippines since the 1950s and translated the Central Subanen New Testament, had a stroke and passed away soon after.

Joshua Mower, the twenty-three-year-old son of Mike and Pat Mower, was killed in a motorcycle accident in the United States. He was serving with the US Marines. Mike was one of our pilots, and we watched Joshua and his sister Elizabeth grow up at Nasuli.

Diane Persons, wife of Gary, one of our regional directors, and mother of six beautiful children, was killed in a car accident when she and Gary were on their way to Manila from Bagabag.

These losses made me realize that life is short. As we grieved for those we loved, we were reminded that it is important to be about the Lord's work and ready to meet Him at any time.

Finallig New Testament Dedication

The Finallig New Testament came off the press in early 2004, and the dedication was set for April 24. Since it was on Luzon and could be reached overland, I decided to attend.

In the mid-seventies, translators Dave and Joan Ohlson arrived in the Philippines and were assigned to translate the New Testament for the people who live in Barlig, located high in the mountains of northern Luzon. Some years later, Takashi and Aiko Fukuda and later Kiyoko Torakawa, all three from Japan, and Lily Pang from Singapore joined Dave and Joan.

One by one everyone except Kiyoko left the project for other assignments. As the translation neared completion, Rundell and Judi Maree from Canada went to Barlig to work with Kiyoko to help with the final revision and see the project through to an end. In the summer of 2003, Rundell, Judi, Kiyoko, and three Finallig mother tongue translators brought the book to Manila where I worked with them to get it prepared for the printer. By April, it was off the press and ready to be dedicated for God's glory.

It had been my privilege to attend the dedication ceremonies for many of the fifty-five New Testaments that we had completed by that time in the

315

Philippines. Along with a number of my SIL colleagues and a group of visitors from the United States and Canada, I traveled to Bagabag on April 22. My housemate, Sharon Dickinson, my downstairs neighbor, Kitty Miller, and I drove to Bagabag in my car. The visitors and other SILers from Manila went on a bus.

We all arrived in time for a wonderful evening dinner in the meeting hall, prepared by women from Bagabag. Rundell and Judi had prepared orientation information concerning the Finallig people and their culture, which they shared with us. Since Barlig had no hotels, we were billeted with families in the community.

Friday morning after breakfast, we got into jeepneys and headed for the mountains. The first stretch was a good paved road, but after an hour-and-a-half, the road turned into gravel but was still in fairly good shape. The women in Bagabag had made sack lunches for us to eat along the way. The weather was beautiful, and we enjoyed the mountains, forests, and panoramic views as we climbed higher and higher toward Barlig.

We came to the town of Talubin. As we turned north deeper into the mountains, the road became narrower, steeper, and rougher. Several times the jeepney had to stop beside a stream to fill the radiator and cool down the engine.

The town of Barlig is located at over six thousand feet. This is the highest elevation of any place in the Philippines where we had a translation team.

Finally, after six hours on the road, we arrived at Barlig. Rundell and Judi met us and walked with us down a long set of steps through the town to the square at the bottom. The town itself had no roads, and the houses were scattered all over the mountainside on both sides of a river.

We gathered in the hall of the Catholic church, where women fed us a delicious rice, sweet potato, and pork meal. The translation team had everything well organized with nametags for everybody and information about where we would stay. Kitty and I stayed with a young family with two school-age children and a baby. The woman of the house met us and took us home with her for the night. One of the children gave us her bedroom.

The dedication program began at 8:00 a.m. with a parade through the town. Almost everyone was represented, carrying banners—the teachers, the health workers, the municipal workers, the school children, regular citizens from each of the divisions of the town, and different churches. Several bands played, and at the front, the New Testament was carried high in a place of honor.

When the parade reached the town square, the ceremonies began. The Finallig New Testaments were placed high in the center of the square under a white cloth. The priest from the Catholic church and pastors from several other churches carried the Book around and set it on a special podium. Prayers of dedication were made, and everyone thanked God for bringing His Word to Barlig. Also on the program were speeches, presentations to the team who had helped with the translation, and much singing by choirs and by the whole congregation of about two thousand people.

During lunch hour and afterwards, the Barlig people put on a cultural presentation with dancing by them and visitors from other cultural communities throughout the mountains. Many wore their handwoven skirts or g-strings with beads and other decorations. Men played gongs for the dancers, and the sound of rejoicing filled the town square.

It was a joy to see a crowd of people gathered around the tables where the New Testaments were sold. Many sat right down to read God's Word in their language. This is what I had spent thirty-seven years of my life for!

Soon it was time to go. We walked five hundred steps up to the road. At an altitude of six thousand plus feet, most of us did a lot of puffing. But we all made it to the top, where a store sold many bottles of water and pop. Then we piled into our jeepneys for the long trip back down the mountain to Bagabag.

Mayoyao Ifugao New Testament Dedication

By November the Mayoyao Ifugao New Testament was also ready to be dedicated. I drove my car from Manila to Bagabag to join those who would attend the dedication celebration. Three busloads of people from England, Australia, the United States, the Philippines, and several other Asian countries traveled to Mayoyao in the mountains of Ifugao Province.

An American couple had begun the work in the mid-1980s but had to leave. Barbara Hodder from the United Kingdom arrived in 1987 to continue the translation for the Mayoyao people. She had a partner from home for a few years but after that had been in Mayoyao by herself, except for a short time when Robyn Terrey from Australia joined her. It was a special treat for Robyn to return for the dedication.

A program on Friday night acquainted visitors with the history of Christianity in Mayoyao and the history of the translation project. The main dedication service was held on Saturday. After the official program of speeches, songs, and a prayer of dedication, copies were given to those who had been involved with the translation project. Adults and school children then entertained the audience with cultural dances.

317

Following the program, more than two thousand people were fed rice, pork, beef, and vegetables. Our bus for Bagabag left at 2:30 p.m., arriving about 8:00 p.m. After a good night's sleep, we set off for Manila on Sunday morning. Between Thursday morning and Sunday afternoon, I had spent twenty-four hours on the road, much of it a very bumpy, steep, gravel mountain road.

Chapter 43
Leaving the Philippines
2004–2006

For a number of years, St. Luke's Hospital in Manila had been offering a special screening program called "executive checkup" for people who wanted to have complete physical examinations. A number of our members had gone through this one-day program and highly recommended it. Since I was now sixty-seven years old, I decided it would be a good idea to do this, since the cost was only two hundred dollars.

I made an appointment in August 2004 and arrived at the door of the hospital at 8:00 a.m. on a Friday. I was assigned an aide who stayed with me all day, taking me from one testing place to another. I had complete blood work done at the lab, checks of my whole digestive tract, upper and lower, an ultrasound of my kidneys, liver, and pancreas, a sigmoidoscopy, a chest x-ray, a visit to the gynecologist, and a treadmill stress test. This took most of the day, but by 4:00 p.m., I was finished and released. I was told to see my family doctor in two days for the results of the tests.

When I arrived at my doctor's office later, he said, "Everything is normal except for one thing. You have tuberculosis."

"What? How can that be?"

After all these years and many brushes with this dread disease, it had finally caught up with me. This was not a serious case, and I had no symptoms, but I would have to take medication for six months. Once I began the medication, I would not be contagious so couldn't pass it to anyone else.

The medications consisted of four large capsules to be taken every morning when I got up, at least a half-hour before breakfast. I had the prescription filled and prepared myself for a handful of pills every day.

I usually walked for half an hour every morning when I first got up, so the first day I took my pills and went out for my usual morning walk. About ten minutes on my way, I felt hot. By the time I arrived home from my walk, I was covered from head to foot with a bright red rash. I was allergic to one of the medications. But which one?

I visited the doctor later that day. He said the only way to find out which medication was giving me a rash was to stop them all and take one for four days, then add one more for another four days until I found the one that was causing the problem. I did that and found it was the fourth tablet that gave me the rash.

After three months, I had a second x-ray that showed considerable improvement in my case. At the end of six months, the lesion was completely healed. I thanked God for His leading to take that checkup. Otherwise, the TB could have become serious before I realized it and would have been much more difficult to eradicate.

The only side effect of the medication for TB was a problem with my thyroid medication, which no longer was effective. By increasing the thyroid considerably, I was able to function until the TB medicine was completed. Then my doctor readjusted my thyroid medication. I didn't suffer much from this imbalance, and soon everything was regulated again.

Back to Amganad with Anne West

In February of 2005, I made a trip to Amganad with Anne West. It had been ten years since I had visited Amganad, and I was eager to see the people I had known in the sixties when I worked there. The children were all grown up by now. My namesake, Funnell, was already thirty-five years old.

Anne and I drove to Bagabag, and Jean Azbell, our accounting department manager, and three Filipina women friends flew in the SIL plane to meet us there. From Bagabag we drove in an SIL van to Banaue, an hour-and-a-half into the mountains. The three Filipinas had not been in this area before, so it was great fun to show them the beautiful rice terraces and introduce them to our friends. Anne was now working as a consultant with the Central Ifugao (formerly Amganad Ifugao) Old Testament mother-tongue translators, helping to train them in translation, and checking their work.

We picked up Hilda Gotia, one of the translators, on the way and visited a man who explained the computer programs he was using to help with his translation work. We stopped to see Hilda Licyag, our Ifugao sister, and then went into Banaue, where we found our hotel before sightseeing.

On Sunday morning we drove down a very narrow, twisting road and then hiked for twenty minutes to a small church in Cababuyan. This town is at the far end of the Central Ifugao language area. Through the New Testament, many had become Christians, and several churches had started in that community. We noticed that many of those attending the church were young people. Pastor Martin preached a very good sermon, and after the service, the ladies of the church graciously cooked us lunch. The Ifugao rice was delicious.

After lunch we hiked back to the van, which I had parked at the end of the road, and returned to Bagabag. It filled my heart with praise to God to see the fruits of our work in Ifugao. Anne and her Filipino coworker, Helen

Madrid, had completed the translation of the New Testament. Even though I had left after two years, I had the privilege of getting it into print.

A month after our trip to Ifugao, we received shocking news. Pastor Martin and a group of young people from the church in Cababuyan had gone on a retreat in the mountains over the Easter weekend. On their way home, they encountered a landslide. When they tried to cross it, the vehicle they were riding in slid over the side of the mountain. Pastor Martin was immediately killed, and eight or nine of the young people and the pastor's wife and child were seriously injured and taken to several hospitals in the area. It was hard for me to understand why God could allow such tragedy and the loss of a pastor who was needed so badly.

Tuwali Ifugao Bible Dedication

Translation work was about to be completed in another Ifugao dialect. Dick and Lou Hohulin translated the Tuwali Ifugao New Testament, which was published in 1991. Then they trained a group of Tuwali believers to translate the Old Testament. Dick and Lou were assigned to SIL's International Headquarters in Dallas, Texas. But they returned for a month or two nearly every year to work with the translators, checking their work and helping them through the difficult passages of the Old Testament. In 2004 they came in March and stayed until the job was done. Now it was time for typesetting, proofreading, and printing.

This was the first complete Bible that I had typeset, and it was a big job. For Dick and Lou, the task of proofreading was even bigger as they read copy day after day and sometimes into the night. We finished in September, and I took the camera-ready pages to the printer. By June of 2005, the job was complete, and the entire Bible in Tuwali Ifugao was available for the Tuwali people.

June 4 dawned bright and sunny as we arrived at the town plaza in Kiangan to witness the dedication of God's Word. The people who came lined the plaza area, sitting under tarps and native-style houses put there on display. It was too hot to sit in the open. People also spilled out of their homes and stores at the edge of the plaza.

The speeches of the dignitaries were exceptional. The air was filled with excitement as both politicians and Christian leaders exalted the entire Bible now translated into Tuwali. Singing and native dancing interspersed the speeches and messages. The main speaker, an Ifugao pastor, was spellbinding as he exhorted the Tuwali Ifugao people to follow the teachings of God's Holy Word.

The highlight of the dedication was the unveiling of the Tuwali Bibles, when the Tuwali Ifugao translators (twenty-two in all) received their own Bibles and read passages that had been assigned to them.

Matima, the oldest translator, painfully hobbled up the steep steps and across the platform, helped by a number of men and women, to read her passage. Her joyful reading of her assigned verses brought tears to the eyes and lumps in the throats of all who listened.

When the program with its speeches, songs, and dancing finally ended, the people lined up to buy their copies of the Tuwali Ifugao Bible. What a sight! By the end of the day, 846 copies had been sold or given as gifts. The entire day was a joyful and festive occasion, perfect in every way.

More than two thousand people participated in the feast that followed. Then about 2:30 p.m., the clouds rolled in, since this was rainy season, and the heavens opened. The rain thundered down as if heaven and all its inhabitants were rejoicing over the grand event.

Two months later, I was involved in a sacred music conference at my church. Our choir sponsored a three-day conference to which we invited directors and five key members from forty local church choirs. Three of the Philippine top choral professors gave lectures.

On the final Sunday evening, we all joined together in a concert of sacred choral music. We felt privileged to host this conference as a service to smaller churches and to provide them with choral music that they could not have afforded otherwise.

Future Housing

On August 16, 2005, I boarded Philippine Airlines for a flight to Vancouver. I had been saving for this trip for some time. After my last furlough, I had informed the director in Manila that this would be my last term in the Philippines. I had made arrangements to transfer to the Canada Institute of Linguistics, beginning in September of 2006, and needed a place to live. While the school is in Langley on the campus of Trinity Western University, I wanted to live in Abbotsford, some 18 miles (30 kilometers) east of Langley. Housing was less expensive, and a number of senior housing societies interested me.

This trip would give me an opportunity to look at these possible places to live and to get my name on their waiting lists. Gordon and Anne Bell met me at the airport and took me home with them for the duration of my stay in Abbotsford.

I had sent a query to Aldergrove Baptist Church to see if anyone would have a car I could borrow for my time there. I received an offer from the assistant pastor. He and his family were planning to be on vacation at that time and would lend me their car. That was a wonderful blessing, since now I could get around without bothering anyone else.

Anne and I visited a number of senior housing societies in Abbotsford. Awana, Avonlea, and Amicus were all similar, two-story fourplexes inside nonsecure compounds. They were close to the city center with malls and grocery stores nearby, which I liked.

Then we visited North Oaks Manor. This was a condominium-type building with sixty-two suites on three floors. The price was a bit more than the others, but I felt the security was better there. The chairman of the board gave me a tour of the building, including his own suite.

I was impressed with the size, 1,030 square feet with two bedrooms, a living room, dining room, a galley kitchen, one bathroom, and a laundry room opening into the bathroom. Each suite had a large storage room, excellent closets, hall storage, and a locker on the ground floor for storing large items.

I had left my name on the waiting list of one or two of the first places we had visited but felt that North Oaks was more to my liking and a better value than the others. So I paid fifty dollars to be placed on the waiting list and went away feeling that God had shown me where I was to live in the future.

After my time in Abbotsford, I returned the borrowed car and caught a plane to Calgary for a visit with Nell and Gary.

While in Calgary, I visited June Spencer. We had kept in touch over the years, and she always said that her time visiting in the Philippines and her trip to Amganad was the highlight of her year's sabbatical trip around the world. She was now in her late eighties and living in a small suite in a military retirement center. Howard was there also, but they had to live separately, since he needed assisted living because of extreme arthritis. June was able to care for herself. They got together for their meals in the dining room.

While visiting with June, I mentioned that I had put my name on the waiting list at North Oaks Manor in Abbotsford. When she asked, I explained that I didn't have enough money on hand to pay for the membership when my name came up. I had been saving for a long time but was still short. Since this was a society, I would not own the unit outright but would receive a promissory note, saying the amount I paid for the suite would be returned to me in full when I left it.

"How much do you need?" June asked.

"About twenty-five thousand dollars."

She thought for a few minutes and then said, "I could easily lend you that much."

I was shocked. I knew that with her teacher's retirement funds, she had some money but hadn't imagined she could part with that much.

When I asked her if she was sure, she got out of her chair and opened a file drawer in a cabinet. Rifling through papers, she found an enveloped marked, "Incontinence." With a grin she said, "I keep my financial records in this envelope, because I don't want anybody to find them. I don't think anybody would look in here."

She pulled out a statement and showed me the amount of money she owned. I was surprised to see she owned more than three-quarters of a million dollars. With thanks, I accepted her offer of an interest-free loan.

"I want you to have this now, but you don't need to start paying it back until you come home to live. Then I would like two hundred dollars a month."

"At that rate, I won't get this repaid during your lifetime. What happens then?"

"Oh, it will be forgiven," she said.

So we drew up a legal promissory note, and I went away with twenty-five thousand dollars to be invested until I needed it.

❦

Paul Sawatsky, Marj and Vic's son, was getting married, so I drove with Nell and Gary to Saskatoon, Saskatchewan, to attend the wedding. Paul was the last of their four children to marry.

Paul's wedding was beautiful. He was marrying Errin, a medical student at the university in Saskatoon. The sun shone all day, and we enjoyed a family reunion, since Art and Bonnie had flown out from Toronto.

Following the wedding, I spent time with Marj and Vic before taking the bus to Calgary and the plane to Vancouver to catch my flight to the Philippines.

❦

When I was visiting my niece, Ann Ryerson, in Saskatchewan, she told me that she and Mark were adopting twin boys from the Philippines. The paperwork was nearly finished, and they hoped they could soon pick them up. In October, the call came, and Mark and Ann arrived in Manila with plans to fly to Tacloban where their eighteen-month-old twins were waiting for them in an orphanage.

Ann and Mark arrived at the Manila domestic airport with their boys in tow. While Mark collected the baggage, Ann walked out of the airport holding one toddler in each hand. At eighteen months, they stepped right along, keeping up with no trouble at all. They were beautiful, healthy boys. Their new parents had named them James and Eric.

At the SIL guesthouse and in our office, James and Eric were the center of attention. Everyone had to see them, play with them, and try to talk to them, but they didn't understand English. They only understood Waray-Waray. It wouldn't be long though, before they understood their new language and adjusted to a very different way of life.

A Publishing Workshop

The months flew by, and soon I was actively preparing to break up my house and return to Canada for good. But before that, I received an invitation to attend a publishing workshop in Dallas in March 2006. With Missy Melvin, who would be taking over my job when I left, and Rex Johnson, our academic publications typesetter, I flew to Dallas for a week to meet with more than forty of our publishing counterparts from other countries around the world. We heard reports and saw demonstrations of new software that would soon be used for typesetting our materials. In addition, we had good times of fellowship, as we got to know each other and listened to each other's joys and difficulties. It was lovely to be in Texas again in the springtime.

Health Checkup

In preparation for leaving the Philippines, I decided to repeat the executive checkup at St. Luke's Hospital that I had had two years earlier when an x-ray showed I had TB. I went on a Friday and spent the day as before, going through many different tests. When I was on the treadmill for a stress test, the technician left and returned very soon with a doctor in tow. The doctor stopped the test and told me to see my doctor as soon as possible. *Now what?* I wondered.

My doctor had Saturday morning clinic hours, so I went to see him. He had already received the report from the tests the day before. Everything was fine this time, except for my stress test. It showed that I had a problem.

He immediately made an appointment for me to see a cardiologist on Tuesday.

When the cardiologist looked at the results of my stress test, he said I definitely had a problem, and the only way to know how bad it was, was to have an angiogram. I could have that in two or three days.

My Last Conference

The following week was our biennial conference, and I didn't want to miss that if I could help it. I asked the doctor if I could postpone the angiogram for two weeks, and he readily agreed that it would be okay. So on Friday I drove a carload of fellow workers to Bagabag to attend our conference.

This was my last conference, and since I always enjoyed them so much, I was sorry to have them come to an end. During our time together, the group gave me a special certificate for having attended every conference since I had first arrived in the Philippines in 1967.

More Physical Problems

While still at Bagabag, I woke up with pain in my chest one morning. I was afraid that the trip had caused some damage, so I called Steve Lynip, one of our directors who was also a medical doctor. He asked a pilot to bring a bottle of oxygen from the hangar in case I needed it. Eventually, the pain went away, and I was fine for the rest of my time at Bagabag.

Two days after returning to Manila, I was admitted to St. Luke's Hospital to have an angiogram. The cardiologist told me that if they found blockage in my coronary arteries, they would do an angioplasty. They would open the artery with a balloon and place a stent in the blocked location.

Since I was awake when this procedure was done, I watched the monitor and saw the blood vessels on the screen. I did have two blockages, one 80 percent and one 50 percent. Since I had struggled with high cholesterol for more than fifteen years, the blockage was hard to get through, and my blood pressure went quite high.

At that point, the doctors gave me a sedative so I would go to sleep. I think they didn't want me to hear what they were saying. When it was all over, they told me they had inserted a stent in the 80 percent blockage but had left the 50 percent blockage, since the blood flow was very good with just one repair.

I was in the hospital for three days before returning home. I lived on the third floor of our apartment building, and when I climbed the stairs, I found I could only make two floors without stopping. I spent a while visiting my second-floor neighbor before climbing the last floor to the top. I was surprised, since I thought that now, with good blood flow to my heart, I should have greatly improved energy also. Instead, it took me a whole month before I felt myself again.

On Friday morning, I woke up with a strange, uncomfortable feeling in my chest. My heartbeat was irregular and very fast. I called the doctor, and he told me to go back to the hospital immediately, so Sharon drove me there. As I approached the desk, the nurse in emergency checked my pulse and got me into a bed quickly. I was admitted again and stayed for two more days, as the doctors tried to see what was happening.

I later learned that I was having an episode of atrial fibrillation. When I asked the cardiologist about it, he said, "What we did on Tuesday was a plumbing job. This is an electrical problem." I was given medication for three months and had no more problems with atrial fibrillation for five years.

Final Packing

Now I had just one week to finish packing to leave the Philippines for good. I had shipped a crate of household and personal items that I wanted to take home, had a yard sale to get rid of many things I could part with, sold my car, trained Missy to do my job, and was ready to go. Two farewell parties were scheduled for June 28 and 29, and I flew from Manila on July 1.

Since I was not allowed to lift anything heavy for a while, I requested a wheelchair in Vancouver so I wouldn't have to handle my baggage. Three others had requested wheelchair assistance also. We were all put on an electric cart and driven to immigration and to the baggage area. At immigration we didn't have to wait but were checked through immediately. A baggage handler was waiting and took me right to Gordon and Anne Bell's car waiting outside. It was the easiest entrance into Canada I had ever had.

On Sunday morning, I woke up with pain in my chest. Anne, who was a nurse, checked my blood pressure and found it quite high. By mid-afternoon, when the pain was still there, Anne took me to emergency at the Abbotsford hospital. The triage nurse listened to my story and told me to take a seat. I asked her how long the wait was, and she said, "About three hours." It was a good thing I'd brought a book. But in about five minutes, I heard my name called and learned later that heart patients are never left to wait.

After a number of tests and a shot of morphine for the pain, I was left to rest for nine hours, after which time I was allowed to go home. By now it was one in the morning, so Anne had to get out of bed to drive me home. The pain went away and didn't return. The doctors didn't find anything wrong. But I am forever grateful to have friends like the Bells to take care of me when I needed them.

Chapter 44
A New Home and Church
2006–2007

The first thing I needed to do after arriving in Canada was to buy a car. I had driven a Toyota in Manila for thirty-four years, so I first looked for one at a Toyota dealer. I planned to buy a fairly late model, perhaps a Corolla.

For some reason, every car I took for a drive was uncomfortable. Perhaps they made Toyotas in Canada to fit tall people.

Next I went to the Honda dealer. Most of Marj's family drove Hondas and liked them. I tried some used cars there with the same experience. They didn't fit me.

Then the salesman said to me, "We have a brand new small car that might fit you better. It's called a 'Honda Fit.'"

"A Fit! That's a strange name for a car."

He grinned. "Well, it's because anything you want to put in it will fit."

I took it for a drive. It fit me perfectly. After hearing good things about this small hatchback and since the price was within my range, I bought it. It was silver, got forty-eight miles to the gallon, and the salesman was right. When the backseats are down, everything fits—my big trunk, a four-drawer filing cabinet, and all my suitcases and boxes (not all at the same time).

I spent the month of July with Anne and Gordon Bell in Abbotsford, getting my strength back and enjoying the summer fruit that I had missed so much in the tropics.

In August I drove to Calgary and spent time with Nell and Gary then drove to Gull Lake to visit with Marj, Vic, and their family. I especially enjoyed seeing James and Eric, the twins, who were now two-and-a-half and beginning to speak a little English. They understood everything but were slow in talking. It made me realize that children learn a language before they begin to talk, and their learning had been in Waray-Waray, so it took them longer to process English.

Back to CanIL

Now it was September and time to begin my new job at CanIL.

I still hadn't heard from North Oaks Manor about a place to live. When I checked with Wilmer Kornelson, the chairman of the board, he said my name wasn't too far from the top of the list, so I shouldn't have to wait much longer.

Eleanor Toews, who lived just a few blocks from North Oaks Manor in a three-bedroom town house, offered to have me live with her until I could get a suite at North Oaks Manor. When my shipment arrived in Vancouver in July, Doug and Phyllis Trick, translators from the Philippines, who had just bought a house in Abbotsford, offered to store my boxes in their garage until I had a place of my own.

With my housing temporarily cared for, I arrived at CanIL the day after Labor Day to begin work as a receptionist on Mondays and an assistant to Don Fama, the director of personnel.

The trip from Abbotsford to the Trinity Western University campus near Langley took half an hour, most of it on the freeway going to Vancouver. Though the traffic was heavy, I didn't begin work until 9:00 a.m., so most of the morning rush was over. In the afternoon when I drove home, the traffic was much heavier. I had to adjust to driving high speeds there. In Manila the traffic was so heavy I was used to driving between 12 to 37 miles per hour (20 to 60 kilometers). On the Trans-Canada Highway, the speed limit was 62 miles per hour (100 kilometers), but hardly anyone drove that slowly.

When I worked at CanIL in 2003, the school was situated in a very old and dilapidated mobile building. In 2005, the new Harvest Centre was completed, so now we worked in a beautiful new three-story building with plenty of space and pleasant surroundings. That fall we had 137 students enrolled in our courses, many training to become Bible translators or literacy workers.

I soon adjusted to my new work and enjoyed getting to know my fellow staff members as well as the students. Several new couples had arrived that fall to begin teaching at CanIL.

Dave and Susan Jeffery had served in Pakistan and Thailand and now had joined the CanIL staff, Dave to teach and Susan as the librarian. Rod and Ellen Casali came from a translation project in Ghana so Rod could teach and Ellen work in member care. Norbert and Karin Rennert had worked in Surinam, and Norbert now joined the information technology team. At a later date, Karin took over as receptionist four days a week. Doug and Phyllis Trick arrived from the Philippines so Doug could teach translation principles while Phyllis continued with their translation project from a distance. In January of that year, John and Wanda Davies joined the staff, Wanda to teach our literacy courses, and Margaret Shields came as academic assistant. All these new people filled the offices in our new building along with the already existing staff.

I still had some vacation time left, so as Christmas drew near, I spent December on the eastern side of the mountains. I flew to Calgary to attend Wycliffe Canada's annual general meeting and then spent two weeks with Nell and Gary. Since it was winter, I was cold almost all the time. After nearly forty years in the tropics, it would take years to adjust to cold weather. I wore five layers of clothes and looked for heating registers to stand beside to get warm.

Nell and I had a great time shopping for Christmas gifts. We attended two Christmas dinners and visited three generations of family.

I spent one afternoon visiting with June Spencer in her retirement apartment in northwest Calgary. I took her my December repayment for the loan she had given me the year before.

She looked at my check and said, "You know, I really don't need this money. Let's just forget it from now on. The loan is cancelled." I could hardly believe that she had just given me a gift of more than twenty-three thousand dollars.

ૐન

After my visit in Calgary, I caught a bus to Gull Lake to spend Christmas with Marj and her family. I attended a family wedding, shopped, went to a church concert, a ladies' Christmas party, and rested.

Christmas was great fun, since all the family was home, except Ruth who had to work. The twins, Eric and James, were two-and-a-half now, happy and energetic children. They did a good job of distributing the gifts on Christmas Day.

ૐન

Back in Abbotsford, I returned to work at CanIL to find that Karen Mathew, assistant to Dale Schatz in development, would soon be taking maternity leave, since her baby was due the end of January. I was to take over her job as Dale's assistant, so I began training to add this to my other work. My jobs in personnel and development were each part-time, so I could manage to do both.

I attended Aldergrove Baptist Church again and enjoyed being part of a ladies' Bible study group of twelve to fifteen women, which met on Sunday morning at 9:45.

Shirley Preece, a retired missionary, was also part of the Bible study group. She had recently given up her car so was riding on the church bus. Since the bus didn't get there in time for Bible study, I volunteered to pick her up on Sunday mornings and take her to Aldergrove. She rode the bus home afterwards because I usually met Eleanor Toews and two of her friends for lunch.

Tina Teichrob and Helga Wiens both attended Central Heights Church, along with Eleanor. These women became my good friends. I knew very few people in Abbotsford, but the others had all lived there for many years so introduced me to their friends.

Abbotsford has a great number of Mennonites living there. Four of the largest churches in the city are of the Mennonite Brethren denomination, so I have made friends with many Mennonites and have learned to appreciate their culture and history.

My New Home

In early February, I received a call from North Oaks Manor, saying that a unit would be available for me by the end of the month. Since two units were available, I went to see which one I liked. I chose one at the back of the building away from the street and facing Horn Creek Park, which has woods and a creek running through it. The building contains sixty-two suites on three floors. We are on a main street only one block from the largest super-market in town and two blocks from a large shopping mall.

I had to set up from almost nothing, since all I had were the contents of my crate from the Philippines and the few things June Spencer had given me when she and Howard broke up their home to move to the retirement center.

At North Oaks, all the appliances belong to the residents, so I would need to buy everything. Ruth Keely, who was moving out of the suite I had selected, asked if I would like to buy her appliances, since she wouldn't need them. She had been one of the original residents at North Oaks when it opened in 1986, so her appliances were all twenty years old. I wasn't sure I wanted to spend money on old appliances, but she said, "You can have everything for $986."

I was amazed. I couldn't buy a new refrigerator for that amount. This included a stove, refrigerator, dishwasher, microwave, chest freezer, washer, dryer, small air-conditioner, and two sets of drapes. I took them all. Although they might not last long, they wouldn't all stop working at the same time, and I could replace them one by one. Once again, God had provided for me in a way I hadn't anticipated.

By the beginning of March, I moved in. Marj came from Saskatchewan to help me unpack and get settled. I had shipped dishes and basic kitchen utensils from the Philippines, and I had china that I had stored at her house. I couldn't have made this move without her help.

We were still unpacking on March 6, my seventieth birthday. Since I didn't know anybody at North Oaks and very few people in Abbotsford, I had no celebration for this turning point birthday. Marj and I simply went out for dinner in the evening.

Soon she left for home, and I went back to work. It took quite some time before I was settled and had everything I needed. But I loved my new home and knew I would be very happy there.

North Oaks Manor - Abbotsford

New car in front of CanIL building

Chapter 45
Travel and Work at CanIL
2007–2011

Because I hadn't seen my supporters in Ontario and the eastern United States since arriving home from the Philippines, it was time for me to visit them. When school was over in late April, I left in my Honda Fit for a seven-week trip, driving 8,290 miles (13,342 kilometers). I traveled through five provinces, ten states, and slept in twenty-two beds. I visited all my supporting churches and almost all of my financial partners, who had been giving so generously through the years. God gave me safety and strength as I drove all that distance by myself for long hours. I thoroughly enjoyed the trip, especially visiting with people I hadn't seen for a long time.

While I was in London, I attended my Bible college reunion, where I saw people I hadn't seen for forty-five years. Did I recognize them? Did they recognize me? Some looked much the same; others I would not have known without nametags.

I returned to Abbotsford to the coldest, wettest June on record. I bought two hanging baskets of petunias for my balcony as well as pots of geraniums and begonias. Now I would have to learn how to grow things, since I hardly ever had plants of any kind in Manila. I tried to grow African violets in the house a few times, but the tropical temperatures were too hot, and they always died. So I gave up.

Summer school started at CanIL in June. A good group of students began their studies, many towards linguistics degrees, which would take two years to complete. I always enjoyed the summer program, since the students had many social and sports activities to which the staff members were invited.

Doris Porter, my friend from the Philippines that I had traveled with through Europe in 1971, had now retired and was living in an apartment attached to her brother's house in Lynden, Washington. I could drive to her house in half an hour, depending on the lineup at the US border. We often got together for lunch or to attend plays in Bellingham, another twenty minutes down the road.

On July 4, she invited me to go to a potluck dinner at the home of a Filipino friend and to watch the fireworks ignited from a barge in the water. They were some of the best fireworks I had ever seen.

At Thanksgiving that year, I had a special treat. Anne West had come home from the Philippines for two months and was visiting her Aunt Beppie in Clarkston, Washington.

Doris and I drove to Clarkston for the weekend to see Anne. I also wanted to meet Aunt Beppie, Anne's favorite aunt. I had heard about her since Anne and I first worked together forty years earlier. We had a delightful time.

Aunt Beppie was in her nineties but very bright and spry. She guided us to a farm in Idaho, where she had lived as a young woman. We crossed the Snake River and drove into the rolling hills. The farm was now abandoned, but we saw the old house and barn.

On the way home, Doris and I spent a night with her sister, Pat, who lived in Richland. This was the first time I had been on the east side of the Cascade Mountains. I was surprised to see the rolling, treeless hills and desert like terrain. When I thought of Washington, I pictured snow-covered mountains and lush green forests, like the area around Puget Sound and the coast.

ॐ๑๑

The Wycliffe women in the Abbotsford and Langley area get together for breakfast one Saturday morning each month. Ruth Snider sponsored this activity soon after she and Keith arrived to teach at CanIL. We have a speaker and enjoy a time of fellowship.

In December for a number of years, we had a cookie exchange. We each brought a dozen of our favorite Christmas cookies and took home a dozen made by other people. Of course, we sampled the offerings as well.

But nobody wanted to eat cookies for breakfast, so in December we gathered on a Friday evening for carol singing, sharing traditions, and the cookie exchange. I have always enjoyed baking, especially at Christmas time, so this was a special time for me. I also enjoyed collecting new recipes, since everyone included copies of their recipes with their cookies. Later, we changed the cookies to appetizers, which we ate at the event, enjoying a lovely Christmas party together.

For the first several Christmases I was back in Canada, I found Christmas to be an emotional time, since I missed the activities in the Philippines where it is such an all-encompassing time of year. I especially missed my church and the choir in which I sang for twenty-nine years. Several of our choir concerts were videoed, and when I watched these productions, I found myself in tears, remembering the good times we had preparing and presenting those concerts as we celebrated the birth of Jesus. Fortunately, He is here too, and each year I can celebrate His birth wherever I am. How wonderful to know that His coming to earth and His death on the cross were for the whole world.

&

In 2007 Bill and Dianne Van der Wal left CanIL for another term on staff at Ukarumpah in Papua New Guinea, where they had served previously. In January of 2008, Kent and Brenda Royer arrived at CanIL from Cameroon, where they headed up the Africa orientation course for new members. They had also worked at a camp in Alberta where Brenda managed the food service and Kent was the camp manager. Their previous experiences made them ideal for their work at CanIL, Kent as finance and office manager and Brenda as donations clerk and in charge of the common room and custodians.

Since I like to cook, it wasn't long before one of my extra jobs became assisting Brenda in the kitchen. Once a month, we prepare a meal for students, followed by a presentation, usually from a CanIL alumnus or a Wycliffe member. All the students and staff are invited to these programs called "M-Files."

Brenda is an excellent cook with innovative ideas for great meals and always receives rave reviews. Sometimes we make two kinds of soup and serve them with rolls and a dessert for "Souper Lunch." No programs are presented at these luncheons, just a chance for everyone to eat together.

We have numerous other occasions during the year to prepare food for our community, and assisting Brenda has become one of the most enjoyable parts of my job.

&

The winter months fly by quickly in the southwestern corner of British Columbia. By late February, the early spring flowers are blooming—snowdrops, hyacinths, and crocuses poke their heads through the flowerbeds and pots of primulas appear in the grocery stores. The first year I lived here, I planted winter pansies in a pot on my deck and kept a few flowers blooming all winter. By March the warmer sun coaxed new buds and soon they were in full blossom again.

I love spring with the early heather, azaleas, rhododendrons, forsythia, and magnolias. Abbotsford has ornamental fruit trees growing on many of its boulevards, brightening the days with their pink-and-white petals. The frogs wake up and sing in the creek outside my bedroom window, sometimes keeping me awake at night. Every morning and evening, a flock of Canada geese fly over. They live at Mill Lake in the middle of town all year long, flying to the surrounding farms to feed during the day.

Each Easter, my church joins with three other churches, one from Abbotsford, one from Mission, and one from Pitt Meadows, for a Good Friday service. We rotate churches. The pastor of each church participates in the service, followed by a potluck luncheon provided by those who attend. This is always a highlight of the Easter season.

In 2008, I joined the hand bell choir at my church. I had never played hand bells before and found it challenging but enjoyable. It's different from singing, since you only play when the note on your bell comes up in the music, making it necessary to count and always watch the music to be ready to play when your note appears. Like anything new, practice is required. I wasn't very good at it in the beginning, but after several attempts, it became easier. Unfortunately, arthritis in my wrist caused me to retire from the choir before I wanted to.

Annual Awards Celebration

As the school year comes to an end in April, part of my job is to help plan for our annual awards celebration when we honor our graduating students. Those who intend to join Wycliffe or any other Bible translation organization are eligible to apply for Ministry Launch Awards which are available when the graduates are ready to leave for their assignments.

I do much of the clerical work for this program, which is held on the evening before the actual graduation for those who have earned a master of applied linguistics and exegesis. Following the program, we host a reception in the CanIL common room for everyone attending. During this reception, we meet and visit with families and friends of our graduates. Part of my job is to assist with the reception. This is always an emotional time for us and for our graduating students as they leave school and friends to begin the ministry to which God has called them.

When school was finished in 2008, Doris Porter and I left in my Honda Fit for southern California. Marge Moran and Judy Wallace had both retired and were now living at Pilgrim Place, a retirement community for long-term Christian workers in Claremont, California. It had been several years since

I'd seen them, so I looked forward to a visit and to see where they lived. Ron and Willie Grable also had recently moved to Pilgrim Place, so we looked forward to a mini-Philippine reunion.

On the way to Los Angeles, we stopped for two days with Don and Carol Dahlheim in Pleasanton, near San Francisco. Carol, who had worked as my secretary in Manila, is Doris's sister. We looked forward to sunny Southern California weather, since we'd had a very cold and wet spring at home, but it wasn't to be. When we left home, it was over 100 degrees F. (37 degrees C.) in Claremont, but by the time we arrived there, a cold front had set in, and the thermometer didn't get over 65 degrees F. (18 degrees C.) the whole time we were there.

Summer Session at CanIL

When we got back from our California trip, it was time for summer session at CanIL to begin again. This year would be different. The Oregon SIL school could no longer use their facilities in Eugene. Now they amalgamated with CanIL and moved to join us, along with a number of their regular staff members, their American students, and their library.

The students found the summer courses heavy, since they took a whole semester of studies in just nine weeks. To help them relax and enjoy the summer, we planned social activities regularly, such as camping weekends, long bicycle rides on Saturday mornings, a pool party and barbecue, a skit night put on by the students and another by the staff, a monthly birthday and anniversary party for staff and students, a picnic on the beach in Vancouver, and a trip downtown to see the Festival of Lights, Vancouver's annual international fireworks display. Three mornings a week, everyone worshipped together in chapel, singing and listening to messages from various staff members, many of whom had worked overseas.

I felt privileged to get to know students and to hear how God had led them to CanIL. Many were looking for His leading for their future ministries, whether in Bible translation or some other aspects of service overseas.

One special summer delight in the Fraser Valley has been attending "Concert in the Park" at Heritage Park just across the Fraser River in Mission. Every summer, starting on June 1 and lasting until September 1, free concerts are held every Wednesday and Friday evening. These feature local and imported groups performing various kinds of music. Although some music is not to our liking, we always find groups that we enjoy.

Eleanor, Tina, and I pack up our lawn chairs and drive to Mission for the one-hour concerts from seven to eight p.m. Heritage Park is a beautiful site, high on a hill overlooking the Fraser River.

Another Visit with Supporters

The months progressed so quickly that soon it was spring 2009 and time for another trip to Ontario to visit my supporters and to attend the LBI/LCBM reunion. I decided that my trip would not be as ambitious as the last one. A student from Manitoba rode with me to Portage la Prairie near Winnipeg, where I picked up Marg Schnurr, now a widow, to accompany me to Ontario.

On the way, we stopped in Calgary and Gull Lake to overnight with my sisters. Marg and I drove south through North Dakota, Minnesota, Wisconsin, Illinois, and across Michigan to reach Ontario.

We enjoyed the reunion again. Each time new people attended that hadn't been there before and whom I hadn't seen for many years. I stayed with Ruth Rowe, a friend from my days at Wortley Baptist Church in London. She was now a widow and living by herself in the old family home. Marg spent time with her sisters in southern Ontario, while I visited supporters.

I spent a weekend with my brother, Art, and his wife, Bonnie. They had already moved onto their boat, where they lived for the summer. It was in the marina under the Scarborough bluffs, a beautiful spot. The weather was chilly though, and I found overnighting on a boat quite uncomfortable, with only a small heater to warm my cabin. Would I ever get over my tropical blood?

From there, I drove to Syracuse, New York, where I visited Bertha Van Amber and Marion Seymour. I also lunched with Bob Laubach and Carolyn Blakely.

Marg and I headed back west on May 25. I was happy to have a companion for the whole trip, except for the leg from Portage la Prairie to Abbotsford. While driving on the highway between Portage and Brandon, I noticed a sign that said this spot was the middle east-to-west point of Canada. I realized I had the width of half the country to drive yet. Perhaps I was becoming a Westerner, since once I passed Winnipeg, I felt as if I were nearing home.

I spent the summer working at CanIL again, enjoying the activities that surrounded the summer program and getting to know the students. In August when school was finished, I had a break again until the fall semester started the day after Labor Day.

&❧

For years I had been saying I wanted to go on a cruise. Nell and Gary had gone on many cruises to various parts of the world and always came home with glowing stories of what they had seen and a camera full of wonderful pictures.

Finally, the time had come. Doris Porter and I decided to take a seven-day cruise to Alaska during my August break. We made reservations on the Holland America line and sailed from Vancouver the last week of August. The sun was shining in the afternoon when we passed beneath the Lion's Gate Bridge on our way through the inner passage, with stops at Juneau, Skagway, and Ketchikan.

We went to bed on the ship and woke the next day to clouds and rain. The next time we saw the sun was when we sailed back into Vancouver one week later. Except for the weather, our trip was great. We saw grizzly bears, whales, and sea otters but not much scenery. One special treat, apart from the fabulous food, was to have Australian friends Pam and Barry Waldeck on the same trip. They were friends and neighbors from Manila whom I hadn't seen for twenty years.

That year I decided to stay home again for Christmas. I had stayed home the year before for the first time, since whenever I went to the eastern side of the Rockies, I was cold. I told my sisters that from now on I would visit them in the summer when the weather is good and stay home in the winter.

My friends and I had many things to do during the holiday season, so I was happy to be home. Early in December, the church ladies sponsored a traditional turkey dinner and program, all prepared and served by the men of the congregation. Every Saturday morning, six of us women from North Oaks went out for breakfast. Two weeks before Christmas, I invited them all to my house for breakfast. I have enjoyed getting to know them, and we have become good friends.

Dan and Leona Goldsmith, who live on the third floor at North Oaks Manor, invited me to join them at a Christmas dinner provided by their church for those who don't have any place else to go. Several hundred folks, many of them street people, attended the beautiful traditional turkey dinner.

Don and Gloria Fama invited me to their home on New Year's Eve. Nine of us from the CanIL staff enjoyed an evening of games, fellowship, and prayer.

The months flew by, and soon the spring semester was over. That year I spent my May break visiting Nell and Gary for ten days and Marj and Vic for two weeks.

Sandy Schneider from Waxhaw, North Carolina, was visiting in Abbotsford. She traveled with me to Calgary but wasn't able to drive. This was the first time I drove the whole trip in one day. I usually stopped off halfway for an overnight, since twelve hours of driving was a bit long for me. The morning we left, we drove through snow in the mountains, but soon it cleared, and the rest of our trip was in sunshine.

When we arrived in Calgary, we discovered they had had a blizzard that morning. We passed a number of cars in the ditch or median on the Trans-Canada Highway before reaching Calgary. The roadway had been cleared by evening when we arrived, so we didn't have any problem but were happy to have our snow boots along when we arrived. After ten days of shopping and visiting, I drove east five hours to Gull Lake to visit my sister Marj's family.

In late May, Marj and her daughter, Jane, were haunting the greenhouses in Medicine Hat, Swift Current, and Shaunavan, looking for bedding plants to get their gardens underway. I loved those trips to see the flowers, dreaming of getting back to Abbotsford and heading for Devan's Nursery to buy plants for my deck. Even though climate wise we were at least a month ahead of Saskatchewan, I didn't buy plants until I returned home the end of May, so I didn't need to find someone to care for them while I was away.

I enjoyed spending time with my niece, Ann, her husband, Mark, and the twins, Eric and James. They were now energetic six-year-olds, who loved to play any sport that was going, and they played them all well. I went to a ball practice one afternoon and was amazed at the powerful way they threw the ball.

On my way home, I drove by way of Summerland, BC, located in the central Okanagan Valley, where I spent an overnight with Bill and Maureen Wills, who were my classmates at Bible college. We had a lot of catching up to do, since it had been quite some time since I'd seen them. This was my first time to visit Summerland.

At CanIL, our summer enrollment was up in 2010, higher than ever before. Everyone survived the grueling regimen of study. Students made new friends, and some began romances. Great times of fun and recreation helped relieve the stress of a concentrated program of study. The weather was exceptionally good—hot and dry. I was still adjusting to the cooler temperatures in British Columbia from the heat I was used to in Manila, so I enjoyed that summer more than usual. The gardeners were not happy though, since we had water restrictions, and the grass turned brown.

The end of June, I drove to Portland, Oregon, to visit Diana Stuhr, my former housemate. I hadn't seen her for ten years. She was now working for the Northwest Region of Wycliffe USA, helping new members through their preparation time before leaving for the field.

Besides spending hours getting caught up with each other, we met Jody Wilson who had also worked with us in Manila. We shopped in Powell's Books, the biggest bookstore I had ever seen, in downtown Portland. It covers a full city block and is two stories high. It has both new and used books and could be very hard on the budget.

Jody's brother-in-law worked at a garden in the middle of the Chinese district. He presented us with complimentary tickets, so we explored the gardens and enjoyed the flowers and architecture. We had lunch at a small Italian restaurant and walked around the district, which had once been train yards but was now converted to upscale town houses.

On Saturday evening, we went to see *The Lion King*, the best musical production I had ever seen. On Sunday afternoon, we drove to George Fox University to attend a hand bell choir concert. This was the conclusion of a five-day convention of hand bell choirs from five states in the Pacific Northwest, which ended with a free concert for the community. Participants included forty choirs with two hundred ringers and over two thousand bells. They covered the entire floor of the gymnasium and produced a glorious sound. Playing eleven numbers, they were directed by the music director from the Union Church of Paris, France.

When summer school was finished, I stayed home during the late August break and saw places in the Vancouver area that I hadn't yet visited. One day I went to Victoria on Vancouver Island with a group of seniors from a church in Abbotsford to see the city and visit a museum. I spent one day with a friend visiting the Vancouver Aquarium and riding in the gondola to the top of Grouse Mountain, a popular skiing venue. We had lunch and saw a couple of grizzly bears behind a fence. On another day, I went with a friend on the Sky Train to attend the Pacific National Exhibition (PNE), Vancouver's big fair. I was beginning to feel like I belonged in British Columbia after four years of residence.

Vice President of Development Dale Schatz retired that year, and in the fall, Judy Friesen arrived to take his place. I enjoyed getting to know her and working with her. She was very energetic and kept me well occupied, which suited me fine, since I don't like to sit around with nothing to do.

We were happy that our student enrollment was up, but as we endeavored to assist our students with the high cost of education, we needed increasing financial aid each semester. Times were hard, and we had been praying that God would provide. And then, in the late fall of 2010, a generous donor promised a matching grant of $102,000 if we could match it by the end of January 2011 in gifts of not less than $3,000 each.

Could we do it? It seemed like a very steep hill to climb. We sent out an appeal with our Christmas mailing, and Judy Friesen contacted people. By the end of January, we had reached not only the required amount for the matching grant but $14,000 beyond. This took us well on the way to reaching our annual goal. God had provided!

Physical Tests

Each year in March since coming home from the Philippines, I visited a heart specialist for a checkup to be sure the stent that had been placed in my coronary artery in 2006 was still functioning. In March of 2011, the doctor saw something in my stress test that he didn't like so sent me to the hospital for a myocardial perfusion test. A technician injected a radioactive isotope into the blood stream, another technician made a scan, and another technician took me through a treadmill stress test. Then after several hours of waiting, I returned for another scan. The whole thing took all morning.

After a few days, I called for the results, but the doctor didn't have them. After two weeks, I checked again. This time the receptionist said she would call back. In twenty minutes, she called to say they had found the report, the doctor had checked it, and he said it was normal. Needless to say, after two weeks of waiting, I was greatly relieved.

෴

In May I went to Calgary again, this time to attend the biennial member conference of Wycliffe Canada called "The Gathering," which was held at a Christian camp northwest of Calgary. One of our CanIL students, Grace Hagenlocher, from Winnipeg, traveled with me, since she was on her way home for the summer. She had recently been accepted as a member of Wycliffe and was eager to attend The Gathering. It was an excellent time to connect with Wycliffe members that I hadn't seen for some time and to hear reports of what God was doing in various parts of the world through our members. At the recognition banquet, I received a beautiful plaque commemorating my forty-five years of service with Wycliffe.

Following The Gathering, Grace and I drove to Portage la Prairie, Manitoba, where her mother picked her up, and I connected with Bible college classmate Marg Schnurr. This was the year to attend the London Bible Institute reunion in London, Ontario, again, so we set out for a two-and-a-half day trip. This year I joined the Golden Milers, those who graduated fifty years ago. We had a blessed time of connecting with classmates from long ago and getting caught up with their lives.

While Marg visited with family, I traveled around southwestern Ontario again, visiting friends and supporters. After a weekend in Toronto with Art and Bonnie, I drove to Syracuse, New York, where I visited with six long-time friends and supporters, all in their eighties and nineties.

Marg and I returned west by way of Iowa, where we spent an afternoon with Dr. Al and Josie Cramer. Al had been our Old Testament professor when we were students. We reminisced about those days but were saddened to learn that Al was manifesting the beginnings of Alzheimer's disease.

I arrived back in Abbotsford after five weeks on the road. My trip meter registered 6,835 miles (11,000 kilometers), all with no problems from my trusty Honda Fit.

Chapter 46
Work in Warm Tucson
2011–2013

Every summer, Eleanor Toews, Tina Teichrob, and I bought seasons passes for Minter Gardens, located just before the mountains begin, some forty minutes east of Abbotsford. Minter Gardens opened in the spring when the early tulips, daffodils, azaleas, and rhododendrons were in bloom, and the gardens closed at Thanksgiving. Our passes allowed us to visit as often as we liked and were cheaper than paying each time if we went more than once.

We enjoyed these gardens at least four times every year, once each season—spring, early summer, late summer, and fall. The rose garden was especially beautiful. About halfway through the walk, a wall of water separated the gardens from a row of benches in a shady place. We usually rested there, enjoying the sound of the falling water and cooling down from our walk.

Minter Gardens was a favorite place for weddings. An outdoor pavilion was perched atop a hillside where almost every weekend during the summer, a wedding would be in progress as we walked past. We usually went on Sunday after church and ate lunch in the cafeteria at the gardens before beginning our walk.

At the end of the walk was a large open area near the restaurant where tables were set up with sunshades. On Sunday afternoons, performers played and sang live music, often from the fifties or sixties. We usually bought ice cream cones from a booth that sold a variety of delicious flavors and listened to the music before returning home.

In 2013, we learned that Minter Gardens was closing, and this would be the last season. We made our final visit just before Thanksgiving and sorrowed along with many others over our loss. This had been a favorite place to take visitors who came to the area, and we would miss our own enjoyment of the beauty of God's creation.

In July, Anne West came home from the Philippines for a month to visit her brother and friends. She came from San Diego with Helen Blair to Manchester, Washington, a short ferry ride from southern Seattle, to visit Fay and Gundy Habich. They had all worked in Ifugao with Send International when I was there in the late sixties. Except for Anne, I hadn't seen any of them since they returned to the States many years before, so I drove with

Doris Porter to the Habich's place for the day, which we spent visiting and reminiscing.

Sightseeing

Since I had spent all of my early life in the East, I hadn't traveled much in the western States. One place I had always wanted to visit was Yellowstone National Park. In the break after summer semester in 2011, Eleanor Toews and I drove through the Cascade Mountains to Spokane, Washington, where we stayed overnight with Neil and Carol Anderson, former CanIL staff members, and then drove on to Yellowstone. The weather was cloudless, and the sights lived up to their reputations. The Old Faithful geyser sent up its great cloud of steam right on time, and the other geysers and boiling mud pools bubbled along the pathways through the park.

From Yellowstone, we spent a day at Craters of the Moon, many square miles of lava fields from a volcano that erupted several thousand years ago. Then we drove on to Oregon to see Crater Lake at the top of a volcano, the deepest lake in North America and certainly the bluest I've ever seen. From there we went north up the Oregon coast and drove back home through northern Washington. It was a delightful trip, which more than fulfilled my expectations.

Central Ifugao Bible

Late in 2011 I received a letter from Anne West, saying that the Central Ifugao translation team was nearly finished with the translation of the Old Testament. They had discovered that the team and the local churches would be responsible for paying half of the publishing costs of the Bible when it was printed. This came to $28,000, an overwhelming amount. Letters went out to people who might be interested, and the national churches looked for sources of funding.

In the meantime, Glenda, Junita, and Ermie continued with the revision and final tasks that needed to be done for the completion of the Bible. Many prayers went up around the world for the financial need and for the translators as they worked through some of the most difficult days of their task. As I had not been back to the Philippines since I left in 2006, I planned to attend the dedication when the book was finished. I set up a savings account, so I would be able to afford a ticket when the time came.

Fund-Raising Banquet

At CanIL I continued my work with personnel and development. In November we held a fund-raising banquet, which was attended by nearly two hundred people and raised $37,000 toward financial aid for our students. A generous donor agreed to match that and any other gifts we received before the end of the year up to $80,000.

The speaker at the banquet was Grace Fabian, a Wycliffe translator who worked in Papua New Guinea. A deranged translation helper killed her husband at his desk, while translating 1 Corinthians 13. Grace spoke of how, by God's grace, she was able to complete the translation and to forgive the one who had killed her husband. God's Word has transformed the Nabak people. She has written her story in a book called, *Outrageous Grace*. Many people were deeply touched by Grace's story that night.

Winter Work in Tucson

Several years before leaving the Philippines, I became aware that my fingers were getting stiff, and I frequently had pain in my lower back. After tests, the doctor informed me that I was developing osteoarthritis. This was not a surprise, since my family is full of it. Both my parents had it, as have my sisters. As the years went by, this disease has progressed until sometimes, especially in the winter when it is cold and damp, I have quite a bit of pain. I have not been able to take the strong arthritis medicine that is available because of my heart problem.

I had been aware for a number of years that the Mexico branch of SIL, which has a center located near Tucson, Arizona, welcomed volunteers to come in the winter to work at different jobs that needed to be done there. Since a number of my friends, who also suffer from arthritis, informed me that the dry warmth of the desert helped them, I thought I should try out some time in Arizona in the winter.

In the fall of 2011, I made contact with Wycliffe's volunteer office to see if I could become part of this program. Eleanor Toews was also interested. I got permission from Don Fama at CanIL to be away from my job for the month of February and applied to work in Catalina, a northern suburb of Tucson, where the SIL center is located. The volunteer office accepted both Eleanor and me, assigned our housing, and welcomed us to the 2012 group of volunteers.

We arrived on February 1 after four days of driving and visiting friends along the way. Judy and Sterling Sloan from Calgary hosted an ice-cream social at their house for all the Canadians on the first night we were there. We stayed in a mobile home right across the street from the administration building, which was very convenient. We could walk to work and every place we needed to go around the center. At the peak of the season that runs from January through March, 140 volunteers lent their expertise in whatever they were skilled at doing. These retirees were still capable of producing much work.

Mornings began with a half-hour chapel service with hymn singing, a welcome to new people arriving, a farewell to those leaving, a speaker, usually a Wycliffe translator working in Mexico, and a prayer time. On our first day, we went on a tour of the center to see what kind of work was being done and where we could fit in.

I chose to work in the archiving department, scanning literacy materials printed in pre-computer days and getting them ready to place on the Internet. Eleanor worked in the sewing department, making repairs and alterations for Mexico branch members and Wycliffe retirees who lived nearby. She also made children's clothing for translators to take to Mexico for their co-translators and neighbors.

Teams of people did a variety of different jobs. One group of women typed New Testaments and Bibles to be placed on the Internet, a group of men put a new roof on the chapel and the daycare building, landscapers put in new beds containing cactus and desert flowers surrounded by rocks, some painted the woodwork on the buildings, others laid new carpet in the computer department, still others repaired and refinished furniture and reupholstered chairs and sofas. A group of women wove rugs, and one couple washed all the windows. Several women worked in the boutique, a large collection of donated clothing that was available free for Wycliffe members. Others made quilts. Three women baked fresh cookies, squares, brownies, or cinnamon buns for our morning and afternoon coffee breaks.

On Fridays we were not scheduled to work, so we could do whatever we liked. Some people went shopping, some played golf, and others of us went hiking. Good hiking trails laced the mountains close to the center. A group of us went every Friday morning to a different hiking area. We visited two state parks that were within easy driving distance. We left about 9:00 a.m., took our lunches, and climbed the mountain trails. We usually got back home about 2:00 p.m. The desert was new to me, so I enjoyed seeing the different kinds of plants, including cacti, trees, and several desert flowers that were already in bloom.

We left for home on March 1 after a very enjoyable and productive month. Our experiment to see if the climate in Arizona would help with arthritis was a success. It did!

On August 12, Margaret Shields went home to meet her Savior. Margaret was a coworker at CanIL for six years and a good friend. She formerly worked as a high school physical education teacher at the SIL school in Papua New Guinea. In January of 2009, she was diagnosed with fourth-stage ovarian cancer and valiantly fought for her life. Twice she was able to return to work after chemotherapy, but eventually the cancer spread to her brain.

Margaret and I were the only single women on staff at CanIL so we often did things together. I had the privilege of helping her during her illness, especially when she could no longer drive and needed someone to take her shopping and to run errands. Since her family lived in Victoria, I was able to help clear her apartment and plan her memorial service. I missed her when she was gone but was happy that she was now rejoicing with Jesus and free from pain. Several of us from CanIL have kept in touch with her mother, who is in her nineties and found the loss of her only daughter very distressing.

In the Philippines, work continued on the Central Ifugao Bible. By the fall of 2012, Anne returned to the States and left the three Ifugao women to continue there. They were in constant touch by Skype, checking back and forth, making changes that were still needed, and wondering if it would ever get done. Anne bought a condo in La Mesa, California, a suburb of San Diego, in the same building as Helen Blair. Anne's brother was not expected to live much longer, so other than some nieces and nephews, she had no family left. Helen's family, who lived close by, took Anne in as one of them and helped her get settled. I was eager to know when the dedication would be held and kept asking Anne what she knew. She did her best to keep me informed, but just when they thought everything was going well and the work would soon be finished, something happened to set them back.

Back to Warm Tucson

In February 2013, Eleanor and I traveled to Tucson again to spend the month as volunteers for the Mexico branch. We worked at the same jobs as the year before. The first year, apart from one man who lived in the Tucson area and came in on Thursdays to work on archiving literacy books and a woman who was there about one week of February, I worked on my own. John Bailey, who had been part of our branch in the Philippines for a number of years before transferring to the Mexico branch, was head of the archiving department. It was good to work with him again. This year Eleanor Akker joined me. Eleanor was the widow of a pastor from Winthrop, Washington. She learned the job quickly, and we enjoyed working together. It was good to have someone to talk to from time to time.

The women working on archiving Scripture were in an office next door to us. Their job was quite different from ours. They actually typed the material on two different computers. Then they put it thorough a comparison program that indicated where there were differences. This way they could find the one with the error and produce a correct copy. They had been working on this for a number of years and now were anticipating finishing that year.

By the end of February, I had processed seventy literacy books to be placed in the branch archives and on the Internet to be downloaded for anyone who wanted to use them.

We enjoyed reconnecting with people we had gotten to know the year before and met quite a few new people. We stayed in a fine mobile home about two miles (four kilometers) from the office. On two Friday mornings, we hiked in the mountains nearby. The weather wasn't as good as it was the first year. We woke up to two inches of snow one morning and had several days with fifty-mile-an-hour winds and temperatures well below freezing at night. The sun did shine, though, even though it was cold.

On our way home, we drove by way of San Diego and spent two days with Anne West. I was glad to see her place and know she was happy in her new home. She was attending a good church, which she enjoyed very much.

While at Anne's place, I made contact with Lois Hummon, who had been a fellow student at Bible college and whom I hadn't seen for fifty-three years. She had been living in San Diego for many years and was now retired, living in a beautiful apartment in a retirement complex. We went to her place and had lunch with her. I'm sure we bored everybody with much reminiscing.

When we left, we also spent a day with Eleanor's brother and sister who live in Los Angeles and an overnight with Dorothy Woodford Arndt at Sonora, southeast of Sacramento. Dorothy had remarried when she returned from the Philippines, but her husband had passed away a few months before.

Visiting Supporters and Family Again

This was the year for me to spend time in Ontario again. I always enjoyed attending the Bible college reunion and took the opportunity to visit supporters and friends at the same time. Previously, I had driven to Ontario by way of Portage la Prairie, Manitoba, to pick up Marg Schnurr. This year Marg had been diagnosed with breast cancer so was not able to go, since she was undergoing chemotherapy. I decided the trip was too long to drive on my own now, so I drove to Calgary, spent a week with Nell and Gary, and then flew to London where I rented a car for the two weeks I spent there. I stayed with Ruth Rowe again and enjoyed her company. She had come to British Columbia the year before to attend her son Paul's wedding, to which I was also invited, so we had much to talk about.

While at Ruth's house, she organized a potluck with a number of friends from my youth when I lived in London. We had a joyful time as we caught up with each other after living apart for so long. I also made my usual trip to Syracuse to see Bertha Van Amber, Marion Seymour, Bob Laubach, and Caroline Blakely. They were all, except Marion, now in their nineties.

Death of Translator Char Houck

From there I drove south to Binghamton, New York, and visited with Char Houck, who was still living in a retirement home there. She was now ninety-five but very bright, and we had a wonderful visit. That would be my last, since she passed away in 2014 at the age of ninety-six.

After completing my visit to London, I flew back to Calgary and then spent a week in Gull Lake with Marj and her family. Vic was not well but was still able to be at home. After he fell and broke his leg a couple of years earlier, he had not regained his strength and was showing signs of dementia. I was glad that Ann and Jane were nearby to help and encourage Marj during this difficult time.

On my way back to Abbotsford, I went by way of Vernon and stopped for a day with Bible college fellow students, Al and Ruth Luesink and their son, David, who was at home then and whom I had not met before. They live in a lovely home on a hill overlooking Okanagan Lake. From there I drove to Kelowna, across Highway 5, and over the Coquihalla Pass to Hope and on home. Now it was time to go back to work, since the summer semester was about to begin.

The Training Ride

During the summer at CanIL we sponsored a fund-raising activity to provide for financial aid for our students. A number of students, faculty, staff, and others from the community participated in "The Training Ride," a choice of two bicycle rides, one 28 miles (45 kilometers), and the other 62 miles (100 kilometers), through the Fraser Valley on a Saturday morning. Participants were required to raise a certain amount of money that would go toward the scholarship fund. This was a very successful activity and greatly enjoyed by all who participated.

353

The riders had three refreshment stops, so my job was, along with Karin Rennert, our receptionist, to set up the refreshments at the first stop. It was located at Aldergrove Park, a half-hour from Abbotsford. We were provided with fruit and food—oranges, bananas, watermelon, energy bars, cookies, an energy drink, and water with which to fill their bottles. The first riders appeared about 8:30, partook of the refreshments, rested for a while, and then were off on the next leg of the journey.

Karin and I packed up the leftovers and proceeded to the home of Lynn and Ron Gamache, CanIL board members, a few miles to the northwest, where we brought the remaining food and drinks and set it up again for the riders' next stop. Lynn also baked a fresh coffee cake to add to what we had.

When the riders stopped at the Gamaches' and were off again, we proceeded back to CanIL, where we set up what we had left to be eaten when everyone returned there. At noon we all went to the dining hall at Reimer Center on campus for a delicious lunch. At this point, awards were given to the riders. The Training Ride was so successful that everyone said we should make it a permanent activity every summer.

After the summer semester was finished, I had three weeks off work. This year I decided to stay home most of the time, except for two short trips and to take advantage of some things that the Fraser Valley has to offer. The first week I attended a potluck luncheon with Lynn Gamache. She attends a Baptist church that has a large seniors' group that I had been attending for a year. I enjoyed getting to know more new people.

Doug Rintoul, who is head of our computer department at CanIL, and his wife, Cindy, who is Eleanor's daughter, invited us to go to a concert in Vancouver at the Queen Elizabeth Theatre. The artist was Celtic singer Loreena McKennett. I love Celtic music, and her concert was a special treat for me. One Saturday I attended a pie social on the lawn of Ed Fast, the Conservative party member of parliament, for our riding. Ed is a fine Christian who is much loved in Abbotsford.

The second week of my vacation, Eleanor and I drove to Redmond, Washington, near Seattle, and spent a couple of days with Kermit and Shirley Ecklebarger. They were on staff at LCBM in the early sixties when I worked there. We had a wonderful time on two cruises, one on Lake Washington and one through the Ballard Locks that take ships and small boats from the salt water of Puget Sound, to the fresh water of the Ship Canal, Lake Union, and Lake Washington. I learned a lot about the Seattle area on that trip.

One day Eleanor, Tina Teichrob, who lives in my building, and I went to the Pacific National Exhibition (PNE). A bus for seniors left at noon and took us from Abbotsford right to the fairgrounds. We spent the day seeing all the things the fair had to offer and were returned home by 9:00 p.m. It was an easy way to go to the fair.

The next day, accumulated air miles allowed me to fly to Calgary where Nell and Gary met me. We drove to Gull Lake, Saskatchewan, by way of Dinosaur Provincial Park, to spend the weekend with Marj and her family. It had been a number of years since we three sisters had all been together.

One other special treat during my vacation was an invitation to attend a Celtic Thunder concert in Abbotsford. Randy and Sandy Evans, who live in my building, took me and two other friends, to see this Irish group. I'd seen them on public television but hadn't expected to ever see them in person.

Archivists 2016

Chapter 47
Back to Warm Tucson
2014–2015

How quickly the days passed by! I enjoyed my work, which had enough variety to keep me interested.

In February of 2014, Eleanor Toews and I made our third trip to Tucson, Arizona, to work with the volunteer program for the Mexico branch. This time we were assigned to stay with Pat Anderson, a retiree who, with her husband, had been a translator among the Chinantec in Mexico. She was now a widow with a lovely home seven miles (11 kilometers) from the center.

I worked in the archiving department again, as I had the two previous years, and Eleanor continued to sew. The year before, the women archiving Scripture had finished all the books that needed to be done. They were asked to move into literacy archiving. This made for a large team of fifteen people instead of just three of us.

Our production that year was encouraging. From January to March, the team processed 567 books consisting of over 17,200 pages. We were told that if we could keep up that kind of production, the task might be finished in one more year.

♊♊

Before my cataract surgery between semesters at CanIL, I drove to Calgary to attend The Gathering, Wycliffe Canada's retreat, which is held every three years. We had an excellent speaker and good workshops. We were updated on some changes taking place within Wycliffe Canada and had opportunities to interact with the leadership.

Summer School

That summer we had seventy-six students, some taking prerequisite courses in order to enter one of the graduate degree programs in the fall, others taking the training track programs, preparing them for work in language survey, literacy, linguistics, or translation.

Our students participated in many extracurricular activities during the summer. The Training Ride provided an opportunity for students, staff, faculty, and interested outsiders to raise funds for student financial aid during the school year. This bicycle ride of either 24 miles (39 kilometers) or 62 miles (100 kilometers) had become a favorite activity after its great success the previous summer. The ride raised $90,000 for CanIL training in 2014.

In early December I received an e-mail from Anne West, saying that the dedication program for the Central Ifugao Bible had been set for May 20, 2015. I had been looking forward to attending this dedication for a number of years. Now I could make plans for a trip to Manila.

Sharon Tully, previously the head librarian at Faith Academy in Manila and now working in the Calgary office, planned to travel with me. Soon after Christmas, we would plan our trip.

Fourth Year at Tucson

After school began in January, Eleanor and I made plans to travel to Tucson for our fourth year of volunteering at the SIL center there. We left on January 25, visited friends along the way, and arrived in Catalina on January 30, giving us time to get settled before beginning work on Monday, February 2. This year we were assigned to live in a three-bedroom mobile home located on the center, about a two-minute walk from the office. It was a perfect location for us, since we didn't need to drive to work every day as we had the two previous years. I worked in archiving again, and Eleanor was sewing as before.

My computer was in the archives library where about nineteen thousand volumes of Scripture and literacy materials are stored. Every morning the archivists got together after the half-hour morning devotions attended by the whole group of about one hundred and forty volunteers. We had a short time of prayer for our work and for personal requests from our group. At 10:00 a.m. we gathered in room 33 for coffee and fresh-baked cookies, squares, cake, or cinnamon rolls, repeated at 2:00 in the afternoon.

This year I scanned books the whole time I was there, completing 252 literacy books. This finished all that needed doing. Then I worked on Old Testament compilations, completing twenty-three volumes.

It was exciting for me to see the end of the literacy books. We didn't think we could complete the job in 2015, but the volunteers were a great group of hard workers. When we departed the end of February, many books still needed to be cleaned up and processed into new books to be placed on the Internet, but Sue, who was now our supervisor, was confident that by the end of the year, they would all be completed.

On our way home from Tucson, we traveled by way of San Diego again to spend a weekend with Anne West. We talked about the Central Ifugao Bible dedication, enjoyed several meals together, and attended her church.

Now all that was left before packing for my trip to the Philippines was a month-and-a-half of work at CanIL, preparing for the awards celebration held the evening before graduation, and saying good-bye to our graduating students.

We will miss them, but some will return at a future date to report to us how God had been using them in the work He's called them to do.

Haida Gwaii canoe in Vancouver airport

Epilogue
2015

I stood waiting by the huge jade carving of a Haida Gwaii (Queen Charlotte Islands) canoe in the middle of the Vancouver, BC, airport, a favorite meeting place for passengers and greeters. Sharon Tully arrived on a connecting flight from Calgary and found me there.

After lunch and the usual long wait in the departure area, we were off on a Philippine Airlines plane to Manila to attend the dedication of the Central Ifugao Bible. Our nonstop flight took fourteen hours, arriving at 8:30 p.m. on Thursday, May 7, 2015. Checking through customs went smoothly, but the wait for baggage was long.

By 9:30 p.m., we were in a taxi heading for the SIL guesthouse in Quezon City. We made a mistake. Instead of letting the taxi driver take us however he wanted, which can sometimes be a long way around, we told him to take us by way of EDSA, the way I had always gone nine years before when I picked up people from arriving flights. He didn't argue and did as we asked. But an hour-and-a-half later, he informed us that if we had let him bring us the way he would have chosen, we would not have been in a terrible traffic jam. We didn't know that EDSA was now gridlocked most of the day and night.

In spite of not having slept on the flight, I woke up before 4:00 a.m. Jet lag has always been a problem for me, and the older I get, the worse it becomes. It took nearly a week before I could sleep normally and awake at a reasonable time.

The first thing we noticed was the intense heat. According to several residents, this had been the hottest summer in a number of years. The temperature was 91 degrees F. (33 degrees C.), with 89 percent humidity, when we arrived. During the next two weeks as rainy season approached, the temperature climbed to 96 degrees F. (36 C.), with the humidity making it feel like 105 F. (41 C.). We were grateful for air-conditioning in our bedroom at the guesthouse.

After breakfast on our first day, we caught a taxi to get a couple of the luxuries we could afford in the Philippines—manicures and pedicures. We found the shop Sharon had frequented before returning to Canada four years before. The staff greeted her with joy, since she had been a longtime customer.

We lunched in a small French restaurant and then stood and sat in line for a taxi to take us back to the guesthouse. The taxi queue consisted of eight seats and a long line of people. As taxis arrived, those sitting on the far end of the row got their rides, and everyone moved down to fill the empty seats seats.

During the nine years since my departure from Manila, our much-beloved Magnolia ice cream plant, where SIL members spent many hours in the air-conditioned ice-cream parlor, moved out of the city. The factory, which occupied a solid city block, was torn down to make way for an upscale four-story shopping mall called Robinson's Magnolia, after the original name of the ice cream.

Back to Union Church

Sunday was Mother's Day. When we entered Union Church, an usher handed each of us a long-stemmed red rose. The service was as I remembered, traditional and reverent. A guest preacher from the States, formerly a teacher at Faith Academy who had become a pastor, brought an excellent sermon, and the men from the choir sang the anthem. It was a tradition at Union Church for the men to sing on Mother's Day and the women to sing on Father's Day, giving the honored sex the day off.

On Sunday evening we attended an outstanding concert at the new performing arts theater at Faith Academy. The award-winning concert choir of the University of the Philippines performed their latest repertoire before leaving on a three-month tour of Europe and the United States.

History of SIL's Publications

Mila Cagape, who was now doing my job in publications, informed me that a workshop for SIL members involved in publishing and typesetting in Asia was going to be held at the Manila center. She asked if I would speak at the opening session on Monday to give the history of printing and publishing in SIL Philippines.

I was glad to do that and enjoyed interacting with the workshop participants, many of whom I already knew and with whom I had worked in Manila. I especially enjoyed seeing Barbara Altork, who now lived near Waxhaw, North Carolina, and who worked with me in Manila for several years, typesetting Scriptures and dictionaries.

Mike Walrod in Abbotsford e-mailed me, asking if I would buy a copy of the Ilokano Bible while I was there, since he needed to give it to an Ilokano speaker. On Wednesday Sharon and I got on a jeepney and rode to Cubao, where we found the Christian bookstore and the bible Mike needed.

We came back on the Light Rail Transit train (LRT) and walked to a grocery store where I bought mangoes. I hadn't had any yet and was craving a taste of that wonderfully juicy fruit that was then at the height of its season. We walked five long blocks home under our umbrellas in the scorching sun.

Faith Academy

People began arriving at the Manila guesthouse in preparation for the Central Ifugao Bible dedication on May 20.

Two of those were brothers Joe and Peter France. Joe had been in my session of jungle camp with his wife Helen and children in 1966. They had then served in the Philippines, Joe as a pilot working out of Bagabag. After they were there a while, Joe's parents with his two younger brothers came for a few years to help with landscaping and other maintenance jobs. John and Peter attended Faith Academy.

Now Peter wanted to see Faith Academy again and arranged for a tour of the school. I too was eager to see the changes that had taken place since I left nine years before. Sharon wanted to visit many of her former coworkers and friends who were still there.

On Thursday morning we walked to the LRT station and rode a train to the end of the line where a taxi took us the rest of the way to Faith Academy. Two staff members gave us an excellent tour of the school.

A number of years ago, a donor gave the school a large grant to build a performing arts theater and a swimming pool. Just recently, they purchased more land and constructed a new soccer field. All of these additions, as well as many other smaller upgrades, have made it a superior school for missionary children.

Following our tour, we had lunch and caught a bus back to SIL. Since the day was exceedingly hot, we were glad to get back to our air-conditioned bedrooms for afternoon siestas.

Central Ifugao Bible Dedication

Monday morning, we left for Ifugao in the SIL van, eleven of us including two Filipina women. One was Anne's friend from Tucson, and the other was the woman's sister who lived in Manila.

It took ten hours to drive to Lagawe, where we stayed in a relatively new hotel for two nights. We had gone one day early because we wanted to visit Amganad and the village where Anne and I first started the translation work.

On Tuesday morning, Ian McQuay, who drove the van, dropped us off at the top of the hill on the way to Huyuk, our village. The last time I was there, the trail was as it had been in 1967, very steep and twisty, almost unnavigable for a group of seniors. This time it was paved so a vehicle could drive down as far as the school. This was unbelievable for me. I couldn't imagine they could make a road out of that trail, but they did.

We visited the beautiful new church that had been built since I was there more than ten years ago, and then we walked on pavement to the elementary school, a bit further down the mountain. From there we walked on a familiar dirt and rocky trail to the village of Huyuk.

The area now had electricity, and we were amused to see a sari-sari store partway down with a sign listing all the frozen meats and fish you could buy. Another sign said you could buy a load for your cell phone there too. Life had changed in the mountains!

Along the way, we met a few people. Some Anne knew and greeted. Most were unknown to me, since the older people who had lived there when I did were now deceased. Most of the adults had either been small children then or hadn't yet been born. We did meet Ongallan on the trail. It was so good to see him again.

At the bottom of the long hill, we finally arrived at Huyuk, which had changed considerably since I lived there. Extremely poor people then now had more resources. Their educated children, who worked in the Middle East or elsewhere, helped them financially.

Houses had been expanded or rebuilt. Grass roofs had completely disappeared. Most small native houses had been removed and larger structures erected in their places.

But the rice fields had not changed. The rice was not yet ready for harvest, so brilliant green terraces spilled down the mountainsides. This area was still one of the beautiful wonders of the world.

Pugong had been a *mumbaki* (pagan priest) and had resisted the gospel for many years, even though most of his family had become believers. Finally, after decades of prayer for him, he gave his heart to Christ and was baptized. He had lived in the house right in front of ours. That formerly small Ifugao house now was large, made of cement, and painted lime green.

Pugong had also constructed a burial house on a dry terrace at the back of the village with his descendants listed on the outside, showing whose bones would be placed there along with his own. Undoubtedly, some were already there, since two of his former wives were on the list.

On our return to the church, the women served us a delicious meal of rice, vegetables, chicken, and fruit salad.

Ian soon arrived at the bottom of the hill in the van with the two Filipina ladies. They were not able to navigate the hike and had gone to Banaue to see the major rice terraces and to shop.

After our meal, we all climbed aboard the van and held our breaths as Ian drove us up the very steep hill to the main road on which we returned to Lagawe and our hotel. We shopped in the local market and then walked down the main street to visit our friend Mary Yogyog. Her daughter, Rachel, had lived with Anne and me in Manila when going to nursing school. We had visited Rachel on our trip to the United Arab Emirates several years earlier.

Later, we all piled into the van again, and Ian drove us to Piwong, where the dedication was to be held the next day. A church near the location of the dedication provided our evening meal and that of the forty-four additional visitors who arrived on a bus from Manila.

Wednesday, dedication day, dawned bright and sunny again, as we once more rode to Piwong for breakfast at 7:00 a.m. The dedication parade was to start at 8:00 a.m. from the main road, about one mile (two kilometers) away. We waited outside the church for it to begin.

Soon the parade came. Members of each church marched, led by someone carrying a decorated banner with the church name. Most women wore their red-and-black woven Ifugao skirts. Some wore tee shirts especially designed for the occasion with Scripture verses or church names. Small drum bands marched at the beginning and in the middle of the parade.

I watched as the parade came around the bend of the road below us. It came and came, a never-ending line of people, some singing, all with smiles as they marched toward an event that gave them great joy.

We joined the end of the parade and walked another half mile to the school gymnasium, which consisted of a roof with no walls. This was ideal, since it was expandable and left plenty of space for the two thousand plus people who attended the dedication service. It also let the breezes through, dissipating the intense heat of the sun, while the roof gave good shade.

The gymnasium was set up with hundreds of plastic chairs. We were escorted to the front where we found seats in the second row.

As master of ceremonies, Herman Dinumla, a local pastor, welcomed the crowd. The program began with the singing of a hymn of praise and welcome remarks before the Amganad Vibrant Evangelical Church choir sang a beautiful choral presentation.

Then Anne gave the wonderful history of the Central Ifugao Bible translation project from start to finish.

Representatives of five churches read selected Scripture portions, mostly from the Old Testament, since this portion of the Bible was new to them. One elderly woman read her verses with great gusto, happy to be part of the celebration.

The director of SIL Philippines, Jason Griffiths, gave the main message. Since the whole program was in the Ifugao language, the master of ceremonies, Herman Dinumla, interpreted Jason's English message so the older people could understand.

Then Pastor Peter Hummiwat prayed the prayer of dedication.

As I listened, only partially understanding what he was saying, my eyes filled with tears as I remembered the dark night in this area when I first heard drunken *mumbaki* shouting and clashing gongs as they called on the spirits to heal a small neighbor boy. In despair, I had prayed silently, *Dear God, what can You ever do in a place like this?* Now I knew! I saw with my own eyes that nothing is impossible for Him.

After forty-eight years of work and prayer, Anne and her coworkers had brought the complete Bible to Ifugao. The result? This huge crowd of believers worshipped the true God and loved His Son, Jesus Christ.

Scattered throughout the program were musical numbers from other churches, a beautiful song from one of the pastors and his family, and cultural drama dances portraying different aspects of the culture and how the coming of the Bible has impacted their lives and those of the surrounding communities.

The master of ceremonies honored Anne and the other translators with plaques and special gold-edged copies of the Bible.

Tony Dasalla, executive director of the Translators Association of the Philippines (TAP); Dr. Romerlito Macalinao, director of Wycliffe Philippines; and Rev. Laurence Nanglegan Sr., chairman of the Ifugao ministerial fellowship, all gave encouraging words.

The program lasted for four hours, followed by a delicious lunch of Ifugao rice, chicken, pork, and vegetables.

The Bibles went on sale afterwards. Many people had paid for their copies ahead of time and now picked them up. We saw them coming down the hill hugging their Bibles, smiles on their faces.

How good that God had made it possible for these people in the northern Philippines to have His whole Word in the language that speaks to their hearts!

After lunch we loaded up our van and headed back to Manila. It was nearly midnight when we arrived, tired and happy that we had the privilege of being present at this once-in-a lifetime event.

A copy of the Central Ifugao Bible now sits on my bookshelf, along with several other New Testaments and Bibles in Philippine languages. I can't understand any of them, but they remind me that God loves Filipinos.

He gave me the unparalleled privilege of helping to give them His Word in languages they can understand.

I can't think of a better way to have spent almost forty years of my life!

Central Ifugao dedication

Central Ifugao Bible

References

Ambassador 1958 to 1966. Yearbook of the London Bible Institute and London College of Bible and Missions. London, ON, Canada.

Atherton, William. *In God's Time and Ours: Philippine Branch History: A Narration 1953–1983*. 50th Anniversary Ed. Manila, Philippines: Summer Institute of Linguistics, 2003.

Baron, Cynthia S., and Melba M. Suazo. *Nine Letters: The Story of the 1986 Filipino Revolution*. Quezon City, Philippines: Gerardo P. Baron, 1986.

Blakely, Caroline, and Robert S. Laubach. *Literacy Journalism at Syracuse University: A Thirty–Year History, 1952–1981*. Syracuse, NY: Lit-J Alumni, 1996.

Elkins, Richard E., and Agnes Lawless Elkins. *Time and Again: God's Sovereignty in the Lives of Two Bible Translators in the Philippines*. Bloomington, IN: WestBow, 2011.

Funnell, Shirley. Letters to her parents. 1967–1989.

Funnell, Shirley. Quarterly newsletters. 1967–2015.

Miller, Carolyn Payne. *Captured: A Mother's True Story of Her Family's Imprisonment by the Vietcong*. Chappaqua, NY: Christian Herald, 1977.

Newell, Len. *Headhunters' Encounter with God: An Ifugao Adventure*. Bloomington, IN: iUniverse, 2007.

Roces, Alfredo R., *Filipino Heritage: The Making of the Nation*. Vols. 6, 9–10. Manila, Philippines: Lahing Pilipino, 1978

Shetler, Joanne with Patricia Purvis. *And the Word Came with Power*. Orlando, FL: Wycliffe, 1992, 2000, 2002.

Made in the USA
San Bernardino, CA
08 July 2016